CREATING THE SUBURBAN SCHOOL ADVANTAGE

A volume in the series
Histories of American Education
Edited by Jonathan Zimmerman

CREATING THE SUBURBAN SCHOOL ADVANTAGE

Race, Localism, and Inequality in an American Metropolis

John L. Rury

CORNELL UNIVERSITY PRESS   ITHACA AND LONDON

Copyright © 2020 by Cornell University

All rights reserved. Except for brief quotations in a review, this book, or parts thereof, must not be reproduced in any form without permission in writing from the publisher. For information, address Cornell University Press, Sage House, 512 East State Street, Ithaca, New York 14850. Visit our website at cornellpress.cornell.edu.

First published 2020 by Cornell University Press

Library of Congress Cataloging-in-Publication Data
Names: Rury, John L., 1951– author.
Title: Creating the suburban school advantage : race, localism, and inequality in an American metropolis / John L. Rury.
Description: Ithaca : Cornell University Press, 2020. | Series: Histories of American education | Includes bibliographical references and index.
Identifiers: LCCN 2019032213 (print) | LCCN 2019032214 (ebook) | ISBN 9781501748394 (cloth) | ISBN 9781501748400 (epub) | ISBN 9781501748417 (pdf)
Subjects: LCSH: Suburban schools—Missouri—Kansas City Metropolitan Area—History. | Suburban schools—Kansas—Johnson County—History. | Discrimination in education—Missouri—Kansas City Metropolitan Area—History. | Discrimination in education—Kansas—Johnson County—History. | Racism in education—Missouri—Kansas City Metropolitan Area—History. | Racism in education—Kansas—Johnson County—History. | Educational equalization—Missouri—Kansas City Metropolitan Area—History. | Educational equalization—Kansas—Johnson County—History.
Classification: LCC LA318.K2 R87 2020 (print) | LCC LA318.K2 (ebook) | DDC 371.0109778/411—dc23
LC record available at https://lccn.loc.gov/2019032213
LC ebook record available at https://lccn.loc.gov/2019032214

Contents

List of Illustrations	vii
Acknowledgments	ix
Abbreviations	xiii
Introduction: Educating the Fragmented Metropolis	1
1. Suburban and Urban Schools: Two Sides of a National Metropolitan Coin	18
2. Uniting and Dividing a Heartland Metropolis: Growth and Inequity in Postwar Kansas City	44
3. Fall from Grace: The Transformation of an Urban School System	76
4. Racialized Advantage: The Missouri Suburban School Districts	105
5. Conflict in Suburbia: Localism, Race, and Education in Johnson County, Kansas	133
Epilogue: An Enduring Legacy of Inequality	157
Appendix: Statistical Analyses and Oral History Sources	185
Notes	195
Index	247

Illustrations

Figures

1.1–1.4 Patterns of metropolitan divergence on selected dimensions, 1940–1980 — 33

2.1 Statistical odds of school success, 1980 — 71

Maps

2.1 Kansas City, Missouri, annexations, 1947–1963 — 47

2.2 Metropolitan Kansas City school district boundaries, 1954 — 49

2.3–2.6 Growth of metropolitan Kansas City's African American population, 1950–1980 — 52

2.7 Metropolitan Kansas City school district boundaries, 1980 — 60

2.8 Geo-spatial distribution of adults with college degrees, 1980 — 66

3.1–3.3 Kansas City public high schools and African American settlement, 1960, 1970, and 1980 — 83

4.1 Districts and schools in Kansas City and South Kansas City, 1980 — 113

4.2 Fifty years of annexations in North Kansas City, 1913–1963 — 121

5.1 Communities and schools upon formation of the Shawnee Mission District, 1971 — 145

E.1 Metropolitan Kansas City African American population, 2013–2017 — 164

E.2 Metropolitan Kansas City, children living below the poverty level, 2013–2017 — 166

E.3 Metropolitan Kansas City, location of college-educated adults, 2013–2017 — 167

Tables

2.1 Postwar population growth in metropolitan Kansas City's four core counties — 59

2.2 Descriptive statistics, 1960: five geo-spatial areas — 65

2.3 Descriptive statistics, 1980: five geo-spatial areas — 65

3.1 KCMPS enrollment by race, 1955–1980 — 84

3.2 Transfers from select KCMPS schools, 1962–1973 — 85

3.3 Results of Missouri Basic Skills testing, 1978, in KCMPS and neighboring districts — 99

4.1 KC metropolitan Missouri districts: growth and resources, 1954–55 to 1974–75 — 108

4.2 KC metropolitan school districts: economic, social, and demographic profiles, 1970 — 109

5.1 Social status indicators, select Johnson County communities, 1960 — 138

E.1 Composite ACT scores and families in poverty for Kansas and Missouri districts in Greater Kansas City, 2012 and 2013 — 170

A.1 Regression analysis, adult education levels, 1960 — 186

A.2 Regression analysis, adult education levels, 1980 — 187

A.3 Binary logistic regression: junior year status or higher, 17-year-olds, 1980 — 191

Acknowledgments

It is an old chestnut that scholarship is a collective enterprise, but that does not make it any less true for this book. I have benefited from a vast supporting cast of other researchers, librarians, colleagues, students, friends, and family over the years of working on it.

Research for this project began in earnest during a sabbatical in the fall of 2011 from the University of Kansas (KU), coupled with a generous grant from the Spencer Foundation, which permitted me to continue working into the following spring and summer months. Aaron Tyler Rife was an intrepid assistant and companion, traveling daily to area libraries and archives, and assisting with interviews and statistical data collection. His work was integral to the project's success, and he extended it with his own dissertation focusing on the Hickman Mills School District.

Aaron and I received vital assistance from librarians and archivists throughout the course of our work. This was especially true of the staff of the Missouri Valley Collections at the Kansas City Public Library and the Kansas City Research Center of the State Historical Society of Missouri, located on the campus of the University of Missouri at Kansas City (formerly known as the Western Historical Collection). We spent months examining materials in these extensive local history collections. Reference librarians at the University of Kansas also provided assistance, especially regarding government (census) documents and the T. R. Smith Map Collection; staff members at the university's Kenneth Spencer Research Library also helped with a number of particular searches.

We conducted a good deal of research in other locations as well. Librarians at the Johnson County Library System's Central Resource Library were quite helpful, as were archivists at the Johnson County Museum. The same was true of librarians at the Kansas Historical Museum in Topeka. The Raytown Historical Society's volunteer staff helped to identify pertinent material in its collections, as did volunteers at the Clay County Historical Society and Museum in Liberty, Missouri. The records department at the Kansas State Department of Education located pertinent school reports and other documents, as did a number of very helpful staff members in the administrative offices of the North Kansas City School District. Librarians at Park University helped locate elusive Missouri School Reports, and librarians at Shawnee Mission North High School aided us in finding materials pertinent to its history.

Individual-level census data were acquired from the Integrated Public Use Microdata Series (IPUMS) sponsored by the Minnesota Population Center at the University of Minnesota. I am very grateful for the availability of this vital resource for quantitative historical research. Social Explorer helped in identifying census tract data and larger spatial patterns of inequality.

Later in the project Jennifer Hurst also provided valuable assistance in locating additional sources in online databases and KU's libraries. Cartographer Darin Grauberger prepared the maps for chapters 2 through 5; Xan Wedel created maps for the epilogue at KU's Institute for Policy and Social Research, where a highly capable staff managed the project's grant funds. Xan also helped identify data sources for the epilogue's analysis of poverty and achievement.

In other regards this study has benefited enormously from the work of scholars who also have written about the history of greater Kansas City. I am especially indebted to Sherry Lamb Schirmer, Joshua Dunn, Peter William Moran, Kevin Fox Gotham, and perhaps most of all James R. Shortridge, for their foundational contributions to the social and economic history of postwar Kansas City and the development of its school systems in particular. Citations throughout the book testify to this, even if I do not always agree with their interpretations or explanations of particular events.

Over the past six years I have presented papers based on this project at various meetings, including those sponsored by the History of Education Society (USA), the American Educational Research Association, the International Standing Conference of the History of Education, and the Social Science History Association. Discussants and audience members in each of these venues provided very helpful feedback, especially Dionne Danns, Ansley Erickson, Karen Benjamin, Jack Dougherty, Tracy Steffes, Emily Strass, Hilary Moss, Walter Stern, Ken Gold, and David Gamson, among many others. I have also presented chapters in various stages of preparation in the Urban Experience Seminar at KU's Hall Center for the Humanities. I found additional responses helpful there and at other venues on campus, particularly from Clarence Lang, Marie-Alice L'Heureux, Bradley Lane, Argun Saatcioglu, Shirley Hill, Shawn Alexander, Bill Tuttle, David Roediger, Steve Obenhaus, Nathan Wood, Barney Warf, Donna Ginther, Derrick Darby, ChangHwan Kim, Jake Dorman, Bill Staples, Bob Antonio, Alan Black, and other colleagues and students too numerous to mention. I also benefited from conversations with Kansas City broadcast journalist Sam Zeff, who offered insightful perspective as well.

Parts of chapter 2 were presented at a 2013 conference on quantitative approaches to the history of education at the École des hautes études en sciences sociales in Paris, and similar presentations also were made at the University of Vienna, the University of Szeged, Soka University of America, the University of Wisconsin–Madison, Arizona State University, and the University of Colorado at Colorado Springs. Useful questions and commentary were offered in each of those instances too, and I am grateful to hosts Daniel Tröhler and Catherina Schreiber, Reka Cristian, Jay Heffron, Bill Reese, Sherman Dorn, and Sylvia Mendez respectively for their hospitality and helpful feedback.

I also received helpful critiques from anonymous readers who reviewed various papers for publication in academic journals. I have benefited enormously from my coauthors on these and other articles that have informed the study, including Sanae Akaba, Aaron Rife, Argun Saatcioglu, and Donna Gardner. Donna's work was especially important in chapter 4. Several publishers considered the book, and their reviewers offered many suggestions for revision. Ben Justice, Dionne Danns, Zoe Burkholder, Bob Hampel, and Jon Zimmerman provided especially valuable feedback on the manuscript as a whole, and Cornell University Press editor Michael McGandy adeptly shepherded the book to publication. Copyediting was very capably performed by Glenn Novak, and production editor Jennifer Savran Kelly managed the transition to print. Hannah Bailey expertly created the index.

Friends, students, and colleagues in Lawrence have been supportive throughout the project, and they have continued to express interest in its findings. This has been especially true in my home department and school, where colleagues and students have endured with unfailing good humor my absences for research and writing. Dean Rick Ginsberg has been a staunch source of support.

Finally, I would like to express heartfelt thanks to my spouse and partner, Aïda Alaka, who has been steadfast in her encouragement of my scholastic predilections, including this long-gestating book. Despite having her own demanding academic career, she has been an invaluable sounding board for many aspects of the project and a fount of encouragement to keep moving forward.

The book is dedicated to my mother, Virginia Gould Rury, who taught me much about inequality and injustice, lessons that have resonated throughout my life and career.

Portions of the following articles have been used in the book with permission from the editors and publishers, for which I am also grateful: "Race, Schools and Opportunity Hoarding: Evidence from a Post-war American Metropolis," *History of Education* 47, no. 1 (January 2018): 87–107 (with Aaron Tyler Rife); "Trouble in Suburbia: Localism, Schools and Conflict in Postwar Johnson County, Kansas," *History of Education Quarterly* 55, no. 2 (May 2015): 133–63; and "The Geo-spatial Distribution of Educational Attainment: Cultural Capital and Uneven Development in Metropolitan Kansas City, 1960–1980," *Histoire & Mesure* 29, no. 1 (2014): 219–46 (with Sanae Akaba).

Abbreviations

FRL	free or reduced-price lunch subsidies
HMSD	Hickman Mills School District
KCK	Kansas City, Kansas
KCKPS	Kansas City, Kansas, Public Schools
KCMO	Kansas City, Missouri
KCMPS	Kansas City, Missouri, Public Schools
NCLB	No Child Left Behind
NKCSD	North Kansas City School District
RSD	Raytown School District
SMSD	Shawnee Mission School District

CREATING THE SUBURBAN SCHOOL ADVANTAGE

Introduction
EDUCATING THE FRAGMENTED METROPOLIS

The Kansas City, Kansas (KCK), and Shawnee Mission (SM) school districts share a border in northeast Kansas, within the greater Kansas City metropolitan area. While geographically contiguous, however, they are worlds away in most other respects. In 2013 the four-year graduation rate in KCK was less than 66 percent, while in SM it was more than 91 percent. The average ACT (college prep) score in Harmon High, the KCK high school closest to the border, was 15.2, about 28 percent below the national mean of 20.9. This level of performance was similar to the district as a whole. On the other hand, the average score in Shawnee Mission North, the SM institution closest to Harmon, was 22.3. This was 7 percent higher than the national standard, with more students taking the test. Other institutions in the SM district posted even better averages.[1]

Less than four miles separate Harmon and Shawnee Mission North, but the outcomes for their students reflect enormous differences in resources, standards of living, and a host of other factors that affect their education. A popular real estate website recently ranked KCK's public schools second to last among the several dozen school districts in metropolitan Kansas City, and the SM schools the third best. This may seem surprising, but it is scarcely unique today. These kinds of stark distinctions have become all too familiar to many Americans, especially those concerned about the welfare of their children. But they are a relatively recent development in the nation's history.[2]

Education is an essential aspect of human development, but it occurs under conditions dictated by specific circumstances of time and place. It may take a village to raise a child, after all, but not all villages are the same. In recent history some communities have marshaled vastly superior resources to devote to their children, which often turns out to make a significant difference in their lives. These assets include financial capacity and the built environment, but they also comprise social, cultural, and political status. As a consequence, such places enjoy decided advantages with respect to education, while others are often labeled underprivileged. In this respect inequality has acquired a palpable geographical dimension in American life, a fact widely recognized today.[3] But just how this happened, and what—if anything—can be done about it, are still not well understood. It is the task of this book to answer these and related questions, but first it is necessary to look back a bit in time.

Inequality in education or any other facet of life is hardly new, of course. There has always been variation in the natural and social resources available in different places. But urbanization and related processes of industrialization and technological change contributed to additional sources of distinction between communities.[4] These developments accelerated dramatically following World War II in the United States, a time of profound changes in metropolitan life. It was an era of suburban ascendancy, labeled a "metropolitan revolution" because of the manifold changes it brought. Families with economic, social, and cultural advantages left the cities for communities that excluded others, adding a spatial dimension to long-standing facets of inequality such as race and social class.[5] Wealth and poverty still existed, but in considerably less proximity. These developments contributed to the differences described in the two high schools above.

A revolution of sorts also occurred in American education during the long postwar era, stretching roughly from 1945 through the 1970s. It entailed consolidation of resources and the deliberate creation of locally defined boundaries, representing a departure from the past. In geographic terms, America's educational center of gravity started in the countryside, moved to the cities after the Civil War, and shifted dramatically to the suburbs during the latter half of the twentieth century.[6] At the beginning of the twentieth century, most people believed city schools to be an improvement over rural institutions, but eventually suburban schools came to be seen as superior to both. There certainly were exceptions to these tendencies, but the direction of historical transformation was unmistakable. By 1980 more children attended suburban schools than either urban or rural institutions.[7] This seismic shift reflected the creation of a decisive suburban educational advantage.

The legacy of these developments remains readily evident today, as the superiority of suburban schools became more or less normalized. To the extent that they think about it, most Americans likely would agree with this characterization. The suburbs, after all, represent an American dream, at least for many families.

Life there is associated with affluence, comfort, and security, attributes that some communities have featured for generations. Less-prosperous suburban areas certainly exist, but they are generally considered exceptions to the rule.[8]

Given this, it is little wonder that suburban schools have become cultural icons. This is especially true of secondary institutions, the popular movie sites of adolescent escapades, middle-class angst, and dreams come true. City schools, on the other hand, are widely associated with far different impressions, such as academic failure, crime, and other social problems; and rural schools can be seen as stifling backwaters, frozen in the past. These have become familiar tropes, rooted in the 1950s if not earlier, and certainly are not entirely accurate.[9] But today much of the public commonly believes suburban institutions to be socially and academically advantageous.[10] Ask most Americans to name a superior school or district, and it is a safe bet they will point to a well-heeled suburb. The historical ascendency of this viewpoint marked a sea change in perceptions of public education.

This book seeks to identify the process by which this occurred, focusing on a particular metropolitan area but also placing it in a national context. It focuses on the three decades following 1950, the long postwar era. It was during these years that the perceived suburban advantage clearly took shape. Systematically excluding people considered to be indigent or members of racial or ethnic minority groups, especially African Americans, was integral to this process. At the same time, white suburbanites occasionally competed with one another for advantage and influence, roiling the placid settings they safeguarded so zealously. The result was a metropolitan region carved into many different locales, distinguished by gradations of wealth and status and bound by few—if any—shared interests. If there were two issues that everyone became concerned with, however, they were race and defense of local prerogatives.

Institutions and Inequality

For better or worse, people today rely on institutions for the orderly performance of everyday functions needed to maintain the social order. The legal system governs commerce and keeps the peace, churches sustain religious and ethical principles, retailers provide goods and services, families raise children, and schools educate and certify academic accomplishment. Countless other institutions perform additional tasks, and all contribute in one way or another to the quality of modern life. Schools are among the most far reaching, however, touching the lives of nearly all members of contemporary society.[11] They also play a pivotal role in the allocation of social status; the credentials they award can open doors and create pathways to success, defined in many ways. But some schools are judged to be better than others, and this too can have important consequences. And as suggested above, educational institutions are intimately connected to their immediate communities, which also contributes to inequity.[12]

Public education in the United States is unique in its local system of governance and funding. Today it counts more than thirteen thousand independent school districts, and thousands of other local governmental units play a role in managing public education systems. As legal scholar Richard Briffault has observed, school districts are governmental organizations under the jurisdiction of states, with authority over a legally defined territory within their boundaries. Historically, tiny rural districts maintained most American schools, and they numbered more than one hundred thousand as late as 1942. Efficiency-minded legislatures reduced the number, but the principle of local control remained inviolate. The political geography of school districts differed regionally, with boundaries often corresponding to municipal and township limits in the Northeast, county lines in much of the South, and typically independent of both in the West.[13] This eventually turned out to hold important implications for patterns of educational inequality.

Local control and funding of education has long been a source of differences in the resources available to schools. This variation extends to financial capacity, social status, and political influence, but also the abilities and dispositions that students bring to class. In 1968 Arthur Wise found that the wealthiest districts in Illinois spent more than two and a half times more per classroom than the poorest ones. Other states reported similar disparities. The postwar metropolitan revolution contributed to telling disparities among school districts. As more-affluent and better-educated families settled in communities attached to particular school districts, inequalities mounted. In this fashion, the geographic location of school systems exerted considerable influence on the types of learning experiences that children received.[14] If the quality of education has been determined largely by instructional time and location, the latter mattered a great deal indeed.

Historians and Suburban Schooling

Despite its magnitude, the change in postwar metropolitan schooling has garnered rather modest academic consideration. Until recently historians have exhibited little interest in suburban schools, perhaps because they seemed so familiar and mundane. As in other disciplines, historical scholarship has focused on big problems in education and the settings where they were most readily evident. The result has been a rich tradition of research on city schools and the manifold challenges they have faced. Along the way, historians discovered that city schools were once seen as the very best institutions. And they amply documented the decline of these systems, sometimes in terms that overlooked their many positive qualities.[15] Even so, historians have generally ignored the suburban schools that emerged at about the same time.

This turned out to have been a serious omission, as the rise of suburban schooling was clearly linked to changes in urban institutions, certainly in the public mind.[16] New highway construction and popular ownership of cars facilitated the movement of families to the suburbs, along with the easy availability of mortgages and a strong preference for selling to whites. Rising birthrates during the "baby boom" led many to seek more spacious and contemporary housing, along with bigger yards and quiescent neighborhoods. The cities were hardly the only locus of change.[17]

Racial segregation, of course, was a critical component of this story, and historians have devoted much attention to it. Through a variety of means, African Americans were systematically barred from most suburban communities, and whites avoided black neighborhoods. This reflected a process of racialization that eventually characterized housing markets in most of the nation's metropolitan centers. For decades prior to the postwar era, blacks were excluded by restrictive deed covenants, discriminatory zoning ordinances, unfair mortgage policies, and a host of other mechanisms. Decades of research has documented this.[18] The suburbs and their schools remained predominantly white as a consequence. As time passed, the result was a widespread pattern of metropolitan racial differentiation across the country.[19]

Most Americans are familiar with these aspects of racialized geography, which now span several generations. They were the product of government policy and private acts of discrimination dating to at least the early twentieth century, if not earlier. And schools eventually played a big role in the process. In the postwar era, urban educational systems became focal points of white flight, a widely observed phenomenon and the object of much commentary. Sociologist Joe Feagin has suggested that these developments were widely associated with a "white racial frame" that held ethnic and racial minorities—and African Americans in particular—to be intellectually, morally, and socially inferior to white people. Another term for this belief is racism, a set of ideas with deep roots in American history and perpetuated by decades of discrimination that helped to prolong myths of minority inferiority. It often hit real estate markets with especially devastating force, when whites ceased to look for housing in areas associated with blacks or other minority groups. This usually resulted in dramatic drops in property value, making it very difficult for African Americans and other minority group members to accumulate wealth through home ownership.[20] Such were the dynamics of a changing metropolitan geography, a process that frequently brought stark changes to schools.

Another side of the metropolitan revolution existed outside the central cities. Suburban schools also had a hand in attracting families to particular communities. Many were drawn to districts touting high scholastic standards or a socially appealing clientele. Such attributes were often linked to affluence, but educational institutions also became a way of comparing suburbs irrespective of wealth. These places were hardly all the same, after all, and competition for prestige could have telling consequences, not least regarding property values.[21] Stability in that regard became a highly prized community attribute.

The long postwar period thus witnessed profound changes in the social organization of American metropolitan life, with predominantly affluent white suburbs ultimately surrounding increasingly poor and nonwhite central cities. Schools often became integral to these developments, both contributing to change and reflecting its consequences. The term "urban education" became associated with racial and ethnic minority groups and high-poverty neighborhoods, while suburban schools were widely presumed to be predominantly white and academically superior. Inequality acquired a distinctive spatial flavor, regarding both schooling and social status in general.[22]

Urban historians have documented many of these developments, at least in broad strokes, and metropolitan inequality has become a familiar feature of American life. But much remains unknown about just how this occurred, especially with respect to schools. A handful of studies have started investigating these questions, but questions remain.[23] One concerns the institutional mechanisms and social practices that contributed to this process. For instance, many African Americans wanted to partake of the benefits of suburban life; how were they excluded, along with others deemed undesirable, from rapidly expanding suburban communities? Where and when were boundaries drawn, and how were they defended? Then, of course, there is the matter of education. What did schools contribute to this process, and how did they help shape new patterns of social inequality? And what were the consequences of educational changes? How did people and institutions respond? To address these and other questions about the character and impact of these events, it is necessary to examine their local manifestations in greater detail.

A Metropolitan Case Study

A fruitful approach to considering specific conditions and practices that contributed to the rise of suburban schools is to scrutinize a particular metropolitan locale. While there have been many studies of individual urban school districts and suburban communities, much less attention has been devoted to change on a metropolitan scale.[24] It makes sense to do this, however, as social scientists have long hypothesized that urban and suburban communities are parts of a greater whole. Developments in one such setting almost invariably resulted in change in another.[25] Urbanist Leo Schnore wrote about this more than sixty years ago, calling for more research on the "demographic and functional composition of the various parts of the metropolitan area" and identifying "other sociological units that constitute the total community."[26] From this perspective, the various parts of a metropolis can best be understood as elements of the larger entity, linked generally in functional terms.

It turns out that this sort of "ecological" approach to understanding urban development is well suited to case-study research, even if its assumptions regarding functionality do not always ring true. Methodologist Robert Stake has pointed out that a case can be productively viewed as a "bounded system," with "working parts" that may well be somewhat illogical but affect one another just the same.[27] In this instance the case is the region organized around a particular city, and the study focuses on schooling as a specific dimension of life. It asks how educational institutions developed there, and how social, political, and economic changes affected them across the region.

The setting is metropolitan Kansas City, a major midwestern hub near the geographical center of the contiguous forty-eight states. It grew to become a nationally significant center for a number of industries, ranking among the twenty largest urbanized areas of the country by 1960. Positioned as it is, Kansas City is neither North nor South, East nor West in its social and cultural orientation. It was settled both from the Northeast and the South historically. While the area featured a good deal of industrial development, it hardly qualified as a major manufacturing center or one long associated with a particular industry. Sprawled across the border between Kansas and Missouri, it grew as a gateway to the West in the nineteenth century, sitting at the juncture of the Missouri River and the eastern terminus of both the Santa Fe and Oregon trails. Kansas City became the site of meatpacking and other food-processing industries, serving an agrarian hinterland that stretched to Texas, Colorado, and the Dakotas and shipping products to the East. Eventually certain other industries took root there, drawn by the central location and transportation lines to regional and national markets.[28]

Kansas City also endured its share of adversities. The state line complicated the area's development, and Kansas City, Missouri, petitioned the state legislature more than once to allow it to be annexed to Kansas. This turned out to be politically untenable, so two quite different Kansas City municipalities subsequently grew on either side of the confluence of the Missouri and Kansas Rivers. The Missouri settlement expanded faster, largely because of advantages in trade to the east and as a terminus for settlers and goods headed west. It became the area's commercial and financial center, while Kansas City, Kansas, developed largely as a manufacturing district, specializing in agricultural byproducts such as oils, soaps, and paints. Population growth on the Missouri side of the rivers, consequently, was considerably more robust, and the principal municipality of the region developed there. In time it acquired a reputation for corrupt city politics, typified by the Pendergast machine, and a thriving jazz scene, emanating from the historic black entertainment and commercial district at Eighteenth and Vine.[29]

Given this history, metropolitan Kansas City is a decidedly apt setting for a study such as this. A recent publication identified it as highly representative of national demographic trends.[30] Located in the nation's farm belt, it grew to more than a million people in the postwar period. Manufacturing surged as local wartime production facilities shifted to autos, steel, and other durable goods. As a result, the region underwent a process of sprawl quite similar to other large urbanized areas. The upshot was a good deal of social and economic differentiation, with some parts of the metropolis becoming blue-collar communities and other, more affluent areas attracting higher-status residents. Geographer Richard Florida listed Kansas City as one of the country's most economically segregated metropolitan areas in 2017, an observation that reflected its history of uneven development, the depth of poverty in certain neighborhoods, and the accumulation of wealth in others.[31] And much of this was related to the question of race.

Missouri was a slave state during the antebellum era, and consequently acquired a strong southern cultural and political orientation. Much of this legacy remained intact well after the Civil War, and it continued to be evident through the twentieth century. Southern influence extended to parts of metropolitan Kansas City, especially north of the Missouri River, but elsewhere too. In these respects, the area can be considered part of a border zone, straddling the country's historic sectional divide.[32] There was a sizable black community on the Missouri side of the river, also dating from the nineteenth century, and a long history of racial segregation and inequality. African Americans migrated to Kansas City, Kansas, too, mostly after the Civil War, in search of opportunity in a state then associated with antislavery activism. They also became segregated and suffered discrimination as the city expanded. These communities grew substantially during the twentieth century but remained largely restricted to the region's two central cities.[33]

In the postwar era, whites left the urban core in large numbers for a variety of reasons, many directly or indirectly associated with race and social class. This process was abetted by highway construction, discriminatory mortgage policies, and aggressive real estate sales tactics. The result was sharp declines in property values, high unemployment due to jobs leaving the cities, and deepening poverty linked to racial segregation.[34] Demographer Douglas Massey and his colleagues have counted Kansas City among the nation's "hyper segregated" metropolitan areas across much of the latter part of the twentieth century, although conditions have improved somewhat recently.[35] It is thus little wonder that the area's city schools struggled with difficult issues of racial isolation and extreme, concentrated poverty. In this regard the fate of these institutions paralleled the experiences of other urban education systems in highly segregated and unequal metropolitan areas. This adversity primarily impacted the region's black residents; greater Kansas City did not have a sizable Hispanic population until the later 1970s.[36]

While segregation and poverty posed big challenges to African Americans, local black communities also boasted many accomplishments. Kansas City was famous for its black musicians, athletes, and culinary entrepreneurs.[37] The *Kansas City Call* became a widely known black newspaper and a stalwart voice against discrimination and exploitation. National black leaders such as Marcus Garvey and A. Philip Randolph visited the city regularly and drew large audiences. Local NAACP chapters actively challenged discrimination in employment, housing, and higher education. And black community leaders also protested unequal and segregated schooling, especially leading up to and following the *Brown* decisions in the mid-1950s.[38] While Kansas City's African American residents faced daunting obstacles in their quest for fairness and equality, their spirit and commitment to progress remained resilient.

This study is principally about the process of suburban development, however, examined in light of the racialization of neighborhoods and institutions, especially schools. As historians have amply demonstrated, suburbanization entailed a massive movement of human and material resources out of central cities, leaving poverty and inequity in its wake.[39] While Kansas City's urban schools struggled with growing numbers of impoverished students, outlying districts grew rapidly and remained predominantly white and middle class. And much of this occurred within the municipal boundaries of Kansas City, Missouri. Given the dynamics of change at play throughout the area, there can be little doubt that schools played a significant role in the process of metropolitan change and contributed directly to metropolitan inequality. This occurred on both sides of the border. In Kansas the schools abetted the success of wealthy and fashionable suburbs, while in Missouri they often became outposts of racialized refuge from real and perceived problems of urban education. In either case they also were the source of considerable conflict and became integral to distinctions between the city and its suburbs. And their leaders became vocal opponents of change. Without the contributions of the schools, there can be little doubt that suburbanization in Kansas City would not have occurred as it did.[40]

Greater Kansas City expanded steadily following the war, abetted by a freeway system that became one of the most extensive in the country. The decision to build a new airport some twenty miles from downtown signaled the willingness of local leaders to abide by these developments, anticipating future sprawl. An aggressive program of annexations helped to keep much of this expansion within the municipal boundaries of Kansas City, Missouri, a response similar to that of cities in western states. But classic forms of suburbanization in surrounding communities also occurred, and this too had educational ramifications.[41] In fact, school districts eventually played a decisive role in demarcating urban and suburban communities, even within the city limits.

The region was also the site of one of the nation's most contentious and ambitious school desegregation plans, the result of a Supreme Court decision that continues to be a source of debate. In an unusual set of circumstances, the complaint was initiated by neither civil rights groups nor aggrieved parents and students. The case, *Jenkins v. Missouri*, began as a suit by the Kansas City, Missouri, public schools against other districts on both sides of the state line. The federal district court changed this, making the Kansas City schools a defendant and releasing the other districts, but not before attorneys on both sides of the litigation had collected a sizable cache of information about local school systems.[42] Local archival depositories preserved much of this material, particularly the Western Historical Manuscripts Collection at the University of Missouri–Kansas City. This rich source of information about the development of schooling in the region is yet another reason why Kansas City is well suited to a study of this sort. While *Jenkins v. Missouri* is not a major focus of the book, the case generated historical evidence that turned out to be especially valuable.

Finally, there is the question of scale. While metropolitan Kansas City is large enough to rank as an important center of culture and commerce, with all the problems of larger urbanized areas, its size is well suited to a case study of this sort. Its suburban communities and school districts numbered fewer than several dozen, unlike larger metropolitan regions that counted more than a hundred. This put Kansas City in the upper half of all urbanized areas with respect to district fragmentation, but it was far from the most extreme case.[43] Studies of urban districts have focused on bigger cities in the past, but these places are often unrepresentative of the norm. Greater Kansas City is more typical in this respect and thus offers a manageable scale for a study of metropolitan dynamics. It permits the use of a geo-spatial frame of reference to identify how the region was partitioned into spaces defined both by race and social class distinctions.[44] This is not to say that the book will deal with all of the many local changes that occurred at this time. It is not an omnibus history of schooling in the region. Rather, its focus is major events and key turning points in the rise of suburban education systems in greater Kansas City, and the manifold changes that they wrought.[45]

Varieties of Localism

As suggested earlier, the metaphorical image of the city as an organism holds considerable appeal. The human ecology school of urban sociology promulgated various permutations of this perspective, influencing social scientists and historians for much of the twentieth century. Amos Hawley was a leading proponent, and his book *Human Ecology* became a foundational text in the field.[46] This viewpoint influenced research on urban growth and change, especially regarding connections between central cities and the suburbs.

Since the ecological perspective holds that metropolitan regions function as an integrated whole, it was logical to see the development of urban and suburban schooling as closely connected. But there obviously was more to the story. It could be misleading, after all, to describe the relationship of schools in these different contexts as functional, at least in practical terms. Suburban schools flourished, while city schools suffered by comparison, at least in the eyes of most observers. In this respect it appeared that these institutions often developed in stark opposition to one another. This observation reveals one of the principal shortcomings of the human ecology perspective: it did not deal well with conflict. In particular, proponents of the integrated metropolis failed to anticipate the salience of viewpoints that favored the local over a region as a whole. It was hardly a trivial oversight.[47]

Conflict wracked the process of metropolitan development in the postwar era, to one degree or another. White racism, of course, was a major source of discord on a range of issues, including housing, jobs, and schooling. But it was hardly the only one. Insofar as suburban development represented a flight from the city, whether due to bigotry or other reasons, it entailed a rejection of urban life. Public discourse made big-city politics and corruption enduring themes, along with crime and grime, that fueled such viewpoints.[48] Given this, suburbanites devoted considerable effort to constructing boundaries, separating themselves from the city and eventually shunning some of their immediate neighbors as well. As sprawl unfolded, the countryside surrounding cities quickly became a complex patchwork of villages, towns, and other jurisdictions. It was hardly a recipe for cooperation and goodwill.[49] Despite outward appearances of peace and tranquility, suburbia also exhibited considerable status anxiety and antipathy alongside its prototypical propriety.

According to human ecology theory and urban planning doctrine, these should have been relatively minor or temporary problems. Such borders were not supposed to exert excessive influence on overall development, and eventually should have given way to shared concerns for orderly and efficient metropolitan development.[50] But boundaries quickly assumed great salience in suburbia. Their creation became a recipe for even more conflict, as communities routinely resisted proposals for reform or greater equity in institutional policies and practices. For better or worse, the rise of the suburbs brought a growing emphasis on local priorities rather than a willingness to abide by larger concerns. As suggested above, suburbanites even could be indifferent or hostile to the interests of neighboring communities. The result was a fragmented polity that valued limited government and direct control of institutions, principles well suited to an ethos of exclusion.

One term that conveys the sentiment animating many suburban communities, particularly the more affluent ones, is *localism*. It is a word with various meanings, but in this context it represents a foreshortening of interests and concerns to exclude matters that did not directly benefit a particular community. When considering a proposed policy or public expenditure, individuals with this perspective would focus resolutely on how it could affect their immediate neighbors and themselves. Consequently, sharing resources was not high on the agenda, and neither was relinquishing control of institutions that served them.[51] Tightly knit homeowners' associations often became a forum for airing such sentiments and organizing in response to perceived threats. In fact, local developer J. C. Nichols made Kansas City a forerunner in the development of such organizations. This sort of localism appeared historically as an aversion to city politics and the large, bureaucratic, and impersonal institutions associated with big municipalities. It contributed directly to the political patchwork of the suburban landscape during the postwar era. These communities may have seemed tranquil and orderly, but they devoted continual vigilance to maintaining such appearances. Property values depended on it, but so did a way of life that many suburbanites were determined to preserve.[52]

Postwar suburban localism represented a sharp break from the views of the system builders who shaped and led urban institutions during the first half of the twentieth century. These men—and a few women—often were cosmopolitan in their thinking, exchanging ideas at the national level to move a shared agenda forward. In education they aimed to create "the one best system," as historian David Tyack characterized it. But similar efforts were made in municipal reform, policing, social welfare, and other facets of urban life. Rather than fracturing the polity in terms of particular neighborhoods and districts, these leaders had sought to serve all the nation's polyglot cities with institutions that functioned efficiently and at least somewhat equitably. There were exceptions, to be sure, especially in deliberate discrimination against African Americans and other racialized minority groups. But urban elites during this era sought to unite much of the rest of their urban constituency, exhibiting a noblesse oblige informed by an ethic of public service. To summon another of Tyack's depictions, they were "managers of virtue," dedicated to improving life for the greatest number of people they deemed possible.[53]

It is safe to say that relatively few postwar suburbanites shared such views. Many found large urban institutions inherently corrupt and inefficient. Large numbers also left the cities to escape neighborhoods undergoing racial transition, and harbored deep animosity toward blacks and other groups viewed as socially inferior. Suburbs settled principally by such residents, especially places proximate to expanding African American neighborhoods, often engaged in a particularly virulent form of localism that has been labeled "opportunity hoarding." Sociologist Charles Tilly coined the term to describe the use of boundaries by members of a group to categorically exclude outsiders, but not necessarily to exploit them. Other scholars have used it somewhat differently, arguing that the effects of opportunity hoarding have been especially pernicious. This study employs it to describe a geo-spatial system of exclusion, typically focused on the segregation of African Americans. In this way, boundary construction by white communities severely constrained the ability of blacks to gain access to schools, jobs, housing, and other valuable collective assets. White suburbanites hoarded these opportunities for growth and advancement, reserving them for friends and families. Historically, a number of factors played a role in these developments, including white supremacy, local resources of social capital, and various forms of status anxiety.[54] This was an especially spiteful variant of localism, one that required a high level of community cohesion to sustain.

Localism and opportunity hoarding are useful concepts for interpreting the behavior of suburbanites during the postwar era. The suburbs that sprang up around American cities did not remain predominantly white and middle class by coincidence. Systematic forms of exclusion clearly operated to maintain a quality of life that suburban residents deemed highly desirable, along with rising property values. This was part and parcel of the suburban experience, to one degree or another. Living in an *exclusive* neighborhood or subdivision, after all, was the height of suburban aspiration, especially one reserved for the most status-worthy residents. As the term implies, the demarcation of geo-social boundaries was indispensable to the affirmation and defense of social standing, along with mechanisms to exclude those deemed undeserving. Identifying these characteristics of suburban schooling is one of the principal objects of this study.

Plan of the Book

The remainder of this account is organized into five chapters and an epilogue. It begins with an overview of suburban development during the long postwar era and the implications that it held for schooling. Beyond that, it explores the development of school systems in metropolitan Kansas City in considerable detail, focusing on the social, economic, and demographic changes that transformed the area's educational landscape. The conclusion summarizes key points from the study and brings the story up to the present. In the end, it appears that events that unfolded in the three decades following 1950 created a new metropolitan system of education, one that resulted in a clear suburban advantage, and which continues to exist today.

Chapter 1 describes the development of educational systems in the United States through much of the twentieth century, and changes in metropolitan life following the Second World War. Patterns of suburban development varied somewhat by region, a process that held important implications for the organization of schooling. In the end, however, there was considerable convergence in the general process of suburbanization. Distinctions between central city and suburban communities became commonplace, especially in larger metropolitan regions. Educational inequities generally paralleled these developments, with few exceptions. By the later 1970s it was quite clear that a new national model of suburban advantage had taken hold, one that has continued to be evident largely to the present.

Chapter 2 introduces metropolitan Kansas City as the site for a case study to examine the dynamics of suburban development and its implications for educational inequality. Following the lead of its city manager Perry Cookingham, Kansas City, Missouri, undertook an aggressive program of annexation to foreclose the negative effects of suburban development on the central city, expanding its boundaries substantially. Cookingham's plan did not include annexation of school districts, however, and as a result the enlarged municipality contained all or parts of more than a dozen districts, a development that would have important consequences. At the same time, suburbanization resulted in population shifts across the area, with affluent and college-educated adults settling in suburban communities, especially in Johnson County, Kansas.

This too would have important educational consequences, giving suburban schools on the Kansas side of the state line a particular advantage in terms of academic attainment and achievement. It also relegated the schools of Kansas City, Missouri, to a range of problems associated with concentrated poverty and declining revenues.

Chapter 3 describes changes in the postwar era to the Kansas City, Missouri, public schools, which went from being considered the very best such local institutions to perhaps the worst. In the 1950s the Kansas City high schools were widely considered to be superior to their suburban counterparts, which were much smaller and offered fewer curricular and extramural options for students. As suburban districts expanded, however, these distinctions began to fade. At the same time, the arrival of large numbers of poor African Americans, most from the rural South, contributed to racial change in the schools. Thousands of white families moved to suburban districts, especially with the advent of desegregation plans in the 1970s. Research on school transfers revealed that most such "flight" headed to the south, remaining largely within the city's municipal boundaries. By 1980 the Kansas City school district's population had fallen dramatically, and only a tiny minority was white, making meaningful desegregation within the system impossible. Meanwhile, neighboring districts had grown enormously, serving an almost entirely white population. A new educational order had emerged.

Chapter 4 deals with changes in the Missouri suburbs, describing their consolidation and growth across the postwar period. Particular attention is devoted to several of these districts, which served as bellwethers of change across the period. They include North Kansas City, which grew rapidly through a process of annexation, eventually more than tripling in size geographically as smaller districts agreed to join it. The other districts are Raytown and Hickman Mills to the south, both of which had been consolidated many years earlier. These districts expanded in population during the postwar era, especially Hickman Mills, which registered the fastest growth rate in the region. They offer an interesting contrast, however, in efforts aimed at excluding blacks and other groups considered undesirable. In particular, Raytown may have represented the period's most active case of opportunity hoarding.

Chapter 5 offers an account of developments on the Kansas side of the border, focusing specifically on the rise of the Shawnee Mission School District. Johnson County became known for the high quality of its schools and attracted the greatest concentration of college-educated adults in the area. This came to represent a significant advantage with respect to the performance of local schools. The district encountered difficulties, however, in achieving consolidation, as wealthy patrons in fashionable communities rejected proposals to join with less-affluent residents in other parts of the area. An act of the legislature eventually forced creation of the district, the only one in the state to require this step. This episode reflected the effects of localism within the suburban context, where status distinctions between communities could make common interests difficult to recognize or acknowledge.

The book's epilogue provides a summary of its principal points and larger implications. Kansas City offers a nearly archetypal case of the metropolitan revolution, with suburban sprawl transforming the region's social, economic, and demographic landscape. At the same time the educational system changed profoundly as well, with so-called suburban districts growing rapidly and the once preeminent central city district suffering a near collapse in significance and stature. It is telling that school district boundaries, rather than municipal limits, became the lines demarking suburban versus urban residential zones. This institutional form of education became a badge of status as a consequence, a telling indication of the power that this particular dimension of metropolitan life came to represent.

Beyond this, the epilogue adds a brief account of the contemporary status of the various entities discussed in the book. It turns out that the Johnson County, Kansas, schools remain the best academically in the region, at least judging by test scores, and the Kansas City schools—on both sides of the border—continue to be considered among the most problem-ridden. Other suburban districts remain somewhere in between but are considered far better than the central city schools. Hickman Mills is the exception, and has become predominantly African American. Somewhat ironically, Raytown today is perhaps the most integrated district in the region. By and large, however, the patterns of geo-spatial inequality that emerged during the postwar years are still clearly evident. The era of suburban advantage appears to be far from over.

In closing, it should be noted that the synopsis provided above represents only highlights of each chapter; it does not begin to convey all their points. The richness and variety of Kansas City history is only touched on in the pages to follow, but hopefully the story of educational inequality in this expansive metropolis will prove compelling. More importantly, it is intended to be informative to readers interested in understanding the past with an eye to forging a better future.

Finally, a note on methodology is in order. This study makes use of a wide range of evidence and thus represents a variety of methodological traditions. Much of it, of course, draws on largely conventional historical documents, including archival records, contemporaneous journalistic accounts, and other such sources. But it also employs statistical data and oral history interviews. The book's appendix offers a discussion of these sources of information and the methods used to analyze them. For the most part, the narrative to follow does not feature technical details of the evidence or methods employed, particularly with respect to statistical analysis. Readers interested in these aspects of the study are encouraged to examine the published articles that I have authored or coauthored that deal with these issues. They are highlighted in the acknowledgments and cited in the endnotes.

1
SUBURBAN AND URBAN SCHOOLS
Two Sides of a National Metropolitan Coin

The 1961 publication of James Conant's landmark book *Slums and Suburbs* sounded a clarion call regarding the new metropolitan social order then emerging across the country. Focusing on schools, Conant depicted urban and suburban institutions as nearly polar opposites, largely reflecting the "status and ambitions of the families being served." Conant suggested that urban institutions represented many of the most vexing problems in American education and were associated with poverty, indiscipline, and low achievement. He warned that "we are allowing social dynamite to accumulate in our large cities." In suburban communities, on the other hand, he described public schools as affluent, well equipped, and representing high academic standards. Few families in these comfortable settings were looking for alternatives, and their chief concerns revolved around sending their children to college. Indeed, many had moved to suburban districts to take advantage of their well-regarded schools. This was especially true for communities where the schools enjoyed a good reputation—deserved or not—for academic excellence. As Conant announced at the book's outset, he offered "a picture of two totally different kinds of neighborhoods and the schools which serve them."[1]

Conant's account set the stage for much commentary on educational inequality in the 1960s and '70s, but it also highlighted a situation that many Americans had not yet grasped. Prior to the 1950s the big-city school systems, and particularly the high schools, were often held up as models. Because of their size, urban districts typically possessed greater resources than their counterparts in smaller communities, especially those in rural areas. Features of modern schooling taken for granted today started in urban settings, such as age grading, uniform textbooks, specialized classes, and summer school, among many others. Historically, big-city schools offered a wider range of courses and specialized programs such as college prep and vocational training. Teachers were better paid in the cities, and as a result schools there generally got the most skilled and experienced educators. Because they often were seen as superior, big-city schools attracted gifted students, many of them from modest backgrounds. Even if some of the worst schools existed in the cities, especially in the most impoverished neighborhoods, so did the very best.[2]

These conditions changed rapidly, however, in the postwar era, when the distribution of wealth and status was "decentered" by the expansion of suburban communities. Much of this was driven by technological change, especially the rise of automotive transportation and construction of contemporary highway systems. But real estate practices played an important role too, along with federal mortgage policies. Politics was a factor, as suburban voters became increasingly decisive in state and federal elections.[3] Schools also contributed to these changes, along with easy financial credit (for whites), extensive residential development, shopping malls, and many other features of metropolitan life. With the arrival of the 1960s, a new geo-spatial order had emerged, as suburban communities became growing sites of partisan power and status. Conant suggested that little recourse existed for such divisions in metropolitan life, and he turned out to be right. But this was just the beginning; the United States was indeed becoming a "suburban nation."[4]

Why did city schools gain and then lose their exalted status as the nation's premier educational institutions? How did suburban development unfold across the country, and what were its effects on schools in these settings? What factors influenced the ways that people in the cities and suburbs respond to change? And how did the school desegregation movement affect metropolitan inequity in education? Answers to these questions expand on the issues that Conant raised in his book. Events that shaped education in specific circumstances, after all, reflected larger historical forces that exerted influence on a national scale.

A Bygone Golden Age of Urban Education?

The city is where public schools acquired much of their contemporary form, as urban education systems came to be seen categorically as the nation's best. But it took decades for the superiority of these institutions to become manifest. American cities expanded rapidly prior to the First World War. Large-scale immigration drove the growth, drawn by industrial development and settlement of the nation's interior. Railways remained the prevailing transportation technology. Factories and other enterprises grew in transportation hubs, which afforded access to labor, materials, and markets for finished products. The nation's largest cities burgeoned: Chicago's population doubled about every decade for nearly a half century, and other cities grew almost as rapidly. These places became sites of wealth and power, along with considerable hardship and distress.[5]

The extraordinary pace of urban expansion placed enormous burdens on local institutions. School authorities scrambled to build new classrooms and staff them to keep abreast of population growth. The *New York Times* reported that some seventy-five thousand children were refused admission to the city's public schools in 1905 because of overcrowding. School officials in other cities faced similar problems, even if on a smaller scale. In the wake of scandals over corruption and mismanagement, political conflict over control of education systems became endemic. Reformers answered by vowing to take the schools "out of politics," creating an elaborate educational bureaucracy to ensure compliance with legal and ethical standards. The governance and administration of city school systems became centralized and routinized, resulting in Tyack's "one best system." A new degree of professionalism dawned in education, and many other institutional domains as well.[6]

Given their size and resources, the nation's urban schools offered students an array of educational opportunities, despite occasional problems such as overcrowding. The rapid growth of high schools and postsecondary institutions became distinctive features of the largest systems. Standardized tests, often intended to measure presumed native ability, were used to assign youth to different curricular "tracks." These included academic courses to prepare certain students for college, and less-demanding vocational classes for others. If the changing urban economy featured greater specialization and a wider division of labor, the schools were ready to respond. Reformers dubbed this "social efficiency," which became the prescription of the day.[7]

Some educators objected to this new organizational ethos, suggesting that it constrained opportunity for many students. But large urban school systems offered the prospect of accomplishment for millions of youth from different backgrounds. Secondary schools in towns and smaller cities usually were modest in scope, but in bigger cities they became expansive and comprehensive. High school enrollments nationally approached half the teenage population by the 1920s, although many fewer graduated. The curricular connection to labor markets helped young women and men find jobs in the growing service sector.

Thousands worked in corporate offices, department stores, catalog houses, government agencies, and similar settings. Many took classes in typing, bookkeeping, and accounting, skills in high demand. It was an exhilarating time to be young and gainfully employed in the vibrant downtown districts of major cities, and requisite training in the public schools made it possible.[8]

Historian Richard Hofstadter once wrote that "the United States was born in the country and has moved to the city." He might have added that others came from abroad. According to the census, by 1920, for the first time, a majority of Americans reported living in urban areas.[9] This included greater numbers of African Americans, as nearly a tenth of the South's predominantly rural black population moved to industrial cities between 1900 and 1930, principally in the North.[10] Larger American urban centers began to acquire some of the features of today's metropolitan infrastructure, including public transportation systems and centralized government services, as well as racially segregated neighborhoods and the early stages of large-scale suburbanization. The first generations of mass-produced automobiles contributed to these changes, even if their impact was still rather limited.[11]

At about the same time, many city school systems began a lengthy period of stability in leadership and organizational form, marking something of an early golden age in urban education. As population growth abated in the wake of war and immigration restrictions, educators ceased worrying about constant expansion. Instead they focused on improving the quality of schooling and increasing access to secondary and higher education. Public confidence in the schools grew as bureaucratic rules and standards helped to ensure wider opportunities for advancement, and at least the appearance of fairness. Even racialized minority groups long denied equal education, especially African Americans, began making headway in spite of ongoing discrimination.[12]

Progress stalled somewhat in the 1930s and '40s, however, largely owing to events far beyond the purview of local institutions. Lasting more than a decade, a period of global economic crisis and war slowed the pace of metropolitan development to a crawl. The Great Depression led to a collapse of the youth job market, boosting high school enrollment rates, and the Second World War triggered widespread migration to cities for employment. Economic calamity in the 1930s placed enormous pressure on school budgets, which saw scant relief during the war years of the '40s.[13] But the configuration of American metropolitan life changed little as a consequence. Major changes did not become evident until peace was declared, when auto and home sales surged and metropolitan highway construction resumed in earnest. A vibrant economy contributed to this, along with government policies favoring suburban development and a spike in the birthrate, the postwar "baby boom." Resources began flowing to education once again. Millions of young families now had money to spend, and new housing beckoned far beyond aging urban neighborhoods.[14]

Schools were a key feature of these changes, even as urban institutions continued to be predominant for a while. As greater numbers of youth graduated from high school, approaching 50 percent by 1950, more Americans came to see education as a vehicle of social mobility and economic opportunity, even if significant racial and social class disparities continued to exist. And events bore them out. Economists Claudia Goldin and Lawrence Katz have estimated that rising high school enrollments represented a major contribution to economic growth, boosting employment in new occupations created by technological advances and the growing service sector. Public schools made these opportunities more readily available, offering better prospects to children from a variety of backgrounds, including working-class families.[15]

Popular support for the schools reached new heights in the decade following the war. Big-city education systems grew with the baby boom. While elementary schools continued to function mainly as neighborhood institutions, urban high schools multiplied and expanded. They also became increasingly cosmopolitan in stature. African American secondary enrollment grew rapidly, sometimes leading to clashes with bigoted whites. Critics of secondary education in the 1950s, most notably James Conant, argued that larger schools were superior. Such institutions could offer a wider range of curricular choices, including academically advanced courses, along with extracurricular activities.[16] It was not until late in the decade that many rising suburban schools began to rival their big-city counterparts in these respects.

Even if the best-regarded city schools typically excluded racialized minority groups, especially African Americans, there was considerable consensus about the value of these systems and widespread support for their leaders. Centralization and bureaucracy remained the prevailing urban organizational ethos, and there was little question about who was in charge. Highly professionalized administrators ruled the roost, their expertise certified by specialized university training and credentials.[17] It would not be long, however, before the social and political context of urban education changed profoundly.

Education and Social Change in the City

As suggested by Conant, the most basic factors in the development of urban school systems were demographic and economic. In the years following the Second World War, the social and financial profile of the nation's cities shifted significantly. While the size of central cities changed relatively little, the thrust of metropolitan development was altered by movement to the metropolitan periphery. At the same time, successive waves of new residents moved to the urban core, many of them members of racial and ethnic minority groups, and large numbers living in poverty. Despite relatively stable population size, the nation's big cities began a dramatic process of social change. The urban population remained culturally diverse, but its composition shifted, and destitution and physical decline transformed certain neighborhoods. In particular, this was a time of especially rapid growth in the nation's racially segregated "ghetto" communities.[18]

Following the hiatus during the 1930s and early '40s, large-scale metropolitan development resumed in the postwar years. Industrial employment fueled migration, notably among African Americans from the South, though suburbanization curtailed central-city growth in the 1950s. Suburban expansion increased to an unprecedented scale, becoming one of the iconic features of the era. Made possible by federally financed new highways, easy mortgage terms for white families, and a boom in home building, it became a driving force in metropolitan development. Neighborhoods in many such communities had long excluded people deemed undesirable by means of restrictive deed covenants, barring property owners from selling to certain social groups—blacks in particular. This, along with federal mortgage standards that largely excluded black families from obtaining loans, virtually guaranteed that the suburbs would remain predominantly white. Even though the US Supreme Court declared restrictive covenants unconstitutional in 1948, their influence lingered. Real estate agents continued to discourage unwanted residents, especially anyone deemed likely to lower property values.[19]

At the same time, a changing southern economy altered life for millions of African Americans in the countryside, stimulating migration to the cities. Mechanized cotton farming triggered some of this, obviating the need for manual labor. Many blacks also hoped to escape Jim Crow segregation, white racial hostility, and impulsive bigoted violence. Within two decades of the war's end, about five million departed to find employment and greater freedom in the North, Midwest, and Pacific states, and millions more moved to southern cities. Most of these places had long-standing black communities, including a modest middle class of teachers, attorneys, doctors, and business owners of various sorts. Migrants, on the other hand, typically were impoverished and poorly educated. Barred from most suburbs and white urban neighborhoods, these blacks were compelled by racial discrimination to take up residence in crowded inner-city ghetto communities, typically in older housing stock. In the new metropolitan geography of the postwar era, poverty became concentrated near the urban core.[20]

These developments had profound implications for life in many communities, a transformation that eventually came to capture national attention. Economist Leah Platt Boustan has estimated that the typical black community in northern cities in 1940 represented just 4 percent of the local population; by 1970 that average had quadrupled to 16 percent, and it was considerably higher in many larger cities. Prior to World War II, nearly half of the African American urban population did not live in segregated neighborhoods, but by 1970 the vast majority did.[21] This rapid influx and high degree of segregation had telling consequences. Poverty became endemic in many neighborhoods, and residents were routinely exploited by landlords and brutalized by police. An emerging African American middle class, abetted by rising graduation rates and liberalizing employment policies, also became subject to greater segregation in highly racialized housing markets. Living conditions deteriorated in the wake of deprivation and crowding, and public services—including schools—often declined perceptibly in perceived quality.[22] These developments led to growing frustration and anger, eventually helping to ignite the "social dynamite" that Conant had warned about.

Beginning in the mid-1960s, violent riots or uprisings erupted in protest of such conditions, resulting in property damage in the millions of dollars and the loss of many lives. The first major disturbance occurred in Harlem in 1964, triggered by a police shooting, and was followed by an even larger riot in Los Angeles in 1965. Major outbursts also occurred in Detroit and Newark in the summer of 1967 and in scores of cities across the country (including Kansas City) following the assassination of Martin Luther King Jr. in 1968. The Kerner Commission, appointed by President Lyndon Johnson in 1967 to investigate these events, concluded that hyper-aggressive police practices had triggered most of them. The commission also found that riots also reflected the dissatisfaction many blacks felt about the poverty and discrimination they endured on a daily basis. But to many whites these were unsettling episodes representing one more reason to abandon the nation's larger cities, or to avoid them altogether.[23]

Black migration to urban areas continued through much of the 1960s, and so did suburban development. Expansive ghetto communities grew in major cities, and as suburbanization accelerated it became associated with the term "white flight." Boustan has calculated that about a quarter of white departures from core cities in this period could be directly attributed to the arrival of African American migrants, and that changes were most clearly evident in the largest metropolitan areas. Housing values typically dropped in central city neighborhoods as a consequence of these events, making suburban communities appear to be a much better investment. White flight, in that case, represented more than just households on the move; it also signaled a shift in wealth to the metropolitan periphery.[24]

There were other reasons for moving away from the urban core, of course. Many families left in search of bigger yards, more closet space, and attached garages, but there can be little doubt that most also were influenced by the increasingly racialized metropolitan landscape. Despite greater segregation, the growth of urban African American communities, along with civil rights activism, posed the possibility of integrated housing and institutions, raising the anxiety of bigoted whites to new levels. Passage of federal civil rights legislation in the mid-1960s manifestly added to these apprehensions, which quickly became evident in cities across the country.[25]

Such sentiments contributed to an escalation of explicitly racist responses to African Americans in certain neighborhoods or communities. In particular, less-affluent—often blue-collar—white suburbs, especially those located close to central cities, frequently exhibited overt hostility toward blacks. Cicero, Illinois, adjacent to Chicago, became a well-known example of this, as did White Plains in New York, Parma, Ohio, and Warren, Michigan. White ethnic enclaves within the cities often responded in a similar fashion, exemplified by the Bridgeport neighborhood in Chicago, home to Mayor Richard J. Daley and his family. Growing intolerance regarding race was evident in the success of bigoted Alabama governor George Wallace in the 1968 Democratic presidential primaries in Michigan, Ohio, and other parts of the metropolitan Midwest.[26]

Whites in more affluent suburban and urban communities may have shared such views but generally had fewer opportunities to voice them, or did so in a less dramatic fashion. In any case, African Americans became acutely aware of racial animosity directed at them, regardless of how it was expressed. This was a powerful incentive to avoid such hostile places and remain in familiar settings, even when moving was financially possible. The number of African Americans in poverty fell dramatically between 1960 and 1968, dropping from more than half to about a third. Those in the highest-paying job categories more than doubled between 1958 and 1973, and those in the lowest categories fell by a third. But segregation did not change appreciably.[27]

White racism remained a palpable barrier to the movement of blacks to certain neighborhoods irrespective of their education or income, limiting their housing choices to a relatively narrow range of options. Sociologist Karl Taeuber calculated in 1964 that 86 percent of African Americans in cities would have to move to less-segregated neighborhoods to achieve complete integration, a figure generally consistent across the country. This reflected a historically unprecedented level of isolation for a significant minority group, and it changed little in the years to follow.[28]

The era of relative stability and confidence in urban schooling, interrupted somewhat by the Great Depression and the war, did not last long. Urban school systems soon became highly segregated because of racialized housing markets and policies that assigned black and white students to separate buildings. Extremely high levels of residential segregation contributed to mounting population densities as black migrants crowded into ghetto neighborhoods. It also led to glaring disparities within city school districts. African American students crowded into schools routinely filled far beyond capacity, often leading to half-day shifts for many of them. High rates of staff turnover also meant that students typically were assigned the least experienced teachers.[29] Such circumstances were hardly conducive to academic success.

Despite these problems, many African American students succeeded in urban schools. Black high school graduation rates increased steadily, even in the biggest cities, testimony to these students' determination and resilience. But that did not mean they were happy about the condition of their schools.[30] Some districts used trailers or other temporary structures to accommodate the influx of students, rather than sending them to less crowded, predominantly white schools. These conditions adversely affected the quality of education for black children and youth, which naturally made many African Americans very angry, including the students.[31]

It was not long before large-scale protests erupted over the clearly unequal educational resources available to black and white students. Some three hundred thousand students boycotted school in Chicago in October 1963, joined by educators, parents, and other community members. Many participated in mass marches to the school board, led by the Coordinating Council of Community Organizations, a grassroots coalition of parents, educators, and community groups. Similar demonstrations occurred in other cities, including New York, Cincinnati, and Boston. Black community groups and civil rights organizations such as the NAACP and the Urban League helped make inequitable public education a national issue. In some cases protests were led by students demanding changes in their schools, such as the dramatic 1966 walkout at Detroit's Northern High School. Eventually these sorts of actions forced district boards to respond. Most offered only token integration measures, however, fearing that whites would abandon the schools if meaningful desegregation occurred.[32] As it turned out, that is what happened anyway.

As middle- and working-class whites left urban neighborhoods, followed by many businesses, the tax base of city governments and school systems began to decline. The proportion of census tracts that were uniformly white in northern cities fell from 67 percent in 1940 to 40 percent in 1970, and the drop was even more dramatic in some of the largest places.[33] Property values in African American neighborhoods were low and appreciated little in the face of racialized dual housing markets. Moreover, most of the newcomers to the cities were very poor and lacked the ability to support higher taxes for schools and other institutions. As a result, local revenues often failed to meet the rising costs of urban schools, and many big-city districts began to face dire budget shortfalls. In 1973 education scholars Raymond Hummel and John Nagle observed that "most urban school systems find it increasingly difficult to raise sufficient financial resources to meet the dramatically increased social and educational demands placed upon them."[34] The problem often became especially acute just as local student populations became predominantly African American or Hispanic. These developments, along with an apparent drop in urban graduation rates and achievement scores, were eventually labeled a "crisis" in urban education.[35]

City schools thus posed a dilemma that drew much attention, both from policy analysts and the political establishment. A study of fiscal disparities in the nation's thirty-seven largest metropolitan areas in 1964 found that suburban schools spent about 27 percent more per student on average than their urban counterparts, despite the fact that the city districts levied taxes at a higher rate. The difference was especially striking in light of higher costs in the cities.[36] With declining sources of local support, schools serving poor children in the cities required help from external sources just to maintain services. Passage of the federal Elementary and Secondary Education Act (ESEA) in 1965, along with increased state aid in some cases, made additional resources available by the end of the decade. Title 1 of ESEA stipulated that schools with a certain percentage of low-income or poor students would receive additional funds to support programs for them, usually in grants administered by the states. Some states also provided aid for districts with lower tax capacity, but such criteria often excluded big-city systems. These sources of financial assistance were helpful but generally failed to compensate for the loss of local tax capacity and the rising costs of urban education. Closing the spending gap with the most affluent suburbs was simply not possible.[37]

Added to this, Title 1 funds eventually went to a very large number of schools, including many outside the cities. As one study of the program declared, "It slathered money over more than nine in every ten districts."[38] While this may have established a firm political base for such support, it placed big-city schools at a competitive disadvantage, especially considering the needs of their less affluent clientele. In 1967 all of the nation's thirty-seven largest urban districts featured pupil-teacher ratios greater than their state average. Reflecting these tendencies, per-pupil expenditures in the cities continued to lag their suburban counterparts. This often meant fewer resources for such perceptible features of the schools as building maintenance, summer programs, and staff salaries.[39]

Money was hardly the only problem facing urban schools, however. The loss of students prepared to excel academically probably was even more significant. The federally funded *Equality of Educational Opportunity* report, written by sociologist James Coleman in 1966, highlighted the importance of family background as a determinant of educational achievement. It was the nation's first large-scale study of these questions, and it clearly demonstrated that higher levels of parental education and social status were associated with accomplishment in school. Coleman's research also suggested that attending schools with well-prepared peers could be a positive influence on achievement.[40]

These findings were borne out in subsequent research and eventually began to inform public thinking about education. Cautioning readers to not place too much emphasis on school finances in assessing districts, the authors of *The New York Times Guide to Suburban Schools* emphasized this point. "What makes more difference in educational achievement than anything else," they wrote, "is the family background of the students. This is as true in New York, New Jersey, Connecticut as it is in Texas, Ohio or Colorado." As a consequence, levels of community affluence became associated with higher-performing schools. White flight deprived urban schools of many students with backgrounds conducive to achievement, a critically important resource for institutional success.[41]

The process of suburbanization thus created two different kinds of problems for city schools. The first was the matter of segregation, or racial and socioeconomic isolation, resulting largely from impoverished black families settling in ghetto neighborhoods while more affluent whites departed. The other was financial: the declining tax base that suburbanization triggered. Consequently, at the same time that urban schools had larger numbers of relatively destitute children to teach, educators had to look farther afield to acquire the necessary resources. Signs of this had become clearly evident by the time that Conant published *Slums and Suburbs*. In the words of one contemporary observer, "the 'educational balance' between the large cities and their suburbs that existed in 1957 had vanished by 1962."[42]

It did not take long for these issues to animate the politics of education. Urban school leaders too often were slow to respond to changing conditions, compounding their districts' problems. Even though board members and administrators were supposed to be impartial and nonpartisan, many habitually enforced policies that maintained racial and ethnic inequity. Historians have documented this in Chicago, Milwaukee, Boston, Detroit, and Newark, among other places.[43] In the South, school leaders actively opposed desegregation, and even when they tried to improve schooling for blacks, true equality of education was almost never achieved in segregated systems. In response to these conditions, activists organized hundreds of demonstrations against school inequity in cities across the country, building on the protests of the early '60s. Directed by African American leaders and involving tens of thousands of community members and students, these events galvanized opposition to city school boards and administrators.[44]

Local politics often became polarized by these disputes, as recalcitrant, prejudiced white defenders of neighborhood schools resisted busing for desegregation or changing attendance zones. Confrontations burst into the open in Chicago, New York, San Francisco, and scores of other cities before coming to a head in dramatic white protests in Boston during the mid-1970s.[45] These developments helped to make schooling a national political issue, a focal point of widespread conflict and anger.

Even if school leaders wanted to support plans to address these problems, large urban districts often proved resistant to reforms. Their bureaucratic organization made it difficult to react promptly to changes in the cities. Long-standing rules and regulations, established to prevent corruption and fraud, frequently were used to undermine demands for improvement, especially for children in impoverished neighborhoods. In his study of the New York City Board of Education in 1968, David Rogers found that resistance from various offices in the system often stymied reform efforts, slowing implementation of plans and leading to the withholding of information and resources. Similar dynamics existed in other large urban systems.[46]

For their part, school boards routinely sidestepped reform proposals in response to constituencies that favored existing arrangements and upholding segregation. Organizational norms such as the neighborhood school provided convenient excuses for recalcitrant administrators and board members, and also hampered the efforts of well-intentioned activists. Consequently, meaningful reform was painfully slow to achieve, and this led to even greater frustration for poorly served urban constituencies.[47]

A National Pattern of Metropolitan Development

While urban districts struggled with growing problems, the suburbs were flourishing. The geographic organization of educational inequality had shifted from a pattern of urban dominance in 1940 to one of suburban advantage two decades later. Public attention to these questions focused on the Northeast and Midwest, where many of the largest cities had been manufacturing centers and experienced rapid change.[48] Vast postwar suburban developments, such as the Levittown communities outside New York and Philadelphia, captured the public imagination by appearing to make home ownership and a middle-class lifestyle widely available. Other such ventures followed suit, and a bustling hinterland of new communities quickly grew up around major American cities.[49]

Suburban developments varied a good deal, of course, ranging from exclusive enclaves to more commonplace subdivisions, depending on location and the types of homes and amenities that builders offered. While suburban school expenditures often exceeded urban levels, there was a great deal of disparity in that regard too. In some districts, cost-conscious suburbanites pushed back against school taxes, as in Long Island's "lower-middle-class" Levittown in the early 1960s. But in more affluent suburbs, residents often enthusiastically supported tax increases for the schools, viewing them as a source of distinction and an investment in the community, especially for augmenting property values. As a result, certain suburban school districts became more highly regarded than others, and this—along with local taxes—could be an important factor in where families decided to purchase homes.[50]

With connection to the urban core made easier by a burst of freeway construction during the 1950s and '60s, suburban growth was partly inspired by the prospect of educational advantage. The postwar-era baby boom, two decades of rapid demographic growth starting in 1945, drove a dramatic educational expansion. It also spurred suburban growth, as families often looked for higher-status communities to settle in, whether they moved from central cities or suburban areas elsewhere.[51] Young parents in particular wanted a safe and comfortable home for their growing families, and good schools to assure their children's future prospects. In surveys suburbanites overwhelmingly claimed that they had moved to improve the lives of their offspring.[52] Before long there was a lively marketplace of school districts for families to consider when shopping for a suburban home. When the *New York Times* published its 340-page *Guide to Suburban Public Schools* in 1976, it was responding to persistent demand for information that could clarify such decisions.[53]

Public attention may have focused on developments in the Northeast, but suburban growth occurred in all parts of the country. Long-standing regional differences in schooling began to change as a result. In particular, the South experienced significant suburban development following the war, and school systems there began to exhibit marked improvement. This occurred in both older and newer southern cities, although more in the former. Metropolitan Atlanta grew to encompass more than eight counties, and Charlotte, Birmingham, Houston, and other larger cities experienced similar if somewhat more modest degrees of suburbanization.[54]

Some municipalities avoided extensive suburbanization by annexing adjacent territory; Jacksonville, Florida, became the nation's largest city geographically in this manner. This was accomplished most readily in the West and parts of the South, as newer municipalities (including Kansas City) grew by annexation, forestalling fragmented metropolitan growth on the scale seen in the Northeast and upper Midwest. Eventually, however, even such prototypically western cities as Los Angeles, Phoenix, and Seattle spawned substantial suburban sprawl, exhibiting many of the same characteristics of disjointed growth that had become apparent elsewhere.[55]

As a corollary of these developments, the emergence of the suburbs as settings of educational advantage became a sign of the times, at least for many whites. As regional differences started to fade, differences within metropolitan settings became more commonplace.[56] A 1965 study of southern suburbanization found its effects to be quite similar to what was happening in the rest of the country, noting that "the exchange between the southern central cities and their suburbs raises the socioeconomic level of the suburban population while it diminishes the socioeconomic level of the city."[57] As a consequence, suburban schools in all parts of the country came to be judged as better than their urban counterparts, making local geo-spatial distinctions more salient than historic regional differences.[58]

This form of metropolitan differentiation may have become unmistakable in the postwar era, but it also was not altogether new. As metropolitan areas expanded during most of the twentieth century, suburban communities often led the way. Historian Kenneth Jackson has noted that urban growth was focused on the outer edges of American cities from at least the 1920s onward. This process contributed to regional convergence in social and economic terms, but also to new patterns of socioeconomic differentiation within metropolitan areas. While shared features of regional development became a widely acknowledged phenomenon, metropolitan growth continued to exhibit common patterns throughout the postwar era. In particular, suburbs became associated with clear distinctions in social status almost everywhere, a broadly acknowledged feature of American culture.[59]

Although the timing and parameters of this process differed from one setting to the next, there could be little doubt about the pervasiveness of metropolitan society. Suburban communities went from a little more than a third of the metropolitan population to nearly two-thirds between 1940 and 1980. It was the suburbs, moreover, that added most new jobs, particularly in the manufacturing sector, a trend spurred by the development of a national highway infrastructure and the replacement of rail by trucks as a principal mode of transportation.[60]

These developments were particularly noteworthy in the South. In these states, the development of metropolitan areas was accomplished with a massive shift from the region's traditional agricultural economy to one dominated increasingly by manufacturing. Early forms of industrial development there had occurred in smaller towns and cities. By 1980, however, a majority of southern factory workers lived in metropolitan areas, which had become the focal point for economic growth. With this development, the region had come to look quite similar to much of the rest of the country, both with regard to local economic development and its geo-spatial organization. At the same time, of course, the metropolitan population grew in other regions as well. By the 1970s it was possible to clearly identify a national experience of metropolitan development, driven largely by sprawling growth at the edges of urbanized areas.[61]

The Social Impact of Metropolitan Differentiation

Historians and social scientists have devoted considerable attention to patterns of inequality within metropolitan areas. Much of this research has focused on differences between central city residents and their counterparts living in surrounding suburbs. Nevertheless, relatively little attention has been given to systematic differences in the educational characteristics of children living in different metropolitan settings. Despite widespread interest in educational inequality between urban and suburban communities, this historical aspect of the spatial organization of schooling has remained under-studied.[62]

Using national data, figures 1.1 through 1.4 reveal some of the indicators of the process of metropolitan segmentation between central city and suburban settings, focusing on high-school-age youth and their families. The first one exhibits a growing divide in adult education levels that distinguished urban and suburban households. Though there was little difference in the rates at which parents—particularly fathers—in urban and suburban communities had graduated from high school in 1940, forty years later suburban parents were nearly 50 percent more likely to have graduated than their central city counterparts. Some of this undoubtedly was due to historically low levels of adult educational attainment in African American communities, resulting from decades of unequal schooling, especially in the South. Given the importance of parental education to school success, long documented in research on attainment and achievement, such differences were hardly inconsequential.[63] This growing divide was a telling sign of suburban educational advantage that emerged decisively in a relatively short time.

The second chart concerns changing racial segregation and concentration in metropolitan areas. African Americans were about 80 percent more likely than whites to live in a central city in 1940 but more than four times (400 percent) more

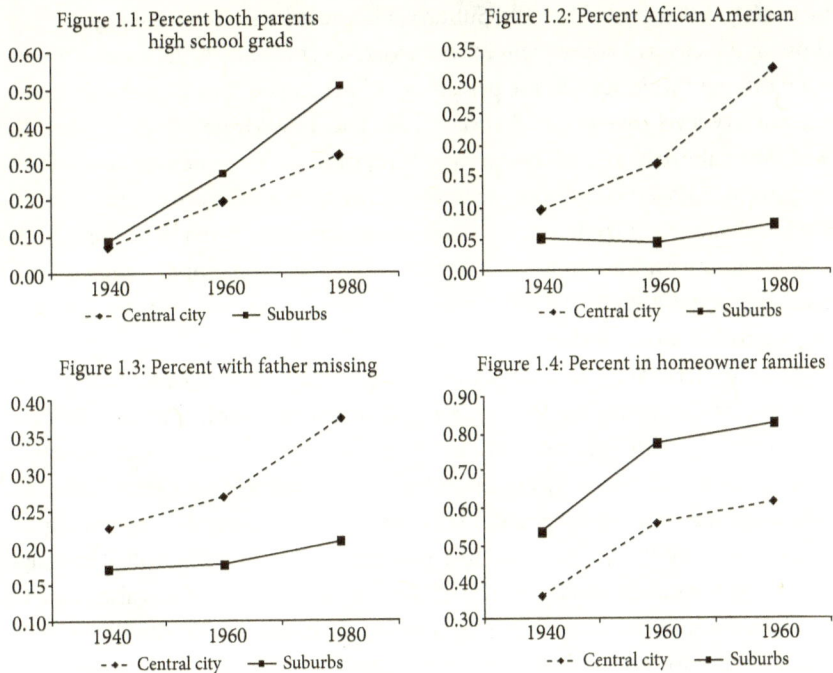

FIGURES 1.1–1.4 Patterns of metropolitan divergence on selected racial and socioeconomic dimensions, 1940–1980. Data include all seventeen-year-olds from IPUMS US census samples for whom metropolitan location is known. Charts created by Argun Saatcioglu.

likely in 1980. Changing urban levels of adult education thus partly reflect the disadvantage of African Americans as their numbers grew in the cities. Figure 1.3 points to a related trend, the rising proportion of households without a male parental figure. Poverty and joblessness contributed to this condition, undermining the stability of marriages. The absence of a male parental figure also reduced the likelihood of school success, as these families often lacked the resources to enhance and sustain academic achievement.[64] While urban youth were slightly more likely to experience this condition in 1940, by the end of the period their odds of it were some 85 percent greater than for their suburban peers.

Finally, figure 1.4 concerns basic differences in affluence. Home ownership—a critical reflection of wealth and status—occurred at a greater rate in the suburbs than in the central city in 1940, but the gap later widens slightly in absolute terms. Of course, acquiring a home was widely seen as the raison d'être of moving to suburban communities, so this is hardly surprising. But it also reflected the greater stability and access to resources that suburban households enjoyed, including well-regarded schools. Suburban home values often were higher than those in the city as a consequence.[65] Poverty rates (not shown) followed a somewhat different trajectory, as the percentage of urban youth in households below the poverty level rose slightly between 1960 and 1980 (from 20 to 23 percent), while the suburban rate fell by nearly a third, from about 15 percent to less than 10 percent. Altogether, growing distinctions between residents of urban (central city) and suburban communities characterized postwar patterns of metropolitan development. This appears to have run contrary to national trends toward greater economic and social integration. All four of these indicators signaled rising metropolitan inequality.[66]

In a number of ways, moreover, these changes reflected broad historical trends. As noted earlier, education levels converged across the country, as did manufacturing employment. But much of this change occurred on the fringes of metropolitan areas, and decidedly not in central cities. Relatively high suburban adult education was hardly a surprise, as these communities generally enjoyed higher income, and by the 1970s many had become centers of white-collar employment.[67] At the same time, a majority of the nation's factory workers also came to reside in the suburbs, according to census data. This was a major shift from 1940, when nearly two out of three lived in the cities. It reflected a well-documented tendency for new economic development to occur on the metropolitan fringe, especially as suburban communities invested in industrial parks, office complexes, and shopping centers to enhance local tax bases.[68] In short, many of the social and economic changes cited as emblematic of the time helped deepen metropolitan segmentation along an urban/suburban divide.

These trends offer a sketch of the shifting contours of geo-spatial inequality. Yet descriptive statistics provide only general indicators of these changes. More rigorous analyses make it possible to examine the effects of metropolitan segmentation on educational attainment. A study of metropolitan high school students across this period offers precisely this sort of analysis. Drawing on a national sample of seventeen-year-olds, it estimated the likelihood of their graduating from high school. In 1940, students in central city schools were 50 percent more likely to do this than their suburban counterparts in the same metropolitan areas, controlling for a host of socioeconomic factors and regional characteristics. Forty years later, the circumstances were reversed. Even though the suburban population had grown enormously and national education levels had risen substantially, youth in these settings were nearly 20 percent more likely to succeed in school than their central city counterparts. In the earlier period it was the big-city students that held the upper hand; by the end of the postwar era they were clearly behind.[69] In addition to the various facets of life represented in figures 1.1–1.4 above, suburban youth gained a distinct advantage in educational accomplishment, independent of their racial and social-class profile. This is not to say that children in these communities did not have problems; growing up is always a challenge.[70] While it had been a plus to live in the city prior to the war, however, four decades later there was clearly a substantial benefit to calling the suburbs home.

A New Suburban Localism

Whatever their advantages with respect to schooling and other factors, suburban communities usually were relatively small in size and stature. They generally resisted consolidation, moreover, into larger administrative or governmental entities. By and large, affluent suburbanites did not want their tax dollars to be spent on goods and services that did not benefit their communities more or less directly. They were not interested in supporting others in this manner.[71]

While consolidation of service agencies and governmental authority had been the prevailing ethos earlier, support for decentralization and local control gained momentum following the war. The change was gradual and affected city residents as well as suburbanites, but by the 1960s the fragmentation of public services and administrative responsibility was widely viewed as a major challenge to suburban development. "Metropolitan problems since the turn of the century have been attributed to jurisdictional fragmentation," wrote a political scientist in 1974, but "voters in most areas have not been convinced of the need for comprehensive reorganization of the local government system."[72] Urban planners and other social scientists argued that the patchwork of small communities that constituted most suburban zones was inefficient and inequitable. Critics of suburban localism called for the creation of larger organizational units for key service agencies, including schools, to assist in creating more rational systems of metropolitan governance.[73] The basic idea was that the communities in each metropolitan region were inescapably bound together as an organic whole, and that their fates were largely shared. But many suburbanites disagreed emphatically and clung stubbornly to a preference for local control. Resistance to consolidation routinely stymied efforts at reform, and schooling was among the most volatile issues wrapped up in such disputes.[74]

Affluent suburbanites exhibited a potent form of localism that extended to many dimensions of governmental authority and local institutions.[75] As a result, suburban areas often became a complex patchwork of different administrative units, including counties, townships, and villages, school districts, water and sewer districts, transportation agencies, library services, park districts, and other entities that frequently overlapped and functioned independently of one another. In 1972 there were more than sixteen thousand such governmental units in the nation's 264 metropolitan areas, excluding school districts. In the largest 33 of these metropolitan areas there were more than six thousand governmental units. At the same time, there were more than five thousand separate school districts across all such areas.[76] If centralization was a theme in the history of the nation's larger cities, especially concerning public education, fragmentation became a major issue in the suburbs that surrounded them.

This problem emerged as a point of concern for policy makers and planners interested in improving the efficiency of local government. Some advocated the development of metropolitan or regional forms of governance to better coordinate services and share costs, along with addressing the inequality then becoming evident. Social scientists debated these questions avidly, spawning occasional efforts to consolidate or combine various dimensions of governmental authority.[77] It was a point of particular interest regarding schools, as suburban districts rarely reached the size of urban systems, raising questions about their efficiency and capacity. In 1968 sociologists Basil Zimmer and Amos Hawley published a large-scale study, funded by the US Department of Education, that shed considerable light on metropolitan attitudes about education. The goal was to identify factors that stood in the way of reforming district organization, but the research revealed much more. The very fact that such a question was posed, of course, was itself revealing in many respects. Suburban schooling was a problem, and federal authorities devoted resources to addressing it.[78]

Zimmer and Hawley were well-known urban sociologists, and they were interested in how people viewed communities and governmental systems in metropolitan settings. Their 1968 study focused on schooling in particular. At the center of the project was a survey of nearly three thousand households, conducted in six northern metropolitan areas: Buffalo, New York; Milwaukee, Wisconsin; Rochester, New York; Dayton, Ohio; Saginaw, Michigan; and Rockford, Illinois.[79] The survey was designed to address sources of resistance to metropolitan consolidation in schools. A widely voiced complaint about metropolitan development concerned inefficiencies in the many small jurisdictions that crisscrossed suburban areas, often with little evident rationale or order. Two other scholars summarized the critique succinctly: "Fragmentation, the critics claim, increases the cost of obtaining coordination among units of government, while overlapping, the same critics claim, results in the creation of an unnecessary duplication of administrative apparatus." Counting themselves among such critics, Zimmer and Hawley found the existing metropolitan order puzzling. They postulated that escalating expense and managerial logic would surely lead to more coherent patterns of institutional development.[80]

By and large, however, their study identified unequivocal lines of suburban resistance to the very idea of consolidating schools across metropolitan areas. In fact, schools provoked greater resistance to change than any other issue in their survey. While the authors steered clear of the question of race, they focused on other factors that proved quite telling. It turned out that the size of metropolitan areas was clearly linked to distinctive suburban attitudes, and to city viewpoints as well. Residents of smaller metro areas did not consider suburban schools quite so superior, especially where urban schools were not judged to be problematic. Perceptions of suburban educational advantage were most pronounced in the larger metropolitan areas, and among certain groups in particular. In addition, it was the highly educated suburbanites, along with locally elected officials, who were most plainly opposed to any changes in the schools.[81]

The latter points represent Zimmer and Hawley's principal finding of relevance to suburban schooling: many suburbanites were steadfast in their resistance to changes in school governance. Furthermore, social class mattered, at least defined in terms of employment, income, and education level. Suburban residents with professional and management jobs, higher income levels, and with college degrees were most likely to believe their schools superior, and were decidedly opposed to changes in the schools' organization. Respondents in these categories also were the most willing to pay higher taxes to support local schools and were most reluctant to accept federal or state money to help them. As James E. Ryan has suggested, suburbanites in such circumstances could be prone to viewing such costs as the equivalent of membership dues.[82] These tendencies were strongest in the larger metropolitan areas. On the other hand, working-class respondents, with lower levels of education, were considerably less likely to see the advantages of suburban schools, and less tolerant of higher taxes. Interestingly, college-educated big-city residents supported urban schools, although social class differences in these settings were quite modest.[83]

Given the fragmentation of suburban communities and attendant variation in wealth and income, there can be little question about the status of the various communities where respondents to Zimmer and Hawley's survey lived. Many of the most privileged respondents undoubtedly resided in districts with high property valuations, with schools widely seen as superior. As Zimmer and Hawley reported, "In the suburban zones of both the large and medium sized areas, the college trained are distinct from all others in the low proportion who would support change." It was this group, after all, that collectively was in perhaps the best position to enjoy the small scale and manifold comforts of suburban life. Their commitment to maintaining these features of localism appears to have been a critical element in suburban development and helps account for the persistent patterns of educational inequality then becoming evident.[84]

School Busing, White Flight, and Changing Cities

The historic *Brown v. Board of Education* decision by the US Supreme Court outlawing racial segregation of public schools made education a hot-button political question nationally. In the decades to follow, civil rights organizations actively pushed local and state authorities to comply with the spirit of the decision. Representing the NAACP Legal Defense Fund, Thurgood Marshall tried more than thirty desegregation cases in this era, and many others were launched by other civil rights advocates and organizations.[85]

Support for integrated education and greater opportunity came from the public too. Survey data in the mid-1960s showed that a majority of Americans were in favor of school integration, and their numbers were increasing. Reflecting this sentiment, President Johnson declared in a 1965 commencement address at Howard University that "the task is to give 20 million Negroes the same chance as every other American to learn and grow, to work and share in society, to develop their abilities—physical, mental and spiritual, and to pursue their individual happiness." Somewhat later, the research of James Coleman and other social scientists demonstrated the positive effects of racial integration on African American school success, helping to sustain support for desegregation among much of the educated public. But there was stubborn resistance as well, especially among those who felt threatened by imminent changes in schools serving their children. The result was a long and highly contentious debate that failed to accomplish much until the 1970s. Since blacks had moved to cities in all parts of the country, urban schools became a focal point of these struggles.[86]

Desegregation eventually realized its greatest success in southern states, where the federal courts finally forced districts to formally end segregated schooling in the later 1960s and the '70s. As a consequence, most black students there attended integrated schools by 1975. Simply redrawing school attendance zones accomplished some of this, but much of it was achieved with busing. Many southern school systems were organized on a countywide basis, helping to accomplish desegregation more easily than in other parts of the country. Such districts often included both urban and suburban neighborhoods. This made white flight more difficult, although it certainly did occur. Urban-suburban distinctions became a point of interest in desegregation cases in connection with these questions.[87]

With the success of integration in the South, institutions in the North and Midwest became the nation's most racially segregated schools, and the sharpest distinctions eventually were drawn between urban and suburban districts. Unlike many of their southern counterparts, urban education systems in these settings often conformed to municipal boundaries and thus did not include suburban neighborhoods. School segregation often resulted from dual housing markets that defined racially distinct neighborhoods. This became known as de facto school segregation, even if it often was triggered by government policies and the real estate industry; and it became the predominant form of racial educational exclusion during the 1960s. Of course, city districts could alter attendance zones or bus children to achieve racial balance in the schools, and sometimes they did. This is what demonstrators often demanded in Chicago, Milwaukee, and other cities. In the early 1960s many such protests were less concerned with achieving racial integration than reducing overcrowding and gaining access to better facilities for black students.[88]

Before long, however, things changed. In the 1970s allegedly de facto segregation became a sore point for civil rights organizations, as it seemed to suggest that dual housing markets were somehow a natural or inevitable development that schools could not address. This led to a series of lawsuits seeking to establish racial parity in urban schools, focused on district policies that abetted segregation. As a consequence, scores of northern city school districts were forced by courts to adopt desegregation plans, often because these districts had helped to sustain segregation by linking schools to racially identifiable neighborhoods and failed to facilitate integration. A crucial case was *Keyes v. School District No. 1* in Denver, Colorado, where the US Supreme Court ruled in 1973 that districts could be held culpable for abetting segregation linked to dual housing markets. This led to a wave of desegregation plans that called for busing students from one school to another, typically black children to predominantly white institutions. Most such efforts experienced limited success, however, even if some students benefited from them initially. White flight often stymied desegregation at particular schools, as many white families withdrew their children to avoid integration. Public opposition to busing eventually became widespread, making it a major political issue.[89]

One answer to metropolitan inequity, of course, was to extend busing programs to suburban districts, many of which had grown enormously in the postwar years. The 1974 desegregation case *Milliken v. Bradley* proposed to do this in metropolitan Detroit. But the Supreme Court ruled in a 5–4 decision that the suburban districts could not be held accountable for segregation in city schools, thus drawing a line at the municipal boundaries with respect to desegregation. Widely decried as a departure from the historic principles of *Brown* two decades earlier, *Milliken* represented a watershed in the movement to integrate metropolitan schools. Urban districts were on their own if they wished to find a solution to racially segregated education. Many did receive financial assistance under the *Milliken v. Bradley* (known as *Milliken II*) decision in 1977, which directed states to assist with the costs of mitigating the damaging effects of segregation. But such aid rarely compensated for the loss of academically well-prepared students. Suburbanites, on the other hand, remained secure in their own districts, sheltered from the supposed threat of racial integration.[90]

A number of developments further aggravated these problems in the '70s. First, government-enforced desegregation plans and middle-class fears about crime and deteriorating urban neighborhoods contributed to ongoing suburbanization in many parts of the country. District efforts to stem these losses with enhanced services and specialized "magnet schools" aimed at attracting middle-class students produced mixed results, although many such institutions did demonstrate that high achievement was possible in urban settings. But the general trend of declining enrollments continued in many urban districts. Second, while black migration from the South slowed, new immigrant groups started to appear in major American cities in large numbers, facilitated by the Immigration and Naturalization Act of 1965. Like previous newcomers, many members of these groups were poor and unskilled, and they too experienced cultural and linguistic exclusion.[91]

The largest groups of immigrants were those who spoke Spanish, most of whom came from Mexico, Central America, or the Caribbean (Puerto Rico in particular). These groups had been important minorities in US cities during earlier times, but their numbers grew dramatically in the latter 1960s and 1970s. By 1980 nearly a fifth of New York's population was Spanish speaking, and Chicago counted more than four hundred thousand residents of Hispanic heritage. Even larger numbers settled in Los Angeles, Houston, and other cities in California and the Southwest. This posed yet a new challenge to the urban schools, one of educating a diverse population of recent immigrants while dealing with long-standing problems of racial segregation and poverty.[92]

In addition to these changes, the economic base of major cities continued to shift as well. In the 1960s, manufacturing employment began to decline substantially, a process often described as "deindustrialization," and it accelerated in the 1970s and into the 1980s. These changes occurred primarily in cities and were linked to industrial competition from abroad and changing manufacturing technology. As suggested earlier, this period also witnessed a sharp rise in suburban manufacturing capacity. Consequently, unemployment in inner-city communities increased significantly. As sociologist William Julius Wilson has noted, the movement of industry out of American cities resulted in large-scale social dislocation. These developments also contributed to the significant decline in tax revenue in many cities.[93]

The resulting loss of employment brought a host of other problems, many with dire implications for education. The number of female-headed households in US cities increased rapidly, as marriages became difficult to sustain in the wake of rising joblessness. Illegal drug sales, violent crime, and teen pregnancy also increased following these developments. And as the popular media amply documented, these were questions that had a direct bearing on children and youth.[94]

The period covered in this book extends only to 1980, but problems facing the cities continued to mount well after that. By 1990 more than half of all black children in large US cities were born in poverty, most of them in female-headed families. With the virtual collapse of urban industrial employment, African American communities that traditionally relied on the factory or other types of manual labor found themselves in a deepening crisis. These developments had a palpable impact on urban schooling, which continued to contend with segregation, white flight, and fiscal difficulty.

In his study of high-poverty neighborhoods in Chicago at the time, William Julius Wilson reported criticisms about the schools that echoed those of thirty years earlier, "ranging from over-crowded conditions to unqualified and uncaring teachers." He quoted one mother complaining that "they don't have the proper books that the children need to study from. That's what holds them back a lot." Given the resources of the United States as a nation, it was telling that such problems continued to plague public institutions, regardless of their immediate circumstances.[95]

While suburbanization changed the economic and demographic profile of the city, problems once restricted to only the poorest areas eventually became far more ubiquitous. Because of unemployment, crime, racial discrimination, and a host of other factors operating in combination, the challenges facing city schools today are arguably worse than those in the past. On the other hand, most of the very best schools still exist in suburban school districts. While the suburbs have become somewhat more diverse, African Americans remain largely excluded from most prosperous communities. Leah Boustan reports that even affluent blacks have been reluctant to relocate to these suburban settings, partly because they fear white hostility, a long-standing concern. Still, many African Americans have benefited from moving to suburban communities too.[96]

Largely African American suburbs have appeared with the growth of the black middle class, but they rarely exhibit the level of affluence found in many predominantly white communities. Some black suburban neighborhoods today experience many of the same problems as in the inner city, including low property valuation, increased poverty, and low-achieving schools. And while suburban settings now account for a large segment of the African American population, many are inner-ring communities contiguous to central cities. Meanwhile, large numbers of African Americans, most of them very poor, continue to live on the urban side of these boundaries. In this respect, the racial ghetto simply has shifted outward to straddle municipal lines. While many African Americans technically have moved into suburbs, their socioeconomic status may not have improved substantially. As a result, patterns of racialized inequality that appeared more than a half century ago continue to be clearly evident, even if the geo-spatial ordering of particular districts and communities has evolved somewhat.[97]

The urban-suburban divide that emerged during the postwar era has proven to be quite enduring. The foregoing has demonstrated how the decline of urban school systems was directly tied to the rise of their suburban counterparts. In this respect it is possible to say that they are two sides of the same metropolitan coin on a national scale. There are two systems of public education in many metropolitan areas today: one for the disadvantaged and disenfranchised in the cities and certain inner-ring suburbs, and the other for those who can afford to live in other suburbs or send their children to a "good" school.[98] In the latter half of the twentieth century, schools were buffeted by the tides of metropolitan change, particularly the settlement of white, middle-class families beyond the city limits, or at least in districts outside the urban core. Those who remained in the inner cities have been disproportionately disadvantaged, both economically and in educational terms. With larger numbers of impoverished minority students in their classrooms, urban schools have acquired a persistent reputation for low academic achievement. These problems are a matter of context; the troubles of the big cities have become the problems of their schools.[99]

Other factors that affected urban education in the postwar era and beyond, such as curricular reform and organizational change (as in specialty magnet schools), have been less important than social context. Once the proud sentinels of academic standards and vehicles of opportunity for generations of students, urban schools eventually came to represent the biggest problems in American education. Hobbled by the concentrated poverty, these institutions have struggled to address the needs of their students. With only modest federal and additional state support directed their way, performance levels in urban schools have continued to lag behind those in suburban school districts. Teachers often prefer school systems with better working conditions and more highly motivated students. And gross inequities in American education continued to sharpen as the twentieth century came to an end.[100]

To answer the questions posed at the outset of the chapter, it is clear that city schools have changed as a result of a historic transformation of urban life. Suburban districts, some of them sites of concentrated affluence, have clearly benefited. They have also firmly resisted efforts to consolidate their resources into larger organizational entities, preferring local control over proximate institutions and related services. The metropolitan revolution extended to all parts of the country, although it took a while to reach the South. And it was there that the desegregation movement eventually realized its greatest success, largely owing to the manner in which school districts were organized in many of its cities.

Elsewhere desegregation principally affected urban schools and actually may have helped to harden suburban resistance to the idea of racial integration, especially following the *Milliken* decision in 1974. The best models for overcoming the metropolitan revolution's geo-spatial inequities appeared in certain southern metropolises.[101] But short of creating countywide school districts, it is difficult to see how similar changes might have been accomplished elsewhere. The result was that the postwar geo-spatial model of urban-suburban educational inequality appeared largely impervious to change in most of the country. At the end of the twentieth century this educational divide remained perhaps the greatest challenge to the egalitarian promise of American public education.

The chapters that follow examine the development of the suburban school advantage, and by extension the urban school disadvantage, in a particular metropolitan context. While all such settings have peculiar characteristics, the historical formation of particular districts and their relationships to one another can shed light on changes that also occurred elsewhere. It is possible, after all, that pathways to productive reform may become more readily evident by examining such developments in greater detail. With this in mind, it is instructive to consider greater Kansas City and its experience with public education and suburban development during the long postwar era. Resolving problems created at that time remains an imperative for the nation's metropolitan regions and represents a continuing challenge to educators concerned with improving the lives of all children.

2

UNITING AND DIVIDING A HEARTLAND METROPOLIS

Growth and Inequity in Postwar Kansas City

In the early spring of 1956, the enterprising city manager of Kansas City, Missouri, L. P. (Perry) Cookingham, addressed the Hickman Mills Chamber of Commerce, highlighting the many advantages to be gained from becoming a part of the big city. Hickman Mills was a quiet suburban community at the time. It had a school district and something of a formal identity as a consequence but never was incorporated as a village, township, or municipality. This made it vulnerable under Missouri law to annexation by Kansas City, or any other adjoining municipality, without a vote of its residents. Cookingham wanted Hickman Mills to join the city and attempted to be persuasive, extolling the lower cost and better quality of its water supply, police and fire protection, and garbage collection, among other advantages. The presentation did not feature schools. While Cookingham may have been less than rousing, greater interest in his entreaties materialized when neighboring Grandview also began to discuss annexation.[1] Becoming a part of Kansas City held considerable appeal under those circumstances.

It was another five years, however, before Kansas City settled the area's fate, formally annexing Hickman Mills. When it finally happened, the community joined a sprawling municipality that eventually spanned more than three hundred square miles, including most or parts of several counties. Following Cookingham's lead, the city had annexed adjacent territory to avoid being constrained by surrounding suburbs. Even though it encountered some resistance, this approach to municipal growth proved largely successful. From a legal and political standpoint, the annexation strategy managed to bind a large portion of the metropolitan region together within a single municipality. As a consequence, Kansas City remained financially viable for decades thereafter. One feature of the local landscape that did not change, however, was the geographic configuration of local school districts. It turned out that this development would have important consequences, eventually dividing the region along lines of race and socioeconomic status.[2] While Cookingham was determined to unite the metropolis as much as possible, schools would become a critical point of dissension.

Changes that shaped metropolitan development and altered the history of American education were readily evident across the country by the 1960s. Kansas City provides an illuminating site for considering these issues. Straddling two states, it served and represented a vast midwestern heartland. Kansas City also had a long history of racial division and discord. Like many other American metropolises, it grew as a center of regional trade and manufacturing and experienced extensive suburban sprawl in the process.[3] It also gave rise to a clear geo-spatial pattern of educational inequity.

Greater Kansas City expanded rapidly in the decades following 1940. Buoyed by a surge in wartime employment and migration, along with the first stages of the postwar baby boom, its population had increased by nearly 19 percent by 1950. In the following decade the pace increased to 27 percent, with population passing a million. Growth slowed thereafter, but by 1980 nearly a quarter million new residents had been added.[4] While development occurred on both sides of the state border, much of it flowed from the urban core on the Missouri side. Kansas City, Kansas (KCK), the principal municipality on the Kansas side of the river until the 1960s, became a manufacturing center but was considerably smaller and lacked many of the social and cultural amenities available in its neighbor to the east. As a consequence, the larger and more cosmopolitan Kansas City, Missouri (KCMO) played a greater role in metropolitan development. In any case, expansion occurred at the margins of development on both sides of the border, with population pushing outward in all directions. Suburbanization quickly took hold as the region changed demographically and geographically.[5] In this regard greater Kansas City remained in step with the rest of the country.

At the same time that it expanded, metropolitan Kansas City became the site of increasing inequality. This was evident in a number of dimensions, including race, wealth, and educational attainment (the highest level of schooling reached by an individual), even if they were closely linked. Each of these sources of social distinction influenced the success or failure of children in schools, and they also became clearly associated with different sectors of the metropolitan landscape. As a result, social and educational inequality acquired a specific geo-spatial form, helping to create winners and losers among the region's many communities. This may not have been altogether new, as uneven development had long been a feature of urban life. But it achieved a new order of magnitude in the era of suburbanization, and education became a more important component of inequality than ever before.

Annexation, Expansion, and the Schools

While Kansas City may have been a typical urbanized region in demographic and economic terms, in certain respects it was anomalous, especially compared to places to the east and north. By the mid-twentieth century, suburban settlements surrounded many older cities, having successfully resisted incorporation into larger municipalities. As a consequence these suburbs constrained central city growth and often were antagonistic—if not downright hostile—to the urban core. St. Louis became a classic example, having rejected proposals to annex neighboring communities in the nineteenth century only to lose population and wealth to them decades later. Kansas City leaders recognized the significance of this.[6]

Soon after the Second World War, Kansas City's municipal authorities began making plans to avoid this fate. City manager Cookingham spearheaded these efforts, which ultimately met with considerable success. With his guidance Kansas City was able to annex vast tracts of adjoining terrain rather readily, eventually more than doubling its geographic footprint. This process of territorial growth went through several phases, beginning in 1950 with some fourteen square miles just north of the Missouri River and an area of similar size to the south and east of the city seven years later. Over the next six years Kansas City added even bigger parcels, extending its municipal boundaries to include large swaths of Clay and Platte Counties and nearly all of southwest Jackson County. By 1963 the city had become one of the country's largest municipalities in geographic terms. More importantly, as new development occurred at the edges of the older urban core, it remained within the city limits, providing vital resources for maintaining public services in the face of social and economic changes that reshaped the historic city center.[7]

Cookingham's plan was brilliant in many respects, and it was executed methodically in less than a decade. In defending it, Mayor H. Roe Bartle declared "Kansas City cannot be hemmed in." As a rationale, he volunteered that "it is the earnest desire of homeowners in the suburbs to have the best in municipal services, although some of them don't want to pay for such."[8] But most of the affected suburbanites had little say in the process; Missouri permitted annexation of adjacent unincorporated areas with just a vote of city residents. Consequently, KCMO was able to acquire territory with relatively little resistance, apart from communities such as Gladstone or Raytown, which hurriedly incorporated themselves to avoid annexation. There was a degree of lingering resentment, to be sure, especially north of the river. But the result dramatically extended city boundaries. Map 2.1 illustrates the scope of these changes. The initial annexation was a relatively modest acquisition immediately north of the river, but larger parcels followed in subsequent years. These additions altered municipal boundaries both to the south and farther north, nearly to Platte City. The result was an expansive municipality, spanning much of three counties, with independent "island" communities located within it, largely or wholly surrounded by the city.[9]

One aspect of Kansas City's metropolitan geography that did not change, however, was the boundaries of school districts. To enable the planned city expansion

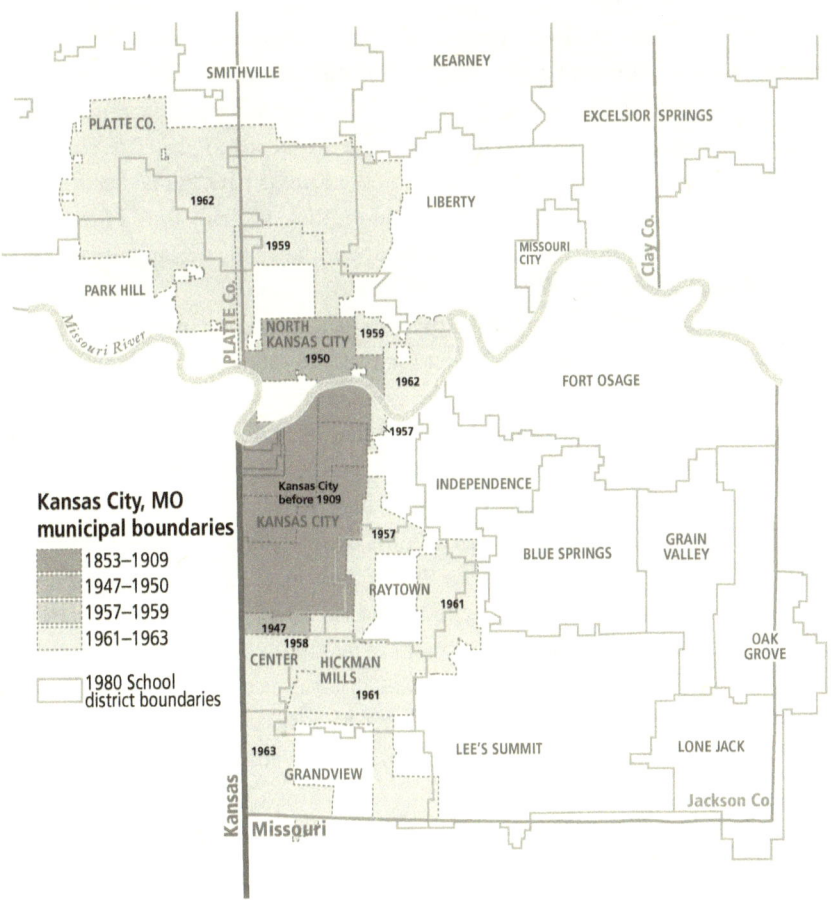

MAP 2.1 Kansas City, Missouri, annexations, 1947–1963, with 1980 school district boundaries

to go forward, in 1957 the Missouri legislature changed a law requiring districts in cities with more than a half million residents to have boundaries conforming to those of their municipalities. Although it did not affect St. Louis, which could not expand geographically in any case, the statute had posed a potential complication to annexation on the western side of the state. Intended to prevent fragmentation of urban school systems, it became an obstacle to municipal plans in Kansas City. By simply increasing the population requirement to seven hundred thousand, however, the legislature kept the law in place and opened a pathway to Cookingham's territorial ambitions.[10]

While some observers may have seen this as problematic, others viewed it as the most expedient way to ensure "orderly expansion plans" for the city as a whole. The *Kansas City Star* editorialized that requiring a single enlarged city school system would "bring complete chaos," chopping off portions of smaller districts or swallowing them whole, causing "confusion and hardship."[11] The president of the Kansas City Board of Education agreed, warning that "bond programs would be endangered."[12] As a result, the expanded city eventually came to include parts or the entirety of more than a dozen school districts, also indicated on map 2.1. The largest of these was the Kansas City Public Schools, but there also were districts to the north and south that suddenly found themselves within the city's boundaries to one degree or another. This was an outcome that would exert a telling influence on the future of the region.[13]

During the 1950s, however, few observers could imagine just how the status of school systems possibly could affect metropolitan development, and keeping existing school boundaries seemed the expedient course to take. As indicated in map 2.2, school systems throughout the five-county metropolitan area were highly fragmented earlier in the decade. Most were elementary districts, often with a single school. Older children from these areas who wanted to continue their education did so at rural high schools or secondary institutions in larger districts. The Kansas City, Missouri, Public Schools (KCMPS) was the biggest system by far, with more than fifty thousand students, and only Independence on the Missouri side of the area had more than a tenth that number. The public school system of Kansas City, Kansas (KCKPS), was also fairly large, with more than ten thousand students, but most other area districts had fewer than a thousand. The region's principal urban school systems on either side of the river were its biggest and most highly developed.[14]

These differences had significant educational consequences. Perhaps the most obvious concerned secondary schooling. Only a handful of high schools with more than a few hundred students existed outside the two central cities. This meant that KCMPS institutions were widely considered academically superior, along with their counterparts across the river in KCKPS. These city schools

MAP 2.2 Metropolitan Kansas City school district boundaries, 1954

offered the widest array of curricular choices and extracurricular activities and generally attracted the most experienced and highly educated teachers. Under the circumstances, it was little wonder that KCMPS leaders failed to express interest in acquiring schools from outlying districts: they would have faced the challenge of bringing these smaller, less academically robust institutions into line with the area's largest and most highly regarded school system.[15] Little did they imagine that within a relatively short time these outlying schools would become potent challengers to their own district's reputation.

As indicated on the map, school districts south of the old city limits in Jackson County were geographically larger than their exurban counterparts elsewhere in the metropolitan region. This reflected the historic movement of population away from the river in the city's development and the success of nascent communities there in creating consolidated districts prior to the postwar era. The Hickman Mills and Raytown districts were the oldest of these, both established long before the annexation proposals of the 1950s. If all the territory of these districts had been subject to annexation by the city, merging them with the Kansas City schools might have been manageable. By the later 1950s, however, several of the Raytown schools were located within the recently incorporated village of Raytown, and a part of Hickman Mills was in Grandview, incorporated years earlier. A portion of the Grandview school district, moreover, fell into newly annexed city territory.[16] All this complicated matters considerably.

Requiring schools in southern Jackson County to merge with the city school system, in that case, would have meant splitting districts and perhaps assuming bond obligations for existing facilities. It also would have reduced the tax base for the remaining suburban districts, weakening them substantially. Since school districts were independent governmental agencies, any mergers would require a vote of their boards and constituents, many of whom were unlikely to assent. Given the many obstacles facing such a change, moreover, there was little incentive for anyone to support it. As a result, there was no pertinent voice to advocate for the creation of a larger, more inclusive school district to serve the expanded version of Kansas City. This was a critical juncture in the region's history that few recognized at the time; it would eventually be seen as a lost opportunity.[17]

Race, Schools, and Metropolitan Development

Race became a major factor in metropolitan development nationally during the postwar era, as it certainly did in greater Kansas City. Black communities on both sides of the river had long histories and had grown substantially earlier in the twentieth century. The larger settlement developed in KCMO, where many African Americans once lived in integrated neighborhoods, mostly near their jobs in the city's stockyards. As black migrants arrived after 1910, however, they began to settle on the other side of town, around Paseo Avenue north of Twenty-Seventh Street. That area soon became known both for it lively music scene and the vice rackets maintained by the city's corrupt Pendergast political machine. This was the start of the larger of two local ghettos, one on either side of the state line. Both were crowded and poor. Violent white resistance to black settlement in adjacent KCMO neighborhoods helped define clear boundaries for African Americans, signifying a new era of racialized residential segregation in the city.[18]

Expansion of the area's black population slowed in the Pendergast era, but it soon resumed dramatically. Migration surged during World War II, and by 1950 the combined African American population of the metropolitan area was nearly seventy thousand. Of that number, more than fifty-five thousand lived in Kansas City, Missouri, and about thirteen thousand across the river in Kansas City, Kansas.[19] But this was just a start, as migration continued through most of the following two decades, and the local black population grew rapidly. It more than doubled by 1970, to nearly 160,000, with about three-quarters living in Missouri. Growth ended soon afterward, a trend consistent with many other urbanized areas outside the South. Despite its numerical expansion, the black share the metropolitan population increased only slightly in the postwar era, from about 10 percent to 12 percent. But African Americans were a considerably larger proportion in the two Kansas City municipalities, eventually representing about a fifth in KCMO and a slightly higher share in KCK.[20] They remained highly segregated in both instances, restricted largely to the two clearly identifiable ghettos in the region's central cities.

The extent of local segregation and the growth of black settlement can be seen in maps 2.3 through 2.6. Throughout the postwar period, most of the region's African American population remained largely restricted to these areas. As in other American cities, this resulted from a process of systematic exclusion of blacks from other parts of the region, leaving them with little recourse to settlement in the oldest, least desirable neighborhoods on both sides of the river. The larger black community started near the commercial center of KCMO and expanded to the south as it grew. The smaller community in KCKS began in the historic Quindaro district, established by abolitionists during the nineteenth century. As indicated in the maps, it expanded to the northwest as the city's black population grew. Other pockets of black settlement appeared in KCK, but across the river the vast majority of African Americans lived in a generally contiguous area bound by Troost Avenue to the west and the Blue River valley to the east. Interstate highway construction and the river blocked northern expansion, so the principal direction to move while maintaining contact with the larger black community was southward. As indicated on the maps, by 1980 the edge of black settlement had nearly reached Raytown.[21] This development would have telling consequences in years to come.

As noted above, the western boundary of KCMO African American settlement historically was a clearly visible line that ran north and south along Troost Avenue. This defined the so-called Troost Wall, representing one of the most distinctive features of racial segregation in metropolitan Kansas City. Some observers have suggested that school district attendance zones maintaining racially segregated institutions created the wall, although it seems unlikely that such a clear and continuous line of racial separation could be simply the product of education policies. There is evidence, for instance, that many African Americans

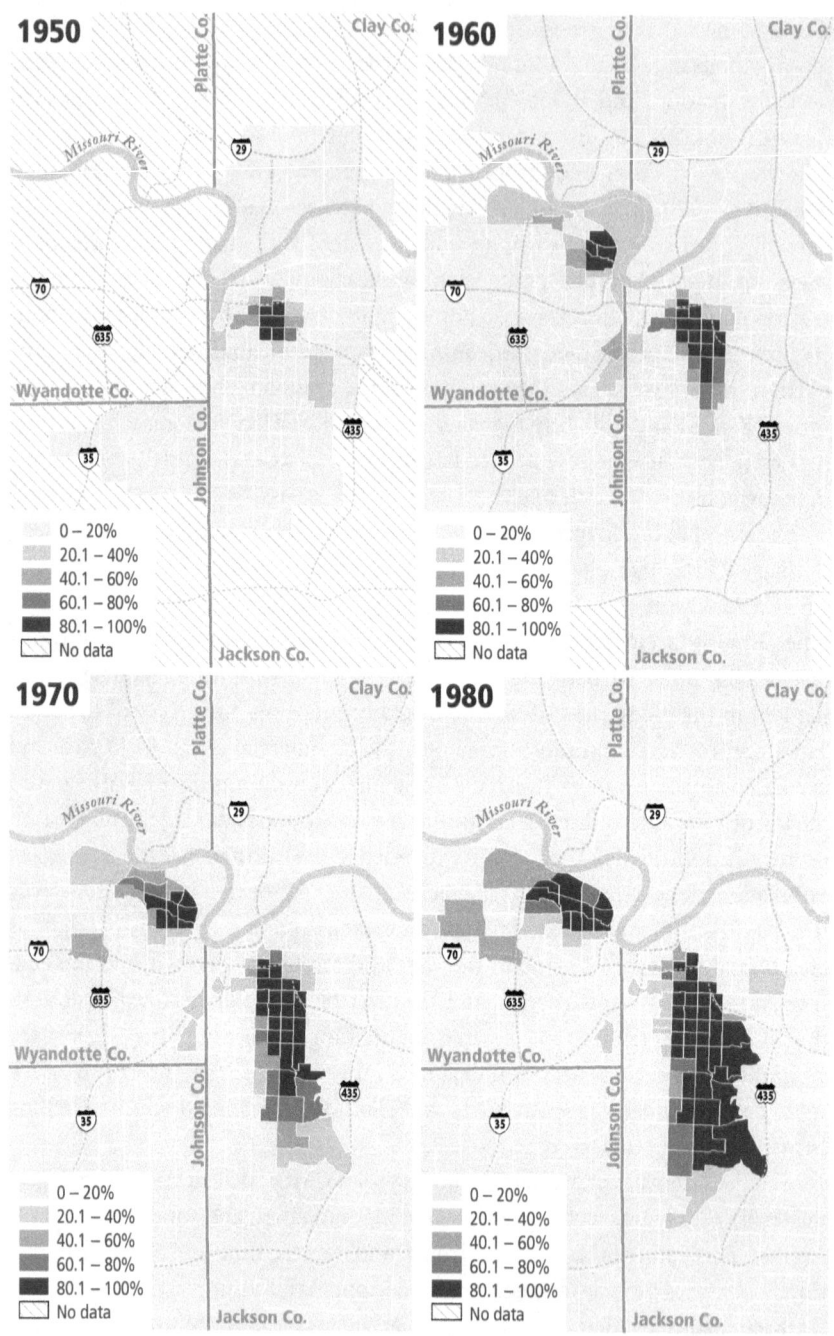

MAPS 2.3–2.6 Growth of metropolitan Kansas City's African American population, 1950–1980 (census tract data)

viewed the neighborhoods to the west of Troost as hostile territory, with boundaries often informally enforced by the police. Susan Hilliard's family, for instance, had moved to Kansas City from Arkansas after the war and lived just east of Troost, near the city center. After walking into a white neighborhood, she and her friends were lined up on the sidewalk by the police and told "we're watching you." Hilliard recalled that such experiences had a "chilling effect," serving as a "powerful disincentive" to leave the black neighborhood. These sorts of racial boundaries were well known to black children and adults alike, as a number of former residents have reported.[22]

Such highly racialized residential patterns did not arise spontaneously. Until the mid-1960s the local real estate board actively discouraged racially mixed neighborhoods, a further disincentive to African Americans moving to the west. Agents became highly cognizant of the informal barrier that Troost represented and feared the consequences of selling homes to African Americans in nearby Westport or other neighborhoods to the southwest. This led many to "steer" blacks in search of better homes southward on the east side of Troost, where a range of desirable and reasonable residences were available and "blockbusting" tactics could persuade whites to leave.[23]

The housing stock west of Troost may have posed another obstacle. Poor whites occupied much of the area north of Forty-Seventh Street, and there was relatively little turnover during the 1950s and '60s, when the city's black population was growing. Writing about the area, historian Peter William Moran observed that "a significant number of residents may have been financially unable to move."[24] Data from the 1970 census confirm that housing values in much of the area generally were no higher than in adjacent black neighborhoods. Consequently, these dwellings may have proved unappealing to more affluent African Americans interested in moving. Financing for such homes probably was difficult to secure, and their low cost offered little incentive to real estate agents, especially if extensive repairs were needed. While racial animosity certainly existed in the area, reflected in school bond election returns, it did not become a major problem in local schools.[25] Westport High became one of the city's most effectively integrated secondary schools during the 1970s, starting with African American students bused in to relieve crowding elsewhere. Additional black students eventually transferred to other institutions west of Troost. These developments gainsay the idea that school policy was primarily responsible for the "wall" observable on the maps, as does evidence of black residential movement west by 1980 (observable on map 2.6).

While shifting enrollments certainly could trigger neighborhood change and did so in Kansas City and elsewhere, other considerations played a role too. Lack of desirable residences may indeed have contributed to the dividing line.[26]

South of Forty-Seventh Street, on the other hand, there appears to have been a different story. More-affluent neighborhoods were able to discourage African American settlement with active homeowner associations and the cooperation of real estate agents, who feared antagonizing potential patrons. As the *Kansas City Star* reported in 1966, "no situation is known in which a Kansas City realtor has negotiated a sale to a Negro of a home in an all-white, middle class neighborhood outside of east and southeast Kansas City."[27] In the end, a variety of factors appears to have maintained the Troost Wall, including historical precedent and long-standing expectations, along with plain racial exclusion. Stanley West grew up on the east side of Troost and observed that "you know where the boundaries are and you simply don't cross them; you just avoid it." In this manner it remained a defining feature of the city's racialized social landscape, one that continues to pointedly distinguish communities today.[28]

Under these circumstances, as the city's black families searched for better housing, they looked to the south, in neighborhoods occupied largely by working-class whites. Natural and man-made barriers to the north and east, including the Missouri and Blue Rivers, along with Troost to the west, left one direction to move. Sociologist Kevin Fox Gotham has documented how unscrupulous real estate agents sometimes took advantage of white fears and bigotry to generate quick sales. Block-busting tactics included selling one or two homes to black families and then urging remaining whites to sell at lower terms. In many instances, however, such measures were hardly necessary. As a child, Marvin Daniels moved into a neighborhood east of Troost that was still predominantly white. Both his parents held good-paying government jobs, so their socioeconomic status was not an issue. But within a few years the area had become almost entirely black. Daniels did not recall overt efforts to frighten white homeowners, but the rate of change in his boyhood neighbors was rapid just the same.[29]

In the end, most whites likely departed regardless of nefarious real estate tactics, which city officials actively proscribed.[30] Other real estate agents just discouraged white families from even considering homes located east of Troost, suggesting that youth there were "thieves" and that vandalism was widespread.[31] For their part, African American families were seeking better residences in secure neighborhoods. Those with greater resources led the advance, while the most destitute generally remained in the ghetto's historic core. On average, black home buyers south of the Eighteenth and Vine commercial strip reported income 20 percent higher than households to the north, and they had higher levels of education too. Susan Hilliard recalled her aunt buying a house about ten blocks south of the black commercial center that seemed like a "mansion" at the time. The lure of such improvements in living standards drew middle-class African

Americans to predominantly white neighborhoods on the periphery of black residential settlement, eventually extending its boundaries.[32]

A survey of African American adults conducted by the Kansas City schools in 1983 found that improved housing was the biggest source of motivation for such moves, but also that most families wanted their children to attend schools with at least some other black students and black teachers. About a fifth also emphasized that it was important not to get "too far out" from predominantly black neighborhoods, for fear of discrimination, harassment, or worse. These responses, of course, meant that most were unwilling to consider buying in outlying parts of the city or the suburbs. Many judged suburban areas as being hostile to African Americans, or feared being isolated from family and friends.[33]

Studies at the time showed that discriminatory real estate practices also excluded African Americans from many parts of the area. A report from the Regional Health and Welfare Council in 1967 declared that "it can be unequivocally stated that the pattern of minority housing does result from discriminatory practices in the sale and leasing of housing." These realities affected the thinking of black families. As Marvin Daniels said about the idea of open housing and moving to the suburbs, "I don't care what the law says, you know, you don't go out there because you're not accepted."[34] The result was an incremental movement largely in one direction, as black families took advantage of favorable real estate values to the south, where real estate agents were willing to show them homes.[35]

Not all African Americans in metropolitan Kansas City lived in the area's two central cities, of course. There were individuals and families that moved out from these areas, and smaller pockets of black settlement existed elsewhere as well. One of the oldest was located in Johnson County, on the Kansas side of the state line. It comprised just a hundred or so families, most of them in the integrated community of South Park, which eventually became part of Merriam, Kansas. Although it was too small to show up on the maps above, this community had an outsize impact on local history. Its members launched a significant school desegregation case in 1948, *Webb v. School District No. 90*, which led the Kansas Supreme Court to rule that the plaintiffs' children had been illegally required to attend a dilapidated separate facility. The decision won the parents the right for their children to attend predominantly white schools nearby.[36]

Somewhat larger African American communities existed in Independence and Liberty, Missouri. They also were too small to register on the maps, but their children attended segregated schools until after the US Supreme Court's *Brown* decision in the mid-1950s. Both Liberty and Independence, along with other outlying Missouri districts, sent black secondary students to Kansas City prior to

Brown, where they attended segregated Lincoln High, sometimes at considerable expense to their home districts.[37] Modest black settlements in Excelsior Springs and Lee's Summit existed in earlier years, but racial violence in those communities drove many away.[38] Wherever they lived in greater Kansas City, blacks were sure to encounter hostility from many whites, and these experiences contributed directly to their desire to live in segregated communities, where they could enjoy a sense of security in the company of family and friends.[39]

The expansion of African American settlements in the larger cities on both sides of the border encountered resistance, as well as the cruelty and greed of unscrupulous white landlords and real estate professionals. Many white families were quick to leave neighborhoods at the first signs of racial change, unwilling to give integration a chance. This was a process similar to that experienced in cities elsewhere, when black communities grew significantly. In Kansas City, educational institutions became a vital component of such white flight, as school desegregation often preceded neighborhood changes, leading many white families to consider relocation.[40] The result was a great deal of movement within the metropolitan area, generally proceeding from the city center to communities on the urban periphery, whether within municipal boundaries or in adjacent suburbs.

As indicated on the maps, black communities expanded outward in rather well-defined pathways. This was a familiar pattern of ethnic settlement, one that housing economist Homer Hoyt had identified in the 1930s. Hoyt theorized that groups moved in corridors, often dictated by lines of transportation, but neighborhood succession was also affected by competing desires for new housing and remaining in touch with family and friends. In the case of African Americans, this entailed moving to the periphery of black settlement, but not too far from it. In Kansas City it meant that the segregated African American residential sector of the city gradually expanded to the south and southeast.[41]

As the city's black neighborhoods grew, so did the area at the urban core marked by severe poverty. This was clearly evident in 1970, at the height of black migration to the city, when poverty levels exceeded 40 percent of families in several predominantly black census tracts and more than 30 percent in five others, all located in the center city. Of the twenty-five tracts with a majority African American population, eighteen registered poverty rates above 20 percent, with an average of nearly 30 percent. And many non-poverty households did not have income levels much higher. There were a half dozen majority white or Hispanic tracts with somewhat comparable poverty rates, but their populations were generally smaller. A similar situation existed on the Kansas side of the border, where black neighborhoods also exhibited the highest degree of deprivation. This was another critically significant dimension of racial segregation, a corollary of systematic discrimination in employment and the job insecurity that contributed to substantially lower income for black families. As a result, African Americans occupied those parts of the city often labeled as "slums," where housing was old, crowded, and often in dangerously poor repair. As noted earlier, poor whites in adjacent neighborhoods also occupied such residences, at least in the 1960s. Because they had relatively few choices with respect to housing, the most deprived families typically were relegated to the least desirable, most neglected neighborhoods. The real estate industry described these conditions as "blight," and they were often accompanied by concentrated poverty and social disaffection.[42]

More affluent African Americans, of course, moved within the city in search of better residential options. Tracts to the south and east of the city center had somewhat lower levels of poverty. Even so, middle-class black families often lived in neighborhoods with poverty levels approaching a third or higher. This was triple the national average for whites, but the dual housing market offered few alternatives. And as housing dropped in value because of racial steering by the real estate industry, so-called slum conditions often followed. The city's African American ghetto grew in this fashion, and persistent poverty with it. The concentrated disadvantage that this represented changed little during the next two decades.[43]

Race and poverty affected the decisions of individuals and families moving into the metropolitan area, especially those concerned with finding the best schools for their children. Real estate agents also played a crucial role in this process, especially for newcomers unfamiliar with the region. Consequently, a good deal of social and economic steering occurred as realty professionals dispensed advice about the best places to live for clients with varied backgrounds and priorities. For bigoted whites determined to avoid contact with African Americans, such guidance was surely welcome, but it probably affected less-prejudiced homebuyers too. This was white "flight" of a somewhat different kind, refusing to consider living in proximity to African Americans.[44] While perhaps not quite as dramatic as families fleeing the city, it may have contributed even more to overall patterns of metropolitan segregation.

Altogether, race came to play an enormously important role in the postwar development of greater Kansas City, just as it did in many other metropolitan areas. As black and white households made crucial decisions about where to live, attend school, work, and join communities, the racial geography of the metropolitan area evolved rapidly. The maps above suggest that extreme, concentrated poverty became a critical dimension of this process as well. Distinct areas within the region were associated with racial identity and varying degrees of socioeconomic status and distress. As metropolitan Kansas City grew, personal and group standing became more clearly linked to household address. An array of social and economic characteristics contributed to this, but schools came to be one of the most significant.

Schools and the Rise of Suburbs

In greater Kansas City, as in many other settings, educational inequality came to be expressed in rather clear geo-spatial terms during the postwar era.[45] While the city could grow geographically, its principal school district did not, and this meant that many different school systems eventually served the expanded municipality. This, of course, could be advantageous in some respects, but it did not mean that schools throughout the city shared a common sense of purpose or commitment to a greater municipal good. Instead, they continued to serve their immediate communities, regardless of where they were located. Outlying districts continued to function essentially as suburban school systems, despite their location within the city limits. They may have been situated within Kansas City, Missouri, but they generally functioned independently from neighborhoods and schools in the central city, if not from one another. Given the dynamics of demographic and social change at the time, this was a policy choice that quickly became associated with race, but wealth distinctions also came into play. With its rapid geographic growth, the city demonstrated how suburban sprawl could continue to be evident within a municipality, especially if critical socioeconomic differences continued to operate there as well.[46]

The development of informal forms of suburbanization within the central city limits, of course, did not preclude the rise of suburbs elsewhere in the region. Despite its growth by annexation, metropolitan Kansas City did experience extensive exurban suburban growth as well. Much of this occurred on the Missouri side of the state line, as older suburban communities also grew, including Independence, Liberty, Blue Springs, and Lee's Summit. Suburbs such as Raytown and Grandview developed from unincorporated areas to the south, largely in response to Kansas City's annexation plans. Most of these suburban communities were largely blue collar, with many residents who worked in the sprawling industrial plants of the Blue River valley and Clay County, or expanding retail and government service centers in South Kansas City. They also were overwhelmingly white.

The other major direction of suburban development was to the southwest of the central city. The region's most renowned local developer, J. C. Nichols, established affluent residential tracts there in the early twentieth century, first in Kansas City, Missouri, and then in nearby Kansas. Nichols was dedicated to ensuring that his communities would retain property values and remain appealing to the most advantageous residents. He was a pioneer in using restrictive deed covenants and homeowners associations to exclude "undesirable" people, and these measures worked quite effectively in keeping African Americans and certain immigrant groups out of his developments. In 1923 he opened Country Club Plaza, one of the nation's first shopping centers and a retail anchor for his housing tracts in the vicinity. Before long the Nichols communities became the most fashionable places to live in the metropolitan area, counting a large share of the region's social and financial elite among their residents. The area embracing his developments in northeast Johnson County, Kansas, eventually gained renown for its public schools, in a district named for the area's historic Shawnee Mission Indian settlement.[47] By 1960 it was one of the fastest-growing school systems in the region, attracting families with an interest in securing the very best educational opportunities for their children, along with thousands of other affluent residents.[48]

As in other major metropolitan areas, suburbanization in greater Kansas City represented a large-scale process of demographic change. The entire metropolis grew significantly across the postwar period, but not at the same pace everywhere. Population increased ubiquitously during the 1950s, largely owing to the baby boom, but later changes reflected new patterns of migration. Following its campaign of annexation, for instance, the municipality of Kansas City, Missouri, experienced relatively modest growth, as did the whole of Jackson County after 1960. This is evident in table 2.1, which documents growth in the region's four most urbanized counties. The population shifted considerably within the city's boundaries, but most growth occurred outside its historic urban core. The same was true of Kansas City, Kansas, the principal city in Wyandotte County, which started to see a reduction in population toward the end of the period.

On the other hand, suburban communities on both sides of the border grew substantially, and the most significant expansion occurred in areas that had

TABLE 2.1 Postwar population growth in metropolitan Kansas City's four core counties

YEAR	JACKSON	CLAY	WYANDOTTE	JOHNSON
1950	541,035	45,221	165,318	62,783
1960	622,732	87,474	185,495	143,792
1970	654,558	123,322	186,845	217,662
1980	629,266	136,488	172,335	270,269

Source: "Population of Counties by Decennial Census: 1900 to 1990," United States Census Bureau. Available at https://www.census.gov/population/cencounts/mo190090.txt, and https://www.census.gov/population/cencounts/ks190090.txt.

experienced relatively little prior development. This was particularly true north of the river in Clay County, which tripled in size between 1950 and 1980. The area of the greatest sustained postwar growth, however, was across the border in suburban Johnson County. Between 1950 and 1970 communities there added about 150,000 people, including large numbers from outside the metropolitan area. This, of course, was home to the Shawnee Mission School District. Altogether, the county's population quadrupled during the long postwar era. No other part of greater Kansas City grew so rapidly. Along with growth in the African American population, this was perhaps the region's most significant demographic event of the era.[49]

At the same time as these changes were under way, many school districts were consolidated, especially in outlying areas. This is when the larger suburban school systems took shape. Map 2.7 shows the area's school districts in 1980, and

MAP 2.7 Metropolitan Kansas City school district boundaries, 1980

comparing it to map 2.2 provides a clear sense of the magnitude of this change. North of the river, for instance, the many smaller districts that fragmented the so-called Northland had been consolidated into a few larger ones. The most significant of these, at least with respect to population size, was the North Kansas City School District, which expanded by annexation of adjacent districts, all quite willing partners. The Liberty School District also grew during these years, moving to the west and north. Both these systems offered their smaller neighbors the opportunity to send students to their sizable high schools and take advantage of the additional resources that a larger district could provide. It was an era of annexation and consolidation in school systems, and bigger was widely seen as better.[50]

There was little change in the eastern segments of the metropolitan area and in Jackson County, as the older school systems there were consolidated many years earlier. Several tiny districts joined to create the Center District just to the south of KCMPS, but it remained a relatively small system even after consolidation. Major changes occurred on the Kansas side of the border, however, with the formation of the Shawnee Mission School District (SMSD) in 1971. This was one of the fastest-growing systems in the region, adding four new high schools within a decade, along with a number of other facilities. Its schools also became known for a high degree of academic excellence, rivaling the very best KCMPS institutions as early as the later 1950s.[51] By the 1970s, the suburban districts—whether within the city limits or not—no longer suffered in comparison with the schools of KCMPS. Instead, they had grown into formidable rivals in nearly all respects. A tide had turned, and scholastic excellence was no longer associated just with central city schools. Suburban educational ascendancy had clearly arrived.

A District in Transition

At the heart of the educational geography of greater Kansas City, of course, was the public-school district of Kansas City, Missouri. As the foregoing suggests, its reputation as the region's premier school system changed dramatically in the postwar era. When more middle-class, mainly white families settled in the suburbs, or in suburban districts within the city, schools in these outlying areas grew and gained a better reputation. Indeed, as several suburban districts became known for educational excellence, such perceptions became a major advantage in their development. This was especially true of the Shawnee Mission schools. It was hardly a coincidence that they served communities built by Nichols and other upscale developers.[52] This too was part of the changing social and educational geography of greater Kansas City. There could be little doubt that the rise of successful school districts was linked to observable advantages in community wealth and social status.

Like many other American urban areas, Kansas City experienced considerable controversy and social unrest due to school desegregation in the 1960s and '70s. The city was the focal point of the *Jenkins v. Missouri* desegregation case, which resulted in nearly $2 billion in improvements to central city schools between 1985 and 1995.[53] But these developments took time to unfold. Conflict over racial segregation did not occur immediately after the historic *Brown v. Board of Education* decision, which had focused national attention on nearby Topeka, Kansas. In fact, after voluntarily ending long-standing legal requirements for segregation in 1955, Kansas City was praised for its seemingly liberal policies regarding school integration. While overcrowded African American schools had been a significant problem prior to *Brown*, the movement of blacks to other institutions relieved some of difficulties that population growth had posed for segregated schools. Unfortunately, however, such positive changes were not lasting.[54]

Despite a seemingly promising start, desegregation in Kansas City proceeded very slowly. In 1960 all but three of the city's nineteen secondary institutions (including junior high schools) remained majority white, and most African Americans lived in an area of several square miles near the downtown business district. The KCMPS neighborhood school policy, coupled with its board's rejection of racial integration as a policy option, soon resulted in a return to overcrowded institutions serving black neighborhoods. The district responded with an "intact busing" policy, which shipped whole classes of black students to under-enrolled schools, where they spent their days in virtual isolation. Local civil rights organizations were understandably incensed by this and demanded that the schools be integrated to end overcrowding and improve education for African American students. As in Chicago and elsewhere, a coalition of groups presented demands to the school board and organized resistance to its policies. Called the Citizens Coordinating Committee (CCC), it became the focal point of activism regarding the schools. While the CCC did not manage to organize large-scale demonstrations, pickets started to appear at the school headquarters in September 1964. When the group threatened legal action to challenge the intact busing policy, the district agreed to a plan that would send black students and teachers to schools throughout the city on an integrated basis. While the board viewed this as a temporary solution to overcrowding, it satisfied most black community demands, at least for a time.[55]

As the city's African American population spread southward, white flight began modestly, and the school system remained majority white through the 1960s. Perhaps because of the busing program adopted in 1964, a sense of urgency regarding race and education was relatively slow to develop.[56] Conflict over desegregation eventually flared toward the end of the decade, however, triggered partly by district decisions to build new schools in black neighborhoods, thereby sustaining racially segregated education. In the meantime, white flight accelerated as the African American population continued to grow. The CCC and other civil rights organizations maintained pressure on the board to end school segregation, but it was not until the later 1970s that the district adopted a clear system-wide desegregation plan, under orders from federal authorities. This entailed busing large numbers of African American students to schools across the city, but the effect was not the same as it had been in the '60s. Many fewer white students remained, making meaningful integration impossible to achieve throughout the system. By the end of the decade a historic transformation of the city's public schools was largely complete.[57]

Southwest High, located near the historic Sunset Hills residential district built by J. C. Nichols, was among the last Kansas City schools to be integrated. It was widely regarded as one of the area's leading secondary schools academically, but the arrival of African American students was seen as endangering its status. Area white families began sending their children to nearby private schools or moved elsewhere.[58] In many respects these changes signaled the end of an era; henceforth the city's schools generally would be judged inferior to their suburban counterparts.

Kansas City thus offers an instructive example of education as a factor related to metropolitan development, in many respects quite similar to other urban settings at the time. It may have differed from places where controversy and conflict over desegregation occurred earlier or on a larger scale, but the broad trajectory of events was similar. In the end, some parts of the metropolitan region acquired reputations for excellent schools, others just the opposite. Most districts, of course, were somewhere in the middle of these extremes. As demonstrated below, however, these differences were also associated with other conditions that affected children's academic success, including wealth, poverty, and the educational levels of proximate adults. As many commentators have noted, these were particularly critical factors in shaping educational outcomes.[59]

Mapping Educational Change

As suggested earlier, social and economic inequality shaped the geography of metropolitan areas, especially with respect to education. Considering the spatial ordering of educational opportunity within a given region, however, requires data that can be identified geographically. Fortuitously, the US Census has provided such information in tract reports, representing relatively small geographic units in both cities and suburbs.⁶⁰ Reliable information about household income and wealth became available for most tracts in 1960, making that year a good baseline for an analysis of geo-spatial inequality. In Kansas City it also preceded major local controversy over desegregation and large-scale white flight. Twenty years later, the 1980 census offered similar census tract data, offering a useful point of comparison. That year also followed the city's first comprehensive school integration plan and more than a decade of declining white enrollment in KCMPS. These two points in time thus provide an opportunity to use statistical analysis in considering changes that occurred between key moments in the historical development of metropolitan Kansas City's urban and suburban schools. Comparing different patterns of spatial differentiation can help identify demographic and socioeconomic correlates of major events in local history: the advent of conflict over schooling and suburban residential development.

For purposes of comparison across decades, it is helpful to divide metropolitan Kansas City census tracts into distinctive groups, roughly corresponding to certain school district boundaries and other identifiable neighborhoods. The geo-spatial structure of demographic and socioeconomic change, after all, is most meaningful in light of the municipal and district boundaries discussed earlier. The discussion to follow will thus focus on five clusters of census tracts as a sampling of important geo-spatial entities. These include the Kansas City Missouri Public Schools (KCMPS), the Country Club district developed by J. C. Nichols (a residential and commercial zone, including Sunset Hills along Ward Parkway, located within KCMPS), the Shawnee Mission School District (SMSD), the Raytown School District, and the North Kansas City School District. Other tracts in Jackson County, Missouri, represent a convenient comparison group. Collectively, these areas can offer a telling profile of the variation in social, economic, and educational conditions evident throughout the metropolitan region. Tables 2.2 and 2.3 provide descriptive statistics for each of them, for 1960 and 1980 respectively.⁶¹

Both the years selected for this comparison reveal unmistakable educational differences. This is apparent in map 2.8, which illustrates broad variation in adult attainment levels. While districts and communities are not demarcated, the shading of the map indicates the percentages of residents who were college graduates in 1980. The heaviest concentrations are located in eastern Johnson County and the several southwest Kansas City tracts adjacent to the state line, the latter located within the Country Club district. As a group they represent neighborhoods planned or inspired by J. C. Nichols. These attainment benchmarks represent a level of social and cultural status at this point in time, a degree of formal education achieved by a subset of the larger population. As many other studies have noted, college education was (and is) a key parental attribute in predicting the educational success of students.⁶²

TABLE 2.2 Descriptive statistics, 1960: five geo-spatial areas (weighted averages of census tract data)

	BLACK POP.		EDUCATION		HOME VALUE		FAMILY INCOME	
	PERCENT		YEARS		DOLLARS		DOLLARS	
KCMPS	25	(34.45)	10.46	(1.38)	9,015	(2,310)	5,231	(1,164)
CC dist.	.4	(.46)	12.8	(.688)	18,990	(5,843)	9,981	(3,604)
SMSD	.2	(.37)	12.7	(.545)	17,598	(5,863)	9,757	(4,940)
Raytown	.01	(.008)	12.3	(.101)	15,156	(5,086)	7,416	(275)
NKC	.02	(.002)	12.25	(.394)	10,293	(5,824)	7,069	(2,733)

Note: Standard deviations in parentheses

TABLE 2.3 Descriptive statistics, 1980: five geo-spatial areas (weighted averages of tract data)

	BLACK POP.		EDUCATION		HOME VALUE		FAMILY INCOME	
	PERCENT		YEARS		DOLLARS		DOLLARS	
KCMPS	49	(40.4)	11.2	(1.21)	19,229	(8,833)	10,848	(3,286)
CC dist.	.4	(.486)	14.2	(1.23)	47,220	(20,933)	21,288	(8,546)
SMSD	.2	(.371)	13.3	(1.14)	59,646	(19,072)	27,162	(11,577)
Raytown	.01	(.008)	12.3	(.718)	58,506	(9,946)	21,036	(2,807)
NKC	.02	(.018)	12.3	(.464)	43,622	(12,393)	20,028	(5,087)

Note: Standard deviations in parentheses

This map also reveals a great deal of inequality across the metropolitan region. With respect to adult educational attainment, the Country Club district of Kansas City exhibited the highest levels, along with adjacent suburban Johnson County, which also featured the region's highest levels of per capita wealth and income. The segment with the lowest level of adult attainment was the remainder of central Kansas City, which largely represented KCMPS. Suburban Jackson County, outside the city limits, was between these extremes. Such differences were emblematic of a historical process of social and economic differentiation that transformed the metropolitan landscape during the postwar years. Indeed, as suggested in comparing tables 2.2 and 2.3, important geo-spatial distinctions grew more dramatic with time.

Additional information from the census underscores this point. It is clear that most of the area's black and low-income population lived within the KCMPS district as early as 1960, even though at the time the district was still widely viewed as effective and in some respects excellent. Not surprisingly, home values were lower there on average, as was overall adult attainment. The principal exception

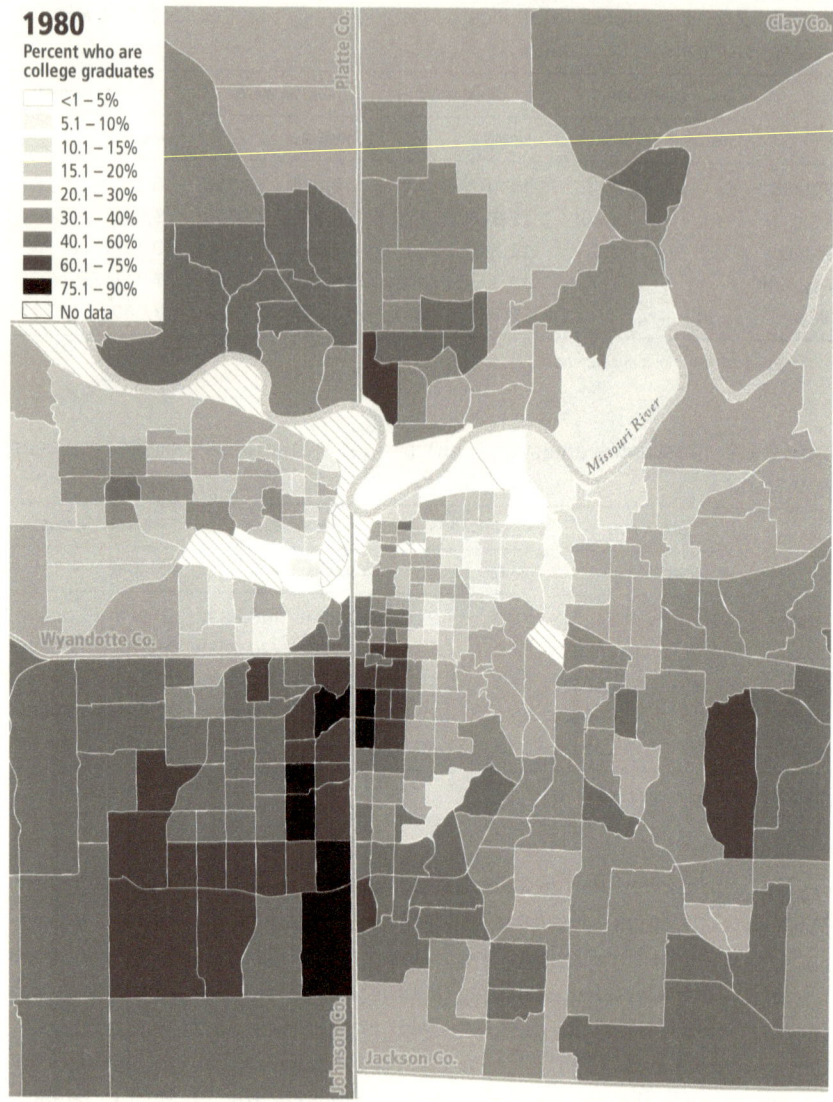

MAP 2.8 Geo-spatial distribution of adults (age twenty-five and older) with college degrees (bachelor's or more) in 1980 (census tract data)

to this, of course, was the Sunset Hills area on the city's southwest side, which featured very high home values, few black or poor residents, and a high level of adult education. The suburban communities included in these tables exhibited a good deal of variation as well. The SMSD area of Johnson County, Kansas, was wealthier and better educated than the Missouri suburbs of Raytown in Jackson County and North Kansas City (a part of Kansas City, Missouri, but not

KCMPS). Raytown was somewhat similar to SMSD in home values, but it was a much smaller community. In general, few African Americans lived in suburban areas, although the SMSD area had more of them than either of the Missouri suburban districts.

Two decades later things had changed in many respects, but stayed more or less the same in others. By 1980 the city's black population had roughly doubled. Overall levels of attainment had gone up, but the Missouri suburbs of Raytown and North Kansas City changed little. Attainment had increased considerably in Kansas City, partly due to rising black graduation rates, while the Sunset Hills area and Shawnee Mission retained the highest levels in the region. Home ownership had also grown, and SMSD commanded the highest property values, with Raytown close behind. With desegregation then under way in Kansas City, extending to the celebrated Sunset Hills area, Johnson County was a logical destination for affluent whites in search of good schools that were unlikely to be racially integrated. Many of those wanting to remain in Missouri headed south to Raytown or other Jackson County suburbs, but overall levels of adult education remained lower there.[63]

These patterns are evident in the levels of adult education evident in map 2.8. It is clear that a substantially greater concentration of college-educated adults lived in the geographically adjacent areas of Southwest Kansas City and Johnson County. Several tracts recorded levels of more than 60 percent, more than double that of most tracts on the Missouri side of the border. Altogether, more than a third of the adult population of SMSD were college graduates, a level considerably greater than for the rest of the metropolitan region. This, no doubt, was a major factor in the high performance and strong academic reputation of schools in the area. Indeed, a statistical analysis in the book's appendix reveals that the numbers of college-educated residents in this quadrant of the metropolitan region were significantly higher than local income levels would suggest. In other words, people with collegiate backgrounds flocked to these neighborhoods, including a disproportionate number of younger adults likely thinking of schools for their children. In this respect, the perceived excellence of local educational institutions was a significant factor in the area's growth. If adult education was among the most important determinants of school success, it is little wonder that students in SMSD did so well. They lived in a large community defined to a great degree by concentrated educational advantage.[64]

The map points to other features of the region as well. To the north and east, within the boundaries of KCMPS, it is possible to see the "wall" represented by Troost Avenue, a vertical line that separated the less-educated black population to the east from practically all white neighborhoods to the west. Not surprisingly, attainment levels were visibly depressed in neighborhoods marked by racial segregation and extreme poverty. This represented yet another dimension of disadvantage for children living in these settings, reflecting the long history of educational discrimination that African Americans suffered in the South and elsewhere.[65]

Across the border in Kansas, the picture was quite different. The area of high attainment extended south and west into the newly established city of Overland Park, which was rapidly becoming a center for corporate headquarters and telecommunications. A few tracts of somewhat lower attainment appeared in the northern section of SMSD, as older housing stock there attracted less-affluent buyers from Wyandotte County and elsewhere. The newly reconstituted Blue Valley School District served children in the southern part of the county and would eventually emerge as the area's premier educational system. Children in this part of the metro area undoubtedly benefited from the accumulation of highly educated adults there too, despite changes in certain tracts in the north and west. On the other hand, little such advancement occurred in Kansas City. At the same time that college-educated adults were clustering in SMSD and other suburban settings, relatively few were evident in the urban core area of KCMPS. Altogether, in that case, the 1980 map of adult educational attainment vividly illustrates a widening socioeconomic divide that fractured the region.

The low adult attainment levels in KCMPS were emblematic of major changes in the district during these years: middle-class white flight, growing poverty, and a declining tax base to support local public schools. Perhaps even more telling, however, was the absence of parents and other adults who had experienced success in the education system. This meant that children in much of the city lacked a vital resource in the quest for an education equivalent to that offered in suburban districts. Given these circumstances, it is no surprise that schools in these parts of KCMPS came to be seen as failing.[66] These conditions also account for much of the frustration and anger that African Americans expressed during the 1960s and '70s. They were well aware of the inequalities that existed across the region. Even within the boundaries of KCMPS, the wealth of the Country Club district and the excellence of its public schools—particularly Southwest High—were persistent reminders that urban education did not have to be inferior. But an intractable school board dismissed calls for integration, keeping most black students in segregated schools serving impoverished neighborhoods. In two decades the condition of African American neighborhoods east of Troost Avenue changed relatively little, and children living there suffered the consequences. To a large degree, they contended with multiple dimensions of concentrated disadvantage.[67]

Altogether, these patterns point to widening inequality in educational aspects of social status across the metro area. If there was a distinctive sector of concerted advantage in the region, it was located in the southwestern quadrant of greater Kansas City. The rest of KCMPS and suburban Jackson County featured fewer social and cultural resources of this sort despite relatively isolated pockets of college-educated residents. In the central city, KCMPS had clearly fallen behind with respect to the resources represented on the 1980 attainment map. The Missouri suburbs were doing better, including North Kansas City, Raytown, and other areas, but still lagged the college education profile of the Nichols neighborhoods. Like many large American metropolitan regions, greater Kansas City was fragmented by race and social class, but it was also sharply divided by the adult educational resources available to children. It is little wonder, then, that schools with the best academic reputations were in Kansas and Southwest Kansas City; it was the result of a process of social and economic differentiation that unfolded over several decades.

Correlates of Educational Inequality

It is clear that considerable unevenness existed in the distribution of highly educated adults across metropolitan Kansas City; but what did that mean for the educational experiences of students? There are many potential dimensions to such a question, but among the most basic is attainment, the levels of schooling reached by individuals. This measure permits estimation of how long students remained in school and an assessment of their chances of graduating. Variation on this count was clearly evident in the experiences of seventeen-year-old youth at this time in US history. Prior research has demonstrated that such a statistical analysis of attainment can offer considerable insight into how geo-spatial patterns of inequality influenced the school experiences of youth.[68] But first it is necessary locate an appropriate body of such evidence.

Fortunately, a ready source of relevant information existed for this study. Using US Census data from the Integrated Public Use Microdata Series (IPUMS), it was possible to identify a sample of seventeen-year-old youth from across greater Kansas City. These data feature a range of demographic, educational, and household characteristics to consider in connection with attainment. With the geographic codes provided by IPUMS, three broad geo-spatial groupings were identifiable in the sample: the city of Kansas City, Missouri (including areas served by "suburban" school districts), suburban communities in Jackson and Clay Counties, and suburban Johnson County. Using logistical regression techniques, it is possible to conduct a comparison of the experiences of youth living in these areas, while considering a wide range of additional issues that affected their lives.

Again, the focal point of this analysis is individual student educational attainment, which considers the progress that each youth in the sample has made toward high school graduation. To do this, the analysis asks whether the youth was still in school and had reached at least eleventh grade, the junior (or penultimate) year of school. This benchmark is required, because the census recorded household characteristics for youth residing at home, permitting consideration of family background factors that most certainly affected attainment. Sixteen was the legally permissible age for dropping out in both Kansas and Missouri, and the census was taken in April, toward the end of the academic year. Most students who were still in school at seventeen and were at least juniors were quite likely to graduate, as relatively few dropped out or pursued General Equivalency Diplomas (GED) or other alternatives. Consequently, this represents a broad indicator of success in school, or attainment of a fixed standard of accomplishment. Using it to compare the success of students in different parts of the metropolitan area permits examination of other factors that may have shaped their school experiences.[69]

To identify such influences, the IPUMS sample offers a range of social and demographic characteristics to consider. These include factors that have been widely used in studies of educational attainment and status attainment research, such as race, gender, economic status, home ownership, family structure, and parental education. The book's appendix provides definitions for these variables, along with detailed tabular presentation of regression results. This analysis highlights their interaction with the geo-spatial factors specified above. The point, after all, is to explore how the uneven distribution of various resources affected the educational experiences of youth at this time.

Within the limitations posed by the IPUMS data, it is possible to identify general patterns of attainment that reflect the larger profile of geo-spatial inequality across the region. Overall, the IPUMS data indicate that seventeen-year-olds in Johnson County were 70 percent more likely to have reached at least their junior year in high school than their Missouri counterparts, whether in Kansas City or the suburbs. There appears to have been relatively little difference in the likelihood of success between Kansas City students and those in suburban Jackson and Clay Counties, probably because of the expansive Kansas City sample. Missouri residents in the sample thus were alike in highlighting the success of students in Johnson County, who exhibited the highest attainment levels in the region. This, of course, is a pattern broadly similar to that observed in the earlier discussion of adult attainment levels.

Figure 2.1 represents the results of the logistical regression analysis, graphically depicting the findings in terms of both positive and negative effects in the likelihood of school success. Factors with lines extending horizontally to the right

Figure 2.1: Odds of school success, 1980

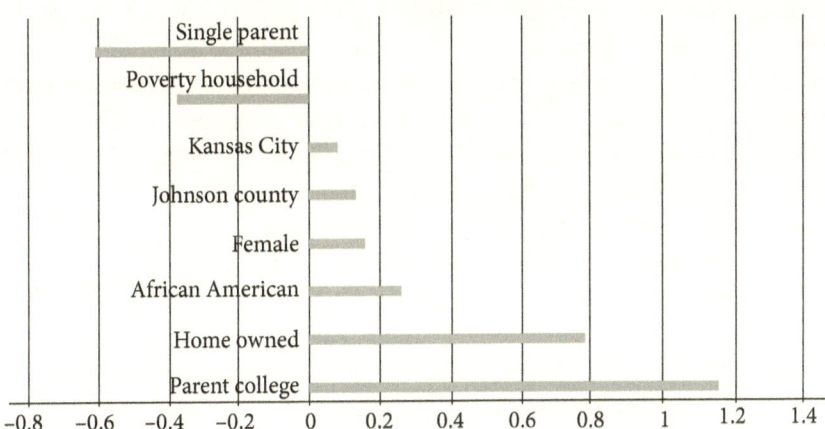

FIGURE 2.1 Results of a logistic regression analysis, using individual-level data from IPUMS. Lines to the right of the 0 axis are factors associated with greater (positive) odds of school success; lines to the left are those associated with lower (negative) odds of success. Numbers on the bottom line represent coefficient values. See the appendix for a step-wise analysis of these variables and their definitions.

of the zero dividing line were associated with a greater likelihood of school success; those with lines extending to the left were linked to lower odds of such accomplishment. Living in a home owned by the family, for instance, more than doubled the likelihood of school success for youth in the sample, while living in a household below the poverty level lowered the odds of attainment by more than 30 percent. These are robust effects, and controlling for them helped to give the African American variable a positive association with school success. Part of the Johnson County advantage in attainment was attributable to the area's high level of home ownership: 93 percent of student there lived in family-owned homes, compared to 75 percent in Kansas City and 78 percent in the Missouri suburbs (calculated from IPUMS data). The effect of being female also was enhanced by controlling for these factors, with girls exhibiting a nearly 17 percent attainment advantage over boys.

The most important factors in the analysis, however, were categorical variables for living in a single-parent, female-headed household and having at least one parent with a college degree. These too represented robust effects: living in a single-parent family represented a 45 percent reduction in the likelihood of school success, and having a college-educated parent increased the odds of attainment by more than a *multiple* of 3 (300 percent). The latter variable, of course, was the focal point in discussing various school districts earlier. In the logistic regression results it exhibited the strongest relationship to student educational attainment, controlling for a wide range of additional variables. Its inclusion dropped the Johnson County variable substantially, reducing the advantage of its resident students over their Missouri suburban counterparts to less than a 14 percent greater likelihood of school success. The family structure variable had very little effect on Johnson County residents, although its inclusion did make the black categorical variable both positive and significant. Holding all these factors constant, African American youth were more likely than whites to succeed in school.

The results of this analysis highlight the importance of a variety of factors as correlates of individual success in school. Poverty, living in a single-parent household, and lacking a college-educated parent were conditions more frequently experienced by black youth, and they were associated with substantially lower attainment. Poverty and lack of traditional family structure were certainly correlated within certain inner-city neighborhoods, and high levels of unemployment contributed to both. Impoverished women headed most single-parent households in these settings, and they frequently struggled to provide basic necessities for their families. In 1980, single women parented about a quarter of Kansas City black families. For the most part, they lacked the economic, social, and cultural resources to help their children excel academically. The extent of joblessness in high-poverty neighborhoods, especially for men, also limited the positive role models for children and youth. These conditions of concentrated disadvantage directly impacted the likelihood of success in school. Even if less than a third of KCMO's black households experienced this degree of deprivation in 1980, and a slightly larger number represented the rising black middle class, a substantial portion of the KCMPS student population struggled as a consequence.[70] And the system's schools were ill equipped to help them succeed.

On the other hand, the positive association of other factors with the Johnson County variable illuminates the manner in which concentrated advantage contributed to higher levels of educational success. In comparison with other suburbs, it was the power of parental collegiate education that distinguished Johnson County youth most clearly. Within the IPUMS sample, fully 40 percent of youth had at least one parent with a college degree, as opposed to 12 percent in Kansas City (including those in "suburban" districts) and 9 percent in suburban Missouri. In other words, students in Johnson County were more than three times more likely than their peers elsewhere in metro Kansas City to have a college-educated parent, and this turned out to be a major advantage with respect to school. These students also had access to many other positive influences in their communities, adults who often were in a position to assist them in achieving their goals, academic or otherwise. The fact that they lived in such an affluent area doubtless was an advantage too. Their families did not struggle to make ends meet, but rather often were able to deploy resources directly to support their social and academic advancement.[71] In short, these circumstances were the mirror opposite of conditions facing many impoverished children in the inner city. It is little wonder that so many more youth succeeded in the Johnson County schools.

In the end, this discussion also points to the significance of geo-spatial differences in wealth, family structure, and adult education, key advantages for students in one corner of the region and, conversely, a disadvantage for others. Johnson County, Kansas, was clearly the locus of great benefits for children and youth, as represented in a combination of conditions. Students who lived there were 70 percent more likely to experience advancement in public secondary schools than their counterparts in the region, and much of this was associated with the area's high levels of home ownership and adult education. Its schools also may have been somewhat better, as Johnson County students were 13 percent more likely to succeed academically even after these factors were controlled, and perhaps students benefited there from highly motivated peers as well, or community norms that emphasized success in school. But much of the observable variation in attainment appears to have been linked to key family background factors, a finding consistent with decades of research. The fact that families with these resources were clustered together in this fashion clearly represented a high degree of concentrated advantage, a feature of metropolitan development that has been discussed a good deal recently but was plainly evident four decades ago.[72]

Conditions were quite different just a short distance away. Poverty, single-parent families, lower parental education, and living in rental property (non–home ownership) clearly were associated with lower likelihood of attainment in other parts of the region, especially Kansas City, Missouri. When these household characteristics—correlates of concentrated poverty—were held constant, African American attainment was actually *higher* than that of whites. For youth in the aspiring black middle class, this suggests that the odds of succeeding in school were very good indeed. But in much of the inner city, an accumulation of conditions forcefully impacted the lives of other young people in a negative fashion. Factors included in the analysis point to the significance of concentrated poverty as a fact of life for many black students, a form of pervasive disadvantage that foreshortened their opportunities for attainment.[73] This was a stark contrast to their peers in Johnson County, whose families' stocks of physical (property) and cultural (education) capital undoubtedly contributed a great deal to their accomplishments. These were significant suburban advantages indeed.

Perry Cookingham worked assiduously to forestall the damaging impact of suburbanization in greater Kansas City, but in the end it does not appear that he succeeded. Like other major US metropolitan regions, rapid growth occurred there during this period, marked by extensive development on the urban periphery. Despite efforts to unify many outlying areas within the municipal boundaries of Kansas City, Missouri, suburban development spilled over to Johnson County, Kansas, and to eastern Jackson County. This process of suburbanization was abetted by racial transition in the center city, resulting is classic patterns of white flight and social-economic inequality. These lines of development mirrored perceptions of area education systems, as suburban districts—both within and outside the city limits—grew in size and outward signs of excellence. Conflicts over desegregation and equity in the central city contributed to these changes, as they did in other metropolitan settings. In all these respects Kansas City reflected national trends, even if certain aspects of its experience were unique.

Schools apparently were a blind spot for Cookingham, and in this respect Kansas City represents an intriguing case of metropolitan development. Given the patterns of educational inequality described above, there can be little doubt that critical geo-spatial disparities came to mark the distribution of these social and cultural resources in the region as well. Race and poverty were critical dimensions of this, along with wealth and other aspects of social status. With respect to education, however, overall attainment levels were an unusually salient element of such differentiation. In particular, adults with college-level education gathered in a distinctive zone of concentrated advantage that was noted for its wealth and style, attributes that apparently proved attractive to (mainly white) parents seeking the very best educational opportunities for their children. Meanwhile, children and youth growing up in the region's poorest neighborhoods, where adult attainment was least evident, endured conditions of concentrated disadvantage that made school success far less likely. These were extremes of metropolitan inequality that emerged relatively quickly during the postwar era.

By 1980 there were clear winners and losers with respect to the degree of school success that children and youth experienced. If some areas in metro Kansas City were seen as good or desirable in this respect, SMSD and the Country Club district were surely at the top of the list. A major part of this status was the proximate accumulation of educational resources, chief among them the attainment levels of the adult population. The absence of such assets in other areas of the region contributed to the high degree of local inequality evident in educational opportunity.

This analysis has demonstrated that this sort of geo-spatial differentiation in education accompanied the emergence of race and segregation as major issues in Kansas City. In particular, African Americans recognized the educational impact of segregation and concentrated poverty, demanding integrated schooling as a means to greater equity in outcomes. By and large, however, they did not succeed in altering the dynamics of socioeconomic differentiation that gave shape to geo-spatial inequality. The cultural and educational attributes of the former J. C. Nichols developments, along with their highly regarded schools, appear to have proven quite attractive to families of a certain economic and social standing. And this more than anything else appears to have accounted for the academic success of its youth. Meanwhile, the departure of middle-class whites from much of KCMPS signaled the rapid decline of crucial assets in that part of the region, and outside of the black community few leaders publicly acknowledged the magnitude of the problem. Local residents live with the legacy of those developments today.

In recent years considerable attention has been given to widening social and economic inequality in the United States, and particularly to the geo-spatial partitioning of various status groups. The evidence herein suggests that this process was evident some fifty years ago and has been an integral aspect of metropolitan development at least since the postwar period. Suburbanization has long been recognized as contributing to social and economic differentiation; but this analysis has demonstrated that educational attainment was also a community characteristic that came to distinguish certain parts of metropolitan regions.

The American tradition of independent school districts certainly made it easier to identify metropolitan zones with different educational attributes. And the history of educational partitioning in Kansas City, Missouri, demonstrates how educational systems could create boundaries that demarcated social and cultural distinctions, even within municipal boundaries. As sociologist Pierre Bourdieu noted, cultural forms of capital such as educational credentials often operate as a telling indicator of dissimilarity, and such differences can become a vital resource in the quest for status distinction.[74] The Kansas City experience demonstrates how these social and cultural forces have operated in recent American history.

3

FALL FROM GRACE

The Transformation of an Urban School System

Speaking to some 340 new teachers at the start of the school year in 1962, Kansas City, Missouri, school superintendent James Hazlett urged them not to believe reports that local suburban schools were better than his district's. The city schools had long been considered the best in the region, especially the system's crown jewel, Southwest High. Noting a "trend towards the suburbs," Hazlett acknowledged that outlying schools were beginning to get more attention, drawing families out of the city with the promise of superior education. In particular, he complained that real estate agents "sometimes say that schools are better in Johnson County."[1] In the past, Kansas City school leaders compared their institutions to those in Omaha, Des Moines, and St. Louis, systems they believed to be peers. The upstart suburban districts, on the other hand, hardly seemed worthy of consideration. But a new day was dawning.[2]

Hazlett objected strongly to the idea of suburban superiority and even arranged a meeting with real estate agents to set the record straight. Observing that people often moved "for status and prestige," he declared that "you can't necessarily apply the word 'better'" to suburban schools.[3] Unfortunately, it was not clear that everyone agreed, as the district was already losing white students. In the years to come, competition from suburban districts would become a major problem for Kansas City, as larger numbers of families left the central city in search of newer, reputedly better, and predominantly white schools. Although Hazlett was loath to admit it, in the early 1960s, questions of race and poverty loomed large in the district's future. Before long they would dictate a dramatic reversal of fortune for a school system that only recently had started to hit its stride.

The "crisis" of big-city school systems became a familiar trope in American education during the postwar era.[4] A similar process of change occurred in metropolitan Kansas City, at least in the eyes of many observers. In particular, the Kansas City, Missouri, Public Schools (KCMPS) underwent a transformation of sorts during the 1960s and '70s. While it was widely considered a venerable school district during the immediate postwar years, by 1980 the reputation of KCMPS had declined precipitously. Like urban educational institutions elsewhere, the public schools of Kansas City suffered a dramatic fall in public perceptions of their quality.

Race and poverty, of course, became major components of these changes. Kansas City's African Americans nearly doubled their share of the city's population between 1950 and 1970, from around 11 percent to 22 percent. As blacks moved southward into areas and schools long occupied by working-class whites, most prior residents departed for suburban districts, especially those located within the city's borders.[5] A growing number of KCMPS institutions became predominantly or wholly African American in composition. By 1970 a slight majority of the system's students were black, and ten years later the number of white students had declined precipitously.

Predominantly African American institutions in Kansas City reported lower graduation rates and test scores than other schools, as they did elsewhere in the country. As district leaders argued at the time, this was largely attributable to the extreme, concentrated deprivation typically found in black neighborhoods, along with historically low adult education levels. At the same time, city school budgets declined as a result of drops in property tax income and state aid. Much of this was linked to plummeting house values, businesses departing the city, and the ill repair of rental properties in slum neighborhoods. If the city schools were in "crisis," it was largely due to the changing circumstances of their settings, partly a consequence of policy choices abetting the flight of human and material resources from the urban core.[6]

For many black students, on the other hand, educational opportunities offered by KCMPS were considerably better than previous generations of their families had experienced, especially those arriving from the South. African American graduation rates improved steadily overall, as they did across the country. Indeed, as noted earlier, black attainment levels were better than those of whites when factors such as poverty and family structure were statistically controlled.[7] But public opinion nevertheless held that the city schools had declined significantly in effectiveness and safety.

Despite their willingness to allow busing to relieve overcrowding, the predominantly white and conservative school board in Kansas City consistently refused to embrace racial integration as a district goal. Their steadfast resistance to black community demands for system-wide desegregation only fueled more such concerns. White flight eventually proved endemic once KCMPS was required to begin desegregating throughout the district. This set the stage for the historic *Jenkins v. Missouri* desegregation case, which prescribed a remedy that did little to alter levels of racial segregation in the schools or popular perceptions of them.[8]

This chapter examines changes in the KCMPS schools in greater detail. It addresses questions about the effects of board opposition to the very idea of desegregation, and popular reactions to attendant patterns of change in the district. What were key moments in its transition from a system serving a racially diverse population to one with a predominantly African American student body? What was the role of the district's leaders in these events, and what could they have done to alter the course of change? How did the process of white flight unfold, and what sorts of conflict did it represent? What were responses of African Americans to changes in the schools? And how did the city's institutions ultimately compare to emerging suburban school systems? The following account of the district's changing fortunes addresses these and other matters, along with their social and political consequences.

A Moment of Prominence

The decade of the 1950s can be considered among the best of times for urban schools in the United States. With the return of veterans following the war, the economy boomed and so did the birthrate. Education systems everywhere expanded, and big-city schools, which historically had greater resources and higher-achieving students than other institutions, benefited. In particular, urban high schools were widely judged to be superior, both with respect to academic offerings and extracurricular activities. They were larger than typical rural or suburban institutions, at least early in the decade, and there were more of them in major urban centers. Outlying communities may have had reputedly good schools, but as a rule their counterparts in the cities were widely regarded as the best.[9]

Much of this was due to the scale of enrollment differences between districts. In 1951 KCMPS enrolled 51,910 students, from a school-age population numbering over 86,000. The next largest district in Jackson County was Independence, at 6,341, and of the eleven remaining only Raytown had more than two thousand.

In Clay County, north of the river, the North Kansas City district enrolled 4,714 students, and Liberty and Excelsior Springs a little over a thousand each. High schools in most suburban districts were tiny, with only Independence and Raytown enrolling more than 250 students in Jackson County, and the latter counted fewer than 600. In Clay County only North Kansas City had more than 300 secondary students.[10] Generally speaking, smaller schools offered few electives or opportunities for more advanced instruction. This meant that they typically provided fewer resources to help students excel academically, including specialized clubs and scholastic competitions. Moreover, many ambitious teachers aspired to work in the big city, where they typically could teach more advanced courses, work with better facilities, and make more money.[11]

In many respects, senior high schools were the crown jewels of educational systems, flagship institutions from which only about half of American youth graduated at midcentury. Bigger was widely considered better, because larger schools offered greater curricular variety and more clubs, teams, and other activities. With nearly twelve thousand students enrolled, Kansas City's senior high schools averaged about fifteen hundred students each, although there was some variation in size. They differed in reputation as well, which tended to reflect neighborhood characteristics and clientele. Near the city's geographic midpoint, Central High was its oldest public secondary institution and enjoyed a venerable academic tradition. Southwest High, located adjacent to the affluent J. C. Nichols development of Sunset Hills, was the most scholastically renowned.[12] It typically registered the most National Merit Scholarship winners each year. Paseo Academy, just to the south of Central, was also celebrated for strong academic programs and an architecturally impressive building. Other schools, such as East, Northeast, Southeast, and Westport, served particular neighborhoods. Lincoln was the city's African American high school and had achieved distinction in science education. Separate technical schools, R. T. Coles and Manual High, also existed for black and white students respectively.[13] Altogether, KCMPS provided students with many options when it came to completing their education, especially for whites.

This is not to say that the system did not have problems, with racially segregated and inequitable schooling perhaps the most obvious. African Americans had long suffered unequal resources in their institutions, and black parents sued the district in 1952 to end overcrowding in segregated elementary schools.[14] When James Hazlett became superintendent in 1955, he confronted these and manifold other difficulties that faced many city districts at the time. Because of the postwar baby boom and in-migration, overall enrollment expanded by about a thousand students annually, adding the equivalent a new school each year. But most new students to the district were black, as white enrollment leveled off in the later 1950s. Overcrowding was a national problem, but in Kansas City it mainly affected African Americans, as whites began to leave the city schools for the suburbs.[15]

At the same time, there was a growing teacher shortage, and the district struggled to recruit and retain educators. In 1956 it dropped the age limit for new teachers, encouraging married women to apply for the first time and urging retirees to return.[16] But competition for teachers increased, and as many as two-thirds of those who were offered positions with KCMPS took jobs elsewhere. The *Kansas City Star* lamented the comparatively low salaries offered by city schools and advocated making teacher compensation equivalent to that in Omaha, Des Moines, and other big cities. The problem was temporarily resolved when a $27 million ($235 million in 2015 dollars) bond issue was approved by voters in 1956, providing funds for new buildings and budget relief to raise teacher salaries.[17] Record budgets were registered in subsequent years, permitting the district to lower class sizes and recruit new staff members. The overcrowding crisis was temporarily averted.

Hazlett also faced issues particular to Kansas City and other districts with a legacy of racial segregation. When he assumed office, KCMPS had just begun the process of dismantling a dual education system that had existed for many decades. By all accounts the process went fairly smoothly and helped resolve overcrowding issues in black institutions. But most previously white schools that gained black students registered relatively small numbers of them. As a result, little meaningful integration was actually accomplished. While there were complaints about black teachers losing jobs as enrollments shifted, most were eventually rehired. By and large, long-standing residential segregation dictated enrollment patterns, since KCMPS remained committed to the concept of neighborhood schools. The fact that the shift to a system that did not explicitly dictate placement by race was accomplished without major discord, however, was taken as a hopeful sign for the future.[18]

As the successful bond levy and growing budgets suggested, along with apparently widespread support for ending de jure segregation, public satisfaction with KCMPS was quite high during the latter part of the 1950s. The district was overseen by a six-member "silk stocking" board, usually elected unopposed and mainly composed of wealthy, civic-minded individuals, so there was little controversy in governance.[19] Despite problems endemic to most public schools at the time, its administrators were widely viewed as competent and forward looking. "Because of Hazlett and board policies of recent years," the *Star* declared in 1959, "the Kansas City Schools operate from a position of strength."[20]

The system's positive reputation had been affirmed four years earlier, when residents of the tiny elementary district of Sugar Creek voted overwhelmingly to be annexed by KCMPS, rejecting entreaties from neighboring Independence. Sugar Creek was the site of a large industrial complex near the Missouri River, and thus offered considerable tax enhancements to its suitors. Its constituents were clearly impressed by KCMPS plans to build Van Horn High School nearby, but they also noted the district's generally good reputation. Within a few years two additional small elementary districts approved annexation by KCMPS in the same area, but that development marked an end to the district's physical expansion for quite some time.[21] The public view of KCMPS would begin to change markedly in the decade ahead.

Race, Poverty, and Education: The Beginnings

Like public education systems across Missouri, KCMPS had long maintained racially segregated schools, but it moved quickly to desegregate following the *Brown* decision in 1954. The board eliminated the dual system by establishing new school boundaries, although the reassignment of students irrespective of race did not occur until 1955, starting in the fall. When the new school year began, forty-three of the district's ninety-two schools had both black and white students, although the numbers of either group that was in the minority were small in most cases. Still, the *Kansas City Call* observed that "the school board has done well as far as the integration of students is concerned." The mixing of black and white teachers was another matter and would take some time.[22]

While the integration of high schools in other cities sometimes led to conflict between students, the process apparently went relatively smoothly in Kansas City.[23] The R. T. Coles vocational programs were shifted to Manual High, which almost immediately became a predominantly black institution. Located near the city's growing black community, Central High also received more than a hundred African American students. As the principal noted after a year, somewhat prematurely, "Those of us who have been privileged to live it have known the determination of students and faculty that the integration program should succeed.... Never once did the leaders of our student body fail to stand fast in their determination that it would succeed."[24] Within a few years, however, integration had turned tenuous, as Central became a predominantly black institution. Still, the initial stage of desegregation was widely considered a momentous step, especially for the schools most immediately affected.

Integration appeared sustainable for a time at some schools, but it was relatively short-lived in most. Most of Central's black students came from impoverished neighborhoods near the city's center, and at the start of the desegregation policy they represented about 10 percent of the city's population. That changed dramatically thereafter, and within four years the school was overcrowded and 70 percent black. Students were given the option of attending Northeast or Van Horn as Central's numbers mounted.[25] Apparently whites many did choose those options, as Central soon became nearly wholly African American, surpassing Lincoln in the number of black students it served.

These changes reflected the movement of African American families southward as their community expanded, but it also meant that whites were moving out of the area. Racial segregation proceeded rapidly as a consequence. Desegregation certainly represented greater opportunities for students in the city's historically black schools, many of which had become extremely overcrowded.[26] But the movement of these students into historically white schools typically resulted in a process of racial transition that unfolded quickly. This experience was akin to that of many urban schools nationally, as they shifted from white to predominantly black in fairly short order.[27]

The process of racial change in Kansas City can be seen in maps 3.1 through 3.3, which illustrate the geographic expansion of African American settlement in relation to KCMPS's principal secondary institutions. By 1960 predominantly African American neighborhoods with high levels of poverty surrounded Central High but had not yet reached Paseo or schools to the south of it. Ten years later they extended south of Paseo but not yet as far as Southeast High, which was beginning to undergo racial change. By 1980 black settlement had expanded all the way to Raytown and started to move into the Center and Hickman Mills school districts. By that time the city's major public high schools east of Troost and south of downtown had become nearly all black, and KCMPS's student population was about two-thirds African American. Kansas City's black community had expanded its geographic footprint significantly but still remained largely confined to highly segregated neighborhoods and institutions.[28] Concentrated poverty existed in pockets throughout much of the area.

Much of this process of change reflected the unwillingness of whites to attend schools with majority black student bodies. In the fall of 1955 the district expected more than 900 white students to attend such schools, but fewer than 120 showed up.[29] By 1960 most black secondary students still attended Lincoln, Manual, or Central, schools located in the city center, while only about 10 percent of new students entering East High were African American, and a slightly higher proportion at West.[30] Institutions serving racially stable neighborhoods occupied by relatively affluent whites remained seemingly immune from integration until the 1970s.[31] This included Southwest High (located far from any black neighborhoods), Northeast, and newly opened Van Horn on the largely white and blue-collar East Side.[32]

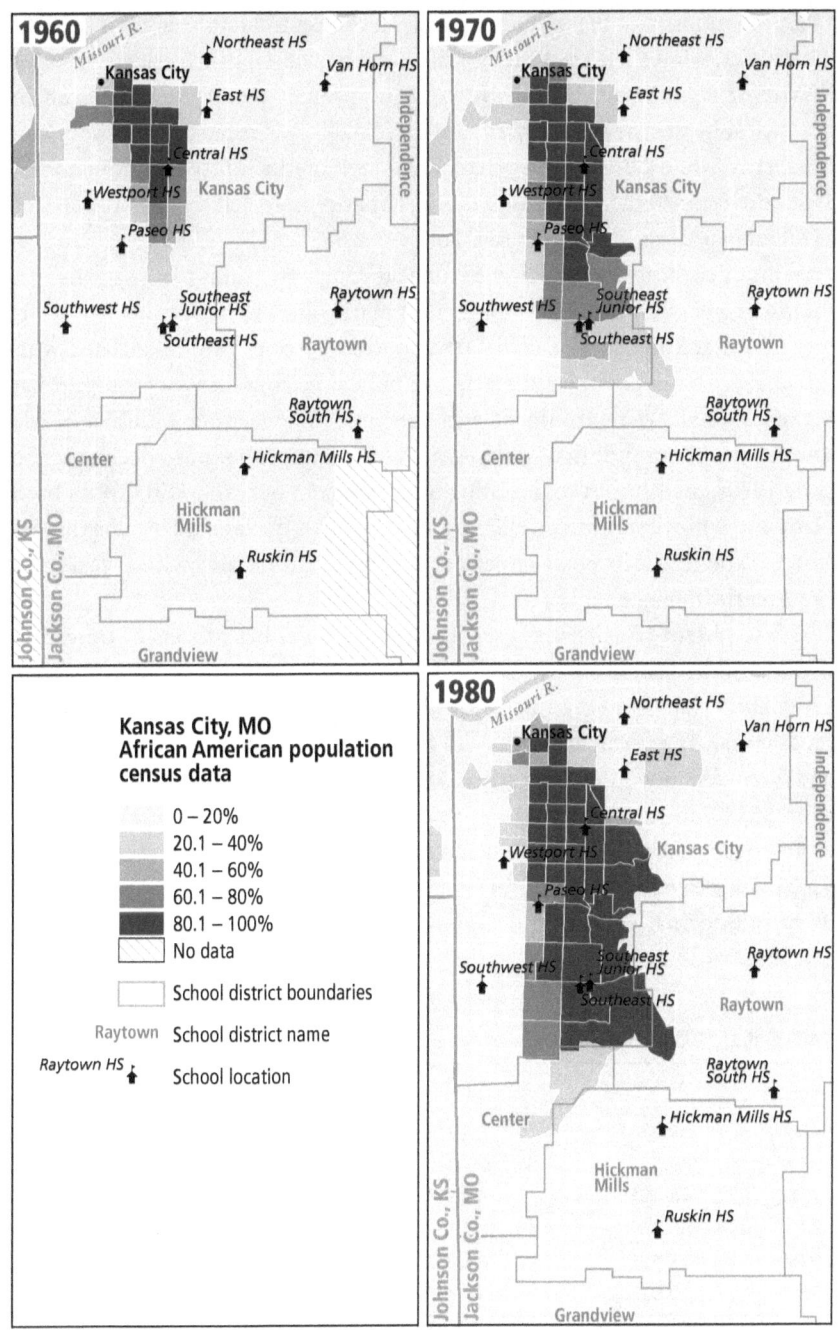

MAPS 3.1–3.3 Kansas City public high schools and expansion of African American settlement, 1960, 1970, and 1980

As the number of black students grew in the central and southeast parts of the district, whites left the system. This is evident in table 3.1, which provides KCMPS student population figures and the proportion African American in five-year intervals. Several patterns are evident. After climbing in the 1950s, the number of white students leveled off at a little more than fifty-two thousand in 1958 and declined thereafter. African Americans represented the major source of enrollment growth in the years to follow.

White departures were fairly gradual through the mid-1960s, at about a thousand per year, but then accelerated markedly. The reduction in enrollment occurred in the face of historically high fertility rates associated with the postwar baby boom, so the actual numbers leaving likely were somewhat higher. Total district enrollment plateaued in 1965, reaching a peak of nearly seventy-five thousand three years later. Black numbers began to decline in the early 1970s, owing both to declining birthrates and out-migration. With both black and white enrollments falling significantly in the later 1970s, the district stood at about half its postwar peak at the end of the decade, with a clear African American majority.[33]

These system-wide changes accompanied a widening process of transition in many of the district's schools. Central and Paseo, located near the city center, experienced rapid integration.[34] As indicated in table 3.2, Paseo High became predominantly African American in 1965. Fueled by migration from the South and high fertility rates, the city's African American population expanded from 55,682 to 83,130 during the fifties, predominantly in central-city areas increasingly perceived as black neighborhoods. Many of these migrants were very poor, arriving from destitute conditions in the South-Central states, and with little formal education or apposite experience in contemporary urban

TABLE 3.1 KCMPS enrollment by race, 1955–1980

YEAR	WHITE	AFRICAN AMERICAN	OTHER*	PERCENT BLACK
1955	49,677	12,274	NA	19.8
1960	48,263	20,040	NA	29.3
1965	44,495	30,304	NA	40.5
1970	35,252	35,504	NA	50.2
1975	21,405	33,001	2,294	62.2
1980	10,923	26,368	1,787	67.5

*Students from other minority groups were counted as white prior to the mid-1970s.

Sources: KCMPS, Department of Accountability and Research, *Twenty-Second Annual Report of the Progress of Desegregation in the Kansas City Public Schools*, 1976. Joshua Dunn, *Complex Justice*, 63.

settings.[35] This movement continued into the next decade as the black population increased to more than 110,000, pushing southward along the infamous metaphorical wall at Troost Avenue.

The dynamics of racial change in schools located in these neighborhoods is clearly evident in table 3.2, which reveals transitions in the student bodies of three secondary institutions. They included Southeast High, just a few miles south of Paseo. By 1969, it too had become predominantly black, and its academic reputation began to change as well. As these figures suggest, along with those for Paseo and Southwest Junior High, inducing white flight from KCMPS schools did not require large numbers of African American students. Departures jumped in the two senior highs when the number of blacks reached a tenth or so. The peak of out-migration, however, appears to have occurred when the number of black students approached a third. This was a widely acknowledge "tipping point" in studies of desegregation and neighborhood change, including research on KCMPS, and district leaders were well aware of it.[36]

TABLE 3.2 Transfers from select KCMPS schools, 1962–1973

LAST YEAR ATTENDED	PASEO HIGH	PASEO PERCENT BLACK	SOUTHEAST HIGH	SOUTHEAST PERCENT BLACK	SOUTHEAST JUNIOR HIGH	SJH PERCENT BLACK
1958	1	4	1	.5	NA	NA
1959	39	6.6	12	1.3	NA	NA
1960	110	9.7	20	1.7	NA	NA
1961	146	16.3	78	2.6	NA	NA
1962	254	23.3	96	5.9	11	9.7
1963	314	36.4	185	8.4	50	18.6
1964	203	50.2	134	13	85	22.5
1965	83	62.4	163	22.2	114	29.5
1966	98	70.1	180	25.2	137	34.4
1967	89	78.1	164	33.2	154	41.5
1968	112	88	178	42.9	134	52
1969	80	97.8	228	59.3	196	73.2
1970	28	99.4	82	79.6	134	85.5
1971	15	99.7	31	92.2	79	91
1972	0	99.9	9	96.5	20	95.9
1973	1	99.8	1	97.9	3	96.9
Total	1,573		1,562		1,117	

Source: Arthur Benson Papers, SHSMO Research Center–Kansas City, UMKC Archives, box 320, file I.R.2. Data from Central High School was also collected. Its student population was more than 97 percent African American by 1961 and registered just 500 transfers in the next twelve years, 63 percent to schools outside the metro area and 20 percent to other KCMPS schools.

Much of this movement, of course, was likely motivated by changes in these students' neighborhoods as much as the schools. But there can be little doubt that the majority of transfers were requested by white students. A study of Paseo students showed that large numbers of whites transferred to Westport or Southwest High Schools, even though district officials did not approve in principle.[37] It also was quite clear that many others were leaving the district altogether.

The only secondary schools that could maintain a relatively stable level of integration for much of this period were Westport, East, and West, institutions located in predominantly white neighborhoods that eventually included black residents in their catchment areas. Although their numbers are not included in table 3.2, Westport and East served a student body that was about 20 to 30 percent African American in 1969 (West opened a little later). The numbers of black students thus did not reach levels that threatened white majorities in these schools, and the direction of black settlement was south rather than west or east.[38] Consequently, white flight was less evident in these cases, as the ratio of racial groups remained more or less constant. It proved very difficult to maintain such a balance elsewhere, however, especially in light of the KCMPS school board's dogged resistance to system-wide desegregation.

By 1970 the KCMPS population was majority African American by a slight margin, but most black students in the system attended schools in neighborhoods east of Troost Avenue where they lived. The result was a highly segregated school district that clearly reflected the racially divided residential geography of the city. Despite a study of the system conducted by urban education expert Robert Havighurst, and a desegregation proposal offered by Hazlett in 1968 to somewhat racially balance the schools, the KCMPS board steadfastly remained committed to neighborhood schools. Given the high degree of residential segregation, this meant that schools also would remain segregated, although the board did permit continued busing to relieve overcrowding in certain cases.

Perhaps reflecting a commitment to "defend" predominantly white institutions such as those feeding into Southwest and Van Horn, and fearful of white flight, KCMPS leaders expressed no interest in busing plans like those undertaken at the time in Charlotte, Denver, and other cities.[39] This offered no encouragement to African American community members interested in sending their children to other schools in the system, and it also abetted opposition to desegregation among whites. There can be little doubt, moreover, that growing status anxieties motivated much of the latter sentiment, often reflecting racist presumptions about black families and their children. The result was a situation rife with growing tension and the potential for conflict, hardly a recipe for attracting new families to the district's schools.[40] Hazlett's retirement in 1969 created a void in leadership that did not help matters. Following his departure after nearly fifteen years at the helm of the system, a "revolving door" of new superintendents attempted to manage the district's mounting problems.⁴¹

Racial Boundaries and Institutional Change

As noted in chapter 2, racial boundaries were clearly established in the minds of Kansas City residents in the postwar era, and they frequently impacted the lives of students. Susan Hilliard had been rounded up by police as a child, and continued to experience such mistreatment as a teenager. Among the first African Americans to attend East High, she recalled walking with her friends to school and "routinely" suffering harassment by the police when they reached predominantly white neighborhoods. Marvin Daniels remembered being threatened by white youth.⁴² Susan's brother was a popular musician at East but was hassled by white students who resented the attention he received. He encountered different kinds of boundaries, those that governed the types of friendships that were acceptable, especially with young women.⁴³

Like Susan, Stanley West also recalled boundaries that barred blacks from the west side of Troost and neighborhoods to the north. He started high school at Manual but transferred to East in the later 1950s and recalled belligerence from some of the white students there. It was intermittent, however, and "nothing that I didn't really expect." He was warned at the end of his sophomore year "not to come back" by a group of them, but ignored such threats and graduated two years later. He found teachers at East to be very supportive, and they helped him feel welcome and to succeed academically. It appears that the staff there worked diligently to accommodate the relatively small number of African Americans they served, and it paid benefits in student experiences.⁴⁴

Marvin Daniels, on the other hand, had a different experience as one of the first African American students to attend Paseo High, where he encountered hostility and indifference from whites and struggled to find friends. His family had moved from rural Kansas, but that hardly made him feel welcome in Kansas City. After a couple of years, he transferred to predominantly black Manual High, the city's public vocational school, where he felt more comfortable, before ultimately finishing at Central.⁴⁵ Patrick Elard also struggled in KCMPS schools when his family arrived in the late 1940s. He was put back two grades because a meager education in Mississippi had left him barely able to read and write. He also recalled the clear boundaries that demarcated racially segregated neighborhoods and institutions at the time. Elard eventually dropped out of high school to join the military, but later graduated from college on the GI Bill and became a teacher.[46] Like West, Daniels, and Hilliard, he managed to navigate the city's segregated education system to a successful conclusion.

White decisions to leave changing neighborhoods reflected fear of falling property values and academically weakened schools, but outright racism too. Popular theories about innate racial differences in intelligence and morality, dating from the nineteenth century, continued to exert a telling influence, particularly for those with less education. The growing use of terms such as "culturally deprived" or "culturally disadvantaged" to describe poor children, typically by social scientists and public officials, was meant to sidestep the question of innate or genetic differences in achievement. But it did not appear to have changed public sentiments as a practical matter. By the mid-1960s these terms became firmly associated with black and brown children, especially in the big cities. As such, they often signaled new dimensions of supposed inferiority, registered in terms of culture and behavior.[47] And they quickly found expression in Kansas City. As one white parent declared in response to the 1964 busing plan, "culturally, our children will not benefit from being reassigned."[48] Parent groups at predominantly white institutions were quick to express such sentiments whenever busing proposals seemed likely to affect their schools.

District officials did not always help matters. In 1963 representatives from KCMPS declared at a Jefferson City hearing that "some 31,000 culturally disadvantaged students" were served by city schools. Establishment of a "Division of Urban Education" to focus on the problem suggested that additional resources and remedial assistance were required for these students' success. Statements such as these signaled that schools with significant numbers of such students could hardly be expected to attain high levels of academic excellence. Eventually programs were developed to assign struggling poor students to schools in "more advantaged neighborhoods."[49] This was intended to help children in such circumstances but reflected a logic that suggested predominantly poor and black schools were somehow naturally inferior.

Changes that occurred at venerable Central High School were symptomatic of a shift in perceived quality that eventually affected the system as a whole. The racial composition of the student body played a role in this, but so did the teaching staff. At the start of the decade only a dozen of Central's seventy-nine teachers were African American, but by 1965 their numbers had increased to nearly half. This was due to increasing staff turnover, partly a result of district efforts to racially balance its teaching force, required by federal authorities and a goal of black community leaders.[50] But it also reflected the priorities of many educators. Patrick Elard observed that more experienced white teachers left Central as it became a predominantly black institution serving many students from impoverished neighborhoods, and their replacements included some "who could not get jobs" otherwise and were "not very skilled" at handling children.[51] Veteran teachers became tougher to recruit, as many avoided schools with "deprived" students, and others were attracted by higher pay in the suburbs. Those that did come often were younger, with less experience. As the student body shifted, consequently, so did the faculty, and this eventually occurred across the district.[52] Whatever the cause, a more racially diverse and less veteran teaching staff contributed to perceptions of a decline in excellence, however unwarranted in many cases.

As the district moved teachers to address federal guidelines regarding faculty integration, parents and teachers sometimes protested.[53] Concerned about the pace of change, district teachers invited the National Education Association to investigate the system. While the ensuing report did not suggest that problems had reached "crisis" proportions, it did note "serious deficiencies" in some schools, including the use of "obsolete and inadequate facilities" and "the increasing problem of attracting and holding qualified educators."[54]

Students sometimes had similar concerns. In the mid-1960s Manny Stevens chose to attend Central rather than East High, where his siblings went, but later regretted the decision because of teacher turnover at the predominantly black school. His family had moved from Louisiana, where black schools had been significantly underfunded, but found educational experiences in Kansas City to be just as problematic. He encountered conflict in the white neighborhoods around East but felt that Central "didn't hold a candle" to his sister's and brother's academic programs. Elard also remarked that the educational climate at Central declined significantly in the later 1960s.[55] These observations were similar to other African American complaints about neglect at schools serving a predominantly black and poor clientele.[56]

Meanwhile, a number of other changes occurred. Participation in extracurricular activities at Central dropped substantially, a development also noted by Stevens and clearly evident in yearbooks from the era. This likely reflected the growing number of students from impoverished households, where such activities may have been less prioritized. The formal curriculum began to shift as well. In 1965 a new wing was added to the building for vocational training and to relieve overcrowding. In subsequent years practical nursing, electronics, and military science programs became more prominent, signaling a move toward job preparation options. This was consistent with national proposals for predominantly black secondary schools, to prepare students for skilled manual labor, but also contributed to the idea that African American students could not meet rigorous academic standards. Eventually Central would be identified as an academically underperforming school, one serving many students labeled "educationally disadvantaged."⁵⁷ By the end of the decade Paseo and Southeast would follow similar trajectories, even if they did not offer as many vocational options.

At the same time that questions of academic quality came into play, recurring reports of vandalism and school discipline problems gained public attention. In 1965 the *Star* reported that KCMPS was sixth in the nation on a per capita basis for destruction of school property, incurring nearly $80,000 (more than $600,000 in 2015 dollars) in damage during the previous year. The incidents went up thereafter, although predominantly white Southwest High reported the highest number, followed by Paseo.⁵⁸ In 1968 the district established a special school for "students who are disciplinary problems," to help "preserve order in the regular classroom."⁵⁹ An estimated $400,000 ($2.5 million in 2015 dollars) was spent on alarms, other security measures, and a special unit of guards trained by the police to address such problems, and eventually vandalism subsided. Although a district study found no statistical relationship to poverty or ethnicity in these incidents, it was not difficult for many observers to imagine that such patterns did indeed exist.⁶⁰ In 1975, following yet another upsurge in damage, one *Star* commentary speculated that it was "one of many symptoms of a school district being deserted by upper middle class families."⁶¹ Given the district's history of racial tensions and the widespread poverty in neighborhoods it served, statements such as this clearly implied that white students were not the problem.

These developments were accompanied by growing fiscal challenges for KCMPS. Most of its budget came from property taxes, and much of the housing in the district had declined in relative value, partly because it was located in the oldest part of the city. A 1980 survey of residential property in the district reported that over half the homes had been built prior to 1940 and 70 percent before 1950.⁶² This, of course, made them less competitive with new developments in suburban districts. Values also declined in tandem with the growth of the dual housing market historically associated with the African American community.⁶³ In particular, the number of residential properties assessed at less than $80,000 (in 2015 dollars) jumped significantly. In 1960 there were twenty-seven census tracts where at least 70 percent of residential properties fell into that category; ten years later the number of such tracts had increased to thirty-six, including the neighborhoods around Paseo and Southeastern High Schools. Combined with variable or declining state aid, partly a function of serving fewer students, and rapidly declining values in downtown commercial property due to competition from suburban malls, this created serious budget problems for the district.⁶⁴

All this put the schools in a precarious position. As early as 1964 public perceptions of the system's quality were beginning to slip, as a survey of local executives found its facilities "less than adequate."⁶⁵ Federal Title 1 funding subsequently helped but represented only about 10 percent of the budget, partly due to rising educational costs. A citywide sales tax increase of a half cent provided additional funds for a few years in the mid-1970s, but hardly enough to offset mounting losses from other sources.[66] Following a successful tax levy vote in 1969, nearly two decades passed before another such increase in taxing authority succeeded in an election, largely owing to opposition among older whites in the district.[67] The result was significant budget cuts, beginning as early as 1969, featuring the elimination of hundreds of staff positions, including teachers, and reductions to physical education, music instruction, libraries, and counseling offices.[68] In the wake of these developments, the state downgraded the district's financial rating in 1971 from AAA, the highest possible, to AA, the second highest. For the once-proud public schools of Kansas City, this was a considerable loss in standing, as it became the only district on the Missouri side of the metropolitan area with such a low assessment. As these issues played out in the press, public confidence in the system was shaken further.[69]

Altogether, it was a time of considerable uncertainty and turmoil for many students in Kansas City, black and white alike, as they negotiated a swiftly changing social and educational landscape. Some fared quite well, such as Marvin Daniels's brothers who attended Westport High to the west of Troost Avenue, or Manny Stevens's siblings at East. Others found a congenial environment at Central, Lincoln, or other schools near the city's center. But there also was a great deal of movement.

As indicated earlier, KCMPS maintained a rather liberal school transfer policy during these years, a holdover from the overcrowded 1950s. The results are evident in table 3.2; students could request transfers to attend a different institution, and these were sought by growing numbers of whites as the population shifted. In 1971 a local task force concluded that "transfer policies have regularly permitted white parents to remove their children from schools in racially changing neighborhoods and place them in predominantly white schools."[70] Although district officials stipulated that such transfers were not to be utilized for "discriminatory" purposes, such requests were rarely questioned. A temporary ban on transfers at Paseo had little effect. KCMPS leaders feared that challenging them on a large scale could trigger a political backlash and the loss of even more whites to outlying districts, outcomes they clearly wanted to avoid.[71] The result was sustained racial segregation and a continuing decline in the student population.

A District Divided

In August 1967 KCMPS superintendent James Hazlett greeted 377 new teachers to the district. This time he did not complain about comparisons with suburban schools, but rather suggested that working in city schools represented a special challenge. These teachers would be "on the frontline," he declared, "in implementing the nation's commitment to elevate disadvantaged and deprived persons." Things had certainly changed in the five years since he had tried to persuade real estate agents of the district's many assets. Now he was seeking foot soldiers ready to figuratively go into battle.[72]

In many respect, KCMPS had turned into something of a battlefield in the intervening years, with lines drawn largely in racial terms. A limited degree of integration had occurred under Hazlett's leadership during the 1960s, but it proved difficult to sustain. He had succeeded in persuading board members to approve busing to relieve overcrowding in primarily black schools, at least temporarily, but their opposition to the idea of integration remained steadfast. In the meantime, elementary schools more proximate to black areas gained greater numbers, making overcrowding a perennial concern for black families.[73] As the African American population grew, the institutions feeding Paseo and Southeast transitioned from white to black, presaging change in the high schools.[74] In this fashion overall levels of segregation across the system remained relatively high.

Not all the district's schools were affected by such challenges, however. Outside of KCMPS's central sector, many were largely untouched by desegregation. Seemingly a world removed from Troost, Southwest High remained the city's most prominent public secondary institution and among the last to be integrated. It continued to be among the nation's top schools in National Merit finalists.[75] A few African American students enrolled there through much of the 1960s, but there was little recognition of the broader issue of racial integration. For schools in this part of the city, along with those clustered with Van Horn and Northeast on the East Side, racial integration scarcely seemed a compelling question, and district leaders did little to change this. Yet just a few miles away, the city's expanding African American neighborhoods were witnessing a steady exodus of whites from other institutions. Prior to the early 1970s just the central part of the district experienced these dramatic changes.

Despite accelerating out-migration, whites still remained the district's largest group of voters, and many proved reluctant to support the schools financially as the African American population increased. Tellingly, in levy and bond elections, the strongest opposition often came from the predominantly white and working-class East Side of the city, while affluent whites in the southwest appeared more supportive.[76] This was a pattern of resistance to school finance measures evident in cities elsewhere too. Kansas City's experience demonstrated how racial integration in larger cities, particularly in the North, quickly encountered residential segregation, escalating numbers of poor students, white flight, and declining school revenues.[77] It became a school system badly divided.

In 1965 the district enrolled more than eighteen thousand high school students, but African Americans were about 20 percent more likely to drop out than whites. As demonstrated in chapter 2, this was largely due to the extreme poverty in segregated black neighborhoods.[78] Responding to low test scores and graduation rates in predominantly black institutions, two years earlier KCMPS announced a "compensatory education" program focused on Lincoln High and its feeder elementary schools.[79] This marked the start of a series of efforts to address educational problems of black students, each well intentioned but also contributing to the stigma attached to predominantly African American institutions. With the arrival of federal Title 1 funds after 1965, compensatory programs expanded to virtually all the district's predominantly black schools. From the standpoint of students who benefited from these funds, these were important programs, and there was evidence that they helped. But test scores remained below national norms, and few middle-class families wanted their own children to attend schools with large numbers of students who were labeled culturally deprived or disadvantaged.[80]

There were other sources of concern that influenced white attitudes. Among the most significant was fear of violence and disorder. This came to the fore after a series of events in April 1968 following the assassination of Martin Luther King Jr. Kansas City did not experience civil unrest immediately following King's death on April 4, as many other cities did, but five days later there was an outburst of violence that lasted for two days. It began with a student walkout and march from Central and Paseo High Schools to City Hall downtown, to protest the district's decision not to cancel classes on the day of King's funeral. When the more-or-less orderly procession arrived to meet with Mayor Ilus Davis, however, police fired tear gas at the crowd to disperse it. This attack angered members of the community, resulting in two nights of civil unrest that left several blocks of Prospect Avenue in ruins. Hundreds of fires were set, more than two thousand National Guardsmen and police were mobilized, many protesters were arrested, and seven were killed. It was the first incident of this type in the city's history.[81]

The "Holy Week Riots" proved shocking to many area residents who believed that racial discord was not a major problem facing Kansas City. The level of violence on display, however, suggested otherwise and raised apprehensions about the possibility of further conflict. The city council passed an ordinance to desegregate housing sales and rentals, addressing a long-standing complaint of local civil rights groups. But other measures to resolve black concerns about public institutions were slow to materialize. At the same time, whites gained a new mindfulness of growing black militancy, especially among youth. For some this made the prospects of school integration even more difficult to abide.[82]

The school board was reorganized in 1970, with nine members elected from separate districts. This permitted greater diversity, including several black representatives, but it also contributed to greater turnover and factionalism. At the same time it made consensus on racial integration less likely. The new board avoided making system-wide desegregation plans until compelled to, under pressure from federal authorities.[83] As noted in a 1971 report, "Plans that may have given encouragement to integration efforts have been consistently rejected."[84] This was frustrating to civil rights groups eager to see improvement in the schools, but it was hardly unusual for large urban school districts of the time. An influential US Civil Rights Commission report, *Racial Isolation in the Schools*, characterized this sort of response as typical. More often than not, the authors noted, school districts tended "to perpetuate, rather than reduce, separation in the schools."[85] Until the US Supreme Court decision in the *Keyes* case involving the Denver Public Schools in 1973, which held the district culpable for long-standing patterns of racial segregation, there was little guidance on the question from federal or state authorities. But even after *Keyes*, the KCMPS board continued to resist efforts to develop a comprehensive plan to integrate schools across the system.[86]

There were other issues regarding the schools, of course. Community groups also protested inadequate funding, demanded curricular changes, and deplored the loss of black educators' jobs with layoffs. Segregation and overcrowding fueled perceptions that the quality of education offered in KCMPS's white schools was better, especially in more affluent parts of the city.[87] Overcrowding was an especially sensitive and long-standing issue for African Americans, and the district's temporary classroom buildings were derisively labeled "Hazlett huts." When complaints led to a 1967 investigation by the federal Department of Health, Education, and Welfare (HEW), however, it did not result in cited violations of the Civil Rights Act, and an investigation by the US Department of Justice a year later also ended inconclusively.[88] The limited busing intended to relieve overcrowding often was uncoordinated and occasionally led to localized conflicts.[89] In 1970, black students being bused to predominantly white Northeast High marched to the district office to protest violence from whites and lack of police protection.[90] School leaders eventually resolved the grievances, but the incident was symptomatic of the district's ungainly and piecemeal approach to problems associated with racial segregation.

Frustrated by lack of progress, the Southern Christian Leadership Conference (SCLC) launched a lawsuit in 1973 against KCMPS for maintaining an illegally segregated school system. The suit was eventually dropped because the local SCLC chapter lacked resources to sustain it, but it signaled the frustration felt by the city's black community with lack of progress on the schools.[91] About six months later, the district received notice from HEW that it was out of compliance with revised desegregation guidelines.[92] As the *Call* noted that year, it was "not too late to build an integrated system," while the district still had large numbers of white students. Describing the failure to adopt Hazlett's plan five years earlier as "a major fumble," the *Call*'s editors worried that KCMPS was "growing more and more segregated."[93] As in other big cities, federal authorities eventually forced the board's hand, mandating a systemic desegregation plan four years later.[94] In the meantime, the racial profile of the district's schools had changed only incrementally.

Too Little, Too Late: Failed Desegregation

In 1970 the numbers of Kansas City white and black high school students were nearly even, but 85 percent of African Americans attended institutions that were 80 percent or more black. Only two of the city's ten large senior high schools, East and Westport, had majority white student bodies and more than forty African Americans enrolled. Just eight elementary and junior high schools had greater than a 10 percent black population in a predominantly white building.[95] Predominantly black schools enrolled large numbers of students from impoverished families, reflecting local conditions of concentrated disadvantage. This high degree of institutional segregation spurred growing complaints from the black community and federal investigations. Paralyzed by worries about angering whites, however, school board members and district administrators deflected or ignored demands for greater integration as a remedy to the educational problems faced by many African American youth. In particular, the board rejected a number of desegregation proposals following the 1973 HEW inquiry.[96]

Fear of antagonizing whites clearly was a major factor in the board's stance, no doubt reflecting pressures that particular members felt from their constituencies. A 1974 report by the Midwest Research Institute found that "a state of caution that bordered on catatonic" existed among educators in the city because of conflict over school integration.[97] A year later, HEW charged the district with maintaining an illegally segregated school system and ordered a cut to federal funds for its schools, demanding a desegregation plan for approval. After fighting the order in court, a decision the *Call* declared "a waste of taxpayers' money," KCMPS eventually launched a desegregation plan that called for every school in the system to enroll at least 30 percent minority students.[98] Starting in 1977, the plan entailed busing nearly twenty thousand students, an expensive proposition for a district already under severe budgetary constraints.[99] After years of resistance, this finally ushered desegregation to outlying schools that had long been sheltered from the very suggestion of racial integration. Unlike previous busing efforts to relieve overcrowding, it also called for white students to be sent to some of the district's predominantly black institutions. This, of course, made it doubly controversial.

Many white patrons of the district were quick to protest, especially on the city's East Side, which had seen relatively few black students in the past. In the Sugar Creek area, which had voted so enthusiastically to join KCMPS in 1955, anger was expressed "with shouts and the jabbing of fingers" as some two hundred parents met to condemn the plan.[100] The Northeast Area Community Council, a major neighborhood organization, also voiced opposition to desegregation, and a new group called Concerned Citizens for Community Schools represented Van Horn High parents "who oppose any bussing of school children for desegregation." Some leaders, such as local priest Richard Saale, urged openness to change, but failed to calm the animosity.[101] At Thatcher Elementary School, the PTA president declared that "I'm not willing to make my children guinea pigs," and other parents agreed, declaring a resolve to leave the district if necessary. Many other residents of the city's East Side doubtless agreed.[102]

Other people felt angry but were resigned to following dictates of board policy while planning to move. The mayor of neighboring Independence appointed a task force to deal with "community tensions" due to desegregation in those parts of his city within KCMPS boundaries, which included Van Horn and its feeder schools.[103] There seemed to be more support for the plan on the city's southwest side, where parents discussed ways to ease the transition to new schools for their children. But some did note that, as one stated, "many of my children's playmates have been put in private schools."[104] In the wake of growing unhappiness about required desegregation, families in areas previously unaffected by it were starting to leave the district in greater numbers.

KCMPS's enrollment figures dropped steadily in the 1970s, as did the population of most school districts, largely owing to the end of the postwar baby boom. But the district was also losing students to other school systems, mostly in Missouri, especially those within the city's municipal borders. Between 1970 and 1980 white students in the system declined by more than two-thirds, to about eleven thousand. African American students decreased as well, but only by about 20 percent, to nearly twenty-five thousand, mostly because of lower post-baby-boom fertility rates. Whites constituted only slightly more than a quarter of the district's population at the end of the decade, making it difficult to achieve a meaningful level of integration in most schools. And their numbers continued to drop thereafter, much faster than declining birthrates.[105]

There can be little doubt that much of this was due to desegregation. A 1975 survey conducted by the *Star* found that the principal reason that families decided to leave the district was to experience "less racial integration," followed by fewer discipline problems and "better instruction."[106] In the two years after the district's desegregation plan was announced, nearly five thousand white students left the system, more than a quarter of their total enrollment. At the same time black enrollments declined by about fifteen hundred, or roughly 5 percent. By 1980 the district was fully two-thirds African American. Whites composed the remainder, along with other minority groups, principally Hispanics who had recently started arriving in greater numbers. Whether because of concerns about the quality of the schools or prejudicial responses to desegregation, in the eyes of many observers, KCMPS had ceased to offer an acceptable educational experience.[107] Budget cuts left buildings in poor repair, and sometimes lawns went unmowed in summer. Given this situation, with whites fleeing and black community leaders complaining about declining standards, it was difficult to avoid the conclusion that most city schools were institutions of last resort, choices that families interested in superior public education would avoid if possible.[108] Such was the stigma attached to public schools in many of the nation's largest cities, and Kansas City was certainly not an exception.

There were yet other factors that contributed to declining enrollments during these years. A lengthy and bitter teacher strike occurred in 1974, and another three years later. Because of the district's severe financial straits, most employees had worked without meaningful increases in pay for years, and KCMPS salaries lagged behind almost all local suburban districts.[109] The schools were closed for six weeks in the first of these disruptive events, and seven in the second. Settlements were eventually reached in both instances, even though KCMPS could ill afford them, but when teachers returned, hundreds of students had left the district each time. The *Star* described parents looking into "district hopping" to find more stable school settings for their children, with Shawnee Mission reporting more than a thousand inquiries.[110] More student departures followed, although it was not altogether clear whether it was the acrimony and disruption of labor conflict or the 1977 desegregation plan that led to the second exodus. Both probably were factors, but given the history of school integration prompting white flight in KCMPS, the threat of comprehensive desegregation unquestionably motivated this wave of departures as well.[111] When the smoke metaphorically cleared in 1980, the district had been reduced to a shadow of its former identity. In less than twenty-five years it had gone from being the strongest public educational agency in the metropolitan region to arguably the weakest.

What did all this mean for Southwest High, the district's best-known school and most academically distinguished? The number of African American students there began to climb after 1970, both as a result of transfers and limited busing, reaching more than a quarter by 1972. Students attempted to make the most of this, although a number of whites left for private schools or adjacent suburbs.[112] In the next two years the proportion of African American students climbed to more than a third, and in the fall of 1977, under the district's new desegregation plan, it jumped to nearly half. Three years later the number of black students had declined a bit (8 percent) but the white student population had fallen by more than half. In relatively short order, Southwest had become a predominantly black institution, although one with a sizable white minority. It also was considerably smaller than it had been during the heydays of the 1950s and '60s, and no longer posted impressive numbers of National Merit finalists.[113] Most of the highly proficient, affluent students who had registered such accomplishments had left. The only senior high schools with majority white student bodies were East and Van Horn, and both were almost half black.[114] Desegregation had finally come to all parts of the district, but it arrived too late to represent a much improved educational experience for most KCMPS students.

Ultimately the district's board tried to enjoin neighboring suburban school systems in a solution to long-standing problems of segregation, finding expression in the federal case *Missouri v. Jenkins*, one of the most ambitious, expensive, and contentious desegregation plans of the era.[115] Metropolitan desegregation plans were widely discussed in the latter 1970s, and a bi-state committee on education, formed by members of the Kansas and Missouri advisory committees of the US Commission on Civil Rights, issued a proposal for combining some nineteen school districts in and around Kansas City. But few suburbanites were interested in such ideas.[116] *Jenkins* ultimately would result in a massive effort to make KCMPS institutions more attractive to suburban district residents. But it did not reverse the fortunes of KCMPS, as affluent, more highly educated adults and their children generally chose to remain in suburban schools. That segment of the region's population was one of the most vital resources that the district had lost in the years following 1950, and three decades later it was far too late to regain its former glory.[117]

A New Metropolitan Educational Order

If anyone had illusions about the relative standing of metro Kansas City school districts by the later 1970s, they were likely dispelled by the results of standardized tests that were then beginning to appear in the news. A budding accountability movement in education at the time placed greater emphasis on quantitatively comparable measures of student learning, seemingly objective portraits of school achievement.[118] In 1978, the *Star* published the results of eighth-grade performance on a state-mandated test of basic academic skills. Even though it did not measure high levels of achievement, just comparing the percentages of students passing the test in each district revealed telling differences. As indicated in table 3.3, about a third of the eighth graders in Kansas City scored high enough to pass, but it was the only district to register less than a 50 percent success rate. Neighboring suburbs such as Raytown, Hickman Mills, and Center to the south, and North Kansas City, Liberty, and Independence to the north and east did considerably better, with nearly two-thirds or better passing.[119] Kansas City high schools did a bit better on a statewide assessment also administered in 1978 but still scored well below suburban institutions.[120] While tests such as these typically underestimated the academic skills of African American students, the district discrepancy in scores clearly reflected the large number of impoverished children served by KCMPS. Given these results, it was no longer possible to suggest that the city's public school system was academically competitive with its suburban counterparts.

Test results such as these helped persuade many white families to leave the district, of course, but some black families as well. Stanley West left Kansas City for a home in Grandview in the early 1970s. His was not the first black family in their new community, but there were not many others at the time. The principal motivation was better schools, and his children eventually graduated from Grandview High. They lived there for more than two decades, with "really good neighbors." West credited his experiences in an integrated high school, in college, and in the military with making the move to a "blue collar" suburb a comfortable experience. He recalled that friends in Kansas City told him "to stay here in the city," but he felt angry about having "been denied access to these areas all my life, and I wanted to be there." If the suburbs did indeed offer a better life, Stanley West did not want his family to be denied it.[121]

Not everyone could leave the area served by KCMPS, of course. For most families that remained, finding an appropriate school for their children became a

TABLE 3.3 Results of Missouri Basic Skills testing, 1978, in KCMPS and neighboring districts

DISTRICT	BASIC SKILLS PASSING RATE (PERCENT)
Kansas City	34.2
Center	71.9
Hickman Mills	65.7
Raytown	71.5
Independence	64.1
Liberty	67.2
North Kansas City	67.3

Source: "Tests of Eighth Graders Shows Few Prepared," *Kansas City Star*, September 15, 1978.

more challenging task. A majority were African American, although significant numbers of whites continued to live in the district and sent their children to private schools. But growing numbers of blacks searched for alternatives to KCMPS as well. The result was a changing educational scene in Kansas City, one that evolved quickly in the face of shifting economic and demographic circumstances.

In the fall of 1982 Susan Hilliard's daughter Maxine became a freshman at Southwest, as the family had moved into an "integrated" neighborhood near the district's southern border. Susan recalled the school acquiring a reputation as a problem institution, but her daughter finished without difficulty in three and a half years. Maxine reportedly was a somewhat indifferent student and did not take the most demanding courses. Although she gave it little thought at the time, Susan believed that the curriculum was divided into tracks that ran largely along racial lines. On parents' night, she remembered, "in some rooms there would be all black parents and other rooms there would be all white parents." She also recalled that Maxine was in ROTC, which also was largely African American.[122] Although schools such as Southwest were integrated for a spell, at least with respect to overall enrollment numbers, classrooms and hallways were often segregated. Integration at the building level in Kansas City public schools was rarely sustained long enough to address the difficult questions of tracking and curricular inequity along racial lines, which eventually became major issues in American education.[123] Maxine Hilliard may have attended a desegregated school, but she did not necessarily have a racially integrated educational experience.

Marvin Daniels's sons attended Central and Southeast in the 1980s, and he recalled that both enjoyed their high school experiences. Like their dad, they reportedly found success in predominantly African American institutions. Patrick Elard, on the other hand, was disappointed with the education his son had received at Central.[124] Manny Stevens, also concerned about the quality of public schools, sent his daughter to school at nearby Catholic institutions. Although he did not state it explicitly, it is possible that his bitter memories of Central disposed him to favor alternatives to KCMPS.[125] Even if the system served a largely poor African American population by the 1980s, Kansas City still offered its residents a variety of educational options. The general public perception of the district may have changed for the worse, but parents in search of viable school experiences for their children often could find workable solutions.

Patterns of Exit

Between the latter 1950s and 1980, KCMPS experienced a net loss of more than forty thousand white students. Despite James Hazlett's worry about the schools of Johnson County, however, it appears that a small minority of those fleeing KCMPS were headed to Kansas. Attorneys in the *Jenkins* case collected data on student transfers from several KCMPS schools and where they were going, each year between 1958 and 1973. These institutions were Paseo and Southeast High, and Southeast Junior High, each of which transitioned from predominantly white to almost all African American during this time.[126] As such, transfer patterns evident at these schools were revealing of just how white flight unfolded in Kansas City, at least prior to the mid-1970s.

Altogether, more than four thousand students transferred from these schools in this fifteen-year period. The largest numbers occurred during the years when each institution's student body shifted from white to black, as district-level data suggested. Many transfers stayed within the KCMPS system, moving to another secondary school, or left the metropolitan area altogether, and little is known about where they went. About 32 percent transferred to suburban districts adjacent to KCMPS within Missouri, and only about 8 percent switched to schools in Kansas. Even if districts in Johnson County received most of these, it was a rather small share of the students leaving KCMPS. Of those staying on the Missouri side of the metro area, about three-quarters went to districts to the south of KCMPS, most within the municipal boundaries of Kansas City.

The districts that received the majority of such students were Hickman Mills, Raytown, Center, and Grandview. Each encompassed at least a part of municipal Kansas City, and all four were growing throughout most of the period in question. Like the neighborhoods that experienced white flight, these were largely blue-collar communities. They were still within easy driving distance of the city's southeast side, where many of the parents likely worked, shopped, attended church, and maintained friendships. In short, propinquity and familiarity appear to have been important factors in deciding where to move, along with the good reputation of local schools.[127] The fact that many could remain residents of Kansas City, with its lower municipal taxes and reliable services, may have been a factor as well. Altogether, for these families the districts just to the south of KCMPS appear to have been a very attractive option.

Of course, the data in table 3.2 end in 1973, before the most disruptive events of the decade. As many as eighteen thousand students left the district in subsequent years, and most were not from the neighborhoods proximate to Paseo or Southeast High Schools. Given the losses evident at Southwest, along with similar declines in white students at Westport in the same period, it is likely that propinquity and familiarity operated in these instances as well. Not surprisingly, significant numbers of Southwest students reportedly transferred to private schools in the area, particularly elite institutions such as Pembroke Academy, the Barstow School, or Rockhurst High, among others. The *Star* conducted a survey of more than two hundred families who left KCMPS schools in 1977, however, and found that most sent their children to suburban institutions on the Missouri side of the border. Once again, Raytown and Hickman Mills were among the leaders, along with Independence and North Kansas City. With desegregation slated to begin on the city's East Side, it appears that families there had started to move as well. White flight, it turns out, was not limited to the city's southernmost reaches by 1977.

The *Star* also found that nearly a third of its survey respondents sent their children to private schools, mainly Catholic institutions within the city. Many of these were African Americans in search of alternatives to KCMPS, and they helped keep local parish schools afloat. While metro-wide diocesan school enrollments declined after 1970, owing to out-migration and declining birthrates, within the city they remained generally stable. Many of the urban parish schools turned from all white to black, serving more children who were non-Catholics. This was a pattern seen in other cities as well, as the African American middle class actively sought better schools. Nearly half the transfers from KCMPS to suburban Hickman Mills were African American as well, as black families started to consider moving to the suburbs.[128] Like Susan Hilliard and Manny Stevens, they too wanted to find the best schools available for their children. It would be a while, however, before their numbers would reach appreciable levels, which eventually would bring important change to these institutions too.

A Tale of Decline and Missed Opportunities

For students of American educational history, particularly postwar urban education and school desegregation, the story of KCMPS in this period is surely familiar. As suggested at the outset, it is strikingly similar to what happened in Detroit, Chicago, Milwaukee, St. Louis, and other districts in the Midwest that were confronted with questions of race and inequality, white flight, and the loss of perceived educational excellence.[129] The arrival of impoverished African Americans in the 1950s and '60s contributed to an exodus from the city's public schools, mostly to suburban districts that enrolled very few black students. Other factors played major roles, especially new residential development, but bigoted responses to integrated schooling also were clearly important. This was evident in the transfer data reported in Table 3.2. As indicated in the subscript, very few—about one per year—of the five hundred students who left Central High after it became predominantly African American went to suburban districts in Missouri.[130] This is an indication of the exclusion that such students faced in choosing where to attend schools. Given this, it is probably safe to say that one of the biggest attractions of suburban schools for many white families leaving KCMPS was the absence of African Americans.

Was KCMPS doomed to enrollment decline and the loss of resources with the arrival of poor African Americans in large numbers? Would white movement to the suburbs have occurred regardless of what district leaders did? The answer to both these questions may well be yes, but is also possible that the course of history might have been different. As Jennifer Hochschild noted during the 1980s, desegregation seemed to work best in school systems that embraced it positively, with leaders who tackled its problems directly and energetically, and more recent studies have suggested this as well.[131] Had the KCMPS board followed James Hazlett's lead in instituting a desegregation plan as early as 1968, while there was still a majority white student population in the schools, it might have been possible to achieve a more sustainable approach to school desegregation. The district may also have been able to better serve the growing numbers of poor students in its schools. This might have followed the model offered by Westport or West High Schools, where blacks represented less than a third of the student body for a number of years.

Of course, as more impoverished African American families arrived in the district, maintaining such a balance likely would have become difficult. But such a plan, in retrospect, would appear to have had much better chances of success than the course taken by the board, which was to resist all systematic attempts at desegregation until it was too late. As the *Call* observed in 1977, "The only thing the Kansas City district can say it has done over these 20 years since 1954 is to delay, delay and to do just enough—and no more—to keep federal funds flowing."[132] It was a pattern of behavior that signaled to whites that their preferences would be valued more than those of black families. Indeed, the very fact that the board unsuccessfully fought HEW orders in court likely suggested to many that desegregation was fundamentally a bad idea, and abetted the racist sentiments of its most diehard opponents. That proved to be leadership of the wrong kind.

James Hazlett's decision to retire from his post as superintendent in 1969 was certainly a loss to the district and may have been influenced by the board's refusal to follow his desegregation plan. His successors in the following decade, Andrew Adams, Robert Medcalf, and Robert Wheeler, lacked his depth of experience and inherited a very difficult situation, although Wheeler did manage to implement the 1977 desegregation plan. Few KCMPS superintendents since that time have remained in office more than a few years.[133] This instability also contributed to the sharp decline in reputation that the district experienced.

For his part, Hazlett later expressed surprise at the course of events following his departure. In a deposition taken in the early 1980s for the *Jenkins* case, he testified that he fully expected enrollments to stabilize during the 1970s and that a successful desegregation plan would eventually materialize. He never expected KCMPS to be negatively compared to suburban districts, or to see outlying districts as competitors or adversaries.[134] Despite his experience and knowledge, Hazlett clearly did not fully appreciate the magnitude of problems the district faced when he left office.

The last major actors in this drama operated largely offstage, hidden from view but exerting a powerful influence. They were the suburban districts, many of which were in fact located within the city limits. As Daniel Levine and Jeanie Keeny Meyer observed in 1977, "white flight" was "most likely to occur in city districts surrounded by largely white suburbs."[135] Kansas City certainly fit this description, and there can be little doubt about the role that many suburban districts played in this period. They were the chief beneficiaries of the crisis experienced by the KCMPS, which sent them thousands of students. It also reduced their chief historical competitor, the once mighty KCMPS, to the status of an educational pariah for much of the public, especially middle-class whites. For some of these districts, their response to this predicament was to erect walls to keep certain types of students out, while encouraging others to enter. In other words, they engaged in a particular form of opportunity hoarding, building their assets while minimizing the risk from dangers that KCMPS had come to represent. The next chapter explores these and other questions on the Missouri side of the metropolitan region.

4

RACIALIZED ADVANTAGE
The Missouri Suburban School Districts

On January 7, 1969, more than fifteen hundred people crowded into the auditorium of Raytown High School to hear officials from several area districts and local politicians denounce a proposal to reorganize school systems throughout the state. "It was obvious," reported the *Kansas City Star*, "that the crowd was violently opposed to the plan." Among their complaints were the insensitivity and unresponsiveness of big-city bureaucrats and a fear of losing local control of their institutions. But race also loomed large as an issue, especially the prospect of school desegregation. "By and large," a local banker stated, "the people who have moved here have moved away from an integrated neighborhood. They moved here for good schools and a segregated society." The city's mayor concurred, declaring that "there are people in Raytown who have moved here to keep their children from going to Central or Paseo." To these men and others, the exclusion of black students from public schools in Raytown and adjacent districts was a critical feature of their community's identity. They also saw it as key to the success of local institutions and crucial to preserving their status. In the wake of desegregation controversies and white flight, many believed these questions to be paramount, especially since their district bordered the Kansas City, Missouri, School District. The very suggestion of changing the local configuration of school systems made many of them hopping mad, and they were determined to oppose it vehemently.[1]

As noted in the previous chapter, many of the families "fleeing" the Kansas City public schools during the 1960s and '70s made their way to suburban school districts, usually wholly or partly located within the municipal boundaries of Kansas City. Although most such districts began modestly, by the end of the 1960s they exhibited clear advantages over their larger urban neighbor. They were also predominantly white and middle class in composition, and as they expanded during the long postwar era, KCMPS mainly served less affluent racial and ethnic minority families. This, of course, was a familiar pattern of development in metropolitan America, but in Kansas City it was school districts rather than separately incorporated suburban communities that often shaped the course of events.[2]

What accounted for this sequence of changes? As elsewhere, the availability of new and better housing spurred the move to outlying areas, well removed from the urban core. Easy mortgage terms for whites, and extensive local highway construction—subsidized by the federal government—clearly helped as well. These developments meant that families with sufficient resources could enjoy an improved standard of living, especially for their children, within commuting distance to employment, shopping, recreation, and other activities. In this respect Kansas City also conformed to the national norm.[3] Schools, of course, were a part of that, but so were race and social status. As suggested in the comments at the Raytown meeting, white families, many clearly motivated by bigotry, left the Kansas City, Missouri, Public Schools when African Americans started attending the institutions their children attended. Eventually thousands of white students departed, and some blacks as well.[4] Suburban districts, consequently, grew significantly, while remaining overwhelmingly white.

The role of race in this process became clear in 1968, when a special commission created by the Missouri legislature investigated the possibility of redrawing district boundaries for greater efficiency and equity in public education. The resulting uproar highlighted many issues that local school leaders held dear, but race was unquestionably paramount in the minds of many suburban district residents. It was this development that prompted the meeting in Raytown, along with many others. Suburbanites made their dissatisfaction quite clear in letters to commissioners and in protests held in Jefferson City, the state capital. Similar reactions were evident during the 1970s and '80s when comparable proposals appeared, calling for school district consolidation across the metro area. Residents of these areas viewed their district boundaries as a bulwark against the threat of incursion by residents of KCMPS, and African Americans in particular. For many the possibility of racial integration in their schools became a highly emotional issue.[5]

This chapter considers suburban school system development on the Missouri side of greater Kansas City. Focusing on the districts of Raytown, Hickman Mills, and North Kansas City, it seeks to illuminate some of the dynamics of their growth. In particular, it highlights mechanisms of exclusion that helped to keep the schools in these areas largely white and middle class in orientation. There is scant evidence of overt discrimination within the schools or by suburban educators, but there can be little doubt that African Americans felt unwelcome in these communities. While reform proposals at the state level stirred racial tensions in suburban districts, local recommendations for metro-wide integration produced similar responses. Localism and opportunity hoarding, it appears, took a particular form on the Missouri side of the state line, and the biggest controversies revolved largely around race.

Kansas City Suburban School Development: North, South, and East

As described in chapter 2, Kansas City grew by annexation during the 1950s, more than quadrupling its geographic footprint and adding substantially to its population base. This was a savvy move by forward-thinking civic leaders, but existing school district boundaries stayed in place. The result was a patchwork of self-described "suburban" education systems within the municipal boundaries of Kansas City, arrayed around KCMPS. This was not considered a big problem initially, but eventually the lines defining the city's various school systems became critically important. During the 1960s and '70s they operated as barriers that permitted—or even encouraged—certain people to enter these spaces, while signaling to others that they were not welcome.[6]

The districts surrounding KCMPS grew rapidly during this period. Table 4.1 provides enrollment numbers for the two decades following the *Brown* decision for the region's Missouri school systems. These are district (not town or city) figures, reflecting changes in the number of households and the size of families, both of which expanded at the time. The table compares enrollment numbers reported a few years after the height of the baby boom, and thus past their peak levels. Even so, suburban district growth outpaced the entire metropolitan area, which expanded by nearly 40 percent.[7] As these figures suggest, almost all this development occurred outside the urban core represented by KCMPS.

A variety of factors contributed to the rapid expansion of these districts. On the leading edge of the baby boom, a wave of new parents moved to suburbs nationally, and there is evidence that Kansas City's outlying districts attracted them too. Most newcomers to the region apparently chose to live in these areas rather than the urban core, unless they were African American. When combined with white out-migration from the city center, the result was rapid growth at the periphery represented by suburban school districts. In this respect Kansas City

TABLE 4.1 KC metropolitan Missouri districts: growth and resources, 1954–55 to 1974–75

DISTRICT	1954–55 ENROLLMENT	1974–75 ENROLLMENT (AND GROWTH RATE)	1974–75 PER PUPIL REVENUE (DOLLARS)	FRL ELIGIBLE 1974–75
Center	1,467	5,220 (256%)	1,235.81	239 (2.6%)
Grandview	1,639	7,177 (338%)	1,201.53	521 (9.4%)
Hickman Mills	1,814	14,657 (708%)	968.39	1,443 (10.5%)
Independence	7,234	16,170 (124%)	899.67	1,344 (8.8%)
Kansas City	67,227	60,147 (−11%)	1,189.15	32,446 (58%)
Lee's Summit	2,218	6,629 (200%)	1,022.86	824 (13.4%)
Liberty	1,450	4,249 (193%)	1,038.74	554 (13.8%)
North Kansas City	6,856	22,882 (234%)	982.06	1,406 (6.5%)
Raytown	5,384	14,380 (167%)	1,018.03	360 (2.6%)

Sources: *One Hundred and Sixth Report of the Public Schools of the State of Missouri, School Year Ending June 30, 1955*, pt. 2, section 4, table A: Enumeration and Enrollment, 1954–55; *One Hundred and Twenty Sixth Report of the Public Schools of the State of Missouri, School Year Ending June 30, 1975*, pt. 2, table A; and Kansas and Missouri Advisory Committees on Civil Rights, "Crisis and Opportunity: Education in Greater Kansas City," unpublished report, 1977, 56 and 57.

was quite similar to other large metropolitan areas, especially as changing technology, favorable government policies, and suburban conveniences made central city housing less attractive.[8]

Yet other factors influenced the development of particular communities. Expansion also reflected the maturity of local communities and their capacity for development. Slower-growing districts, such as Independence, Liberty, and Raytown, were located in areas that had long been settled. Independence tripled in population between 1950 and 1970, partly because of annexation, but about a quarter of the city was served by KCMPS. Many students leaving schools in Kansas City's center moved east to attend institutions in the Van Horn High cluster rather than Independence district schools.[9] The city of Raytown grew rapidly, too, but half its school district was located in bordering Kansas City neighborhoods that did not develop quite as quickly.[10] North Kansas City realized much of its population growth through annexation of neighboring districts. The most dramatic expansion, on the other hand, occurred in districts located in the city's southwest quadrant: Center and Hickman Mills, along with Grandview. This reflected the area's booming growth following the war, when it became a focal point for manufacturing, retail investment, and new military installations. This was especially true after a US Air Force base opened there in 1955. Some families moving to these communities may have been attracted by the schools, but most were interested in reasonably priced new homes and proximity to jobs, shopping, and the other amenities of recently annexed parts of the city.[11]

If suburban districts differed in growth, there also was a good deal of variation in their revenues and the families they served. Calculated on a per-pupil basis, residents of Center and Grandview were the most generous supporters of their schools, reflecting higher incomes and commercial development that helped boost the local tax base (Center's district revenues were nearly $6,000 per pupil in 2015 dollars). Table 4.2 provides statistics on median family income levels for each district in 1970, with the two largest Kansas systems included for comparison. While the students in wealthy Shawnee Mission clearly benefited from well-educated parents, other districts lacked its tax base or failed to reach consensus on school funding. Raytown did not have large-scale commercial or industrial development but enjoyed relatively high household income. Independence had limited assets on either count, as did Liberty, but residents of both worked in nearby plants. In Hickman Mills, a persistent opposition to school funding increases managed to defeat such proposals in levy elections, despite the district's relatively high level of household income.[12] Overall, the result was relatively modest financial support for the Missouri suburban schools, with only Center and Grandview spending more per capita than KCMPS.

Funding differences of this sort may not have mattered much, however, if the students in these districts were generally homogeneous with respect to wealth or income, parental education, and minority status, all potentially significant factors affecting school success. As indicated in table 4.2, only the two urban

TABLE 4.2 KC metropolitan school districts: economic, social, and demographic profiles, 1970

DISTRICT	POPULATION	MINORITY PERCENT*	MEDIAN INCOME (DOLLARS)	ADULT HS GRADS (PERCENT)
Center	33,581	2	12,630	71
Grandview	17,894	3	10,906	70
Hickman Mills	47,882	1	11,712	72
Independence	67,643	2	10,684	60
Kansas City, Kansas	155,923	40	9,024	47
Kansas City, Missouri	370,109	35	8,803	50
Lee's Summit	21,749	1	11,132	67
Liberty	16,014	3	10,498	64
North Kansas City	87,451	1	11,470	66
Raytown	59,586	1	12,120	67
Shawnee Mission	182,470	1	14,037	83

Source: "Crisis and Opportunity: Education in Greater Kansas City," 29 and B-3.

* 1972–73 estimates

core Kansas City districts served large numbers of minority families, most of them African American. KCMPS reported that a majority of its students were enrolled in the federally funded Free or Reduced Lunch Program (FRL), and similar numbers participated across the river in Kansas City, Kansas. This, of course, reflected levels of household income, which were 16 percent lower in KCMPS than in Liberty, the poorest of the suburban districts. Adult education levels, reflected here in the proportion of adults with high school diplomas, also were lowest in the urban core districts, with half or less attaining that level of education. The long history of discrimination that African Americans had faced in schools accounted for much of this difference. It was a combination of factors that did not bode well for the children in the city schools, whose needs for school resources were considerably higher than those of most of their suburban peers. Given these circumstances, it is little wonder that KCMPS students scored relatively low on standardized tests. Suburban students started each school year in a considerably stronger position to succeed.[13]

On the other hand, resources did seem to make a difference outside the urban core. Most suburban students may not have been poor, but their background characteristics and school funding did seem to have a bearing on learning outcomes, or at least those measured by standardized tests (reported in table 3.3). The Independence School District, for instance, registered relatively low adult education levels and modest median family income, likely reflecting the blue-collar industries where many of its residents worked.[14] It also generated the least revenue per student of any district in the area. The same was true of nearby Liberty, although its revenue level was somewhat higher. It is hardly a surprise, in that case, that in Independence proportionately fewer students passed the 1978 Missouri basic skills test (by a small margin) than in any of the other suburban districts. At the other end of the scale was Center, with the highest levels of income and revenues among the Missouri districts, and second in adult education. As indicated in the previous chapter, it also had the highest passing rate on the basic skills test. In this respect it was followed closely by Raytown, another relatively high-income district, although one with adult education and revenues closer to the suburban average. Penurious Hickman Mills possessed fairly high income and attainment levels but chose to spend comparatively little on its schools. Less than two-thirds of its students passed the basic skills test in 1978. North Kansas City passing rates were about average for the suburban districts, as were its other characteristics, aside from revenues.

While it is likely that a range of factors affected the performance of suburban students, the differences between them were relatively minor, especially in light of the test-score chasm that separated each of them from KCMPS. Compared to the many problems that beset the city schools, especially by the later 1970s, suburban institutions doubtless appeared to be islands of tranquility and proficiency. But the fact that performance on a basic standardized test would parallel student characteristics so closely, even at a high level of aggregation, suggests that there may not have been much variability in the performance of these institutions. They all appear to have contributed to student success in similar ways. The lack of substantial distinctions in this respect, of course, fits the observation of James Coleman in his famous report of 1966, and of many other researchers hence, that schools contributed relatively little to differences in student achievement.[15] If this was true in suburban Kansas City, it could be evidence that the chief resources these schools possessed were the students they served. School funding levels might have contributed as well, but may have reflected local attitudes and preparation for education as much as differences in institutional capacity.

As the foregoing suggests, the area's Missouri suburban districts were hardly the same with respect to a variety of social and economic characteristics. But if there was one feature that they shared, it was their racial profile, particularly its whiteness, which differed very little. In this regard they also stood in sharp contrast to KCMPS, which became increasingly African American.[16] The Missouri suburban districts also worked together, playing one another in sports leagues and sharing information through a local coordinating council that did not include KCMPS. Created in 1962 at a meeting held in Raytown High School, this organization was initially called the Greater Kansas City Suburban Association of Co-operative Schools, with representation from twelve districts.[17] Its leaders clearly did not believe that they faced the same issues as their colleagues in the city system and felt that their districts had more in common with one another despite their differences. It is also telling that they referred to themselves as suburban districts, when so many of them, to one degree or another, were located within the municipal boundaries of Kansas City. They clearly wanted to avoid any confusion with the institutions of KCMPS.

Much of this perception, of course, concerned questions of race and poverty. Given the rapid growth of Kansas City's black population, it is striking that so few African Americans found their way to these school systems. Some did, of course, as suggested in the previous chapter. But their numbers were small, at least until the 1980s.[18] These districts also served a relatively modest population of poor students, as indicated by their FRL numbers, although there was more variability on that count than race. Still, the pattern suggests that the distribution of African American and poor children was hardly indiscriminate. Poverty and minority status, like wealth and adult education levels, clustered unevenly across the metropolitan landscape. This suggests a purposeful pattern of policy decisions and active exclusion rather than a natural or unintentional geo-spatial arrangement of status and individual choice. Local manifestations of this, of course, also differed from one setting to the next.

Raytown and South Kansas City: Contrasting Patterns of Racial Exclusion

The southern reaches of metropolitan Kansas City were relatively slow to develop in the early twentieth century. Mainly composed of farmland, the area lacked the industry, commercial development, and access to transportation that settlements closer to the region's major rivers enjoyed. When annexation talk began to stir in the postwar years, consequently, communities immediately south of Kansas City and Independence were still unincorporated and thus vulnerable to appropriation. It was in response to this situation that local leaders established the tiny municipality of Raytown in 1950, counting little more than five hundred residents in three square miles.[19] In the following decade Raytown expanded through a series of its own annexations, soon more than tripling in size and adding some fifteen thousand residents.[20] Access to nearby freeways made commuting relatively easy. Ten years later its population had doubled, peaking at more than thirty-three thousand.[21] Map 4.1 depicts the district's boundaries and secondary schools, along with the neighboring Hickman Mills district and the rest of South Kansas City.

As was often the case in rural areas, the local school district pre-dated incorporation of the community, and in this instance it was among the first in the state to be consolidated. In 1903 seven rural districts joined together, becoming the second consolidated district in Missouri, following their neighbors immediately to the west by a year (later to become the Hickman Mills district).[22] An advantage to consolidation was the ability to pool the resources and students of constituent districts to establish a secondary school. The addition of yet more rural schools in subsequent years contributed to the district's growth and the size of its high school, which was accepting nonresident students from other rural schools by the start of the Second World War. It was shortly after the war's end that the district began offering transportation to its schools, soon amassing a fleet of nearly fifty new buses to serve its expanding clientele.[23]

Growth came quickly in the 1950s. As indicated on the map, the Raytown School District (RSD) became one of the most expansive geographically in the region, comprising twenty-seven square miles and about twice as large as Raytown itself at the end of the decade.[24] Enrollment records indicated that new students arrived from all parts of the country, and growth meant that classes sometimes had to be held in bus garages or even on buses while facilities were constructed.[25]

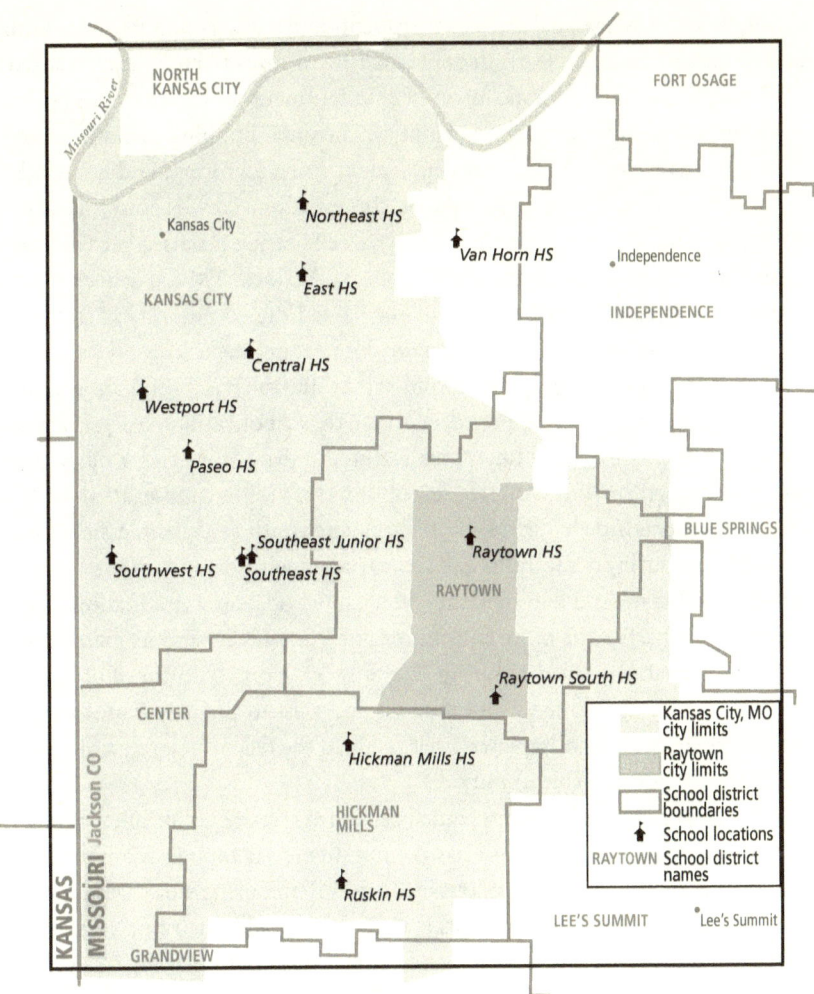

MAP 4.1 Districts and schools in Kansas City and South Kansas City, 1980

Public support for the schools was fervent, however, with seventeen bond issues approved by voters between 1946 and 1961. These funds helped to construct seven new schools, and a new wing added to Raytown High, permitting an enrollment of more than twelve hundred. Even so, overcrowding resulted in a second high school in 1961, Raytown South. Four years later the district enrolled more than fifteen thousand students, twelve times its 1945 number, and it added nearly two thousand more by the end of the decade. Falling birthrates eventually led to declines, as in other districts, but there could be little question that Raytown had become a significant component of the local educational scene.[26]

Despite its rapid expansion, former students and teachers in Raytown warmly recalled the intimacy and warmth of its small-town atmosphere. The city lacked a movie theater and other public forms of entertainment, so school events became important social outings for many families. The only shopping mall was a modest "thrift center" with a discount department store, a grocery, and a few other shops serving a local clientele.[27] Athletic contests drew crowds, and graduation ceremonies and school plays were popular as well. Jeanne Harrison recalled teens organizing dances in the high school gym or the local YMCA, where movies occasionally were projected on a wall. She valued the community's "closeness" and never recalled her parents locking the doors at night.

In 1962 the local newspaper proclaimed that "Raytown is a good place to live," reporting that the city was "proud of the AAA school rating," a sign of fiscal strength.[28] Its modest downtown area featured a drug store and a dairy stand that served ice cream, but it offered few options for kids to congregate outside of school. There was little trouble with misbehaving youth as a result. A small man-made lake, featuring a sandy "beach" constructed with help from the Raytown High football team and run by Coach Ted Chitwood, was a destination during summer months. For the more adventuresome, Kansas City and its many attractions was a relatively short drive up Highway 50, along with the Blue Springs Mall. Later it was possible to motor south and west to the new Bannister Mall near Hickman Mills. But Raytown itself retained the feel of a closely knit, lower-middle-class bedroom community.[29]

With respect to social status and local norms, residents recalled Raytown being a blue-collar or working-class community, even though many residents held managerial or professional jobs.[30] Most of the housing stock was relatively modest ranch homes or bungalows.[31] One former administrator recalled the town having a "redneck" reputation and being viewed as something of a cultural backwater.[32] Most adults were high schools graduates, but their numbers were proportionately lower than in districts to the west, including Shawnee Mission across the state line. Perhaps reflecting this, some thought the local high schools offered a "no frills" curriculum that favored the college bound but offered relatively few advanced courses. This apparently was fine with many parents, even as district expenditures on secondary education reportedly trailed national averages.[33]

The Raytown schools were probably better known for sports than academic excellence, in any case. Ted Chitwood at Raytown High and Bud Lathrop at Raytown South became legendary coaches in football and basketball respectively. It was the first district in the region to build a stadium that seated more than five thousand spectators.[34] Games with such traditional rivals as neighboring Blue Springs or Lee's Summit typically were highlights of the season. Competitive athletic teams also were maintained by elementary schools, feeding the high school programs. This added to the popularity of sporting events, helping to sustain support for the system as a whole.[35]

Given the high level of interest and involvement in the schools, the district became a vital source of local identity and a point of community pride. There was relatively little else, after all, for residents to share collectively. The reputation of the schools, moreover, was linked to local property values, which were rather high. But there was more to local support for the district than housing markets. Communal interest in schooling became a potent source of relationships and social bonding. Many adults, after all, came to know one another through children and youth and the institutions they attended. Involvement in school-related activities was a widespread norm, and public interest in the system remained robust throughout the period.[36] This became especially evident when residents felt the schools coming under attack, and their response could be forceful indeed.

Continuity in leadership also contributed to the district's success. The fact that it had one superintendent, Joe Herndon, ensured stability in the system for most of this period. Herndon provided a steady hand and inspired confidence in the schools.[37] When he retired in 1974 after nearly thirty years, the district launched a new vocational center named for him. His apparently easygoing and personal style of leadership was well suited to the community's intimate atmosphere.[38] Herndon's departure opened the door to new leaders to address the difficult process of downsizing during the 1970s, which did not entail the conflicts that it engendered elsewhere. It that respect, the trust and goodwill that Herndon had cultivated served the community well. Local support for the schools eventually wavered a bit, with failed bond and levy votes in the wake of declining enrollments, but school closings occurred without undue rancor or debate.[39] Compared to nearby districts, Raytown was largely free of controversy.[40]

Hickman Mills, on the other hand, offered a telling contrast. That district (HMSD) struggled to find financial support in the community and suffered painful leadership disruptions, school board conflicts, and mismanagement scandals. Voters routinely failed to pass levy increases and bonding issues by the required two-thirds margin, and superintendents came and left recurrently.[41] While the local community's economic and social profile was quite similar to Raytown's, it lacked a comparable sense of cohesiveness and shared purposes in supporting the schools. As historian Aaron Tyler Rife has argued, it "was in actuality a collection of neighborhoods that identified themselves with the school district."[42]

When Perry Cookingham visited Hickman Mills in 1956 to propose annexation, residents found it difficult to rally around incorporation as an independent municipality, as Raytown had done.[43] Entreaties from Grandview to the south made the prospect of joining Kansas City, with its lower taxes, more appealing.[44] While residents were quite clear in refusing to join KCMPS, they lacked the sense of familiarity and sociability that sustained Raytown's commitment to the schools. The area known as Hickman Mills, consequently, surrendered much of its identity to the collection of communities called South Kansas City.

Some of this may have been due to other differences that distinguished the two places; Hickman Mills was less a classic bedroom community than Raytown. Major investment in retail, manufacturing, and governmental facilities brought thousands of jobs to the area, and many of its residents worked there. Because there was no local government to exert control over residential development, moreover, rapid growth yielded a haphazard pattern of subdivision building rather than a coherent municipal plan. As a result there was a tendency for residents to identify more strongly with their immediate neighborhood and place of employment than the larger community. Such as it was, Hickman Mills took an identity from the school district and little else, and not everyone agreed that education was a priority. For instance, Carla Baker moved there in 1954 primarily for affordable housing and proximity to her husband's workplace. For her, as for many other residents who arrived at the time, the schools were an afterthought.[45] This reflected a set of priorities quite different from those of neighboring Raytown, or Shawnee Mission across the border. The school system was not a major source of local distinction or pride. In the end it appears that most HMSD residents were content with schools deemed good enough to sustain a broadly positive reputation—certainly better than KCMPS, but not enough to become known for their academic excellence or athletic prowess.

If there was one characteristic that residents of both RSD and HMSD shared, however, it was determination to keep poor and minority families away from their schools and communities. Raytown became particularly infamous in this regard, as its police department, led by Chief Marion Beeler, was notorious for hounding African Americans who happened to drive there.[46] In 1962 a black family purchased a home just east of the city and had a Molotov cocktail thrown onto their property.[47] This did not go unnoticed in Kansas City's black community, which was likely one of the objects of such provocations. Manny Stevens echoed the sentiments of other African Americans when he proclaimed, "Hey, by Raytown, I'll just drive around it. I won't go through Raytown."[48] Patrick Elard recalled an especially vivid memory of racial incitement when stopping for food there: Oh, yeah, yeah, Raytown was bad. I used to have to drive through there on the old 50 Highway, and I would stop at some of those restaurants like Smacks and get some takeout or something. I remember one night I almost, I was called names. I had gone in for food for my family and all I could do was just eat crow and take 'cause my family was in the car.[49]

Racial tensions were aired publicly in 1972, when an incident between students from Raytown and Kansas City's Central High at a state tournament basketball game in Marysville flared into a brawl. Central was banned from the following year's tournaments as a result but was declared eligible after its students and administration expressed remorse for the affair. Raytown's Superintendent Herndon, however, announced that his district would not permit its teams to play Central if scheduled to meet again in the tournament, citing concerns for student safety. This, of course, evoked images of black youth as unruly or violence-prone and a threat to whites, which did not sit well with Kansas City's black community. As the *Kansas City Call* observed, Raytown's students were never held responsible for their role in the 1972 fracas, and the district's leaders were "poor sports" for their unwillingness to play after Central's repentance.[50] Other suburban districts also may have been loath to play city schools, but this incident underscored Raytown's reputation as being particularly hostile to blacks.[51] The district's well-publicized reaction, moreover, suggested this was just fine with most of its constituents. If residents of Raytown wanted to maintain firm boundaries with Kansas City's black community, this certainly helped to bolster them.[52]

For some Raytown residents, racial exclusion apparently was a source of pride. Sally Westbrook recalled being shaken when a local real estate agent proclaimed that "you don't have to worry about blacks in this town" as she and her husband were house hunting. The comment was offered unabashedly as a positive quality of the community, suggesting it had been an effective selling point before. Other longtime residents reported hearing similar stories.[53] Vigilance against unwanted intruders from the city extended to the schools, as the district posted observers at certain bus stops to report on youths from KCMPS seeking to attend RSD institutions.[54] As Kansas City's African American population edged southward, gradually approaching Raytown and other South Kansas City communities, awareness of these issues was inexorably heightened. As maps 2.6 and 3.3 indicate, by 1980 the southernmost extent of African American settlement had reached the northwest corner of RSD.[55] This undoubtedly contributed to racialized white anxieties. Given its collective resolve to avoid or resist racial integration of any kind, Raytown became known as a bastion of bigotry in maintaining its generally white small-town identity.

Raytown's reputation regarding race was similar in many respects to that of other blue-collar suburbs bordering on cities in the North that became known for hostility and aggression directed at African Americans. Like in Cicero, Illinois, or Warren, Michigan, that reputation proved quite effective in deterring black settlement, maintaining effective boundaries that defined exclusion largely in racial terms. As suggested by the January 1969 mass meeting at the high school, these sentiments apparently were widely shared, a point of collective identity.

This was localism of a particularly virulent form, which can aptly be described as opportunity hoarding. Not all suburban communities or school districts in these circumstances were able to achieve this level of consensus around such issues, however.[56]

Many residents of Hickman Mills may have harbored sentiments comparable to their Raytown neighbors, but they lacked the resources and power of municipal sovereignty to prevent African Americans from settling in their vicinity. They did reject a proposal to merge with KCMPS in 1964, which the school board had proposed in a somewhat desperate quest for additional resources. Citing the dangers of "31,000 culturally deprived children" in Kansas City schools, the figure touted by KCMPS officials, opponents of the annexation proposal succeeded in defeating it.[57] Area residents also mobilized for concerted action against low-income housing during the 1960s and 1970s, which was somewhat successful in maintaining the area's middle-class appeal.[58] But even the most prejudiced whites could do little to keep minority families from settling in the area, especially those with the means to buy homes or rent at market rates. Insufficient consensus existed for collective action on that score.

Because South Kansas City was served by the Kansas City Police Department, along with other city services, local residents also lacked institutional capacity to racially profile African Americans and others deemed less than desirable, as often was done in neighboring Raytown. Eventually, this restricted the ability of bigoted whites to deter African American home buyers in a systematic fashion, and middle-class blacks began to settle in the district. These families, of course, were seeking the same amenities that whites had pursued decades earlier, and some were associated with the military, which continued to be a major employer through most of the period.[59] It was in this fashion that the suburban districts of South Kansas City began to be racially integrated. This included Raytown, which counted 78 African American and more than 170 other ethnic minority children in 1976, mostly in portions of the district proximate to KCMPS. Hickman Mills counted more than 200 black students at the time.[60] It would be another decade, however, before the arrival of larger numbers of African Americans, including less affluent families, would begin to change the area's identity more significantly.

North Kansas City: Growth by Annexation

The municipality of North Kansas City began as a planned industrial district in 1912. Located in Clay County, on the north and east banks of the Missouri River at the turn, it looked across the water to Kansas City, Kansas, on the west and

Kansas City, Missouri, to the south. Factories, warehouses, and other businesses occupied much of its land, situated between two railroad lines, along with homes built expressly for the families of men who worked there. The river posed a formidable barrier to the daily movement of people, limiting the city's growth and settlement of the surrounding countryside. Consequently, North Kansas City remained a relatively small factory town through much of the twentieth century, limiting its population to "better" workers, which generally meant whites. For most African Americans who found employment there, mainly as domestics or service workers, it was a "sundown town," requiring them to leave at nightfall. By 1940 it boasted a residential population of 2,688, although a much larger number worked there every day.[61]

With a relatively small resident population and a tax base bolstered by industry, the North Kansas City School District (NKCSD) had a promising future when it was formed in 1913 from the merger of two elementary districts. It grew by fits and starts, but when it opened a new high school building in 1926, the district gained a resource unique in its immediate vicinity: a free-standing secondary institution with the capacity to offer a varied curriculum. Within a year the school added courses in home economics and business, and students from surrounding districts began attending. In little more than a decade, better than a third of the enrollment consisted of tuition-paying residents of surrounding districts. The high school, it turned out, became an inducement for local educators and students to look to NKCSD for expanded opportunities to learn.[62]

One obvious way for neighboring districts to take advantage of the benefits that the North Kansas City schools offered was to join them through annexation. Missouri law at the time made such mergers relatively simple, just requiring positive votes by the school boards involved.[63] Beginning in the mid-1920s, NKCSD spurned a number of overtures to this effect, preferring to marshal the resources available within its original boundaries.[64] Residents who attended the schools in this period recalled the small-town intimacy of the community and the busy social scene at "Northtown" high school.[65] At the outset of the postwar era, however, the district began to undertake annexations with neighboring districts, quickly expanding its geographic footprint. Its well-regarded senior high school remained a powerful inducement to the smaller elementary districts surrounding it.[66] Under the leadership of Superintendent H.W. Schooling, the district added four adjoining districts in 1949 and 1950, boosting enrollment and the number of schools significantly. By 1952 it counted some 5,000 students and nearly 150 teachers, more than a fourfold increase in two decades.[67] But its growth was far from finished. The area's industrial economy continued to advance in the postwar era, providing a firm foundation for the local public schools to develop as well.[68]

When Schooling left the district to take a faculty position at the University of Chicago in 1955, the North Kansas City schools enjoyed a good reputation. The *Kansas City Star* commended the departing superintendent for the district's expansion, accomplished without controversy, and its progress academically.[69] Schooling's successor, R. B. Doolin, continued the system's approach to growth through annexation, adding four adjoining districts in 1959, one in 1960, two in 1961, and another in 1963. Within that time frame the number of schools nearly tripled, and enrollment climbed to seventeen thousand. Like other districts at the time, NKCSD struggled to find classroom space for its surging population, teaching students in shifts at the high school and hiring scores of new teachers each year.[70]

Echoing local pride reminiscent of Raytown, in 1962 a Northland newspaper declared that "North Kansas City is a good place to live." It also noted that the local school system "did not hesitate to take in surrounding rural districts, which were having great difficulty in providing for themselves."[71] This may have reflected a bit of hubris, but it also represented a distinctive approach to expansion. In this manner the district quickly extended its boundaries north to rural Smithville and east to Liberty. Map 4.2 documents the timing of these annexations. As a consequence of these developments, a second senior high school, Oak Park, opened about eight miles to the north of the first in 1965, and a third, Winnetonka, was erected five miles to the east in 1971. Each was carefully planned, both with respect to future educational needs and architectural and landscape design.[72] Popular support for the system remained high, and elections for levy increases and bond issues during this period were consistently successful. The district's enrollment peaked at more than twenty-two thousand students a few years later and declined slightly thereafter.[73] The era of growth by annexation ended, and the postwar baby-boom generation finally passed through all the schools, as it did in other districts.

Following Doolin's retirement in 1977, his successor, Raymond Waier, dealt with the difficult problem of closing and consolidating schools, a process fraught with potential pitfalls. There was evidence of friction between different parts of NKCSD following Oak Park's opening, as the newer school quickly established a local reputation for innovation and progressivism. Closer to Liberty and the working-class community of Claycomo, Winnetonka High offered yet another source of internecine rivalry in the 1970s.[74] Waier, however, managed to overcome such potential discord and led the district through a sweeping reorganization in 1980 that accomplished the tasks of downsizing and consolidation without much controversy. Bitterness lingered over some of the school closings, particularly Northgate Middle School, but NKCSD emerged a leaner, more efficient school system. Enrollments declined until the mid-1980s, after which they began to climb again with the area's continued development.[75]

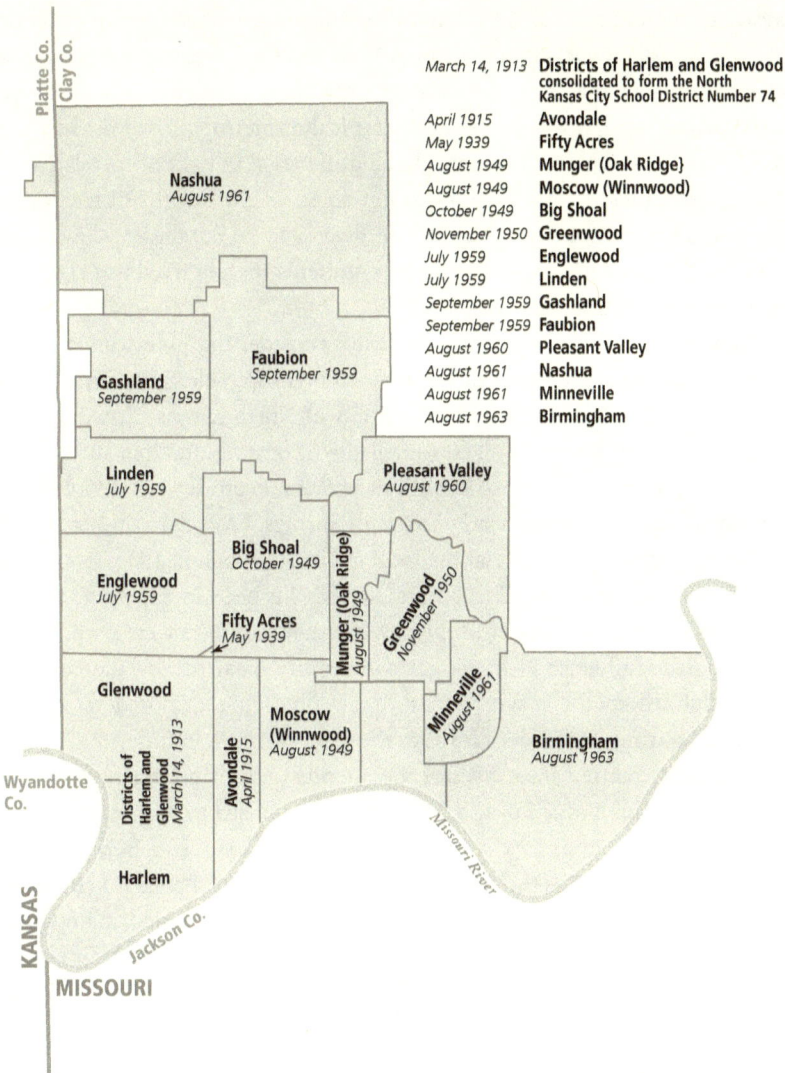

MAP 4.2 Fifty years of annexations in North Kansas City, 1913–1963

At the height of its expansion, NKCSD stood as the largest of the area's Missouri "suburban" school districts, spanning more than seventy square miles and serving a population of nearly ninety thousand. While most residents saw it as broadly middle class, there was a good deal of diversity in social status as well. The district included relatively wealthy areas such as Briarcliff in the northwest, working-class neighborhoods in the older industrial quarter to the south, and a mixture of middle-class and blue-collar communities to the east.[76] As table 4.1

indicates, a bit more than 6 percent of its students qualified for free or reduced-price lunch, slightly less than Hickman Mills and Grandview, and its educational expenditures were among the lowest in the region. Judging from proficiency scores at the time, it was academically typical of metropolitan Missouri suburban districts, which could be considered quite good in light of its relatively low per-student spending. By 1980 it was not an especially wealthy district on a per capita basis, which was hardly a surprise, given its size. But the very low numbers of African American and other minority students that it served was right in line with other local suburban systems.[77]

By and large, African Americans did not consider the large segment of metropolitan Kansas City north of the river to be hospitable. They generally were not welcomed in the planned industrial city of North Kansas City, and very few ventured into the largely rural and small-town communities that surrounded it. Clay County had a history of hostility to blacks, expressed most violently in a 1925 lynching by a mob in nearby Excelsior Springs.[78] An angry throng also killed an African American inmate at the local jail in St. Joseph in 1933, less than fifty miles north of the county line, before burning his body in effigy.[79] Generations of blacks had lived in the city of Liberty, but their numbers were small, and they wielded little influence in the larger community. That part of the county had long exhibited southern sympathies, reportedly flying a Confederate flag over the local courthouse five decades after the Civil War.[80] As in Independence to the south, black children there historically attended a separate elementary school, extending through much of the 1950s, and were bused to Kansas City for high school.[81] North Kansas City counted just a few black students in the early years and sent them all across the river to KCMPS rather than allowing them to attend local district schools. As longtime educator Gary Littlefield noted, many whites in the district harbored a deep-seated animosity toward blacks, even if it was rarely expressed in public.[82] Other area residents agreed, suggesting that a substantial portion of the area's white population had left KCMPS during the 1950s and '60s because of racial change in city neighborhoods.[83]

This situation was clearly acknowledged in the comments of blacks who shared impressions of growing up in the area. For Manny Stevens, it was similar to suburbs to the south with respect to racial attitudes. "Well, along the same line into Raytown," he observed, "to be aware, it's, you know, it was not a written rule but you kind of, you just kind of sensed you weren't welcome."[84] Echoing the concerns of others, Marvin Daniels worried about natural barriers: "You know, you had to cross that river. And the transportation of that made a big difference." He added that there was a clear sense of being cut off from the black community and perhaps the difficulty of flight from peril. Susan Hilliard worked in North Kansas City for a time but found it forbidding. "I don't remember anybody sitting at break with me, really odd. It was the worst place in the world to work. I was just desperate for a job." She left after finding employment in downtown Kansas City, describing the experience as "not the best six weeks of my life."[85] Patrick Elard agreed with these sentiments, adding a qualification: "So North Kansas City was not seen as a pleasant place you'd want to be. You probably didn't want to be driving over there too much because you could get stopped for little or nothing. In fact, I guess, I think that it's been seen basically as kind of a hostile place until, oh, we had some people that were working for TWA who moved up there, and they seemed to do all right."[86]

Cookingham and other leaders in Kansas City, however, made grand plans for development in the Northland, most of which took considerably longer to bear fruit than initially imagined.[87] Locating a new airport there in 1956, some fifteen miles from downtown Kansas City, was intended to spur settlement, but the pace of growth was slow. The airport eventually stimulated some economic activity, especially after new terminals were completed in 1972, but there was little industrial investment or office development through much of the period. Consequently, the Northland became a patchwork of subdivisions with relatively little in common to bind them together. The municipality of Gladstone, surrounded by Kansas City's annexations, offered a modest sense of community for its residents but not the larger area. A bedroom community similar to Raytown in some respects, hastily incorporated to avoid Kansas City's reach, it lacked a separate school district to provide a more distinctive identity.[88]

As the sprawling North Kansas City school system grew by annexation, in that case it lost much of the intimacy and easy familiarity that had characterized its early years. In this respect it was similar to Hickman Mills on the city's south side, but considerably larger. The North Kansas City schools also did not experience a comparable influx of African American residents, probably owing to the physical and social barriers that many blacks perceived.[89] The area also did not have a ready stock of older homes that real estate agents could offer to lower-income families, which represented the largest number of black households. Many would have had trouble securing mortgages for homes in that part of the city in any case.[90] Altogether, the Northland was not seen as a welcoming part of the city to most African Americans, and few were willing to venture so far from the city's traditionally segregated neighborhoods to try it out.

Given these circumstances, it is little wonder that NKCSD enrolled so few minority students, just 1 percent. In 1976 the district counted just sixty African Americans, less than a third of 1 percent of its student population. This was proportionally the lowest number of all the districts that directly served municipal Kansas City. In absolute numbers it was less than Raytown or Center, both considerably smaller systems. Like Raytown, NKCSD schools enrolled larger numbers of Hispanic and other minority group students, about 350 altogether. This was less than 2 percent of the district total, but it made the low number of African Americans especially striking. If indeed black employees at the airport lived in the district, as Elard suggested, their children may have accounted for a large proportion of its entire African American population. This was compelling evidence of the power of racial exclusion that operated in Kansas City's Northland. Residents of NKCSD might not have been as resolute or frank about their views as many in Raytown or elsewhere on the south side, but they were just as effective in keeping African Americans out of their schools.

Controversy over Race and Resources: The Spainhower Commission

Like many other states during the postwar era, Missouri faced the challenge of consolidating school districts to realize greater efficiency and improved educational opportunity, especially in rural areas where small schools with relatively meager resources predominated. While certain suburban districts such as North Kansas City were able to grow through annexation, large school systems were unusual outside of the state's principal metropolitan areas. Recognition of this problem led to the formation of the Missouri School Reorganization Commission in 1967, led by James Spainhower, chair of the Missouri Assembly's Education Committee. Given a budget of $125,000 (over $800,000 in 2015 dollars), Spainhower's commission set about studying the issue and making recommendations. A report released in the following year suggested reorganizing Missouri's school districts into 133 local units, nested within twenty regional school districts of generally equal enrollment size.[91] This obviously would have been a radical change from existing arrangements, and generally speaking it was not well received. Local school leaders and their communities across the state responded sharply to the very idea of surrendering any control over their institutions. In many respects it was a direct challenge to the principle of localism, and it did not sit well with most districts and their constituents.[92]

The commission recommended two metropolitan-wide school districts, one each for greater Kansas City and St. Louis, combining city schools with surrounding suburban districts to create more equitably financed institutions. These "urban" regional districts also would have opened the possibility for greater racial integration. This, of course, immediately raised red flags.[93] As one commission member pointed out regarding the public reaction, "The predominate interest is on the integration question."[94]

In June 1969 the commission published another report stemming from its work on metropolitan schools, titled *Equal Treatment to Equals: A New Structure for Public Schools in the Kansas City and St. Louis Metropolitan Areas*. While the report failed to address the history of segregation in either of the state's major metropolitan areas, it did call for mixing students from urban and suburban schools. In doing so, it made a straightforward plea for educational equity, arguing that Missouri's two metropolitan areas needed region-wide remedies to address the problems of urban education. It suggested that the suburbs and cities had a "common destiny" and called for solutions driven by "communal self-interest."[95] The principal conclusion was that economic inequality contributed to specific urban problems and that public finance equity was needed, a theme in other studies at the time.[96] It was a position very much in line with the thinking of urban sociologists and planners, who had long called for integrating urban and suburban institutions to provide more coherent governance and policy options in metropolitan settings. The response of residents in suburban school districts, however, was a different question altogether.

The commission's report proved to be a potent provocation for its staunchest critics. Missouri's suburban communities did not want school integration, and they certainly did not want to share their tax wealth with other school districts. Race quickly became a focal point of resistance to the plan. Correspondence regarding the idea of large consolidated districts reflected this, much of it written in response to a Missouri Assembly bill that Spainhower introduced to initiate discussion of the commission's proposals. While most opponents did not make explicitly racial statements in their letters and petitions, there could be little doubt about their intent. They typically employed proxies for such ideas, such as opposition to busing and the dangers of urban schools, which signaled racially charged sentiments. As one letter stated, "You can [not] push onto the people in a few years what has been going on for a hundred years," suggesting that busing had made the Kansas City schools worse.[97] Another Kansas City area couple was more direct, expressing doubt that Spainhower would want his son "bussed into a slum district of Kansas City or St. Louis."[98] Other writers made it clear that they had moved to the suburbs for the express purpose of avoiding the Kansas City schools. As one noted, "¾ of our adults work in K.C. and by each one's personal choice desire to raise our children away from K.C."[99] But some did put intimations aside and openly opposed integration, as in a letter from another Kansas City suburb: "It seems to us that this country is losing the democracy on which it was founded. . . . Why should all citizens be made to suffer and pay for the troubles of a few? You are really just trying to force integration down people's throats, as well as trying to expose our children to conditions which can endanger their lives."[100]

In addition to letters, eight communities in greater the Kansas City area submitted petitions to either the commission, Spainhower himself, or the legislature, and another Kansas City suburb sent a resolution. The statements in most such documents expressed general opposition to reorganization, but two petitions went further, asserting clearly that they did not want to be a party to solving "urban" problems. Representing thirteen residents of the Raytown, Center, and Grandview districts, one stated that "we have fought the Kansas City School system for years to keep our school system separate from theirs. Now we are not having any say in the matter."[101] Writing from a nearby rural district, yet another group elaborated a bit more: "This is a good way for St. Louis and Kansas City to attempt to solve their problems at the expense of the rest of rural Missouri. We do not have a solution to their problems, but we do know this plan is designed for the two large cities of Missouri, and we do not like it."[102]

Opposition in metro Kansas City was stronger than in St. Louis, as reflected in the January meeting at Raytown High. One observer there noted that a "unanimous feeling was expressed on the part of the crowd that this bill and everything about it is a piece of shoddy, misrepresented and dangerous work."[103] In many respects Raytown became an epicenter of opposition, as reported in the *Kansas City Star*, and race was a major factor indeed. Raytown school records indicated that a large number of students had transferred from Central High in Kansas City during the 1950s, and others had come from Paseo and Southeast High more recently. While most residents reportedly felt a firm determination to preserve the community's small-town sensibility and to retain local control of schooling, they also acknowledged that concerns about race were widespread.[104] Raytown sent busloads of people to the state capitol building to testify and demonstrate against the commission's recommendations. One commissioner later noted that hostility to the very idea of district reorganization was especially virulent there.[105] As Spainhower himself observed, many people "moved to Raytown for the purpose of getting away from the problems of the Kansas City School District and were quite upset with the possibility of being exposed once again to [those] problems."[106]

Not all the correspondence responding to this question was negative, however, and supportive letters even were sent by residents of Raytown. Mrs. Margie McCoy, for instance, argued that "especially we in the suburbs cannot turn our backs on the problems of the city. For us not to work out a fair plan for all schools is impractical and shortsighted."[107] Similar letters were written by residents of other suburbs. Not surprisingly, the strongest endorsements of the Spainhower recommendations came from Kansas City. KCMPS board member Homer Wadsworth was forthright in his support for the commission's ideas: "We cannot have equality of opportunity in education unless we have a relatively equal investment per child in educational plant and program. This we do not have and as a consequence the rich districts get richer and the poor districts get poorer."[108]

While many others in the urban core shared this view, and KCMPS superintendent Hazlett cautiously endorsed the commission's plans, the vast majority of suburban correspondence was decidedly hostile.[109] Most such letters, petitions, and other accounts made it clear that many suburbanites had abandoned the cities to avoid integration. Moreover they felt justified in resisting change because of the perceived problems and hazards of the big cities.[110] It was these residents who responded most vehemently to the Spainhower Commission's recommendations. They were happy with the homogeneity of their communities and paying taxes for their own schools. From their perspective it was the rural and urban districts that clearly had problems demanding to be solved. They did not need or want state interference in their own institutions. They had no interest in racial diversity and certainly did not want to share their financial resources with city schools.

At the same time that racial animosity animated much of the opposition to the Spainhower Commission, many suburbanites also expressed a proprietary view of their schools. They saw these institutions as part and parcel of the local community, an investment that should be preserved. A mother writing from North Kansas City reflected this sentiment: "We taxpayers and concerned parents bought our homes in this community only after carefully considering the nearby schools, school district, teaching staff and their qualifications. Our children should be allowed to attend their . . . neighborhood schools."[111]

Statements such as this suggested that educational assets were a critical aspect of the decision to move for many suburbanites. Such amenities, of course, were seemingly threatened by the idea of admitting potentially low-performing or morally suspect students.[112] These suburbanites believed their institutions to be superior to those in the city or in rural areas and were determined to maintain that advantage, along with local property values.[113] In the opinion of many, school problems elsewhere stemmed from corrupt or incompetent management, or irresponsible residents, especially in the cities. A suburban superintendent from Cass County opined that unequal funding for urban schools was not the problem: "We . . . find it difficult to believe that our tax money could have been spent for such a recommendation! It is pointed out that the 'poor' central cities have been left in bad condition due to the flight to the suburbs, [but they are better funded than our district]. . . . Some reorganization was to be expected, but if our lawmakers pass this into law, then God pity us! Surely you do not expect this to receive serious consideration."[114]

Another suburban Kansas City letter writer was even more explicit in locating the blame for the problems of city schools, suggesting forcefully that local institutions deserved the advantages they enjoyed. "This bill . . . is hypocrisy in its highest form. . . . to force the people who care enough to educate their children, by working long, hard hours to pay higher taxes so other able bodied men and women can shirk their responsibility, or the money to go into the pocket of a so-called 12 man advisory board, elected by the people of the big city, you say that is fair."[115]

Suburbanites also opposed funding equalization in order to protect their schools, which they viewed as having earned a better reputation than urban institutions. Like the opponents of racial integration, they blamed the urban schools and big-city residents for existing problems, rejecting the notion that there was a viable metropolitan or statewide solution to social inequality and related school questions. They were principally concerned with maintaining the status quo, with little acknowledgment that their own actions contributed to a larger process of social change. The immediate response was to secure the existing boundaries that district lines represented. They believed the advantages represented by local school systems depended on these barriers, and they were determined to defend them from any and all threats.

The Specter of Metropolitan Coordination

Spainhower's bill failed to even find a second sponsor in the Missouri legislature and thus died ignominiously, but the idea of a metro-wide educational system did not disappear entirely. By the later 1970s there were two additional attempts to involve the suburban districts in plans to address the problems of KCMPS schools. Somewhat coincidentally, they occurred within months of one another in 1977. The first was a proposal to create two large districts that would embrace public school systems on either side of the state line. The second was a lawsuit to enjoin surrounding school systems to participate in metropolitan desegregation plans, launched by the KCMPS board (and eventually leading to *Jenkins*). Not surprisingly, the leaders of suburban districts greeted both with open hostility, reflecting viewpoints quite similar to those expressed nearly a decade earlier.

The Kansas and Missouri advisory committees of the US Commission on Civil Rights offered the first proposal. It called for voluntary cooperation of some nineteen districts in an effort to foster wider participation in school desegregation across the metropolitan area. The committees' report did, however, include the threat of "legal proceeding" if voluntary action was not forthcoming on its recommendations. Declaring that "remedies for racial isolation probably require some movement of pupils," it offered a straightforward analysis of the problem facing public education at the time. "Racial isolation and lack of exposure to the multiracial and multicultural characteristics of the area are problems for both cities and suburbs. The Central city districts are segregated, of themselves. But as districts they are also segregated by comparison with the suburbs around them. Real contact, in light of existing demographic patterns, requires multidistrict involvement."[116]

Following soon after this report, the KCMPS lawsuit was announced in May 1977, the first in the country to feature an urban district suing its suburban neighbors to establish a metropolitan solution to school segregation. It also named political figures on both side of the state line and several federal agencies as defendants. This was the first step in the case that eventually resulted in the *Jenkins v. Missouri* school desegregation decision, which would come seven years later. That decision, of course, did *not* require the suburban districts to participate in the ultimate plan to integrate KCMPS schools.[117] But the original suit offered an opportunity to gauge how suburban educators in both states would react to the idea of interdistrict cooperation for desegregation.

Predictably, suburban school leaders did not welcome either of these developments, and they were certainly not prepared to accept the logic of the advisory committees' recommendations. Garland Smith, a school board member from Bonner Springs in Kansas, predicted that such measures would result in "chaos," adding that "nothing can be forced along this issue and make any real gains." On the other side of the metropolitan area, Lee's Summit board president Robert J. Gourley stressed the importance of "keeping the autonomy of the local school districts." In nearby Independence, board president Carlton Milby declared that he "would oppose any change that would reduce the influence of our patrons over the educational policies of this district." For his part, James L. Robinson Jr., president of the Raytown board, worried that local levy elections would fail because of fears about funding being used for desegregation. In short, local control was considered paramount everywhere, and vehement opposition to the possibility of racially integrated schools was likely to make metro-wide school desegregation impossible.[118]

Perhaps the most telling response to the report and recommendations, however, came from North Kansas City. In February, board president Bob Raines announced that a letter would be sent home with all students declaring that the district "has no intention of voluntarily participating in any plan which would dissipate the resources of the district or reduce the quality of education in the schools by any proposal which would alter our obligations to our patrons and students." In particular he stressed that NKCSD has "never been involved" and "[has] no plans for the future to be a party to the Bi-State Advisory Committee." This, of course, suggested that area residents had expressed concern about the possibility of NKCSD's involvement in metropolitan desegregation plans, enough that the board felt it necessary to communicate directly with every family in the district. Raines also worried that an upcoming vote to increase district operating funds might be jeopardized by fears about school integration.[119] If suburban school leaders across the metropolitan area were clear about their opposition to the idea of interdistrict cooperation for desegregation, it was partly because they dreaded the response of their constituents. In particular, if they could not reassure residents that the districts were going to continue excluding African Americans and other students from the central cities, their school systems could lose popular support.

As before with the Spainhower report, educators and activists in Kansas City's urban core were supportive of the advisory committees' report. James Lyndon, KCMPS board president, described it as "uplifting." Julia Hill, president of the local NAACP chapter, was "happy to see that someone is interested in obeying the law," declaring that "at least someone is trying to do something voluntarily instead of waiting for the courts to force them."[120] On the other hand, suburban districts on either side of the state line expressed no interest in voluntary cooperation. However compelling the arguments arrayed in favor of a wider approach to achieving desegregation may have been, these districts remained resolutely committed to maintaining the status quo.

With respect to the lawsuit launched by KCMPS against the suburban districts, there was a fixed resolve to fight it across the board on the part of area superintendents. As in responses to the advisory committees' report, they stressed the importance of following the wishes of their constituents. Robert Atkin of Raytown emphasized that his district would oppose it "because [doing so] reflects the desires of the community." Other district leaders expressed similar sentiments. Most declined to comment because of the impending litigation, but their responses were generally consistent with those offered weeks earlier regarding the advisory committees' report. From their point of view, there was no reason to consider assisting the city schools. Their constituents had little sympathy for the plight of urban students and were opposed to permitting them access to local institutions. In the years since the Spainhower episode, little seemed to have changed. Suburban antipathy to the city and its residents continued unabated.

Purposeful Racial Exclusion

The unwillingness of suburban residents to participate in metropolitan efforts to desegregate schools represented a classic expression of localism, especially with respect to their repeatedly expressed preferences for home rule in decision making. This, of course, reflected a time-honored principle in American education, embodied in its tradition of autonomous school districts extending back to the nineteenth century. But it also epitomized a highly discriminatory form of opportunity hoarding, specifically with regard to racial exclusion. Suburban residents who sought to prevent school integration were trying to preserve the advantages that their predominantly white and middle-class schools afforded them, at the expense of children and youth who did not have access to comparable opportunities. Many saw students from the city, and African Americans in particular, as threats. And this included members of the growing black middle class.

The prevailing white racial frame in many of these communities depicted African American students as sources of contamination, regardless of their economic status, who could diminish the advantages of local institutions. Thus, when school district leaders declared their resolve not to weaken the quality of education, it signaled opposition to racial integration for their constituents, and to Kansas City's black community. Statements about honoring the wishes of local residents likely played a similar role. Such declarations often reflected a form of "dog whistle politics," employing coded terms to express a commitment to racist exclusion and discrimination that could be deemed unseemly if stated plainly. But there could be little doubt about their effect. These words helped to mobilize a solid wall of racialized opposition to the very suggestion of integrated schooling.

Opportunity hoarding in the suburbs, of course, meant a restriction of opportunities elsewhere, particularly in the urban core. This was a classic pattern played out in metropolitan areas across the country. Race was a principal question, and metropolitan Kansas City suburbanites expressed little concern for African American students, even if their districts also were within the city limits. A metro-wide desegregation plan could well have spread the city's black students across the region's schools so that overly large concentrations of them might have been avoided. This would have posed little danger to quality of education in any of the participating districts and likely would have helped to improve schools in the central city. Something akin to this had proved quite workable within KCMPS during the 1960s, and worked elsewhere in the country, particularly in the South.[121]

But suburban intransigence made such a plan unfeasible, virtually guaranteeing that urban-suburban inequity would continue to plague metropolitan education for decades to come. Active exclusion was abetted by natural barriers such as the Missouri River and inaccessibility in the case of North Kansas City, and antagonistic confrontation and policing authority in Raytown and doubtless elsewhere too. But it was mainly due to widespread opposition to integrated schooling among white residents of these districts, signaled in a variety of publicly accessible forms. For their part, African Americans were well aware of these sentiments, and it affected their decisions about where to live and send their children to school. As a result, school district boundaries became one of the region's principal racially defined geo-spatial dividing lines in this period.[122]

As noted earlier, so-called suburban districts on the Missouri side of the metropolitan area were hardly the same. They differed in size, in resources, and in the social and economic status of the families they served. If there was one attribute they shared, however, it was a commitment to the perceived virtues of localism, proximate control of resources and institutions, and the segregation of African Americans. As the Spainhower letters and subsequent statements of school leaders suggested, there was a strong sense of common interest in maintaining this dimension of inequality. In Raytown this bond was strong enough to mobilize considerable effort in opposing proposals to change existing forms of district organization. That community's robust commitment to the schools may have represented a distinctive form of social capital, shared values and interests that proved quite effective in drawing and defending racial boundaries. One sign of this was local norms that found expression in opposition to integration. It became especially forceful when residents felt threatened, as the response to Spainhower's proposals clearly illustrated. This was probably the area's most active and unambiguous reflection of opportunity hoarding at the time.[123] There could be little doubt, on the other hand, that many other suburbanites would have responded just as readily if they felt sufficiently apprehensive. Few questions brought putative suburbanites together as vehemently as did race.

The ongoing crisis in urban schooling was historically rooted in this period, a legacy of the responses that James Spainhower and the advisory committees' report engendered. Districts such as Raytown and North Kansas City may have enabled their residents to experience a fulfilling and productive childhood and education, but they also contributed to the problems encountered by children growing up in concentrated poverty in KCMPS. That was the injustice inherent in the racial advantage enjoyed by the area's Missouri suburban school districts across the long postwar era. And to a large extent, it continues to be evident today.[124]

5

CONFLICT IN SUBURBIA
Localism, Race, and Education in
Johnson County, Kansas

In February 1966 Donald Sewing moved his young family to the tasteful J. C. Nichols community of Fairway in Johnson County. A thirty-five-year-old college graduate and Korean War veteran, Sewing had become a successful real-estate broker and banker in Wyandotte County and wanted a better home and superior schools for his children. Like thousands of other parents who decided to settle in the area, he was seeking an improved standard of living and a chance to provide for his family's future. But in one important respect the Sewings were different from their neighbors in Fairway and adjacent communities: they were African American.[1]

Donald Sewing's decision to purchase a home in suburban Johnson County, Kansas, caused quite a stir in the normally placid pace of life there. A "traffic jam of cars driving past" quickly ensued, and a single picketer appeared in front of the house, who was invited in for a soda. But Fairway mayor Neale Peterson ordered the street blocked off and posted a police watch to ensure the family's safety. Eventually life returned to normal, and Sewing later opened a real estate office in nearby Overland Park, although it closed before long owing to lack of business. He had purchased the Fairway home directly from the owner to avoid obstacles that blacks typically encountered from banks and real estate agencies. Sewing saw himself as "one of the active spearheads" of a movement to integrate suburbia, but his efforts ultimately had little effect on the racial composition of Johnson County. Despite his determination and a relatively small number of like-minded African American residents, the area remained overwhelmingly white.

As a consequence, local controversies over schooling did not revolve around race as a major issue in that particular corner of metropolitan Kansas City.[2]

While discord focused on questions of segregation and inequity on the Missouri side of greater Kansas City, schools on the Kansas side became embroiled in a somewhat different set of problems. It was not that race lacked salience as a social issue there, as Sewing's experience suggested, but rather that it did not pose an immediate challenge to local schools. Instead, suburbanites in affluent Johnson County struggled to find unanimity on a range of other questions, not least the need for a large and comprehensive school system. As in other wealthy communities, education became a critical element in suburban struggles to create and sustain distinctive local identities. These developments paralleled events elsewhere in the country, perhaps most notably in Southern California, when suburbanites asserted their independence as property owners in order to control neighborhood institutions. Such conflicts became perhaps the clearest manifestation of "localism" in suburban political culture when race was not an immediate or predominant concern.[3]

The Shawnee Mission School District (SMSD) in metropolitan Kansas City offered a window on these questions as it became a rapidly growing and widely admired school system during the postwar era. As noted in chapter 2, SMSD is located in Johnson County, Kansas, just over the state line from the affluent Sunset Hills neighborhood in southwest Kansas City, Missouri. Embracing communities such as Mission Hills, Fairway, and Prairie Village—all planned by J. C. Nichols, Kansas City's legendary suburban developer—along with parts of Overland Park and other municipalities, it became both large and wealthy. It also contributed directly to the county's rise as the region's premier site for residential development.[4] All was not well in SMSD, however. Many of its residents resisted the district's consolidation as a unified school system in the 1960s, before a special act of the Kansas legislature finally compelled its formation in 1971. The struggle over the district's organization yields insight into the politics of suburban schooling at the very time that it was becoming predominant across the country.

The Shawnee Mission schools provide a telling case of these dynamics in metropolitan Kansas City. A dozen small elementary districts served the various municipalities that Nichols and other builders had founded as separate housing developments, most launched with neighborhood associations that eventually became formal or informal branches of local government. These communities opposed efforts to create larger administrative units in the 1950s, expressing a preference for local control and an aura of exclusiveness that many strived to maintain. The Shawnee Mission High School District had long served the area, a source of immense local pride and positive publicity, not to mention high property values. But creating a single, large school system out of the area's smaller elementary districts threatened the sense of intimacy and proximate influence that many SMSD residents prized. The subsequent disputes point to the conservative, inward-looking political culture of the area's well-heeled communities. Nichols helped to foster a lifestyle that featured an ethos of neighborhood control and status consciousness that militated against the authority of larger governmental entities. For those concerned with maintaining a sense of privilege and extending advantages to their own children, the creation of a single school system spanning multiple communities threatened "bureaucracy at its worst."[5]

Nichols's upscale developments had appealed to growing desires to escape the city, creating a "bourgeois utopia" that contributed directly to the area's growth.[6] In the postwar era there can be little doubt that many Johnson County residents settled there to avoid the growing black and working-class population in the two Kansas City municipalities, one across the state line to the east in Missouri and the other just over the county line to the north in Kansas. These boundaries helped to shelter the suburbs from desegregation litigation in the 1960s and '70s, and the area remained predominantly white.[7] For all practical purposes, race was not a major factor in the school controversies that eventually afflicted northeast Johnson County.

Apart from distancing their suburban enclaves from nearby urban centers, the most affluent residents of SMSD also were concerned about maintaining status distinctions between themselves and neighboring suburban communities. Like suburbanites across the border in Missouri, they saw public schooling in proprietary terms, a limited resource to be supported and controlled for the benefit of residents in its immediate setting. This, of course, differed from the views of urban educators, planners, and political leaders, who had campaigned in earlier decades for greater bureaucratic control of schools and the development of centralized systems of governance and administration. Once ensconced in the suburbs, it seems that wealthy patrons of public education became devotees of home rule and the virtues of neighborhood institutions.[8] They rejected the idea of larger, bureaucratically organized school system when it became a threat to their personal interests. Suburban fragmentation, after all, required more than just antipathy toward the big city; it also meant that some suburbanites had to distrust their neighbors. Creating large suburban school systems, consequently, was not always easy; as the history of SMSD demonstrated, it was sometimes fraught with conflict.

Suburban Development in Northeast Johnson County

For most of the first half of the twentieth century, Johnson County, Kansas, remained a largely agricultural enclave abutting the southwest border of Kansas City, Missouri. With the emerging industrial city of Kansas City, Kansas, immediately to the North, its truck farms served the region's growing urban markets. Johnson County also presented a tempting prospect for developers seeking fresh territory to accommodate Kansas City's growing middle- and upper-class population seeking refuge from the rough-and-tumble city. As a 1919 advertisement for Merriam, Kansas, put it, "If you desire a quiet, dignified home for yourself and family with pure country air, sunshine, shade and removed from the dirt and noise of industrial life and from the nervous strain and confusion of business centers and commercialism, this is the place for you."[9] Jesse Clyde (J. C.) Nichols was among the speculators selling such visions, a native of nearby Olathe, Kansas, who found the idea of developing suburban tracts in unincorporated Johnson County quite intriguing.[10]

Nichols eventually became well known for developing the "Country Club" district in southwest Kansas City and the Country Club Plaza, a retail showcase and one of the nation's first shopping malls. He began building homes in Johnson County in 1909 and launched his first major development there in 1913, Mission Hills. Bordering Kansas City and just a short distance from the Ward Parkway mansions he was erecting for the Kansas City elite, it was intended to offer the appeal of living in "a restricted residence" neighborhood on the Kansas side of the border. Nichols planned Mission Hills to conform to the somewhat variegated contours of the land without a conventional street grid, unlike developments in Kansas City. He also built it in conjunction with a country club and golf courses, with memberships linked to home purchases. This became an inducement to the wealthy, and Nichols offered some of his most expensive and expansive homes in Mission Hills. Working with landscape architect Sid J. Hare, he "created a wonderland of irregularity" with pedestrian walkways, statuary, and abundant trees and other plantings. By the 1920s it was a great commercial success and opened the door to the development of other communities to the west and south in Johnson County in years to follow.[11]

Like other leading developers of his time, Nichols recognized that building successful "exclusive" communities involved at least two critical steps: getting the right people to purchase homes to start, and protecting property values once they did. This meant keeping the wrong people out, as Nichols had seen many Kansas City neighborhoods decline in value when less socially desirable groups began to settle nearby. He became a pioneer in the use of restrictive covenants written into property deeds that dictated building standards and forbade sales to blacks, Jews, and certain other ethnic or religious groups. Perhaps even more importantly, he insisted on membership in local neighborhood associations for all residents of his developments, a key enforcement mechanism for covenants and other exclusionary measures, including zoning provisions. While Nichols may have been a bit more open-minded than some of his real-estate magnate peers, occasionally selling homes to upstanding Jewish families, he was resolute in the principle of defending new developments from any threats to future market viability.[12]

Ringed by golf courses, Mission Hills was shielded from the possibility of encroachment from bordering communities. But Nichols left little to chance and soon moved ahead with plans to develop new communities to the west and south. These included Westwood, Fairway, and Prairie Village, all somewhat less extravagant than Mission Hills but with costs still well above average for the metropolitan area. Here, too, Nichols made restrictive covenants a key element of the development process, and apparently it helped to spur home sales. The association with Mission Hills and Nichols's reputation for high-quality houses and planned development also contributed to the company's success. It won national acclaim for community planning and design in Prairie Village, the last of these developments and by far the largest. Launched after the Great Depression, it grew rapidly in the initial postwar housing boom.[13]

Nichols stressed the importance of home rule, and initially this fell to the neighborhood associations he required home buyers to join. To one extent or another, these groups eventually gave rise to local governments. By design, they focused almost exclusively on domestic concerns, especially matters linked to the future attractiveness of the community.[14] This came to have important implications for the schools, as neighborhoods became linked to particular institutions, and residents often identified closely with them.

Nichols's communities in northeast Johnson County helped to set the tone for the area's subsequent development. With Westwood and Prairie Village, he contributed to an image of affordable distinctiveness that came to characterize much of the area. Not everyone could live in Mission Hills, after all, but communities immediately around it benefited from its proximity. Judging from studies of the local social register, a very high proportion of the greater Kansas City elite lived in Nichols developments.[15] Other builders followed his lead in launching similarly attractive developments in the vicinity, particularly the Kroh brothers, who established Leawood to the east and south of Prairie Village. In the years following World War II, thousands of families poured into the area, filling out these communities, but also neighboring Roeland Park, Mission, Merriam, Shawnee, and other small municipalities and unincorporated areas to the west.

While almost all these communities were predominantly white and middle class, there was a good deal of perceived and real status distinction as well. Some were former farm villages, and others were elegant and relatively new suburbs.[16] Table 5.1 offers statistics on adult education levels, the proportion of men in professional and management jobs, and median household incomes, and they are quite telling. A range of differences are readily evident: residents of the Nichols

TABLE 5.1 Social status indicators, select Johnson County communities, 1960

COMMUNITY OR AREA	MEDIAN ADULT YEARS OF SCHOOLING	PROFESSIONAL OR MANAGEMENT EMPLOYMENT (PERCENT)	MEDIAN FAMILY INCOME (DOLLARS)
Mission Hills	14.3	80	10,000 + *
Fairway	13.1	57	10,000 + *
Prairie Village	14	56	10,000 + *
Leawood	13.5	62	10,000 + *
Overland Park	12.8	40	8,013
Roeland Park	12.5	38	7,961
Mission	12.6	45	7,889
Merriam	12.4	33	7,711
Shawnee	12.3	26	6,895
Urban Kansas	12.1	27	5,856

Source: United States Census Bureau, *Census of Population: 1960 Kansas*, vol. 1, pt. 18, *Characteristics of the Population* (Washington, DC: Government Printing Office, 1961), section 4: General Social and Economic Characteristics.

*The published census tables in 1960 did not provide median income figures above $10,000 (about $73,000 in 2010 dollars).

communities and Leawood were clearly better educated, more likely to hold high-status jobs, and enjoyed higher income levels than their neighbors to the west. In the area's older communities, such as Mission, Merriam, and Shawnee, income and education levels were well above those of urban areas across the state but substantially below those of the wealthiest neighborhoods.[17] In short, the area embraced a range of social and economic categories, creating the possibility for dissension. One feature that all its residents shared for many years, however, was a single public secondary school.

Shawnee Mission Rural High School

In the opening decades of the twentieth century, Johnson County offered few opportunities for secondary schooling. Some students living near the northern county line attended the large, well-respected public schools in Kansas City, Kansas, particularly Wyandotte High. Smaller, somewhat makeshift institutions served districts to the south. Families living in Mission Hills often sent their children to private schools, which Nichols had helped to establish, mostly on the Missouri side of the border. Eventually many attended Southwest High, located in Nichols's nearby Sunset Hills neighborhood and the jewel of the Kansas City, Missouri, system. What the developing northeast portion of Johnson County lacked, however, was a comprehensive high school of its own.[18]

This void was filled in 1922 with the opening of Shawnee Mission Rural High School, established by a slim majority of local voters a year earlier in a special election. The school's name reflected the two principal communities it served, Shawnee and Mission, and not the nearby site of the county's original Shawnee Indian settlement, as students often imagined. The school was established as a rural secondary district serving a number of smaller primary districts scattered across the area, most with just a single school. This was a conventional approach to providing secondary schooling in rural parts of the state and elsewhere in the Midwest.[19] What was unknown at the time, of course, was that northeast Johnson County would eventually experience rapid residential development, leading to calls for a larger, unified school system.

Shawnee Mission Rural was somewhat small at the start but eventually grew to more than a thousand students as enrollment mounted gradually through the 1920s and '30s. The number of students began to increase rapidly, however, with the area's development following the war, especially the Nichols communities to the west and south of Mission Hills. A student petition drive led to the "rural" designation in the school's original name being dropped in the late 1940s, although it continued to appear in state reports. By the early '50s the school was running a double shift, and there were discussions about the need for expansion.[20] Within a relatively short time, the question of how best to organize the area's rapidly growing schools demanded immediate attention.

In 1944 Howard McEachen arrived to serve as the rural secondary district's leader. He was an admirer of progressive superintendent Carlton Washburn's work in suburban Chicago, and local businessmen recruited him from downstate Pittsburg to strengthen local schools and promote the area's development. McEachen remained the district's superintendent for nearly a quarter century, overseeing its expansion and marshaling support for its eventual consolidation with local elementary schools. He was an experienced administrator interested in building a well-organized school system out of the area's patchwork of districts. From the beginning, it seems, he realized that the task would not be easy, but he had big plans and set about energetically pursuing them.[21]

Among the first problems McEachen faced was rapid expansion in the area's population. He had studied at Teachers College, Columbia University, and in 1952 he arranged for a team from that institution to conduct a survey of the district and make recommendations for its future. The visitors from New York examined many aspects of the local schools but focused on the area's growth, especially the many "households with small children." Moreover, they commented on the type of people who were moving to the district, and what it meant for the schools: "The people who have moved to Shawnee Mission have not done so because they sought the lowest cost housing and living conditions; they wanted something better. This desire for a higher standard of living should carry over to the school system, and from present evidence the people want exactly that."[22]

Calling on experts from afar, of course, was a tried-and-true strategy for tilting local opinion in favor of greater investment in education, but it was only partially successful in the case of Shawnee Mission. As McEachen no doubt anticipated, the Teachers College team called for integration of the existing twelve school systems into a single district, arguing its necessity for purposes of efficiency and consistency in programming and standards. Certain elementary districts rejected the idea, however, as an abrogation of local control, reflecting the long-standing principles of home rule that Nichols had promulgated. Other recommendations received a more positive reception. McEachen's former adviser Paul Mort led the team, which recommended establishing junior highs to relieve secondary enrollment pressure, and the eventual building of an additional high school as numbers increased.[23] After a period of discussion, local voters approved the junior high proposal by a 3–1 margin, including construction bonds totaling more than $6 million, and within a year the plan was put into action.[24] Shawnee Mission thus entered a period of rapid physical and geographic expansion, a time when it also would begin drawing national attention as a highly successful suburban school system. As suggested by reactions that greeted the recommendation to form a single district, however, finding a consensus on just how to organize such a system would not be easy.

Race, Education, and Suburban Affluence

The state line may have sheltered residents of Johnson County from racial strife on the Missouri side of greater Kansas City, but there was a history of local controversies over race and inequality to consider as well. African Americans had lived in the area since the nineteenth century, working on local farms and as domestics in more prosperous white households. While black and white children attended the same school for many years in Johnson County District No. 90, such integration ended in 1912, when whites moved to a larger, newer facility. As a result, the old building, named after businesswoman C. J. Walker, became the area's only segregated black institution. By the latter 1940s it served more than forty students in two classrooms, one of which was taught by an uncertified teacher. When the district built an even larger and more modern building for whites in 1947, the local black community objected to its much older, dilapidated facility. Boycotting the Walker School for more than a year, they enlisted the assistance of Esther Brown, a local Jewish housewife, who helped them to raise money and eventually take their complaints to the Kansas Supreme Court.

With assistance from the NAACP, in 1949 the case of *Webb v. School District No. 90* was decided in favor of the plaintiffs, ending segregated schooling in Johnson County and establishing an important local precedent for the *Brown v. Board* decision five years later.[25]

The successful challenge to segregated schooling in *Webb* soon meant that the Shawnee Mission Rural High School District became modestly integrated, to the extent that the one hundred or so black families who lived in the area represented a substantial minority population. But it did not mean that everyone was happy about it, or willing to abide by any measure of integration in other aspects of community life. It took nearly a decade for the city of Merriam to incorporate the African American neighborhoods, providing them fire and police protection, and they still had to petition to be included in the local water district. Black students interested in attending high school were bused to Sumner Academy in Kansas City, Kansas, until the *Webb* decision; by 1950 some twenty of them were enrolled in Shawnee Mission High. This was a small fraction of the school's student body, but more than could be found at most other suburban secondary institutions in the region. In this respect Johnson County was also a leader, however ambivalently. The area's black population did not grow appreciably in years to come, signaling continued opposition to residential and social integration; African Americans generally were not welcome.[26]

A revealing case of such racial exclusion occurred in Westwood, a small, middle-class enclave in the northeast corner of the county, set between affluent Nichols neighborhoods and Kansas City, Kansas. A black couple, both teachers in the Kansas City, Kansas, schools, purchased a home there in 1964 with the assistance of a third party. While they were moving in, several men approached and asked what they had paid for the house, and offered to buy it for more than twice the original cost. They were reluctant to comply but soon learned that they were required to live within the school district where they worked in any case. They subsequently sold the house to another black family, who eventually agreed to accept the terms extended to the previous buyers. Although the details of this transaction were not fully reported in the press, it was almost certainly the work of a local neighborhood association determined to prevent African Americans from moving into the area. The fact that the original buyers were solidly middle class and college educated apparently did not matter. The opposition they encountered involved neither threats of violence nor public protest. Instead, it was quiet but also quite effective. It was a clear example of how African Americans who might have imagined that Johnson County could be welcoming were met with determined opposition from local white homeowners. Judging from the area's very small black population throughout this period, less than 1 percent of the total, this approach to exclusion seems to have proved very effective.[27]

An incident such as this also sent a message to local real estate agents. If they were interested in remaining involved in the lucrative Johnson County housing market, they could not afford to represent African American home buyers. The *Kansas City Star* reported in 1968 that black families could not find a real estate agent to show them homes in Prairie Village or Mission, and those who managed to settle in other parts of the county were ignored by their white neighbors.[28] In 1970 Donald Sewing opened his office in Overland Park. Located in a bungalow, it quickly became an object of controversy. He reportedly received threats, and a smoke bomb was tossed through a window, causing little damage. Sewing managed to sell homes to a small number of black families in the area but ultimately proved unable to persuade enough white homeowners to list their properties to make the office viable. While hardly a major event in local history, this episode underscored the perception of African Americans that Johnson County was not a hospitable environment for them.

Although local authorities may not have exhibited the sort of explicitly antagonistic attitudes associated with certain communities across the border in Missouri, they clearly did little to encourage blacks to consider settling there. The area's comparatively high cost of living and its lack of proximity to black settlements on either side of the border certainly did not help. As a consequence, Johnson County, Kansas, remained overwhelmingly white throughout the long postwar era, without significant controversy over racial questions during the tumultuous 1960s and '70s. This, of course, was yet another factor that doubtlessly added to its appeal among prospective home buyers, particularly those new to the area and with children.[29]

A Local and National Leader

From an early point in the postwar era, Shawnee Mission High School began to gain a reputation for excellence, as did other schools in the communities it served. This may have been partly due to McEachen's leadership and publicity surrounding the Teachers College survey. Mostly, however, it was probably due to the school's association with such desirable communities as Mission Hills and Fairway, among others. As indicated in chapter 2, the area featured the highest concentration of college-educated parents in the region, which accounted for much of the success of its students. This was clearly evident as early as 1960, which means it had been building during the preceding decade. Those fortunate enough to attend the high school would rub shoulders with the sons and daughters of the affluent and socially prominent families in the premier Nichols developments. It did not take long for the real estate industry to recognize the potential appeal of this to prospective home buyers. Home advertisements in the *Kansas City Star* featured references to Shawnee Mission High more than any other school from the latter 1940s through most of the following decade. As one real estate agent put it in 1958, "Johnson County has the tops in schools."[30]

The rapid growth of area schools in the wake of suburban development gained attention across the metro area. In January 1955 the *Star* ran a story about the completion of Shawnee Mission's four new junior highs and the expansion plans of many of the area's elementary school buildings, also mentioning high school plans for the local parish in Roeland Park, St. Agnes.[31] Three years later another *Star* article described plans to add a second high school, highlighting the local support Shawnee Mission experienced at the time. Noting that the *Nation's Schools*, a trade magazine, had featured the district, the *Star* reporter marveled at the willingness of local residents to pay higher taxes and vote for bonds, and a dozen districts collaborating on a junior high curriculum. "They establish high standards of quality, space and design for their school buildings," he exclaimed, "and still pay all of their teachers and administrators top salaries."[32] In other words, education meant a great deal in this segment of metropolitan Kansas City, and its residents were prepared to support it generously.

The high level of fiscal support for schools in northeast Johnson County reflected the area's considerable wealth. As the *Star* noted, the district's assessed valuation was fourth-highest in the state, and it was increasing. Local household income at the end of the 1950s, the highest in the five-county metropolitan area, was nearly double the national average. The district's residents had higher levels of education, more white-collar workers, and greater home values than any other comparable area in the region. Located less than ten miles from downtown Kansas City, its communities attracted thousands of managers, professionals, and businessmen who commuted from the city center. Johnson County was the most rapidly developing residential area in greater Kansas City.[33] These were conditions that many people were beginning to associate with highly desirable suburban schools, and Shawnee Mission certain seemed to fit the bill.

If there was any doubt about the quality of Shawnee Mission as an educational institution, it was dispelled in the fall of 1957 when both *Time* and *Newsweek* magazines declared it one of the best thirty-eight high schools in the country, based on the number of Merit Scholarship finalists it enrolled that year. With twenty-one students in this category, Shawnee Mission tied with Kansas City's Southwest High, which was only about half as large, and had one more than Topeka High in the state capital, also featured on the list. Regardless of the proximity of these other institutions, Shawnee Mission's inclusion in this exceptional national group added significantly to its luster. It was a distinction that no other suburban institution in the metropolitan area could claim.[34] This could only make the district even more attractive to prospective home buyers interested in finding the very best schools for their children.

The year after Shawnee Mission received this recognition marked the end of an era, as the district opened its second high school in 1958, Shawnee Mission East. There was a debate about the name of the new school, with Shawnee Mission students petitioning McEachen and the board to give the new school a different name. They did not want their own institution to receive a new one, Shawnee Mission North. McEachen, on the other hand, argued that the new school would benefit from association with the Shawnee Mission reputation, and that his goal was to maintain the same level of excellence throughout the district. Consequently, the original high school became North, and its new sibling institution served the area's wealthiest communities, including Mission Hills and much of Prairie Village. With this development the high school district lost some of its cohesiveness, an eventuality that McEachen hoped to forestall with a common point of identity.[35] The dispute about school names, however, was yet another sign of rifts that would pose challenges in the years ahead.

Rapid growth characterized the years to follow. By 1960 the Shawnee Mission High School District enrolled more than eight thousand students and served an area population of over one hundred thousand. In two years enrollments increased by nearly 20 percent, as more families poured into the district's growing communities, especially to the west and south of the historic J. C. Nichols developments. A third high school, Shawnee Mission West, opened in 1963, and two others were established in 1966 and 1969, South and Northwest. By the latter date the general population of the district had doubled, and more than forty thousand students were enrolled in all of the area's public schools, nearly half in Shawnee Mission junior or senior high buildings. Altogether, the district embraced some seventy-four square miles, spanning the fashionable Nichols communities to the northeast and less exclusive, sparsely settled developments at its western edge. Although there was a long-standing pocket of black residents near the district's center, the entire area was overwhelmingly white and middle class.[36] Map 5.1 offers a depiction of the district at the peak of its enrollment in 1970, including its constituent communities and their schools.

There can be little doubt that the excellent reputation of the Shawnee Mission schools contributed to the area's growth. In 1970 a local newspaper reported that Shawnee Mission East was among the top ten schools in the country for National Merit semifinalists, and that nearly eight out of ten district graduates went to college. In the years to follow, the district enrolled more than three out of four Johnson County students, and some observers suggested that the schools added as much as 20 percent to local property values.[37] Only Wichita counted more high school students in Kansas, and Shawnee Mission

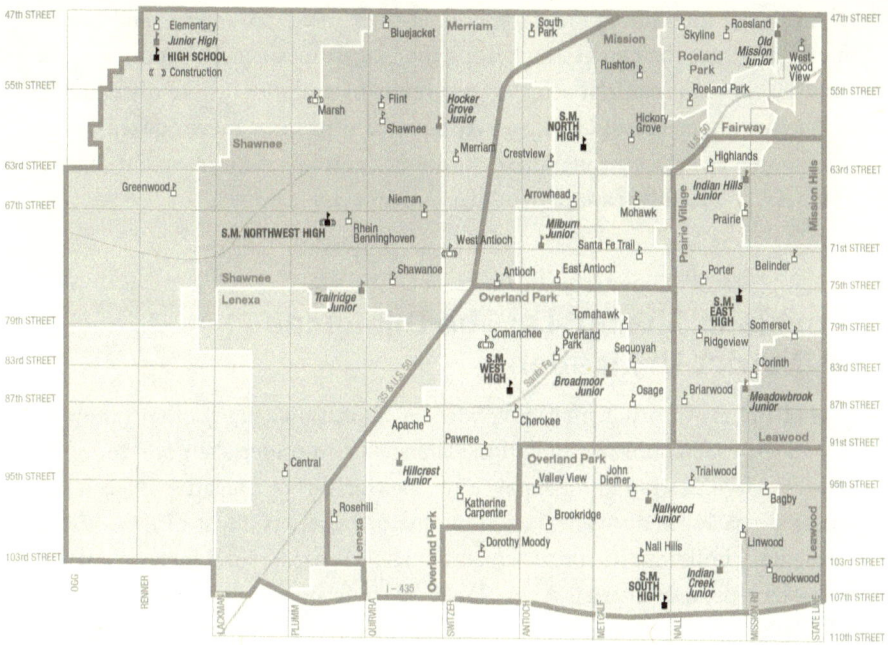

MAP 5.1 Communities and schools upon formation of the Shawnee Mission District, 1971. Heavy lines demarcate high school attendance areas, reflecting the more sparsely populated communities to the west.

had much higher taxable income and assessed valuation. Just two Kansas districts had greater household income levels, and both enrolled fewer than one hundred students. Household income also was higher than in any other Kansas City metropolitan district, on either side of the border. Even within Johnson County, Shawnee Mission income levels were double those of other districts.[38] From the standpoint of financial and academic resources, it was in a class by itself.

By the 1960s, real estate ads in the Kansas City newspapers featured fewer mentions of Shawnee Mission schools, perhaps because their reputation was so well known, and quality seemed similar throughout the district. This pointed to the success of McEachen's strategy of establishing Shawnee Mission's association with educational excellence. The district's standing was evident in teacher applications; in 1961 more than fifteen hundred applicants vied for forty-eight positions.[39] It was widely seen to be the best school system in the metropolitan area. Despite rapid growth, SMSD approached the pinnacle of achievement for an American suburban educational system. This was reflected in the local press; in 1967 the *Kansas City Star* ran an effusive six-part series on "the schools of northeast Johnson County," describing their many advantages and posing questions about their success.⁴⁰ Among the biggest problems, however, was the fact that they still had not achieved the status of a unified school district. The well-known high school district served an area with more than a dozen public educational agencies, posing questions about coordination in programs, hiring practices, and facility management that remained unanswered.

Trouble in Shangri-La: The Dilemma of District Unification

One of the major problems facing postwar Kansas, like many other midwestern states, was school consolidation. The state had undertaken one round of school reorganization immediately after the war, but by the latter 1950s it still counted nearly twenty-eight hundred separate districts, most of them single elementary buildings with rural constituencies. Separate rural high school districts served these districts, typically in sparsely populated areas. Following a failed attempt in 1961, the state legislature passed a measure calling again upon districts to consolidate. The goal was to make all of them larger than four hundred students, less than two hundred square miles in size, and with at least $2 million in assessed valuation. It was an act clearly aimed at the state's many tiny rural districts, but it also held important implications for northeast Johnson County.⁴¹

The school consolidation legislation required that all proposed mergers be approved by a majority of registered voters living in affected districts. This was meant to protect smaller districts from being compelled to join larger ones against the wishes of their constituents. In practice, it became a form of veto power in the hands of opponents to consolidation, but the state legislature made it clear that only unified school districts would be eligible for additional state aid. This proved a powerful incentive, and despite considerable opposition in the state's western districts, most did merge with others, reducing the total to just 311 by 1969. As a consequence, the average size of a Kansas school district rose from 167 students in 1958 to more than 1,700. By the later 1960s, enormous progress was made in bringing greater efficiency and uniformity to the state's public schools.⁴² The principal exception, however, was the twelve districts in northeast Johnson County, all operating within the attendance boundaries of Shawnee Mission's secondary schools.

School consolidation was controversial in rural areas, and not just in Kansas. Historians have documented the bitter disputes that it sparked in Iowa and other states.⁴³ But northeast Johnson County was quite unlike the rural districts that typically resisted such measures. As indicated earlier, many of its residents were affluent, highly educated, culturally sophisticated, and likely familiar with the principles of efficiency and standardization associated with school consolidation. The values of localism and home rule, however, became a counterweight. A study group of superintendents from the district had considered changes for the future in 1962 but expressed considerable skepticism about unification. "We do not agree," they wrote, "that weaknesses or inequities exist in all schools because of the reasons given in the state survey." They also rejected the idea that greater coordination was necessary to connect the area's high schools to the elementary districts, asserting "we fail to find in the schools of the Shawnee Mission District, any interruption in the educational program as children pass" from one level to the other.⁴⁴ Even though the report was only informational, such statements were a troubling portent.

The Kansas legislature took up school consolidation again in 1963. New regulations called for a planning committee in each of the state's counties, and a special one for the Shawnee Mission area, making a total of two in Johnson County. These were groups of local citizens, typically excluding educators and board members, charged with drawing up proposals for consolidation that voters could decide on. In the case of Shawnee Mission, the planning committee drafted a proposal to merge the area's twelve elementary districts with the Shawnee Mission High School District, and to call the newly consolidated system the Shawnee Mission School District. Despite objections from certain elementary boards and misgivings on the planning committee, recommendations seemed to proceed smoothly, and the local election was scheduled for June 2, 1964, in conjunction with similar ballots across the state.⁴⁵

On the eve of the voting it was difficult to predict the outcome in northeast Johnson County. The report of the planning committee noted the variability in programs and resources that existed across the twelve elementary districts, arguing that consolidation promised greater uniformity and coordination of resources and curricula. Supporters of the plan included Shawnee Mission district leaders, naturally, but also several area elementary boards, the League of Women Voters, and the *Kansas City Star*. On the other hand, at least five of the elementary boards passed resolutions opposing the plan, claiming that it did not make a clear case for the advantages of unification, and additional critics raised other objections, including concerns about rising costs. The *Star* reported that some observers predicted that the proposal would fail, noting the spontaneous applause that its opponents received from mothers at local information meetings. Despite this, there was no organized opposition spanning the area, and Shawnee

Mission officials suggested that unification was unavoidable even if local voters rejected it, because of sentiment in the state legislature. Once a majority of counties approved local plans, they believed it was only a matter of time before unified districts would be mandated everywhere.[46]

Local school leaders may have been prepared for a defeat in some of the area's elementary districts, but they doubtless were surprised by the one-sided tally when all ballots were counted. In a rather light turnout, voters rejected the plan to create a single school district by a nearly 2–1 margin, 5,733 to 2,954. While the vote was close but favorable in some of the western elementary districts, along with the older communities of Shawnee and Merriam, it failed heavily in others, including those where boards had opposed it. The local press provided daily coverage of the election but revealed only glimpses of the opposition. Much of it reportedly involved fears about loss of local control over the elementary schools that served the area's many separate municipalities. Some residents also expressed concern about the creation of a large district comprising more than forty schools and forty thousand students, fearing loss of "special programs" and "rapport between mothers and school officials." It was a big change from the highly localized, personal, and treasured experiences of schooling that many associated with their immediate communities. As much as residents valued the advantages of the Shawnee Mission's secondary schools, many felt no compelling reason to heed the call for system building.[47]

Given the criteria used by the state to guide consolidation, most districts in the area met basic requirements for independence in terms of enrollments and expanse and hence probably felt little urgency regarding unification. They all had sufficient resources, but some residents reportedly feared that joining the high school district would result in higher taxes by bringing all personnel under a single compensation plan. It is telling, however, that the core of opposition to the unification plan was located in the Roesland, Corinth, and Prairie elementary districts, along with District 110, which all served communities established by J. C. Nichols in the northeast quadrant of the area. This included Mission Hills, Prairie Village, Fairway, and Westwood, among others.[48]

These communities had a history of resistance to other forms of governmental unification and reorganization. A decade earlier citizens of Mission had resoundingly voted down a proposed merger with Roeland Park, which county officials hoped would lead to larger municipalities in the area.[49] In 1956 the mayor of Prairie Village rejected the idea of merging with other communities, noting that "Johnson County residents moved to escape large cities." Another proposal in 1957, to combine water districts, met "vigorous opposition to consolidation from councilmen in Mission Hills, Prairie Village, Fairway and Mission

Woods."[50] Many residents of these areas preferred government on a small scale and rejected efforts to create larger administrative entities, sentiments that apparently extended to the schools.

Elsewhere in the state, school consolidation met the greatest resistance in rural districts faced with the prospect of merging with adjacent urban areas. Voters in these areas often balked at paying for upgrades to local institutions in order to meet higher standards. On the other hand, consolidation succeeded in areas that had undergone significant population growth, and where the number of school districts was high, similar to system-building campaigns in the cities in earlier years.[51] Johnson County was the principal exception to both these rules. In the case of the proposed Shawnee Mission consolidation, it was the oldest, most urbanized areas that rejected unification and not the least-populated districts. Johnson County had more separate school districts (thirty-nine) than any other comparable part of the state, and one-third of them were within the boundaries of the Shawnee Mission High School District. Its population also was growing very rapidly. Given these circumstances and responses elsewhere, unification should have been approved handily.[52]

But despite complaints from planners and school officials, most people in the wealthiest portions of the proposed Shawnee Mission district were quite happy with the existing order of things. They apparently saw little advantage to creating common standards and expectations across area schools, or reorganizing administrative systems for greater uniformity. And some worried that consolidation would mean loss of control and a new school bureaucracy, a big change from the intimate connections that many felt with local institutions. Boards of local residents governed the elementary districts, fostering a sense of familiarity and informality that many in these communities did not want to lose.[53] Notwithstanding arguments about the need for a more coherent organization of schooling, they had little interest in pursuing a best or better system. Their affluence undoubtedly made the prospect of state aid for area schools less alluring as well.

The lopsided negative vote appears to have caught school leaders off guard, creating considerable uncertainty about just how to proceed. Initially there was talk of holding another election, but the state attorney general's office ruled that a second ballot would have to consider a different proposal, such as organizing the district some other way. Some voices called for breaking the secondary district into pieces, perhaps four or five, each with its own high school, to form smaller unified districts. "We all wanted more local control," declared one representative of an elementary district, "and [this plan] comes closest to that." Expressing a fear of centralized control that would have been quite uncharacteristic of affluent school patrons fifty years earlier, she added, "in my opinion, a 9-member single unified board puts too much power in the hands of too few people." Other opponents of unification were more plainspoken, outraged at the prospect of having their views ignored. "We're having unification rammed down our throats," declared one, "and we should have a chance to vote whether or not we want it." When the local election's negative vote did not settle the question, it seemed that the democratic process had been thwarted, contributing to indignation. But no one seemed to know what to do next.[54]

The unification planning committee rejected the idea of breaking the district into pieces, as did Shawnee Mission's board and administration, along with other proponents of the original unification plan.[55] The result was an impasse that lasted for several years. Many observers dismissed the idea of a second vote, describing it as "doomed to defeat," and an alternative plan was slow to develop.[56] Opponents of unifying the area's elementary districts with Shawnee Mission had succeeded in blocking the initial proposal for a single school system. Whether they could ultimately prevail in staving off consolidation altogether, however, was another question.

The initial wave of school consolidation ballots across the state of Kansas in 1964 turned out to be momentous, as voters in thirty-four counties approved the formation of unified districts. The other districts in Johnson County unified quite readily. Elsewhere patrons of particular schools objected to consolidation plans and eventually negotiated more acceptable terms of unification, and in some instances unification proposals—as in Shawnee Mission—were rejected outright.[57] The direction of change was clear, however, and within several years the vast majority of the state's districts had been reorganized. These new school systems were assigned the title Unified School District (USD) with three-digit numbers starting with 100 and counting up in order of their dates of formation. As more districts moved ahead in the process, it appeared that the plan for rationalizing and simplifying the state's educational system was a success.[58] By 1968 just a few areas had managed to avoid consolidation, and the largest one by far was in northeast Johnson County.[59] Shawnee Mission was the last big piece preventing the school organization puzzle from being completed, and it turned out to be a complicated one.

Given the resoundingly negative result of the SMSD unification ballot, the state legislative delegation from Johnson County was reluctant to endorse a move by the legislature to require unification of area districts. Local resistance continued to be evident in 1968, when a bill was introduced to force the remaining unconsolidated districts in the state to complete the amalgamation process. At least two elementary districts, Prairie and Roesland, issued statements calling for another election to approve new consolidation plans. Proponents of alternative proposals bandied them about, but none could gain support of a majority of the districts. Like opponents of unification elsewhere, protesters complained about the idea of a single district being "forced" on them.[60] Once again, they expressed fears about "losing identity in a larger district," and rising taxes, especially for funds to pay for schools in other communities.[61] Local legislators heard appeals for one plan or another, sharply dividing some communities. But others in Topeka were losing patience with the "emotionalism" opposing unification in the last major area in the state to complete the process.[62]

As legislation to require unification moved forward in 1968, Shawnee Mission leaders asked for additional time to commission a study. They feared that simply mandating consolidation could inflame its opponents, creating bitterness that would last for years. Consequently, a "national consulting firm" conducted a survey to make recommendations about how best to organize the local schools. The final report, written by Emerson Mitchell, a New York expert on school board organization, called for the formation of a single unified district, quite similar to the proposal voted down in 1964. Although opponents of unification criticized it, the report provided local legislators with a rationale to go forward with consolidation.[63] A complex process of negotiation resulted in a "compromise" plan, calling for a board elected partly from five attendance areas and establishing "local advisory boards" to ensure greater "neighborhood voice."[64] This unique governance structure proved acceptable to a number of opponents to consolidation. Although considerable unhappiness about it still existed, there was little the opposition could do. The acceptance of unification elsewhere, the failure of alternative proposals, and action in the state legislature all contributed to a sense of inevitability in the decision. Finally, in 1971, a special act of the legislature created the consolidated Shawnee Mission School District, USD 512—the highest-numbered public school district in the state.[65]

Unification took longer to accomplish than local leaders had planned, but the new district emerged as the leading suburban school system in the metropolitan area and probably the best in Kansas academically. Skeptics continued to express doubts about the wisdom of turning their cherished local schools over to such a big organization, and predictions of tax increases turned out to be prescient in several of the elementary districts, as teacher and administrator pay scales were standardized and facilities were improved. Howard McEachen retired in 1967, and it is possible that his departure defused some of the controversy over unification. His successor, Arzel Ball, brought a somewhat different style of leadership and a sense of openness to innovation.[66] The district remained one of the wealthiest in the nation, and overall levels of satisfaction with its schools were high. The years to come would bring further change, and although few may have realized it at the time, unification was just one step in an ongoing series of conflicts. New challenges lay ahead.

The End of an Era: Decline and Displacement

Despite predictions of continued growth that alarmed opponents of unification, Shawnee Mission experienced declining numbers of students during the 1970s, along with controversies over school closings and reductions in staff. This occurred in other districts too and was principally due to the end of the baby-boom era, when diminishing birthrates led to smaller school-age cohorts.[67] It was a new experience for most residents of northeast Johnson County, however, as their numbers had increased for more than twenty-five years, often rapidly. Perhaps even more disconcerting, new residential development shifted south of the district, especially after large office complexes appeared there in the 1980s. The rise of Overland Park as the county's principal economic engine, with a growing downtown business center just beyond the district's southern boundary, signaled a new chapter in local history.

These changes, however, did not alter the concerns that opponents of the district's unification had expressed, and rancor continued to exist. In 1973 Representative Earl Ward of Mission Hills introduced a bill in the legislature to break the district into five smaller ones, each with a high school. "There are a lot of people living in the district who think they don't have control over their school matters anymore," he declared, and he also reported considerable unhappiness with rising taxes. Superintendent Ball intimated that Ward's constituents were concerned about paying for schools in the growing western reaches of the district, highlighting tensions that had long existed. But the controversy also pointed to the aging population in the wealthiest communities, perhaps contributing to less interest in the schools.[68] Eventually the emergence of the Blue Valley School District to its south would challenge Shawnee Mission's status as the region's premier school district. Serving much of Overland Park and Leawood, Blue Valley began developing a reputation as the metropolitan area's most academically high-performing system in the 1980s.[69]

Enrollment losses are always difficult for school systems, but the experience turned out to be especially trying for Shawnee Mission. Many of its patrons continued to view schools as vital local institutions, and this provoked sharp opposition to school closings. In particular, area residents aggressively resisted the suggestion that neighborhood schools should be shuttered. Protests of school closings are commonplace, but in Shawnee Mission it was particularly contentious. As before, the reaction appeared most visibly in the district's older, more affluent neighborhoods. Residents filed lawsuits to prevent any buildings being closed without a vote of affected patrons, which would effectively block the closings. It turned out that the legislation creating the district did not clearly establish its authority to close schools without such votes, and the threat of legal action was successful in blocking district plans.[70] Protesters were unmoved by arguments citing the inefficiency of low-enrollment schools, some noting that enrollments had been low before the district's unification, and no one had suggested closings then. They also argued that smaller classes contributed to a higher-quality educational experience. When the district suggested that some facilities were outdated or in ill repair, parents hired their own consultants to evaluate the buildings and disputed the board's claims. Once again, there was a strong tendency to view local educational institutions in largely proprietary terms and to depict district leadership as a threat to neighborhood prerogatives.[71]

Eventually district leaders had to turn again to the state legislature for a special bill authorizing them to close schools without a vote of local constituents, a power normally granted to urban districts but not rural ones. Here, too, the tentativeness of legislators pointed to the range of reactions these questions spawned in particular communities. Constituents felt protective of neighborhood institutions and often viewed the district as usurping local authority. In the eyes of some, it was an example of big government at work on a local scale. If they were being asked to pay such high taxes, many asked, why were they being told that their schools had to be closed? As a board member pointed out at the time, the closings affected less than 3 percent of the district's students, yet the protests effectively stymied the district's authority. It took several years for Shawnee Mission to finally gain approval to close schools without a local referendum, once again through special legislation in Topeka.[72]

Yet other signs of restiveness appeared. In the 1980s a levy ballot was somewhat close for the first time in district history, apparently because older residents in wealthy Mission Hills and surrounding communities voted against it. Many of these households no longer had children living at home or attending public schools, and some doubtless were disenchanted with recent conflicts over school closings. New superintendent Raj Chopra noted that younger families with children were moving into neighborhoods to the south, particularly the more rapidly growing developments in Leawood and Overland Park, mostly served by Blue Valley schools.[73] Once the premier school system of the region, Shawnee Mission was racked by conflict and dissension and was losing population to neighboring districts that did not have to contend with such contentious issues.

Despite these problems and reports that the district was losing status, it had not declined as much as some constituents may have feared. Its schools were still widely admired, and even after the school closings they were widely considered to be among the best in the region. In the early 1980s the district won national recognition for its board and leadership, and three-quarters of its students exceeded national norms on achievement tests.[74] But there can be no question that other parts of Johnson County began to rival it, both in terms of school quality and in general measures of community affluence, civic involvement, and political influence. The political infighting had done little to advance the district to new heights of distinction, and as Johnson County's population continued to expand in the 1980s and beyond, new centers of scholastic excellence were destined to emerge.[75]

The Shawnee Mission Experience in Perspective

Northeast Johnson County developed as a patchwork of communities, reflecting a variety of income and social status positions ranging from very affluent to merely middle class. It also was a hodgepodge of small school districts, dating to the years when the area was principally rural and agricultural. This system of highly localized governance and community control contributed to high levels of financial support for the schools and parental involvement in education. But considerable inequality existed between communities, and this created the possibility of dissension as well; status distinctions divided the district. As communities grew in the 1950s and '60s, both because of rapid in-migration and the baby boom, schools expanded and new buildings were erected to keep pace. But not everyone agreed that creating a single comprehensive public education system was desirable. High-status residents of the J. C. Nichols communities apparently had doubts about it, even though they included significant numbers of the greater Kansas City social and economic elite. As controversies over district unification and school closings suggested, the size of the system and loss of control proved disconcerting to many area residents, especially those who valued local prerogatives. Unlike earlier generations of metropolitan elites, they were not proponents of bureaucratic efficiency and expert control. They preferred local authority in school affairs and resisted plans to establish a highly centralized and professionalized administrative structure for the district as a whole.[76]

As reported in chapter 2, sociologists Basil Zimmer and Amos Hawley found that affluent suburbanites in large urbanized areas during the later 1960s experienced a "localization of daily life" that influenced their attitudes about consolidation of governmental authority. Compared to city residents, or even suburbanites in less affluent communities, those living in wealthy areas like northeast Johnson

County expressed the greatest opposition to the consolidation of local institutions or service organizations. This was especially true regarding schools, an issue that produced the greatest divergence in urban/suburban attitudes measured by Zimmer and Hawley's survey. Highly educated, affluent suburbanites heavily favored local control of schools, without state or federal involvement, and were willing to pay higher taxes to support them.[77] As the Shawnee Mission experience demonstrated, they even resisted consolidation with other suburban schools. They preferred small, intimate education organizations, where direct involvement and influence in academic issues could be realized most easily. For many of these suburbanites, schools became an amenity reflected in the price of a new home, analogous to a membership in the local country club. Consolidation threatened that, even if it promised to strengthen the educational system and ultimately improve outcomes for greater numbers of children.

As suggested earlier, the controversies in Shawnee Mission exhibited political dynamics similar to those described by historians in other suburbs during this era. Like the affluent suburbanites who expressed outrage at the prospect of their children being bused in the South, or the "suburban warriors" who dominated school board elections in Southern California, they viewed the schools as part and parcel of the life they purchased in these communities. They actively opposed proposals that appeared to threaten or compromise local control of these resources, including racial integration on a large scale. The resistance of area school leaders to the 1977 metropolitan school coordination plan offered by the Kansas and Missouri advisory committees of the US Commission on Civil Rights was yet another example of this type of response. As such conflicts demonstrated, these suburbanites had little interest in suggestions that schools should serve such larger purposes as promoting greater social understanding or bridging the racial and socioeconomic divisions that fractured most metropolitan areas.[78] They were even opposed to arguments based on the need for creating uniform standards of performance and greater efficiency, ideas that had animated earlier generations of affluent metropolitan residents. Instead, they favored local autonomy, the preservation of neighborhood values, and the full utilization of proximate resources for the schools, even at greater cost. At bottom, it was an attitude fundamentally at odds with the ideal of "equality of opportunity," reflecting wider conflicts in American culture at the time. It also was a repudiation of bureaucratic, professional principles that had guided the development of American public education for most of the twentieth century, even if it did not ultimately succeed in the case of Shawnee Mission.

In the end, the development of SMSD was symptomatic of social and cultural forces then shaping the development of high-status suburban school districts. Howard McEachen's insistence on maintaining a common Shawnee Mission identity for all the area's secondary schools, and the importance of the district's reputation for local residential development, established a logic of consolidation that promised to extend benefits to some areas at the expense of others. Those with the least to gain from this change, the prosperous communities whose educational and cultural advantages were already clearly established, resisted it the most. Some objected to paying for schools in neighboring communities and may have resented sending money to Topeka to support schools elsewhere. And they were often unhappy with a district leadership seen as remote and bureaucratic. These constituents rejected the administrative cult of efficiency, wanting to maintain a suburban idyll that preserved localist privileges. The fact that they failed to stop the district's formation does not diminish the significance of their resistance. Their dogged commitment to localism signaled a distinctive logic regarding public education, linking it firmly to a particular place and proximate control.

Shawnee Mission may have been unique in the state of Kansas, both with respect to its degree of wealth and the severity of local opposition to consolidation, but it reflected impulses that were evident elsewhere in greater Kansas City. Localist initiatives surged in other local suburban districts. But a state legislature focused on rural school consolidation, and unwilling to countenance affluent suburban preferences, constrained resistance to change in Johnson County. Even so, conflicts along the lines of social class and income continued to be evident for many years, reflecting community distinctions that J. C. Nichols had established decades earlier. As indicated earlier, race did not appear to have been a critical factor in these events, despite the significant role that racial exclusion played in the immediate area's development. Indeed, the foregoing suggests that racial conflict was not a necessary component of localist perspectives on schooling in the suburbs.

Many observers celebrated the success of Shawnee Mission's schools, but gaining consensus on the district's policy priorities and any number of other questions proved extremely difficult (and often remains so today). Shawnee Mission suffered from a fractured education polity, defined by the particular cultural and economic identities of the places its residents called home. This, of course, was contrary to long-standing principles of shared public responsibility in schooling and the democratic ideals of the common school, not to mention the mechanisms of bureaucratic control and centralized authority. As such, it foreshadowed the widening social and economic inequality that came to increasingly characterize education in American metropolitan life in years to come.

Epilogue

AN ENDURING LEGACY OF INEQUALITY

In the fall of 2016 newly appointed Kansas City, Missouri, Public Schools superintendent Mark Bedell presided at a celebratory event staged to announce that, for the first time in nearly three decades, the district had scored high enough on the state's evaluation metrics to be eligible for full accreditation. State officials were a bit less sanguine, however, stating that another year's worth of data would be necessary to determine if the district's gains represented sustainable progress. Even so, it was a hopeful moment for a school system that had long struggled with enrollment losses, dismal test scores, and staff turnover.[1] In most important respects, KCMPS never recovered from the crisis of the later 1970s, when white flight escalated and the *Jenkins v. Missouri* desegregation case took center stage.

When Bedell arrived in Kansas City, KCMPS schools enrolled about fifteen thousand students, fewer than half the number in 1980, and charter schools served some ten thousand additional children and youth in the district.[2] Suburban districts had grown, especially those farther from the city; Johnson County schools alone enrolled more than one hundred thousand students. School systems north of the river and in eastern Jackson County also had gotten bigger. Some of this was due to continued population movement out of the central city, a long-standing national trend, but it also represented a sustained lack of confidence in the city schools. They remained failed institutions in the eyes of many across the region.[3]

KCMPS's loss of provisional accreditation in 2011 became national news, but it also triggered alarm through the metropolitan area.[4] Under Missouri law, families living within the district's boundaries could send their children to adjacent systems, with the cost borne by KCMPS. Local commentators labeled the anticipated budgetary impact on city schools as "crippling," and suburban districts balked at the prospect of poor minority students arriving on their doorsteps. Area school boards and superintendents urged state officials "to reward Kansas City for its recent progress and give it provisional accreditation." Suburban school leaders were deeply ambivalent about accepting children from the inner city, despite the prospect of gaining additional funds for new students and an opportunity to serve a more diverse population.[5] Several districts subsequently mounted legal challenges to the state's transfer rules.[6] In this respect little had changed since the Spainhower controversies of the later 1960s, even if the rhetoric was far less inflammatory. Status distinctions between suburban and urban schools remained largely intact, and many suburbanites wanted to keep it that way.

Kansas City was not unusual in this regard. Across the state in metropolitan St. Louis, white suburban residents protested at the prospect of African American students transferring to their institutions when the struggling Normandy school district also lost its accreditation. In a scene reminiscent of Raytown more than forty years earlier, a raucous crowd in a school gym cheered when one parent declared herself "concerned about my children's education and safety," evoking stereotypes of black students as low achieving and violence prone. As in Kansas City, suburban districts resisted the idea of accommodating African American students seeking a better education. Eventually, students who had found placements in adjacent districts were required to return to Normandy when its schools regained provisional accreditation.[7]

Elsewhere, predominantly white and affluent areas within racially diverse school districts have attempted to split away by forming their own school systems. This has occurred chiefly in the South, where many districts are organized on a county-wide basis, but it represented a localizing impulse similar to that observed in Kansas City. In most of these cases, whites sought to create boundaries that would exclude poor and minority students from gaining access to their schools.[8] These instances offer compelling evidence that potent forms of localism continue to function nearly a half century after the controversies described in this book.

National statistics on the distribution of population within metropolitan areas indicate that suburbanization has continued to be a defining force in the spatial organization of institutions and opportunity. While 40 percent of metropolitan residents lived in central cities in 1980, and they held 50 percent of all metropolitan jobs, by 1990 those numbers had fallen to 37 percent and 45 percent respectively. The latter figure was especially significant, as it marked the first time that most metropolitan employment was found in the suburbs. These distributions have proved persistent, as the suburbs continue to count most of the nation's metropolitan residents and jobs today. Following a relatively brief shift in growth to central cities after the recession of 2008, in recent years suburbanization has resumed, especially at the outer extremities of larger metropolitan areas.[9] In this respect, the postwar era's dramatic changes in the geo-spatial organization of metropolitan life continue to be manifest. For better or worse, the United States has become a largely suburban nation.

These developments inevitably affected schools, as a suburban education advantage remains evident in most metropolitan areas, especially larger ones. Much of it, moreover, was linked to deteriorating conditions in the cities. The closing years of the twentieth century witnessed a deepening crisis of urban education. A 1996 report from the National Center for Educational Statistics (NCES) found that "urban children were more than twice as likely to be living in poverty than those in suburban locations (30 percent compared with 13 percent in 1990)." It added that "urban students were more likely to be exposed to safety and health risks that place their health and well-being in jeopardy, and were less likely to have access to regular medical care," while also being more likely to engage in such risky behaviors as unmarried teen pregnancy.[10] As poverty became more pervasive in the cities, other social problems mounted.

City schools often struggled in the wake of these challenges, especially in hyper-segregated African American communities such as Kansas City's. Urban institutions generally reported the lowest achievement levels and highest dropout rates in the country.[11] The NCES report indicated that standardized test scores in high-poverty schools were 20 percent lower on average than those in more affluent institutions, in both urban and suburban settings. Perhaps even more disturbing, less than three-quarters of urban high school students graduated on time, compared to 84 percent of suburban students, which also reflected differences between high- and low-poverty institutions. High-poverty urban high schools reported the lowest graduation rates; only about two-thirds of their students finished in four years. Most of these schools, furthermore, were predominantly or wholly African American, typically in settings of extreme deprivation.[12]

Sociologist William Julius Wilson has argued that most of this inequality was due to growing "concentrated poverty," when the number of households below the federal poverty line approached 40 percent. Wilson and other social scientists attributed this to the profound impact of unemployment in these neighborhoods. This was a problem during the 1960s and '70s, but it grew worse in many respects with time. The ongoing flight of industrial jobs led to massive job losses, aggravating racial segregation, deprivation, and delinquency. The neighborhoods most directly affected were principally African American, as housing and employment discrimination made it difficult for blacks to follow jobs to the suburbs. Debilitating poverty also inhibited movement out of ghetto neighborhoods. As work disappeared, conventional social norms often shifted, family structures fractured, and troublesome behavior mounted. In particular, the sale and use of illicit drugs became more widespread, especially following the onset of the so-called crack epidemic of the 1980s. Rising arrests and harassment by police did not help matters and in many instances aggravated them. And these were events that affected young people disproportionately.[13] It is little wonder that urban graduation rates stagnated and achievement levels lagged national norms.

In the wake of these developments city residents continued to depart for surrounding suburban communities, including African Americans with the means to do so. As in earlier years, they wanted newer houses, more property, and other amenities of suburban life, but schools continued to be an attraction too. This resulted in a higher degree of socioeconomic variety in the suburbs, with certain areas becoming predominantly black. Demographer William Frey has identified many "melting pot suburbs," although relatively few had large African American populations.[14] Much of this change appeared in western states, where a growing Latino population contributed to diversified suburbs. Substantial numbers of Asian Americans lived in these areas too. There was greater black suburbanization in the South, but considerably less elsewhere. In older metropolitan areas of the Northeast and Midwest, suburbs remained predominantly white, with isolated pockets of racial and ethnic diversity.[15]

While suburban schools generally benefited from comparisons to urban institutions, relatively few earned reputations for consistently high levels of achievement. Some districts, typically white and affluent, had long been known for academic excellence, such as Shawnee Mission in greater Kansas City. Writing in the 1990s, economists Peter Mieszkowski and Edwin Mills observed that "once high-quality school districts became established, they became magnets for further suburbanization and attracted other households that placed a high value on education, furthering their quality and reputation."[16] In other words, ostensibly excellent suburban schools typically attracted the types of families whose children assured their continued success. In this fashion, localized centers of educational distinction continued to dot the metropolitan landscape, contributing to the aura of suburban superiority, even if a limited number of districts enjoyed such prominence. At the same time, of course, the allure of academic reputations added to internecine suburban rivalry, occasionally fueling a lively status competition.[17]

As metropolitan population expanded, considerable variation appeared in school characteristics and outcomes, especially in so-called inner suburbs. While few suburban institutions experienced the problems of urban ghettos, new pockets of poverty did pose challenges to the suburban image. Certain communities experienced conditions similar to inner-city neighborhoods, such as Compton in California, Ford Heights in Illinois, or Paterson in New Jersey, to name a few. Most were predominantly African American and were located close to central cities, or in so-called satellite cities at some distance. As the suburbs became more variegated, these places defied conventional stereotypes about the schools, but they also represented exceptions to the rule.[18] The majority of suburban schools have remained predominantly white and middle class. This was especially true in outlying communities, as most minority families leaving the central cities found homes where costs were lower and housing more readily accessible. While most African Americans who made such moves did experience a better standard of living than those who remained in central cities, their children often encountered problems in suburban schools. This was especially true in predominantly white institutions, where problems related to academic tracking and racially disproportionate discipline came into play. Thus, although more poor and minority families left the cities following the 1980s, many continued to experience discrimination and exclusion. And general perceptions of suburban advantage remained secure.[19]

The tendency to favor suburban schools continued to be robust in the twenty-first century, despite a renewed interest in urban living among younger, well-educated whites. Spurred by the "Great Recession," city growth surpassed suburban areas nationally for a time after 2010, leading James E. Ryan, Richard Florida, and other observers to declare a potential revitalization of the larger cities. But this shift in urban fortunes did not endure, and by 2017 momentum had swung back to the suburbs.[20]

It appears that many young urban residents longed to own a home and enjoy the comforts of suburban life, and city schools also may have been an important factor in their thinking. Most did not have children when moving to the cities, but when offspring did enter the picture, these families often relocated to different school districts. Sociologist Ann Owens has demonstrated that improved educational opportunities became a decisive factor in many such decisions.[21] Urban school systems offered special schools and magnet programs to retain students, but the opportunities that these institutional options represented were limited in number. In the end, city schools continued to find it difficult to compete with suburban institutions on a large scale.[22]

The movement of young, successful professionals into the cities may not have restored the former glory of urban school systems, but it occasionally did create pockets of affluence within them. It thus became more commonplace to find particular neighborhoods with better-performing schools and other amenities. This, along with the deepening poverty and related problems in highly segregated black communities, resulted in widening inequality within the cities, too. Rising arrest rates for black males, along with a corresponding increase in female-headed households, made inner-city deprivation even worse.[23] As Richard Florida has recently documented, indices of dissimilarity along lines of income and wealth have increased in the nation's major cities during the past decade.[24] Similar trends have been evident in the suburbs as well, with communities farthest from central cities exhibiting greater affluence than many inner-ring suburbs. The result has been rising metropolitan geo-spatial inequality, including inequity between cities and their surrounding suburbs.[25]

In the wake of these changes, distinctions between urban and suburban schools continued to be readily evident. Examining test data from 2004, sociologist John Logan and his collaborators found substantial differences between urban and suburban institutions, most of which were associated with poverty, parental education, and other socioeconomic factors. And variation between schools was substantial indeed. Some 60 percent of urban schools were classified as "high poverty, with more than 55 percent of their students eligible for free or reduced lunch subsidies (FRL), compared to 26 percent of suburban schools." On the other hand, just 17 percent of urban schools were judged low poverty, with less than 25 percent FRL eligible, compared to 42 percent of suburban districts. These differences contributed to a clear suburban advantage in achievement results, both in math and reading, largely due to geo-spatial sorting of students by income and parental education. Race was a factor too, although highly correlated with poverty.[26]

In a different line of inquiry, researchers at Johns Hopkins University reported that the number of high schools with "the lowest level of success in promoting freshmen to senior status on time" had increased by 75 percent in the decade following 1993. Labeling these institutions "dropout factories," the authors declared that "graduating is at best a 50/50 proposition" for their students. Not surprisingly, most such schools were found in larger cities, serving predominantly poor neighborhoods and a principally black or Latinx clientele.[27] Once again, this designation highlighted the problems facing urban institutions, reinforcing the impression of suburban educational advantages that most Americans continued to harbor.

To summarize, little has occurred in the past four decades to change prevailing public attitudes about the status of metropolitan educational institutions. This is testimony to the enduring images that still distinguish urban and suburban communities after the dramatic shifts of the postwar era. Big cities may have represented the height of wealth and cultural sophistication during the 1950s, but they were eclipsed by suburbs in the decades to follow. Suburban ascendancy was well established by 1980, abetted to no small degree by the readily apparent superiority of schools and other local institutions. These impressions were amplified by conflicts over school desegregation and housing, and found widespread expression in the popular media. Events in the intervening years have continued to reinforce such associations more or less continually up to the present. Developments in greater Kansas City, in that case, represented a much more widespread and sustained pattern of metropolitan growth and social change. The advent of a profoundly deep and debilitating urban poverty, affecting African Americans in particular, and the growth of affluent and largely white suburban communities marked a change in metropolitan life that has proved enduring.

Continuity and Change in Metropolitan Kansas City

If suburban advantages in schooling and many other facets of life continued to be evident nationally, they certainly remained palpable in Kansas City. School district boundaries became crucial markers of social status and racial exclusion in the 1960s and '70s and continued to be salient decades later. At the same time, growing numbers of African Americans and members of other minority groups found their way across these lines, especially in districts to the south of the city center. In this respect, Kansas City came to exhibit a pattern of change emblematic of the era. Putatively inner-ring suburbs, most within municipal Kansas City, Missouri, witnessed a racial transition as African American families began arriving in greater numbers. Some of these areas eventually became predominantly black, as many whites moved out—or ceased to move in—and property values declined. Since most such changes took place within the city, it may be apposite to say that formerly "suburban" districts "became urban."[28]

Black population movement continued after 1980, and within several decades African American settlement extended nearly to the city's southern border. As indicated on map E.1, in the years following 2013 black households were located throughout the metropolitan area but remained clustered on the city's south side. This meant that school districts that previously had excluded blacks began to serve a rapidly diversifying clientele. Hickman Mills was predominantly African American by that time, and Raytown—once an epicenter of racial exclusion—served a sizable black population. The movement of more affluent blacks to the east of Raytown, into Independence, Lee's Summit, and Blue Springs, is a hopeful sign of improved racial tolerance and integration. Indeed, by 2017 the region's segregation index had dropped 15 percent since 2000, among the largest such shifts in the country.[29] Even so, most of the region's African American residents remained grouped in census tracts where they represented a clear majority, and there has been mounting evidence of racial tensions in the suburbs. The black population in central city neighborhoods declined somewhat, shifting to the south and east. Like other metropolitan areas, Kansas City had acquired a sizable black middle class, along with somewhat lower levels of residential segregation, but concentrated poverty continued to be evident as well.[30]

Meanwhile, most of Johnson County and North Kansas City remained predominantly white. The dynamics of racial integration, constrained by barriers

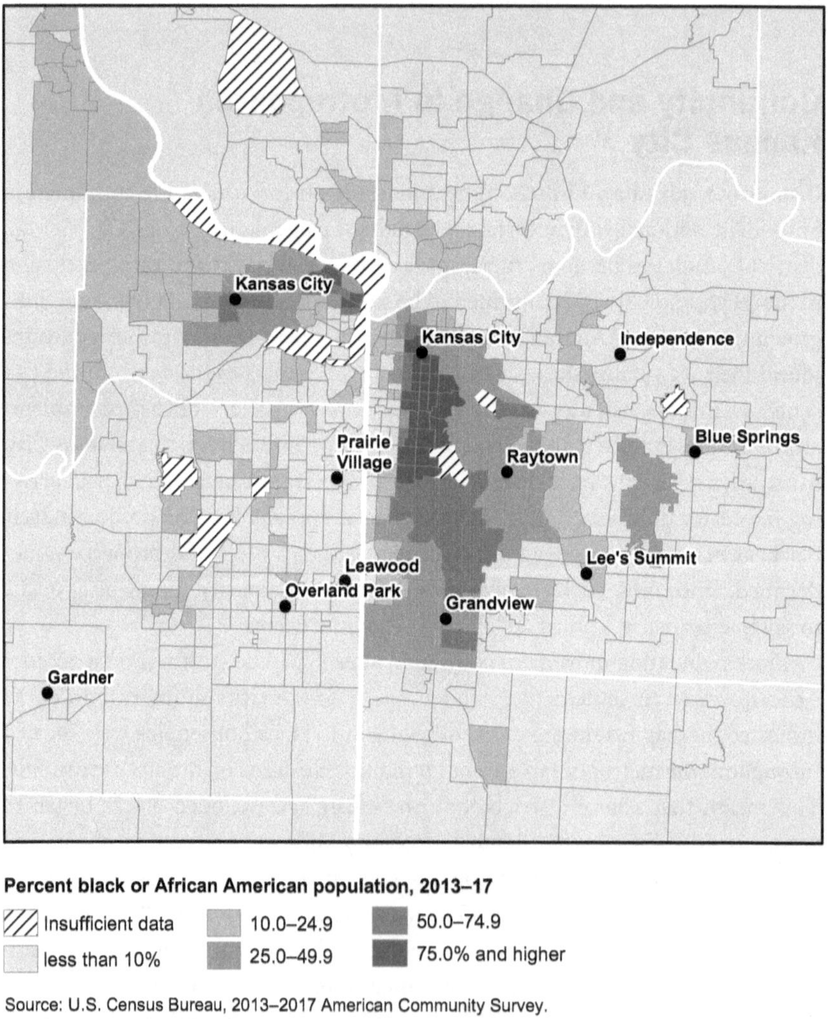

Percent black or African American population, 2013–17

▨ Insufficient data	10.0–24.9	50.0–74.9
less than 10%	25.0–49.9	75.0% and higher

Source: U.S. Census Bureau, 2013–2017 American Community Survey.

MAP E.1 Metropolitan Kansas City African American population, 2013–2017 census tract averages (American Community Survey)

such as the river or the state line, continued to reflect concerns that influenced earlier generations of blacks in assessing the metropolitan landscape. They did not see these parts of greater Kansas City as welcoming, Johnson County in particular. Despite the efforts of Donald Sewing and other middle-class African Americans decades earlier, that affluent and highly educated corner of the region continued to evade meaningful racial integration. While its black population grew to 4 percent by 2010, it was the lowest level of the area's principal counties. The absence of African Americans was especially evident in the older J. C. Nichols communities of Prairie Village and Mission Hills, long known as fashionable enclaves with a somewhat liberal social orientation. The fact that so few blacks lived in these neighborhoods almost certainly was not an accident.

The same was undoubtedly true of communities north of the river, many of which were considerably more affordable than stylish Johnson County. The black population of Clay County in 2010 was just 5 percent, despite its proximity to the city center. The presence of so few black families in the Northland also suggested they were not generally welcomed there, likely reflecting the reluctance of real estate agents to show them homes. And within the urban core, the legendary Troost Wall was still clearly evident in 2010. While blacks had moved into census tracts west of Troost to the north of Forty-Seventh Street and south of Seventy-Fifth, prosperous neighborhoods around the Country Club Plaza and Brookside continued to count relatively few of them. This too was not a coincidence; neighborhood associations likely remained vigilant there too, keeping real estate agents in line regarding sales to those deemed undesirable.[31]

The geo-spatial distribution of poverty adds another dimension to these matters. As indicated in map E.2, the greatest concentration of household deprivation affecting children remained in the city's oldest African American neighborhoods to the east of Troost, extending directly to the south of the city center. Census tracts extending into the Raytown and Hickman Mills school districts exhibited somewhat lower numbers of poor households, but still well above the national average. This included areas of black settlement and portions of the south "suburban" districts that resisted African American settlement in the 1960s and '70s. Lower poverty rates represented evidence of the black middle class, which had moved out of older black neighborhoods to the south and east. One of the highest concentrations of poverty households existed in the southwest corner of Jackson County, where more than 60 percent of the families in one census tract reported income below the federal poverty threshold. Interestingly, a significant number of whites lived in these neighborhoods as well, representing about a quarter of the population. In these parts of the region, it seems, concentrated poverty did not affect only African American children.[32]

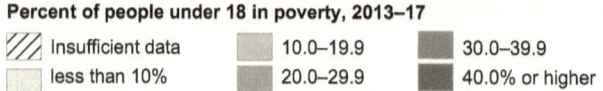

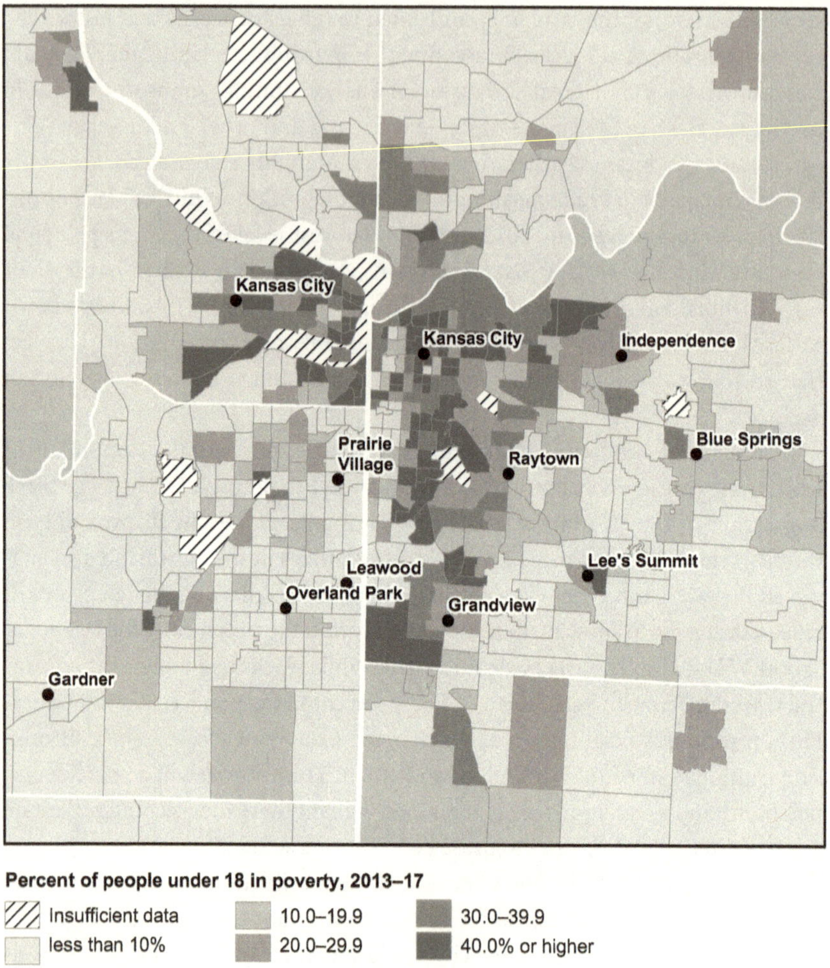

Kansas City
Kansas City
Independence
Blue Springs
Prairie Village
Raytown
Lee's Summit
Leawood
Overland Park
Grandview
Gardner
Percent of people under 18 in poverty, 2013–17
Insufficient data
less than 10%
10.0–19.9
20.0–29.9
30.0–39.9
40.0% or higher

Source: U.S. Census Bureau, 2013–2017 American Community Survey.

MAP E.2 Metropolitan Kansas City, children below the poverty level, 2013–2017 census tract averages (American Community Survey)

Most of the area's child poverty, however, remained squarely within the Kansas City, Missouri, School District, and another large concentration existed across the river in Kansas City, Kansas. The region's two central cities counted the clear majority of its poor families, and in this respect Kansas City was similar to other major metropolitan areas. The historic black commercial center at Eighteenth and Vine Streets had been reduced to a few museums and restaurants and little other activity, despite considerable public investment to sustain its cultural heritage. Many middle-class African Americans departed, and poverty rates remained stubbornly high. These were telltale signs of the continued association between race and concentrated deprivation. In many adjacent neighborhoods poverty levels ranged between 25 and 40 percent, and large numbers of students in local public schools lived in these areas.³³

High poverty rates also existed for children in other racial and ethnic groups, most of whom also lived in one of the region's central cities. This was readily evident, for example, in the growing Hispanic community located in the southeast quadrant of Kansas City, Kansas.³⁴ But deprivation for African Americans was

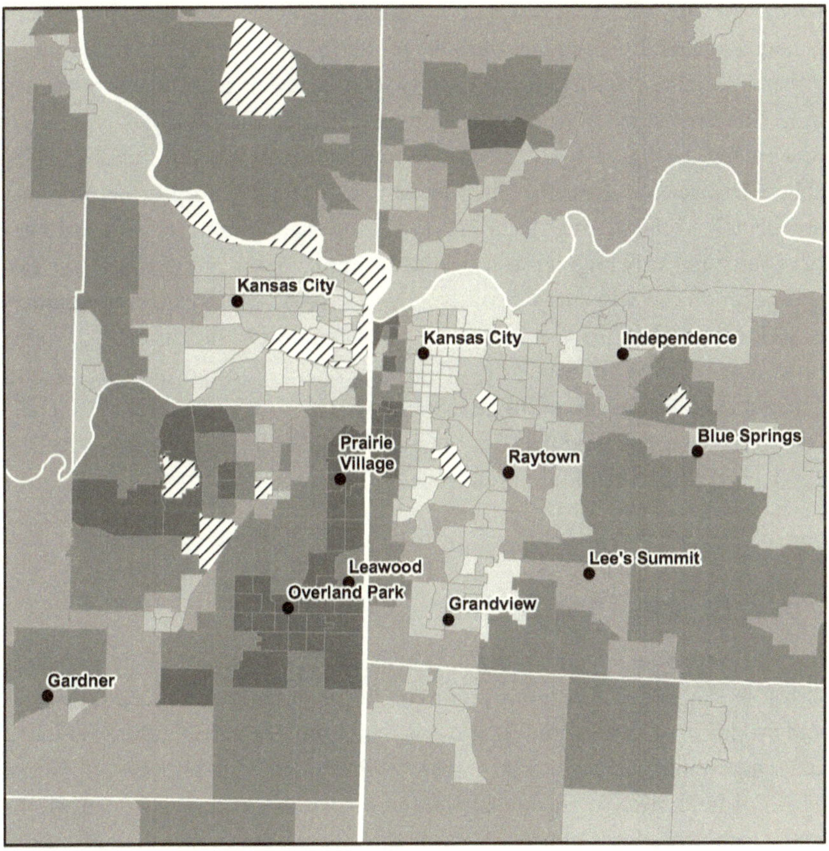

Percent of people with bachelor's degree or higher, 2013–17

Source: U.S. Census Bureau, 2013–2017 American Community Survey.

MAP E.3 Metropolitan location of college-educated adults (age twenty-five or older), 2013–2017 census tract averages (American Community Survey)

clearly more severe than for whites and most other minority groups, abetted by much higher levels of residential segregation, and this continued to be readily evident in the twenty-first century.[35] More than a quarter of the households in these neighborhoods were headed by single parents, most of them women. As the analysis of school success in chapter 2 suggested, these were circumstances with significant implications for educational inequality. It can aptly be described as concentrated disadvantage.[36]

Yet another dimension of educational advantage or disadvantage in the past, of course, was the geo-spatial distribution of adult educational levels, particularly those with a bachelor's degree or higher. Map E.3 displays the location of greater Kansas City's college-educated adults in 2010, and the distribution is remarkably similar to that observed in chapter 2. The greatest numbers of such individuals remained in Johnson County, especially in the J. C. Nichols communities along its eastern edge, extending south into Leawood and the Blue Valley School District. Decades after the postwar era, this segment of the metropolitan area remained the premier local site of concentrated advantage, with low rates of poverty and very high levels of adult education. Outlying suburbs to the east and north on the Missouri side of the region also had acquired telling numbers of well-educated adults, but not to the same degree. On the other hand, most of KCMPS, along with much of Independence and other portions of Jackson County, exhibited many fewer adults with this level of attainment. These circumstances compounded the effects of poverty and other disadvantages faced by children and youth in these communities.

Poverty and Test Scores

In the era of school accountability, only in its infancy during the 1970s, standardized tests scores have become a common means of comparing school districts and making judgments about their status. This is no less true in Kansas City than other metropolitan areas, although the state line makes comparison of schools in Missouri and Kansas somewhat difficult, since each uses a unique assessment system.[37] Families seeking "good" schools, in that case, often rely on other indicators, including college readiness exams. In the Midwest most high school students interested in college take the ACT, including 75 percent of seniors in Kansas and 74 percent in Missouri.[38] In multistate metropolitan areas, assessments such as this offer a convenient means of judging the academic standing of local education systems, even if they provide an incomplete picture of student achievement.

Using tests such as the ACT to compare schools or districts is tricky, as the number of students taking them can vary. Also, factors such as parental education, poverty, and family structure affect achievement a great deal, so test scores are not always a good reflection of what schools contribute to student learning. Even so, parents interested in preparing their children for college often look for institutions with high scores, creating an expedient map of the metropolitan education marketplace Media outlets understand this and occasionally publish composite ACT scores to compare districts or schools. In 2013 the *Kansas City Star* did just that, listing test results for most of the area's public high schools.[39]

As presented in the *Star* article, the ACT scores also offer a revealing point of contrast between urban and suburban schools. Since institutions were grouped by district, these differences were hard to miss. Table E.1 provides test results for area districts, listed by state, with the percentage of families living below the federal poverty line in each one. These are composite ACT scores derived from averaging school-level results for 2012 and 2013. While not a complete list, it represents the range of such indicators throughout the region, along with district poverty levels in 2012. The correlation between district poverty levels and ACT scores was −.95, indicating that higher levels of deprivation were strongly associated with lower district-wide test performance.

Examining these data, it is immediately evident that the lowest composite scores in both states were found in the central cities. Most institutions in these settings served large numbers of poor and minority students, including many who had experienced severe hardship. Their levels of poverty were the highest in the region, approaching 40 percent of all families. Magnet schools in these districts performed much better than these averages, but they enrolled relatively small numbers of students. Lincoln High was one such institution in KCMPS, serving a predominantly black population of high-achieving youth; Sumner High in KCK was another.[40]

At the other end of the geo-spatial spectrum were districts serving affluent and highly educated constituents, located in the well-heeled communities of Johnson County, Kansas, or in more remote districts in the Missouri suburbs. Districts to the south—Center, Raytown, Grandview, and Hickman Mills—had seen mounting poverty since 1980 and exhibited generally lower scores. The same was true of Turner, a small Wyandotte County district adjacent to Kansas City, Kansas. In Johnson County, the venerable Shawnee Mission schools still made a good showing, even if their Blue Valley neighbors had the highest scores in the region. Olathe and De Soto to the west did well too, reflecting their relatively low numbers of families in poverty. It was telling, however, that Blue Valley had the lowest poverty levels of all. By and large, the highest-performing districts in both states had poverty rates under 10 percent, far below the national average at the time.

TABLE E.1 Composite ACT scores and families in poverty for Kansas and Missouri districts in Greater Kansas City, 2012 and 2013

DISTRICT OR REGION NAME	COMPOSITE ACT SCORE	FAMILIES IN POVERTY, 2012 (PERCENT)
United States average	20.3	21
Missouri State average	21.6	20.6
Kansas City, MO	16.2	38
Hickman Mills	17	31.8
Independence	20.5	24.8
Grandview	18	24.4
Center	18.4	23.8
Raytown	19.8	21.2
North Kansas City	21.1	14.5
Blue Springs	23	11.5
Lee's Summit	23.1	9.4
Park Hill	23.6	8.9
Liberty	22.3	6.7
Kansas state average	21.9	17.2
Kansas City, KS	16.6	36.5
Turner	18.9	30.7
Shawnee Mission	23.6	9.9
Olathe	23.6	7.5
De Soto	23.1	4.7
Blue Valley	24.9	3.1

Sources: Kansas City Star, August 23, 2013; US Census, Small Area Income and Poverty Estimates, Ages 5 to 17 in Families in Poverty, https://www.census.gov/data-tools/demo/saipe/saipe.html?s_appName=saipe&map_yearSelector=2012&map_geoSelector=aa_c&menu=grid_proxy&s_measures=5_17_fam_snc&s_district=2010140,2005490,2918540&s_state=20,29&s_year=2012.

As the test scores and poverty levels suggest, crucial distinctions between urban and suburban schools continued to be evident in the twenty-first century. Since these are mainly scores for high school seniors, they represent the cumulative results of education in these systems for many students. Suburban districts with large numbers of poor and minority students also had lower test scores, such as Center, Turner, and Hickman Mills.

Raytown had become an integrated school system with middling poverty levels, and its test scores were just slightly below the state average. The older suburban districts of Independence and North Kansas City were just a bit higher. It was affluent and highly educated Johnson County, Kansas, on the other hand, that exhibited the most significant suburban advantage. Schools in Park Hill, Liberty, Lee's Summit, and Blue Springs, at a somewhat farther remove from the urban core, also did well. As a rule, in that case, it was the outlying districts that showed the highest levels of ACT performance, those with the greatest wealth, parental education, and other attributes to support their students.

As these data from greater Kansas City indicate, the metropolitan educational hierarchy that was forged during the postwar era remained largely intact nearly a half century after the desegregation controversies of the 1970s. The geo-spatial distribution of academic achievement that John Logan and his associates identified nationally was clearly evident across the region. The area's black population remained highly segregated within both of its central city municipalities, and poverty was concentrated in many of the same neighborhoods.

This was highlighted in the fall of 2017, when KCMPS once again failed to reach basic accreditation standards established by the state of Missouri, dashing the optimism that Superintendent Bedell expressed a year earlier.[41] As the *Kansas City Star* noted, the district's major difficulties included its poor attendance record and the many students switching schools each year, problems endemic to high-poverty neighborhoods.[42] On the other hand, concentrated wealth had accumulated in other sectors of the metropolis, especially in Johnson County and certain locations in Jackson, Platte, and Clay Counties in Missouri. By and large, these areas lay well outside the central cities, providing resources for community schools that continue to exclude most poor and African American children. It is hardly an exaggeration to say that the experiences of growing up in these widely disparate urban and suburban settings held very little in common. And that could hardly bode well for the future.

These are the contemporary dimensions of social and educational inequality manifest in geographic terms, and they reflect national trends.[43] They are quite stark, and also have proved to be enduring. But these patterns were neither inevitable nor entirely predictable at the start of the postwar era. How did this happen?

Creating and Maintaining the Suburban Advantage

In 1983 James Hazlett, former superintendent of the KCMPS, speculated about factors that prevented African American families from moving to the suburbs, dispersing themselves across the metropolitan landscape in the same manner as whites. He acknowledged that they were concerned about questions of safety and wanted to feel welcome in a new neighborhood. But he also suggested that suburban districts could have signaled a willingness to serve African American students by hiring black teachers, which they generally did not do. At the same time, Hazlett asserted that there was little evidence of outlying districts actively excluding African Americans while he served as superintendent. Despite this, he readily affirmed that the continued segregation of black families in the area's central cities was the principal challenge facing education, along with attendant problems of poverty and social instability. When he assumed the district's helm in 1955, things had been quite different.[44]

Metropolitan Kansas City experienced a wrenching process of social change between 1950 and 1980. As the local population grew, whites and blacks arrived on different pathways to the metropolis. African Americans, of course, mainly settled in the central cities on either side of the border, but principally in Kansas City, Missouri. Whites steered clear of those places, mostly heading for surrounding "suburban" communities, many within the city's municipal boundaries. These were choices dictated by a variety of factors, but racial prejudice and status aspirations—including ambitions for children—clearly played major roles. Many families who lived in Kansas City to start left for the suburbs to find newer homes and better schools, among other things; but racial animus also often was a decisive element in such decisions. The result was a racially divided metropolis with impoverished African Americans, along with more affluent blacks, crowded into a relatively small sector of a sprawling metropolitan landscape. The ensuing concentrations of deprivation eventually had a dire effect on city schools, creating the crisis of urban education that has continued more or less unabated to the present.[45]

This is how the current configuration of Kansas City's metropolitan social geography got started in earnest, but how did it continue or become accentuated? If African Americans had settled in the urban core, after all, what prevented them—or their children—from moving to suburbs for better homes and schools just as whites did? The answer, as indicated earlier, is that firm and unambiguous boundaries were drawn to prevent them from doing so. This also was done elsewhere in the country, of course, often with the formation of sovereign suburban communities that opposed urban expansion. But in Kansas City it was school district lines, and not necessarily municipal borders, that separated many white "suburbs" from an increasingly black city. These boundaries proved decisive, at least for a time. While they occasionally coincided with barriers such as the river or a state or county line, the district borders often held greater salience. In the absence of politically distinctive suburban municipal entities, the region's public-school systems gave shape to local identities.

The sociopolitical foundation of these developments, of course, was informed by the belief system described herein as localism, and not just in Kansas City. Postwar suburban development embodied a widespread conviction that immediate community interests were far more important than larger metropolitan or regional concerns. As Amos Hawley and Basil Zimmer found in 1966, these views were especially prevalent in high-status communities, where residents felt that local resources should be mainly devoted to proximate institutions. This was expressed in a wide range of governmental domains, from water and sanitation districts to fire and police services, but public education clearly became one of the most important. It apparently held true irrespective of racial animus, although bigoted beliefs and sentiments certainly contributed a great deal to it.[46]

The American tradition of locally governed school districts, which long predated suburbanization, suited the rise of localism in metropolitan life like a well-fitted glove. This became doubly significant as suburbanites began to see schools as local assets, contributing directly to a community's attractiveness and property values. The logic of these historical developments dictated that communities and their school districts should ever seek to improve their own status, regardless of the effect on others. And if affluence—or whiteness—was a desirable quality, residents and education leaders often became determined to sustain it. This naturally meant that they gave correspondingly little regard to ideas of shared regional interests or metropolitan harmony, especially if it incurred a cost. In this context, racial integration became anathema.[47]

Localism of this sort eventually helped to differentiate greater Kansas City communities according to perceptions of prominence and appeal. As a consequence, the region's educational landscape became clearly defined by the 1970s. The high number of affluent and college-educated adults that settled in Johnson County, Kansas, was a key element of this, effectively creating a higher-education sector of the metropolis. James Hazlett observed in 1983 that "the state line was a symbol" of "two things" that existed to its west: "a superior school system" and "the most active real estate development," which combined to produce "magnetic appeal" for prospective home buyers.[48] The fact that so many of that area's new homeowners were highly educated meant that its schools probably were destined to perform very well.

As indicated in chapter 5, area real estate agents actively steered families interested in superior schools and housing in that direction. The result was a classic case of the dynamics that Mieszkowski and Mills described, as reputedly excellent schools attracted the types of families that could sustain the academic advantages of local institutions. It started with the rise of the Shawnee Mission District in the later 1950s and has continued since, as indicated by local ACT scores today. Given this, there can be little doubt that school systems there contributed directly to the growth of those suburban developments. This was reflected in housing advertisements featuring local schools and the extent to which college-educated adults flocked to that corner of the region. It also reflected localism at work. Purchasing a home in such a setting meant joining the local district's constituency and gaining access to everything it could offer, an opportunity denied to those who could not live there. Once settled, of course, newcomers to the area had an interest in maintaining its exceptional reputation and deterring threats to its status, and by extension their own.[49]

The academic standing of schools was one aspect of the educational landscape, but race was another. Widely interpreted by whites as a threat to local aspirations, black families were actively discouraged from moving into most suburbs. And when they did—as the experience of Donald Sewing and others demonstrated—they were almost never greeted with open arms. As a consequence, African Americans had little choice in where they could decide to live and the schools their children could attend. White families, on the other hand, enjoyed many options with respect to both housing and schools, depending on their income and sociocultural preferences. And when they settled into a community of their choice, they often benefited from the many amenities of suburban life, including newer housing stock, orderly neighborhoods, and convenient services, along with well-regarded schools. Insofar as whites denied African Americans and other members of ethnic or racial minority groups access to such benefits, along with poor people in general, the erection of boundaries represented a virulent form of localism, which can be described as opportunity hoarding.[50]

As described in chapter 4, Raytown in the 1960s and '70s offered a clear example of this. In this respect it was quite similar to communities elsewhere, such as Cicero, Illinois; Parma, Ohio; or Warren, Michigan. These too were inner suburbs in large metropolitan areas, largely blue-collar communities that also developed reputations for racial animosity and exclusion. In many such places, actively discouraging African Americans from settling and enrolling their children in local schools helped to sustained whiteness as a point of community identity. With respect to Raytown, testimony about the community's reputation for antiblack hostility clearly reflected this. The effectiveness of such attitudes and actions meant that the advantages afforded by its well-regarded institutions were reserved for the community's overwhelmingly white residents. And given the centrality of the local schools to the community's life, it is clear that the schools were a key component of suburban development in South Kansas City. This contributed to the high degree of mobilization against the possibility of integrated schooling, a telling instance of defending boundaries to dominate a vital resource. In this case it was made possible by an ongoing campaign of confrontation and harassment directed against blacks. Its effect was evident in the very small number of African American students registered in district schools prior to the 1980s, despite the proximity of predominantly black neighborhoods.[51]

Not all suburban communities were able to maintain boundaries so effectively, of course. As also seen in chapter 4, residents of Hickman Mills were less successful in barring black families in search of better neighborhoods and schools. Unlike whites in Raytown, they lacked the cohesion and political power to accomplish effective exclusion. Bigoted whites there were unable to erect effective obstacles to African Americans interested in relocating to the suburbs. While generally the same size and demographically similar to Raytown, Hickman Mills did not exhibit the same degree of consensus and mobilization around the local schools and racist ideas about who should attend them. Educational institutions were somewhat less significant in the area's development. As a consequence, opportunity hoarding was much less viable, and the area eventually became integrated, before finally becoming predominantly African American decades later. Hickman Mills thus became an attractive destination for black families interested in better housing and schools for their children, at least until the effects of racial segregation and concentrated poverty eventually became evident there too.[52]

Another point of comparison, of course, is the Shawnee Mission School District (SMSD), located just a few miles west in Johnson County. It became the leading school system in the region, at least with respect to academic performance. But it also experienced problems in unifying the many communities it embraced. This was partly because of perceived and real differences in wealth and other dimensions of status, but also because the logic of localism fostered a vigorous skepticism of large organizations. Despite attempts to resist consolidation of the district or to break away from it, however, dissatisfied residents did not succeed in forming a new system that could have excluded their less-affluent neighbors. Had they accomplished this, it might have been described as a form of opportunity hoarding. Since they did not, however, it seems more appropriate to label their efforts a somewhat more benign species of localism, a stated or implied preference for the preservation and control of their own institutions.

Contrasting these quite different districts at the time offers an important insight about the dynamics of social change. Boundary construction required a high level of agreement about social distinctions and degrees of exclusion to prove effective. It turned out to be far more difficult to gain a consensus about the significance of social distinctions between groups of whites than it did to reach agreement on the bigoted exclusion of African Americans. Attitudes and behavior associated with systemic racism, or the "white racial frame," proved crucial to the viability of clear and durable boundary creation in Kansas City.[53] And a sense of imminent threat may have helped as well, as the case of Raytown suggested. SMSD was shielded from the prospect of black settlement by geographic distance and the state line, and sustained opportunity hoarding proved quite difficult to accomplish there. Johnson County whites did exclude blacks interested in living there, but with less fanfare and little officially sanctioned or publicly acknowledged antipathy. This made the Raytown experience all the more telling.

Localism of the sort seen in Johnson County may very well represent a precursor to opportunity hoarding but was hardly its equivalent. The crucial distinction, of course, was the ability to erect and maintain barriers to exclude certain parties from the benefits of access to the resources in question. Residents of SMSD living in such well-heeled communities as Mission Hills, Prairie Village, and Fairway, among others, were unable to do this. The widely acclaimed success of SMSD undoubtedly militated against such separatist sentiments. After all, Johnson County as a whole, and SMSD in particular, gained a national reputation for academic excellence that benefited everyone, and local norms abetting this undoubtedly represented a potent form of social capital in support of schooling. Even if they disliked bureaucratic organizations, the district's wealthiest families were still able to send their children to highly regarded local institutions. Localism may still have been a dominant perspective, but the dangers to neighborhood status and institutions were not considered dire enough to warrant mobilization of the social and political resources necessary to block the district's consolidation, even though attempts were made. It was in this respect that race possibly played a role there. As long as African Americans were not seen as posing an immediate and substantial hazard, residents of Johnson County could appear to hold liberal views on questions of race and other social issues, while high property standards, taxes, and real estate professionals helped to keep less-educated whites at a distance. That was enough to sustain the area's educational advantages well into the future.[54]

The more obvious hoarding community, Raytown, exhibited a high degree of consensus and cohesion around the idea of excluding African Americans, who were framed as direct threats to the status and repute of area schools and—consequently—the community itself, including property values. It benefited from the use of local governmental power, in the form of police, to make blacks feel unwelcome, and this was reinforced by real estate agents and apparently even local school personnel. Many Raytown residents, furthermore, responded to the possibility of African American encroachment because of personal perceptions of the Kansas City schools, and the movement of black settlement to the south, in their direction. Their active endorsement of exclusionary policies—and implicit support for signals such as the district's decision not to play Central High in basketball—gave substance to popular impressions that Raytown was openly hostile to African Americans.

Whites in other communities may not have felt the need to undertake such measures because of natural barriers to African American migration, or the state line. Racially motivated exclusion, and even opportunity hoarding, in these settings may have been somewhat easier to accomplish, without the degree of community mobilization seen in Raytown. This was likely the case in North Kansas

City, where the Missouri River represented a formidable impediment in the minds of African Americans and whites alike. The response of North Kansas City residents to the Spainhower Commission and other desegregation proposals, however, left little doubt about their own antipathy to blacks. But they probably did not feel an imminent threat of African American settlement to the same degree as residents of Raytown, and consequently were collectively less vociferous in their racial animus.

The North Kansas City School District (NKCSD) was somewhat different in other respects too. As described in chapter 4, it grew by means of annexation, but as it became larger the district did not experience the sort of conflict that made the formation of SMSD so difficult. It appears that the socioeconomic and institutional dynamics of the two settings were quite different, and that may have been decisive in their respective experiences. The area north of the river on the Missouri side of the border lacked a comprehensive rural high school district to serve its scattered elementary schools, and this made joining NKCSD an attractive option for smaller districts. The area also did not have the significant differences in wealth and status that characterized northeast Johnson County, even if it did include both affluent and blue-collar communities. This made the process of creating a large, centralized, and somewhat bureaucratic school district a good deal less contentious than it was for SMSD.

Such differences, of course, underscore the points made by Zimmer and Hawley, who argued that it was the most affluent and well-educated suburbanites who were especially adamant in their opposition to school district reorganization. Johnson County clearly had accumulated a critical mass of such residents, who became quite effective in making their opinions known to school leaders and the larger public. While controversy did surface occasionally in NKCSD, especially regarding school closures, it did not reach the scale evident across the border to the southwest. As a consequence, the robust renditions of localism voiced by residents of SMSD did not become a major factor in the expansion of NKCSD, nor in its subsequent development.

As indicated in chapters 3 and 4, a number of proposals offered the opportunity to devise metropolitan solutions to the problem of social and educational inequality in greater Kansas City. While educators in the urban core typically were receptive to these ideas, suburbanites immediately rejected them, often vehemently. In districts outside the city center, these proposals represented a direct threat to everything that localism had seemed to promise, including the power to exclude groups and individuals judged undesirable. This was clearly seen in suburban responses to the Spainhower Commission recommendations, as well as the 1977 Civil Rights Commission proposal and the *Jenkins v. Missouri* desegregation case.[55] The mere suggestion that local districts could have been consolidated with KCMPS was enough to induce panic and anger.[56] Raytown may have represented something of an extreme in this respect, but whites throughout the region undoubtedly agreed. And so did school district leaders on both sides of the border. Their public refusals to entertain the possibility of greater integration of schools throughout the region represented clear evidence of their complicity in the creation and maintenance of metropolitan educational inequity.[57] In that regard Hazlett was wrong. His suburban colleagues contributed directly to the racial and socioeconomic segregation that became so endemic in the latter half of the twentieth century. They too were beneficiaries of the boundaries that district lines represented and were determined to defend them.

In the years since then, greater Kansas City's suburban school districts remained vigilant in their maintenance of barriers to entry.[58] Not all of them have been successful, as the geographical expansion of the area's poor and black population suggests. But most outlying districts have remained predominantly white and affluent, sustaining advantages they have enjoyed for nearly a half century. Altogether, this set of circumstances reflects the high degree of inequality that continues to characterize American life, and the inequitable educational opportunities it represents are an ongoing threat to the nation's democratic heritage.

Prospects for Change?

This is principally a history book, but it is important to devote at least some attention to potential answers for the contemporary questions it has broached. If the problem today is a long-standing pattern of concentrated poverty in the center of American metropolitan areas and the accumulation of wealth at the peripheries, solutions would seem to necessitate the movement of people and resources to mitigate the negative effects of such arrangements. Despite recent declines in racial segregation evident in greater Kansas City, large numbers of African Americans remain trapped in high-poverty neighborhoods, where local schools struggle to serve their children. And most other metropolitan areas have not experienced the same degree of improvement in racial isolation. As sociologist Douglas Massey, along with many other observers, has pointed out, the geographic distribution of affluence and deprivation is a key element of the widening inequality that characterizes American life at present.[59] Insofar as they affect educational opportunities, these spatial dimensions of inequity threaten to perpetuate this problem well into the future. But given the long-standing national myths regarding individual freedom to choose where to live, and by extension whom to live with, along with investment in local communities, it is an open question as to how such changes can be effected.[60] Fortunately, there are a number of potential answers to consider.

Before turning to possible solutions, however, it is important to briefly discuss educational reform policies that have *not* addressed these problems. One important example is the movement for greater school accountability, culminating in the No Child Left Behind legislation at the federal level in 2001. Local, state, and federal policy initiatives that have made use of standardized test scores to identify "failing" schools, or to subject them to sanctions, may have contributed substantially to increased interdistrict inequality rather than ameliorated it.[61] While such data can be useful in identifying patterns of inequality, as suggested by the discussion of ACT scores above, to be helpful they must be linked to reforms that address the underlying problem. Similarly, offering students alternative schooling options without considering underlying conditions of concentrated urban disadvantage and suburban advantage is unlikely to resolve the question of metropolitan educational inequality. Until "choice" extends to high-status districts outside central city limits, opportunities for impoverished children in the cities and segregated suburbs undoubtedly will remain limited.[62]

Fortunately, there are a number of other policy options to consider. One that dates to the era discussed in the book is good old unfashionable school desegregation. This has long been considered impractical, if not impossible, partly because most large urban core districts are predominantly minority, making significant desegregation within them difficult to achieve. Another reason is deeply rooted suburban hostility to the very suggestion of desegregation. The *Milliken v. Bradley* Supreme Court decision in 1974 effectively ruled out the possibility of making suburban districts a party to metropolitan-wide desegregation plans, ensuring continued exclusion and thus suburban advantages in schooling for decades to follow.[63] Nevertheless, certain districts have achieved a good deal of success in desegregating across the urban-suburban divide, at least for a while. As Genevieve Siegel-Hawley has shown, there have been notable cases where this has occurred, mainly in the South with county-wide districts, but progress has slowed in recent years, and there is little evidence of it recurring.[64]

Elsewhere, a small number of interdistrict transfer programs between cities and suburbs have offered interesting models to consider, mostly outside the South.[65] Beginning during the desegregation era, often in conjunction with legal settlements of federal lawsuits, these examples of limited urban-suburban cooperation have pointed to the possibilities that cross-district enrollment plans can offer. In Kansas City most suburban districts rejected the idea of a voluntary transfer option that would have permitted students from KCMPS to attend their schools, closing the door on the possibility of a similar program in the region.[66] Elsewhere, programs such as Chapter 220 in Milwaukee, the Indianapolis

Suburban Township Desegregation Plan, and the Voluntary Interdistrict Transfer Plan in St. Louis have provided opportunities for thousands of urban students to attend affluent suburban school systems, opening pathways to higher education and professional success that may not have been available to them otherwise.[67] These programs provide a degree of racial and socioeconomic integration to the host institutions as well.

On the other hand, relatively few students nationally have benefited from these programs, which mainly are holdovers from the desegregation era. While thousands of black children have attended outlying schools, relatively few white suburban students take the opportunity to enroll in center city institutions. Even with the development of well-regarded magnet programs, urban education systems historically have held little appeal for suburbanites, a testimony to the real and imaginary barriers that continue to fracture metropolitan landscapes across the country. And suburban resistance to the enrollment of even small numbers of city students has become a problem as well.[68]

Given this, the prospect of large-scale movement of poor and minority students from central city to suburban school systems seems an unlikely scenario, at least in the immediate future. As two scholars recently noted in a systematic review of transfer programs, "The student assignment plans in place today, then, are much weaker than desegregation plans of the 1960s and 1970s that substantially integrated many schools."[69] The painful conflicts associated with the 1960s and '70s have left a legacy of ill will in many respects. As recent events in St. Louis have demonstrated, suburban resistance to the very suggestion of large-scale integration of students perceived to be "urban" in character can produce a vehement response. While limited cross-district integration plans may be positive examples, they probably do not represent a pathway to large-scale socioeconomic integration of metropolitan schools, at least presently.

The same is likely true of other forms of interdistrict cooperation that have been discussed lately. The sharing of information and certain resources is one thing, after all, but mixing student bodies is another. While it is promising when school systems work together on common problems, it is necessary to build bridges between central city and outlying suburban districts to make a significant difference. Other forms of interdistrict collaboration typically deal with cost-sharing arrangements and are a far cry from establishing equitable school experiences for most students, especially considering the extremes that often exist in rather close geographic proximity.[70] After all, the dictates of localism as a general proposition, and community control of schools in particular, hold that local interests must always take precedence over shared regional concerns or the problems of other districts. Despite a few promising examples of interdistrict cooperation, it seems likely that much time will be necessary to realize significant changes in existing patterns of educational inequality in most large metropolitan areas.

Despite the limitations noted above, some observers have recently touted school choice plans as an answer to metropolitan school inequities. Michigan has been something of a leader in this respect, and metropolitan Detroit has become a kind of laboratory for determining how offering families greater choice in where to send their children to school will affect things. As it now stands, students from the city can attend certain suburban districts, but transportation is not provided. This means that most poor families are effectively excluded, as the distance to cooperating school systems is often considerable, and area public transportation systems are not well developed, especially outside the city.[71] Providing an affordable and reliable means of conveyance is absolutely necessary in sprawling, fragmented metropolitan areas such as Detroit or Kansas City if "school choice" plans are to become a viable solution to geo-spatial inequality in education or other aspects of life for local children. And suburban school districts would have to agree to participate, or be compelled to, which could be politically difficult for legislators to even contemplate. Short of measures creating improved transportation and widespread suburban participation, school choice plans typically work to make educational inequities even more pronounced.

While institutional solutions inevitably run into difficult questions of localism and control of educational resources, perhaps the most promising avenue of change is simply moving families. The national model for doing this is Moving to Opportunity (MTO), which began as an experiment in Chicago during the 1980s and became a federally sponsored program in a limited number of other cities in years to follow. MTO offered families living in inner-city neighborhoods with concentrated poverty the means to relocate to a low-poverty area, often in a nearby suburban community. While there has been debate about its effects, the most recent studies find that MTO has had a very positive impact on the lives of younger children who make such moves, resulting in better school experiences, less problematic behavior, and more positive outcomes later in life. These are very important developments and have been verified in longitudinal studies conducted with careful controls. MTO thus offers a promising policy option for addressing the problem of concentrated poverty, and its problematic educational effects, in many central city neighborhoods.[72]

To date, relatively few families have benefited from this sort of relocation program, however. Whether MTO represents a large-scale solution to concentrated urban poverty thus remains an open question. There are other policy options for addressing these issues, of course. Sociologist Matthew Desmond has recently pointed out the crisis of evictions in many poor urban neighborhoods, arguing that housing vouchers would provide greater stability for families living there.[73]

But the question then becomes the viability of proposals to make such housing options available in suburban areas. Historically, as seen in Hickman Mills and other suburban communities, local opposition to low- or even mixed-income housing can be quite fierce in suburbs, especially those with high property values and highly regarded schools. More recently, efforts to link affordable suburban housing to school desegregation in the South have proved difficult to sustain, despite initial progress.[74] Thus, while this is a critically important issue to address, it is unlikely to resolve the problem of racial segregation and concentrated poverty that continues to plague the nation's largest cities.

The same is true of calls to devote greater resources to city schools. This would undoubtedly help these institutions a great deal and prove beneficial to many students, and should be undertaken for those reasons alone. But such efforts are unlikely to resolve the crisis of extreme poverty in many neighborhoods, at least in the foreseeable future. Schools have little power to address these issues and should not be held accountable for them.[75] To fundamentally change these conditions, people must move away from ghettos and other areas of concentrated poverty, and eventually it must be large numbers of them.

In the end, there does not appear to be a ready or convenient policy "fix" to resolve the long-standing problem of metropolitan inequality that this book has described. All the efforts described above can help to mitigate its effects, helping a number of fortunate families and children to escape its worst effects. But as long as local prerogatives take precedence over metropolitan—or even state and national—concerns, the existing geo-spatial organization of resources and status of metropolitan life is unlikely to change significantly. Localism dictates that school districts are neither required nor expected to consider the plight of impoverished minority students in setting their policy priorities. It is noteworthy that the successful urban-suburban school integration plans described by Siegel-Hawley and other scholars have occurred when district boundaries were eliminated. A recent study by Jennifer Ayscue and Gary Orfield indicates that states with the greatest fragmentation of districts have higher levels of educational inequality, largely between rather than within school systems. As long as separate districts define a fragmented metropolitan landscape, boundaries can be utilized for purposes of exclusion and hoarding opportunity.[76]

Given these realities, and the long-standing American system of local district control of important decision-making authority, the likelihood of significant change in the short term appears dim. The current situation did not develop overnight, even if it did unfold rather quickly in historical terms, and it will not be easily altered. The promising programmatic approaches to overcoming the urban-suburban divide are too modest in scale to produce major change in the foreseeable future. Gradual shifts in residential segregation of the sort that William Frey and other demographers have documented may eventually make integrated schooling more possible, but it will probably take a long time. Efforts at more rapid change will likely require a social and political movement of momentous proportion to realize meaningful progress.[77]

In the end it may require a major shift in public attitudes about education to change the geo-spatial dynamics of educational inequality that emerged so decisively in the long postwar era. As David Labaree has noted, many Americans today view schooling as a source of social status, or "mobility" in his terms, a classic positional good in sociological parlance. Given this, it is little wonder that they seek to hoard educational opportunities, or exclude others deemed likely to threaten their aspirations. If schools have become crucial instruments of status acquisition or maintenance, after all, defense of geo-spatial boundaries to restrict access makes considerable sense. On the other hand, the restriction of opportunity that inevitably follows from such viewpoints and behavior, and the fragmented approach to school organization that logically also follows from it, can hardly be described as conducive to democracy, or even a region's collective welfare. Opportunity hoarding, after all, contributes directly to inequality, which undermines the possibility of effective democratic forms of association and realizing everyone's productive potential equitably.

As Labaree suggests, Americans must come to view education as a social good in order for a democracy to succeed, and equality of opportunity will be necessary to realize that goal.[78] In the case of metropolitan education, this could mean a fundamental change in the way school districts are organized, a move that likely would meet fierce resistance from many suburbanites. But until that is done, the dynamics of metropolitan educational inequality are unlikely to change in essential ways. Interdistrict transfer programs and MTO certainly can help, and if sustained for an appreciable length of time they can produce incremental advances. Short of a more fundamental shift in localist attitudes, however, the basic structure of metropolitan inequality in education—and in many other spheres of life—is unlikely to change. Hopefully, this book and other studies can play a role in stimulating conversation about this situation, which has created the most significant and persistent problems of educational inequality in the contemporary United States. Then it is up to citizens and leaders in the political system to begin making changes that can restore the egalitarian promise of the nation's schools and its democratic heritage.

Appendix
STATISTICAL ANALYSES AND ORAL HISTORY SOURCES

This study relies on evidence from a variety of sources. Most are cited in the book's endnotes, but it is helpful to discuss some of them further. This brief appendix provides additional details about the statistical analyses described in chapter 2, along with information about oral history sources used throughout the book.

Statistical Analysis of Uneven Educational Advancement

As the maps and data discussed in chapter 2 indicate, educated adults were distributed quite unevenly across the metropolitan Kansas City landscape in both 1960 and 1980. There can be little doubt, however, that these patterns were highly correlated with wealth, race, and a number of other factors. One way to establish this is to explore spatial dissimilarities with the use of ordinary least square (OLS) regression.

To identify the spatial organization of adult educational attainment in each of these years, I created fixed dummy (binary categorical, 0–1) variables with the assistance of Sanae Akaba to represent the principal geographic units discussed in chapter 2. We ran separate cross-sectional regressions for each year, with the percentage of college-educated adults (those with any college in 1960 and at least four years in 1980) as dependent variables. We then added a number of additional factors to control for the effects of race and the age structure of the adult population, and home ownership and wealth (property values) across 120 census tracts in each year. The results are presented in tables A.1 and A.2.

In conducting this analysis, we ran three models in stepwise fashion for each point in time, displayed from left to right in tables A.1 and A.2. The first features just the five geographic areas discussed in chapter 2, which roughly correspond to four school districts and the Country Club district (a residential and commercial area located within the boundaries of KCMPS) established by J. C. Nichols in southwest Kansas City. Suburban Jackson County, excluding Raytown, serves as the comparison category. All results are expressed in the form of standardized regression coefficients (Beta) with tolerance coefficients (Tol) to indicate inflation of standard errors.

As can be seen in both years, this analysis reflects patterns readily evident in maps throughout the book. In 1960, adult attainment levels were lowest in KCMPS, even before desegregation controversies had occurred there and well before it had become majority African American. Adult attainment was highest, on the other hand, in the Country Club district and SMSD, areas developed by J. C. Nichols and associated with highly regarded secondary schools. The coefficients are positive, modestly robust, and highly significant. This was the "higher education sector" identified on map 2.8, and it is clearly evident in the first models in both tables A.1 and A.2. The two other suburban districts in these models, on the other hand, are not appreciably different from the comparison Missouri suburban tracts, failing to achieve significance in either table. Altogether, these

TABLE A.1 Regression analysis, adult education levels, 1960 (census tract data)

OLS REGRESSION	MODEL 1		MODEL 2		MODEL 3	
PREDICTOR	BETA	TOL	BETA	TOL	BETA	TOL
KCMPS	−.355**	.409	−.294**	.373	−.136	.299
Country Club Dist.	.357**	.634	.319**	.585	.155*	.515
SMSD (JoCo)	.407**	.614	.374**	.580	.250**	.542
Raytown SD	−.085	.730	−.088	.730	−.127*	.721
North KC SD	−.116	.724	−.107	.720	−.035	.702
Percent black			−.134*	.791	.051	.749
Young adult			−.122	.772	−.064	.684
Home value					.560**	.443
Homes owned					−.072	.591
Adjusted R²	.582		.621		.740	

Dependent variable: Percent of adults over 25 with any college attendance

* Significant at .05 level

** Significant at .005 level

TABLE A.2 Regression analysis, adult education levels, 1980 (census tract data)

OLS REGRESSION	MODEL 1		MODEL 2		MODEL 3	
PREDICTOR	BETA	TOL	BETA	TOL	BETA	TOL
KCMPS	−.287**	.446	−.133	.382	.145	.297
Country Club dist.	.421**	.677	.432**	.672	.397**	.669
SMSD (JoCo)	.372**	.626	.332**	.616	.175*	.557
Raytown SD	−.016	.659	−.022	.628	−.122	.608
North KC SD	.012	.709	.002	.685	−.010	.683
Percent black			−.276**	.603	−.142*	.542
Young adult			.118	.832	.116*	.808
Home value					.607**	.403
Homes owned					.049	.647
Adjusted R²	.485		.546		.720	

Dependent variable: Percent of adults over 25 with four years or more of college

* Significant at .05 level
** Significant at .005 level

fixed geo-spatial dummy variables account for about half the variation in adult attainment in both years, though slightly less in 1980, and all tolerance coefficients are satisfactory.

The picture changes in models 2 and 3 in both tables when additional variables are included. Controlling for race (proportion black in each tract) and adult age structure (adults ages 25 to 35) increases the explained variance somewhat, but only race is significant in both years. Not surprisingly, the sign is negative, and the effect size is about twice as large in 1980, when the African American population was greater and resided in more tracts. Including race in the analysis also reduced the negative coefficient for KCMPS in both tables, more appreciably in 1980, when it became insignificant. This reflects changes that had occurred in the region's urban core, such as white flight, declining property values, and growing perceptions of school problems, all associated with race. Controlling for race made adult attainment levels in KCMPS statistically similar to suburban Jackson County in 1980; in other words, it was the African American population, much of it from the South, that accounted for much of its negative association with attainment levels in model 1. This is clear evidence of the impact that segregated southern educational systems, white flight, growing numbers of poor minority students, and other issues associated with social inequality had on this dimension of educational resources in the urban core.

Tellingly, the other geo-spatial dummy variables in these analyses were affected much less dramatically by the inclusion of race in model 2, particularly those for the Country Club district and SMSD. They represented areas, of course, with much smaller African American populations. Coefficients for the latter areas were reduced substantially, on the other hand, by the inclusion of a wealth variable (home values) in model 3 for both years. This too is hardly a surprise, as these areas had relatively high property values, especially the prestigious Country Club district. Controlling for home values reduced the coefficient for this area more substantially in 1960 than in 1980, and the reverse was true for SMSD. As noted earlier, there had been turnover in certain census tracts in northern Johnson County, which was still growing faster than the older neighborhoods of southwest Kansas City. This may have accounted for somewhat less change in the college-educated adult population on the Kansas side of the border. It is revealing on this count that the raw (uncontrolled) variable for SMSD is slightly less robust than the coefficient for the Country Club district in 1980, whereas the reverse had been true in 1960. This suggests that there was a higher tendency for college-educated adults to settle on the Missouri side of the border by 1980, at least in this part of the metro area.

It is noteworthy, of course, that the coefficients for both these wealthy areas, one inside the city limits and the other an adjoining suburb, remained positive and significant after controlling for race and property values, along with other factors. This was true for both years, although the magnitude of this independent effect varied, as noted above. Both areas—together comprising one contiguous sector divided by the state line—exhibited high levels of adult educational attainment, even controlling for economic status and key demographic factors. This part of the metropolitan area was wealthy, to be sure, but its residents were also highly educated, beyond the level generally associated with their "economic capital." In short, they were better educated than their property values alone suggested.

A bit farther to the east, the rapidly growing community of Raytown offers a telling point of comparison. As noted earlier in table 2.3, property values were relatively high there in 1980, but adult education levels were considerably lower than in SMSD, and median income was less too. Raytown's predominantly white schools were known as good academically but not as exemplary as the SMSD institutions, which received national recognition. Raytown was a largely blue-collar town, solidly middle class but not nearly as fashionable or sophisticated as some of the neighborhoods in SMSD. Its inhabitants may have possessed considerable economic capital, reflected in the value of their homes, but they lacked the cultural capital of SMSD and Country Club residents to the west. In this respect, the legacy of J. C. Nichols and his success as a developer was clear; his communities continued to be associated with a degree of refinement and status that other places lacked.

Other factors that contributed to these differences are not altogether clear. Perhaps it was the allure of high-quality schools in the vicinity of the wealthier neighborhoods, particularly two high schools rated among the best in the country in the later 1950s, one on either side of the border. On the other hand, perhaps it was a more subtle form of influence, with individuals and families deciding to settle in these areas because people with similar tastes and backgrounds already lived there. Whatever the reason, the result is plain to see in model 3 in both tables A.1 and A.2. In addition to considerable economic wealth, this quadrant of greater Kansas City clearly contained its most educated segment of the population.

As a final point, it is noteworthy that the coefficient for the "young adult males" factor in model 3 for the 1980 analysis is positive and statistically significant. This suggests that areas with larger numbers of these individuals and their young families exhibited higher levels of adult education. The areas with the highest numbers of residents in this category were SMSD and the Country Club district, with levels about 25 percent higher than the rest of the metro area. This group represented the leading edge of the baby boom generation, born between 1945 and 1955, and they were starting families during the 1970s. The fact that they were settling in larger numbers in Johnson County and the adjacent Country Club district is evidence of the attraction this "higher education sector" held for families in search of educational opportunity. This group of younger adults also would be most likely to exhibit higher four-year-college levels of attainment than older adults. This was evidence that the next generation of collegiate adults was choosing the very best-educated neighborhoods to settle in and raise their children.

The sign on the KCMPS variable in model 3 is positive, although it failed to achieve significance. This may be due to a portion of the urban core that exhibited higher levels of educational attainment than normally associated with the relatively low stocks of economic capital (property wealth) that existed there. This was certainly evident in the higher levels of adult education exhibited to the west of the notorious "Troost Wall" in Westport and other neighborhoods in its immediate vicinity. Much of this area was undergoing the early stages of gentrification in the latter 1970s, and this may have accounted for some of this effect. In short, once race and property values were held constant, there were parts of Kansas City, Missouri, outside of the Country Club district that exhibited levels of adult education similar to that seen to the south and west in the metro area.

Statistical Analysis of Educational Success

The book's analysis of the likelihood of graduation considers whether seventeen-year-old youth are enrolled at the junior year or higher, including having graduated, or not. It thus indicates whether they have been successful in school, having kept more or less on track to graduate and not dropped out. At the national level, this variable is correlated with nineteen-year-old graduation rates at .9, accounting for more than 80 percent of the variation across states.[1]

Because the dependent variable is dichotomous, binary logistic regression was used to assess the likelihood of high school success for individuals in the sample. This technique produces odds ratios to express the chances of such outcomes, net of other factors in the model. These are expressed as coefficients by exponentiation to produce values, with positive and negative signs for odds greater or less than even. Each coefficient (or odds ratio) is an expression of the likelihood that a given characteristic is associated with the outcome in question, controlling for other specified factors. In this case, the question of interest is odds of school success for seventeen-year-olds in Johnson County, Kansas, and urban and suburban settings in metro Kansas City, Missouri.

The dependent variable is coded as a binary measure, with 1 for enrollment in grade 11 or 12 or graduated, and 0 for enrollment in a lower grade or out of school without a diploma. It is thus a broad measure of success in school, or attainment of a fixed standard of accomplishment. To address this question of who succeeded in school and why, this analysis was conducted in a stepwise fashion with four models. Model 1 includes the two geo-spatial dummy variables described above, and other factors are added in successive stages. The final model includes all variables in the analysis and exhibits odds ratios for each of them. This approach is useful for identifying how various factors influence one another, and particularly their interaction with the geo-spatial variables in model 1. The results are presented in the table below.

To begin, model 1 leaves little question that major differences in school success distinguish youth in these places. Seventeen-year-olds in Johnson County were 70 percent more likely to have reached their junior year in high school or better than their Missouri suburban counterparts (the comparison group for geo-spatial factors), and the same was true of their success compared to youth in Kansas City, despite the fact that the latter group included many students attending suburban schools.

Subsequent models in the analysis introduce additional factors, all of them characteristics of students or their families. In model 2, race and gender are added, with binary categorical variables for being African American (as opposed to white) or female (as opposed to male). As noted in chapter 2, being black was associated with nearly 25 percent lower odds than whites of school success in 1980, and controlling for this improved the odds of attainment in Kansas City to almost 10 percent greater odds than suburban Missouri residents. Since more than 90 percent of African American youth in the sample lived in Kansas City, their

TABLE A.3 Binary logistic regression: junior year status or higher, 17-year-olds, 1980

VARIABLES	MODEL 1	MODEL 2	MODEL 3	MODEL 4	ODDS RATIO
Johnson County	.540***	.538***	.362***	.129*	1.137
Kansas City	−.022	.091*	.120**	.076	1.079
African American		−.279**	.023	.257***	1.293
Female		−.015	.154***	.154***	1.166
Home owned			1.039***	.782***	2.186
Poverty status			−.630***	−.375***	.687
Single parent				−.608***	.544
Parent college				1.147***	3.148
Nagelkerke R^2	.010	.014	.086	.132	

N=958

* Significant at .05 level
** Significant at .01 level
*** Significant at .001 level

lower odds of success clearly affected overall city attainment levels. The inclusion of these variables, on the other hand, had no meaningful effect on the odds of school success in Johnson County, where few blacks lived at the time.

The picture changed somewhat in models 3 and 4, however, where socioeconomic, educational, and family structure factors were introduced, each in binary categorical (0–1) form. Here too, the results conform closely to findings of other studies of educational attainment in the postwar era and beyond. Living in a home owned by the family more than doubled the odds of school success for youth in the sample, compared to renters, while living in a household below the poverty level lowered the odds of attainment by nearly 50 percent, compared to families above it. These are robust effects, and controlling for them reversed the negative sign on the African American variable and reduced it to insignificance, along with boosting the fixed Kansas City dummy. Controlling for poverty and home ownership, also binary variables, African American youth were just as likely to experience school success as whites, and Kansas City residents were nearly 13 percent more likely to be successful than their Missouri suburban counterparts. The effect of being female was enhanced as well, with girls exhibiting a nearly 17 percent advantage over boys in this respect. Controlling for these factors also reduced the advantage exhibited by Johnson County youth to about 44 percent greater odds of school success, especially the home ownership variable, which accounted for much of this change alone. As noted in chapter 2, part of the Johnson County advantage in school success was attributable to the area's high level of home ownership.

In the final step of the analysis, model 4, the picture changes once again with the introduction of categorical variables for living in a single-parent, female-headed household (compared to two-parent households) and having at least one parent with a college degree (compared to those without one). These too are very robust factors. As also noted in chapter 2, living in a single-parent family was associated with a 45 percent reduction in the likelihood of school success, and having a college-educated parent increased the odds of attainment by more than a *multiple* of 3 (300 percent). A college-educated parent exhibited the strongest relationship to student educational attainment, with a wide range of additional variables controlled. Its inclusion dropped the Johnson County fixed dummy substantially, reducing the advantage of its resident students over their Missouri suburban counterparts to less than 14 percent greater likelihood of school success. The family structure variable in model 4 had very little effect on the Johnson County dummy, although its inclusion did make the black categorical variable both positive and significant. The effect of home ownership was reduced as well, along with Kansas City residence.

From the standpoint of this analysis, however, the interaction of parent collegiate education with the Johnson County dummy helps to demonstrate the manner in which parental education affected the high levels of educational success attained by local students. As argued in chapter 2, it also points to the implications of this for geo-spatial differences in educational attainment in the Kansas City metropolitan area. Johnson County, Kansas, was clearly part of a "higher education zone" in the region. Kansas City, Missouri, on the other hand, was marked by the lack of such attributes, as demonstrated by its rise to significance when they were controlled in the analysis above. Much of the observable variation in attainment appears to have been linked to these family background factors, a finding consistent with decades of research on such questions.

Oral History Sources

In the course of the study I conducted interviews with thirty-one individuals who lived in greater Kansas City between 1950 and 1980 and were connected in one way or another with the region's public schools. They included former students, teachers, administrators, board members, and community members (including family members of people who worked in the schools). About a third were African American, and the remainder were white. They had lived in all major parts of the metropolitan area and were identified by school district personnel, local historical societies, and by other interview participants. Most of the interviews were conducted with a single subject and lasted between forty minutes and an hour. Others included two or more subjects and took somewhat longer. All were recorded digitally and professionally transcribed. I performed checks of the transcriptions, along with the several transcribers employed on the project.

Per University of Kansas IRB guidelines, the names of oral history subjects were changed to pseudonyms for use in the book. I believed that it was important to guarantee participants anonymity in order to increase the likelihood of open and frank discussion of race, inequality, and related issues, even though several stated that using their identities would be fine. These are socially sensitive topics, and a large body of research suggests that people are often reluctant to discuss them in public forums.[2] While anonymizing the interviews surely did not remove such inhibitions entirely, it did reassure some subjects that there would not be repercussions for their remarks.

Validity checks were performed by comparing oral history interviews across subjects, and with other sources of historical perspective, including newspapers and other documentary materials. While just a subset of the interviews are quoted in the book, all offered background information about the period and its educational controversies that was very helpful. As suggested in the narrative, the interviews were especially useful for identifying distinctive black and white perspectives on education and the changing geo-spatial organization of the metropolitan area.

In addition to oral history interviews, depositions of school district leaders, other school employees, and expert witnesses of various sorts conducted by plaintiffs' lawyers in the *Jenkins v. Missouri* desegregation case also proved to be very helpful. Since the case began as a suit against the suburban districts by the Kansas City, Missouri, Public Schools, much of the questioning in these depositions focused on issues quite pertinent to this study. In particular, the *Jenkins* lawyers were especially interested in any behavior of suburban districts or their personnel that could be construed as discriminatory or racially biased, and thus contributing to extant patterns of racial segregation in the schools and the region.

As often occurs in such depositions, many of the participants assumed a largely defensive posture, answering very briefly, but in some cases the responses were quite revealing. Again, much of this provided background for the book, even if such sources are quoted just a few times. Altogether, nine of these depositions were reviewed closely for purposes of this study. This put the total number of oral history sources at forty, representing a substantial contribution to the project.

Notes

INTRODUCTION

1. Data for both districts, including school addresses, can be found on the Kansas State Department of Education website, http://ksreportcard.ksde.org/home.aspx?org_no=D0500&rptType=2. About 90 percent of KCK students were labeled "economically disadvantaged," compared to a little more than a third of Shawnee Mission students. The vast majority of KCK students represented various racial and ethnic minority groups, compared to about a third of Shawnee Mission students.

2. For rankings of local schools see Niche, at https://www.niche.com/k12/rankings/public-school-districts/best-overall/m/kansas-city-metro-area/, which provides a complete list of Kansas City districts on both sides of the state line. For a discussion of similar disparities elsewhere see James E. Ryan, *Five Miles Away, a World Apart: One City, Two Schools, and the Story of Educational Opportunity in Modern America* (New York: Oxford University Press, 2010), pt. 1.

3. See, for instance, Tiffani Myvett, Rebecca Medley, and Phase 2 Project, "Urban and Suburban School Systems," at https://sites.google.com/site/susantmichelle/web-text, or "Why Are Suburban Schools Usually Better Than City Schools," Act for Libraries, at http://www.actforlibraries.org/why-are-suburban-schools-usually-better-than-city-schools/ (both accessed June 10, 2017). For greater context see Peter Dreier, John Mollenkopf, and Todd Swanstrom, *Place Matters: Metropolitics for the Twenty-First Century* (Lawrence: University Press of Kansas, 2014), chaps. 1–3.

4. On changing dimensions of inequality in the past, for example, see Carl F. Kaestle and Maris A. Vinovskis, *Education and Social Change in Nineteenth-Century Massachusetts* (New York: Cambridge University Press, 1980), chaps. 5–8. Also see Carl F. Kaestle, *Pillars of the Republic: Common Schools and American Society, 1780–1860* (New York: Hill & Wang, 1983), chaps. 7 and 8.

5. Jon C. Teaford, *The Metropolitan Revolution: The Rise of Post-urban America* (New York: Columbia University Press, 2006), introduction and chaps. 3–5; Kenneth Fox, *Metropolitan America: Urban Life and Urban Policy in the United States, 1940–1980* (New Brunswick, NJ: Rutgers University Press, 1985), chaps. 1–3.

6. There were schools in all three settings historically, of course, but the educational center of gravity changed with time. On the early stages of this grand process of change see Kaestle, *Pillars of the Republic*, chap. 4, and David Tyack, *The One Best System: A History of American Education* (Cambridge, MA: Harvard University Press, 1974), pts. 1 and 2. Also see Tracy L. Steffes, *School, Society, and State: A New Education to Govern Modern America, 1890–1940* (Chicago: University of Chicago Press, 2012), chaps. 1 and 2, on the transition from rural to urban schooling and consolidation campaigns. On the shift to suburban schooling see Campbell F. Scribner, *The Fight for Local Control: Schools, Suburbs, and American Democracy* (Ithaca, NY: Cornell University Press, 2016), chaps. 1–6.

7. Perceptions of schools in these settings are discussed in Laura Lippman, Shelly Burns, and Edith McArthur, *Urban Schools: The Challenge of Location and Poverty* (Washington, DC: National Center for Educational Statistics, 1996), introduction. In 1980 there were more than 16 million suburban students, while students in urban and rural settings numbered 24 million altogether, with about 10.5 million in central cities (p. 4).

8. On the history of suburbanization and perceptions attached to it see Kenneth T. Jackson, *Crabgrass Frontier: The Suburbanization of the United States* (New York: Oxford University Press, 1985), and chaps. 13–15 on the postwar boom. Also see Dolores Hayden, *Building Suburbia: Green Fields and Urban Growth, 1820–2000* (New York: Pantheon, 2003), part 1; and Andres Duany, Elizabeth Plater-Zyberk, and Jeff Speck, *Suburban Nation: The Rise of Sprawl and the Decline of the American Dream* (New York: Farrar, Straus and Giroux, 2000), chap. 3, as well as Fox, *Metropolitan America*, chap. 2.

9. On images in cinema see Robert C. Bulman, *Hollywood Goes to High School: Cinema, Schools, and American Culture*, 2nd ed. (New York: Worth, 2015). See also two books by Timothy Shary: *Teen Movies: American Youth on Screen (Shortcuts)* (New York: Columbia University Press, 2005), chap. 2, and *Generation Multiplex: The Image of Youth in American Cinema since 1980* (Austin: University of Texas Press, 2014), chap. 2.

10. On this point see Trevor Thompson, Jennifer Benz, and Jennifer Agiesta, *Parents' Attitudes on the Quality of Education in the United States* (Chicago: Associated Press–NORC Center for Public Affairs Research, 2013), 3, which shows that suburban parents express higher levels of satisfaction with their schools, which typically perform a bit higher than rural schools. Also see, for instance, CBS Moneywatch, "What It Costs to Live in the Top 10 School Districts in the U.S.," September 1, 2015, http://www.cbsnews.com/media/what-it-costs-to-live-in-the-top-10-school-districts-in-the-u-s/.

11. David Baker, *The Schooled Society: The Educational Transformation of Global Culture* (Stanford, CA: Stanford University Press, 2014), introduction and chap. 1.

12. This is a long-standing question, of course. For a recent popular discussion see Alana Semuels, "Good School, Rich School; Bad School, Poor School: The Inequality at the Heart of America's Education System," *Atlantic*, August 25, 2016, https://www.theatlantic.com/business/archive/2016/08/property-taxes-and-unequal-schools/497333/.

13. Richard Briffault, "The Local School District in American Law," in *Besieged: School Boards and the Future of Education Politics*, ed. William G. Howell (Washington, DC: Brookings Institution Press, 2005), 25; "State and Local Government Special Studies: Governments in the United States 1951," *Property Taxation 1941*, US Census Bureau, G-SS-No. 29, March 1952, 2.

14. For discussion of this during the postwar era see Arthur E. Wise, *Rich Schools, Poor Schools: The Promise of Equal Educational Opportunity* (Chicago: University of Chicago Press, 1968). For a more recent popular account of these questions also see Jonathan Kozol, *Savage Inequalities: Children in America's Schools* (New York: Random House, 1991). For a somewhat more positive assessment of school districts in the United States see William A. Fischel, *Making the Grade: The Economic Evolution of American School Systems* (Chicago: University of Chicago Press, 2009), chap. 1.

15. Early examples of this literature include Carl. F. Kaestle, *The Evolution of an Urban School System: New York City, 1750–1850* (Cambridge, MA: Harvard University Press, 1973); Stanley K. Schultz, *The Culture Factory: Boston Public Schools, 1789–1860* (New York: Oxford University Press, 1973); Marvin Lazerson, *Origins of the Urban School: Public Education in Massachusetts, 1870–1915* (Cambridge, MA: Harvard University Press, 1971); and Selwyn K. Troen, *The Public and the Schools: Shaping the St. Louis System, 1838–1920* (Columbia: University of Missouri Press, 1975), along with Tyack's *The One Best System*. More recent contributions include William J. Reese, *Power and the Promise of School Reform: Grass-Roots Movements during the Progressive Era* (New York: Routledge, 1986); Jeffrey Mirel, *The Rise and Fall of an Urban School System: Detroit, 1907–81* (Ann Arbor: University of Michigan Press, 1993), and Ronald D. Cohen, *Children of the Mill: Schooling and Society in Gary, Indiana, 1906–1960* (Bloomington: Indiana University Press, 1990).

16. Jack Dougherty, "Bridging the Gap between Urban, Suburban, and Educational History," in *Rethinking the History of American Education*, ed. William J. Reese and John L. Rury (New York: Palgrave Macmillan, 2008), 245–60.

17. These processes are described in Teaford, *Metropolitan Revolution*, chaps. 3–5. Also see Jackson, *Crabgrass Frontier*, chap. 13; and Kevin M. Kruse, *White Flight: Atlanta and the Making of Modern Conservatism* (Princeton, NJ: Princeton University Press, 2005), chap. 9 and epilogue. On black migration and settlement in cities see Leah Platt Boustan, *Competition in the Promised Land: Black Migrants in Northern Cities and Labor Markets* (Princeton, NJ: Princeton University Press, 2017), chaps. 1 and 2; and Isabel Wilkerson, *The Warmth of Other Suns: The Epic Story of America's Great Migration* (New York: Vintage, 2010), pt. 1.

18. Richard Rothstein, *The Color of Law: A Forgotten History of How Our Government Segregated America* (New York: Liveright, 2017), chaps. 3–6; Thomas J. Sugrue, *The Origins of the Urban Crisis: Race and Inequality in Postwar Detroit* (Princeton, NJ: Princeton University Press, 1996), pts. 2 and 3; Arnold Hirsch, *Making the Second Ghetto: Race and Housing in Chicago, 1940–1960* (Chicago: University of Chicago Press, 1983), chap. 1; Robert O. Self, *American Babylon: Race and the Struggle for Postwar Oakland* (Princeton, NJ: Princeton University Press, 2003), pt. 2; and Clarence Lang, *Grassroots at the Gateway: Class Politics and Black Freedom Struggle in St. Louis, 1936–75* (Ann Arbor: University of Michigan Press, 2009), chaps. 3–5.

19. Douglas S. Massey and Nancy A. Denton, *American Apartheid: Segregation and the Making of the Underclass* (Princeton, NJ: Princeton University Press, 1993), chaps. 1 and 2; William Julius Wilson, *The Truly Disadvantaged: The Inner City, the Underclass, and Public Policy* (Chicago: University of Chicago Press, 1987), pt. 1; Paul A. Jagowsky, *Poverty and Place: Ghettos, Barrios, and the American City* (New York: Russell Sage Foundation, 1997), chaps. 1–3; Patrick Sharkey, *Stuck in Place: Urban Neighborhoods and the End of Progress toward Racial Equality* (Chicago: University of Chicago Press, 2013), chaps. 2–4.

20. Joe R. Feagin, *The White Racial Frame: Centuries of Racial Framing and Counterframing*, 2nd ed. (New York: Routledge, 2013), chaps. 1 and 7. On the growth and evolution of racist ideology see Derrick Darby and John L. Rury, *The Color of Mind: Why the Origins of the Achievement Gap Matter for Justice* (Chicago: University of Chicago Press, 2018), chaps. 2–5. For discussion of property value loss due to racial bias in housing markets see Chenoa Flippen, "Unequal Returns to Housing Investments? A Study of Real Housing Appreciation among Black, White, and Hispanic Households," *Social Forces* 82, no. 4 (June 2004): 1523–51; and Colin Gordon, *Mapping Decline: St. Louis and the Fate of the American City* (Philadelphia: University of Pennsylvania Press, 2008), introduction.

21. On these points see Mathew D. Lassiter, "Schools and Housing in Metropolitan History: An Introduction," *Journal of Urban History* 38, no. 2 (March 2012): 195–204. His essay provides a very good overview of relevant literature, including essays by Jack Dougherty, Karen Benjamin, and Ansley Erickson published in the same issue of the journal. Also see Bethany L. Rogers, "Integrating Education History and Urban History: The Politics of Schools and Cities," *Journal of Urban History* 34, no. 3 (July 2008): 855–69.

22. For an overview of this shift see Argun Saatcioglu and John L. Rury, "Education and the Changing Metropolitan Organization of Inequality: A Multi-level Analysis of Secondary Attainment in the United States, 1940–1980," *Historical Methods* 45, no. 1 (2012): 21–40. On portrayals of urban and suburban schools see Jonathan Kozol, *Shame of the Nation: The Restoration of Apartheid Schooling in America* (New York: Three Rivers, 2005), chaps. 2 and 3.

23. Few books take a metropolitan perspective in considering education, and those that do focus for the most part on desegregation in the South. The most thorough and comprehensive is Ansley T. Erickson, *Making the Unequal Metropolis: School Desegregation and Its Limits* (Chicago: University of Chicago Press, 2016), which examines metropolitan Nashville, Tennessee. Richmond, Virginia, is profiled in Ryan, *Five Miles Away, a World Apart*, which considers particular urban and suburban schools and places them in a national context. A comparative analysis can be found in Genevieve Siegel-Hawley, *When the Fences Come Down: Twenty-First-Century Lessons from Metropolitan School Desegregation* (Chapel Hill: University of North Carolina Press, 2016), which assesses desegregation experiences in four metropolitan settings. And a somewhat more schematic and personal study is offered in Gerald Grant, *Hope and Despair in the American City: Why There Are No Bad Schools in Raleigh* (Cambridge, MA: Harvard University Press, 2009).

24. For case studies of urban school districts see note 15 above. Studies of suburban communities are less common, but there are a number of recent examples. Emily Strauss explores a suburban district that shifted to being considered urban, with a racial transition in clientele, in her book *Death of a Suburban Dream: Race and Schools in Compton, California* (Philadelphia: University of Pennsylvania Press, 2014). On the other hand, Daniel L. Duke describes the rise of a suburban district to academic prominence in his book *Education Empire: The Evolution of an Excellent Suburban School System* (Albany: SUNY Press, 2005). Paul *Mattingly's Suburban Landscapes: Culture and Politics in a New York Metropolitan Community* (Baltimore: Johns Hopkins University Press, 2001) deals principally with an earlier period, without focusing specifically on institutionalized education. Along these lines also see Zane Miller, *Suburb: Neighborhood and Community in Forest Park, Ohio, 1935–1976* (Knoxville: University of Tennessee Press, 1981).

25. A classic statement of this can be found in Leo F. Schnore, *The Urban Scene: Human Ecology and Demography* (New York: Free Press, 1966), pt. 1. For a more recent version of this perspective see Bruce Katz and Jennifer Bradley, *The Metropolitan Revolution: How Cities and Metros Are Fixing Our Broken Politics and Fragile Economy* (Washington, DC: Brookings Institution Press, 2014), chap. 1.

26. Leo F. Schnore, "Metropolitan Growth and Decentralization," *American Journal of Sociology* 63, no. 2 (September 1957): 177.

27. Robert E. Stake, *The Art of Case Study Research* (Thousand Oaks, CA: Sage, 1995), chap. 1.

28. The most comprehensive account of metropolitan Kansas City's development is James R. Shortridge, *Kansas City and How It Grew, 1822–2011* (Lawrence: University Press of Kansas, 2012). Also see Rick Montgomery and Shirl Kasper, *Kansas City: An American Story* (Kansas City, MO: Kansas City Star Books, 1999).

29. John Simonson, *Paris of the Plains: Kansas City from Doughboys to Expressways* (Charleston, SC: History Press, 2010), chaps. 1 and 2; Montgomery and Kasper, *Kansas City*, chaps. 10 ("Thoroughly Modern") and 11 ("The Town That Tom Ruled"); proposals to append Kansas City to the state of Kansas were made in 1855 and 1879 and are discussed in Shortridge, *Kansas City and How It Grew*, 8.

30. Jed Kolko, "Normal America Is Not a Small Town of White People," *Five Thirty Eight*, April 28, 2016, http://fivethirtyeight.com/features/normal-america-is-not-a-small-town-of-white-people/. The article ranked metropolitan Kansas City tenth among metropolitan areas that most closely resemble the demographic profile of the nation as a whole.

31. Richard Florida, *The New Urban Crisis: How Our Cities Are Increasing Inequality, Deepening Segregation, and Failing the Middle Class—and What We Can Do about It* (New York: Basic Books, 2017), 100. Florida puts Kansas City among the top twenty American

metro areas on inequality overall, but in the top ten for larger metropolises. On local industrial development and socioeconomic differentiation see Shortridge, *Kansas City and How It Grew*, chap. 5.

32. Robert M. Crisler, "Missouri's Little Dixie," *Missouri Historical Review* 48 (April 1948): 130–39; Jack Dingle, interview by John Rury, March 22, 2014.

33. The growth of the city's African American population is described in Sherry Lamb Schirmer, *A City Divided: The Racial Landscape of Kansas City, 1900–1960* (Columbia: University of Missouri Press, 2002), introduction.

34. These factors, along with racial conflict and transitions, are discussed in Kevin Fox Gotham, *Race, Real Estate, and Uneven Development: The Kansas City Experience, 1900–2010*, 2nd ed. (Albany: SUNY Press, 2014), chaps. 1–5. Also see Shortridge, *Kansas City and How It Grew*, chap. 6, and Teaford, *Metropolitan Revolution*, chaps. 2–4.

35. Douglas S. Massey and Jonathan Tannen, "A Research Note on Trends in Black Hypersegregation," *Demography* 52 (2015): 1025–34; see also Douglas Massey and Nancy Denton, *American Apartheid: Segregation and the Making of the Underclass* (Cambridge, MA: Harvard University Press, 1993), 67–69. Massey and Denton note that Kansas City had one of the lowest black suburbanization rates in the country during the 1970s. Kansas City also was one of just five metropolitan areas to appear both on the Massey and Tannen list of hypersegregated areas and Richard Florida's list of the most economically segregated areas in the country. On recent declines in metro-wide racial segregation see Eric Alder, Mará Rose Williams, and Savanna Smith, "KC Area Has Been One of the Most Racially Segregated in America. But Not Any More," *Kansas City Star*, January 6, 2019, 1.

36. US Census Bureau, *Historical Census Statistics on Population Totals by Race, 1790 to 1900, and by Hispanic Origin, 1790 to 1990, for Large Cities and Other Urban Places in the United States*, https://www.webcitation.org/69hd5KAIE?url=http://www.census.gov/population/www/documentation/twps0076/twps0076.html.

37. Shortridge, *Kansas City and How It Grew*, chap. 4; Charles E. Coulter, *Take Up the Black Man's Burden: Kansas City's African American Communities, 1865–1939* (Columbia: University of Missouri Press, 2016), chaps. 3–6.

38. Schirmer, *City Divided*, chaps. 6–8; G. S. Griffin, *Racism in Kansas City: A Short History* (Traverse City, MI: Chandler Lake Books, 2015), chaps. 3 and 4. On the role of women in local school desegregation battles see Rachel Devlin, *A Girl Stands at the Door: The Generation of Young Women Who Desegregated America's Schools* (New York: Basic Books, 2018), chaps. 1, 4, and 5.

39. See the studies cited in note 17 above, along with John L. Rury and Jeffrey E. Mirel, "The Political Economy of Urban Education," *Review of Research in Education* 22 (1997): chap. 2.

40. These points are discussed in considerable detail in chapters 2, 4, and 5.

41. Shortridge, *Kansas City and How It Grew*, chap. 6. Montgomery and Kasper, *Kansas City*, chaps. 13 ("Big League") and 14 ("Winds of Change"). On the development of school districts in the West see Fischel, *Making the Grade*, 203–9.

42. For somewhat different accounts of *Jenkins* and circumstances leading up to it see Peter William Moran, *Race, Law, and the Desegregation of Public Schools* (El Paso, TX: LFB Scholarly, 2005) and Joshua M. Dunn, *Complex Justice: The Case of* Missouri v. Jenkins (Chapel Hill: University of North Carolina Press, 2008). For a contrary interpretation of the case see Preston C. Green III and Bruce D. Baker, "Urban Legends, Desegregation and School Finance: Did Kansas City Really Prove That Money Doesn't Matter?," *Michigan Journal of Race & Law* 12, no. 1 (2006): 57–105.

43. On the number of school districts and resulting competitive dynamics in metropolitan areas see Fischel, *Making the Grade*, 186–91.

44. Geo-spatial can be defined as relating to or denoting data associated with a particular location or locations, representing how geography is divided to identify certain spaces as linked to social groups, natural events, or activities of various sorts. See Brian J. L. Berry, Daniel A. Griffith, and Michael R. Tiefelsdorf, "From Spatial Analysis to Geospatial Science," *Geographical Analysis* 40, no. 3 (July 2008): 229–38.

45. While this study may thus have some of the limitations of prior historical research on urban education, it features a case that is considerably more representative than many such works. I should add that convenience also played a role in deciding to study this site, since I live and work within fifty miles of downtown Kansas City, Missouri. This, however, does not detract from the many other qualities that make this midwestern metropolitan region a very good candidate for a project such as this. Of course, as a case study this account is necessarily limited with respect to making generalizations about the questions that it addresses, and this would be true even if it was an ideal site. For a discussion of problems associated with recent case studies in the history of education see John L. Rury, "The Power and Limitations of Historical Case Study: A Consideration of Postwar African American Educational Experience," *HSE: Social and Education History (Historia Social y de Educacion)* 3, no. 3 (2014): 241–70, doi:10.4471/hse.2014.15 (published online).

46. While Hawley's original book on human ecology was published in 1950, the final articulation of his ideas found expression in Amos Hawley, *Human Ecology: A Theoretical Essay* (Chicago: University of Chicago Press, 1986). For more recent discussions of this perspective see the essays in the collection edited by Markus Nauser and Deter Steiner, *Human Ecology: Fragments of Anti-fragmentary Views of the World* (New York: Routledge, 1993), and Robert Dyball and Barry Newell, *Understanding Human Ecology: A Systems Approach to Sustainability* (New York: Routledge, 2015).

47. For further discussion of these questions see John L. Rury and Jeffrey E. Mirel, "The Political Economy of Urban Education," *Review of Research in Education* 22 (1997): 49–110. For a broad critique of the human ecology perspective see John R. Logan and Harvey L. Molotch, *Urban Fortunes: The Political Economy of Growth* (Berkeley: University of California Press, 1987), chap. 1.

48. Steven Conn, *American against the City: Anti-urbanism in the Twentieth Century* (New York: Oxford University Press, 2014), chap. 6. On questions of uneven distribution of services, an overview is provided by Deirdre A. Oakley and John R. Logan, "A Spatial Analysis of the Urban Landscape: What Accounts for Differences across Neighborhoods?," in *The Sociology of Spatial Inequality*, ed. Linda M. Lobao, Gregory Hooks, and Ann R. Tickamyer (Albany: SUNY Press, 2007), 215–32.

49. Jon C. Teaford, *City and Suburb: The Political Fragmentation of Metropolitan America, 1850–1970* (Baltimore: Johns Hopkins University Press, 1979). These themes are also evident in many studies of suburban development, beginning with Jackson, *Crabgrass Frontier*, chap. 15, but also including works such as Kruse, *White Flight*, chap. 9, and Matthew D. Lassiter, *The Silent Majority: Suburban Politics in the Sunbelt South* (Princeton, NJ: Princeton University Press, 2006), chaps. 4 and 5.

50. This is expressed in Amos H. Hawley and Basil G. Zimmer, *Metropolitan Community: Its People and Government* (Thousand Oaks, CA: Sage, 1970); also see Katz and Bradley, *Metropolitan Revolution*, chap. 1.

51. I have derived this term from Basil Zimmer and Amos Hawley in their important but now largely forgotten study of urban and suburban attitudes regarding education, *Metropolitan Area Schools: Resistance to District Reorganization* (Beverly Hills, CA: Sage, 1968), chaps. 8 and 9. For a more recent use of the term in this light see Kathryn A. McDermott, *Controlling Public Education: Localism versus Equity* (Lawrence: University Press of Kansas, 1999), chap. 3. Advocates of localism have used a Tiebout frame of analysis to suggest that

competition among localities can produce greater efficiency in governance and related services. For critiques of this see Sheryll Cashin, "Localism, Self-Interest, and the Tyranny of the Favored Quarter: Addressing the Barriers to New Regionalism," *Georgetown Law Journal* 88, no. 6 (2000): 1985–2048, David D. Troutt, "Localism and Segregation," *Journal of Affordable Housing & Community Development Law* 16, no. 4 (Summer 2007): 323–47, Erika K. Wilson, "The New School Segregation," *Cornell International Law Journal* 49, no. 3 (2016): 139–210, and Richard C. Schragger, "The Limits of Localism," *Michigan Law Review* 100, no. 2 (November 2001): 371–472.

52. Mark Baldassare, *Trouble in Paradise: The Suburban Transformation in America* (New York: Columbia University Press, 1986), chaps. 3 and 4; Basil G. Zimmer, "Suburbanization and Changing Political Structures," in *The Changing Face of the Suburbs*, ed. Barry Schwartz (Chicago: University of Chicago Press, 1976), 165–202; and Ann Lennarson Greer and Scott Greer, "Suburban Political Behavior: A Metter of Trust," in Schwartz, *Changing Face of the Suburbs*, 203–20. Also see Jon C. Teaford, *The American Suburb: The Basics* (New York: Routledge, 2008), chap. 4. On the role of J. C. Nichols in Kansas City see Rothstein, *Color of Law*, 79.

53. Tyack, *One Best System*, pt. 4; David Tyack and Elisabeth Hansot, *Managers of Virtue: Public School Leadership in America, 1820–1980* (New York: Basic Books, 1982), chaps. 11 and 12.

54. Charles Tilly, *Durable Inequality* (Berkeley: University of California Press, 1998), 10. This term has been directly tied to suburban development by Kevin Kruse and Thomas J. Sugrue in the introduction to their edited volume, *The New Suburban History* (Chicago: University of Chicago Press, 2006), 6. For a somewhat more systematic analysis see John L. Rury and Argun Saatcioglu, "Suburban Advantage: Opportunity Hoarding and Secondary Attainment in the Postwar Metropolitan Northeast," *American Journal of Education* 118, no. 3 (May 2011): 307–42.

1. SUBURBAN AND URBAN SCHOOLS

1. James B. Conant, *Slums and Suburbs: A Commentary on Schools in Metropolitan Areas* (New York: McGraw Hill, 1961), 1–2. On contemporary conditions that mirror the disparities that Conant described see Linda Lemasters, "Disparities between Urban and Suburban Schools," Educational Facilities Clearinghouse, June 11, 2015, http://www.efc.gwu.edu/library/disparities-between-urban-and-suburban-schools/. Also see Sarah Butrymowicz, "Struggling Cities and Excelling Suburbs: A Repeated Pattern around the Country," Hechinger Report, September 28, 2015, http://hechingerreport.org/struggling-cities-and-excelling-suburbs-a-repeated-pattern-around-the-country/. Also see Jon C. Teaford, *City and Suburb: The Political Fragmentation of Metropolitan America, 1850–1970* (Baltimore: Johns Hopkins University Press, 1979), chaps. 5–8; and James E. Ryan, *Five Miles Away, a World Apart: One City, Two Schools, and the Story of Educational Opportunity in Modern America* (New York: Oxford University Press, 2010), chaps. 1 and 2.

2. On this point see Jeffrey E. Mirel, *The Rise and Fall of an Urban School System: Detroit, 1907–81* (Ann Arbor: University of Michigan Press, 1993), esp. chap. 2. Also see the essays in John L. Rury and Frank Cassell, *Seeds of Crisis: Public Schooling in Milwaukee since 1920* (Madison: University of Wisconsin Press, 1993), esp. chaps. 1 and 3–6. Also see David L. Angus, Jeffrey Mirel, and Maris Vinovskis, "Historical Development of Age Stratification in Schooling," *Teachers College Record* 90, no. 2 (Winter 1988): 211–36.

3. Jon C. Teaford, *The Metropolitan Revolution: The Rise of Post-urban America* (New York: Columbia University Press, 2006), introduction; Kenneth Jackson, *Crabgrass Frontier: The Suburbanization of the United States* (New York: Oxford University Press, 1985), chaps. 9–14; William Frey and Aldon Speare, *Regional and Metropolitan Growth and*

Decline in the U.S. (New York: Russell Sage Foundation, 1988), pt. 2; Robert Bruegmann, *Sprawl: A Compact History* (Chicago: University of Chicago Press, 2006), chaps. 3 and 4. See also Kenneth Fox, *Metropolitan America: Urban Life and Urban Policy in the United States, 1940–1980* (Oxford: University Press of Mississippi, 1985), chap. 2.

4. Conant, *Slums and Suburbs*, introduction; Andrés Duany, Elizabeth Plater-Zyberk, and Jeff Speck, *Suburban Nation: The Rise of Sprawl and the Decline of the American Dream* (New York: North Point, 2000), chap. 1.

5. Howard P. Chudacoff, Judith Smith, and Peter Baldwin, *The Evolution of American Urban Society*, 8th ed. (New York: Routledge, 2016), chap. 4.

6. David B. Tyack, *The One Best System: A History of American Urban Education* (Cambridge, MA: Harvard University Press, 1974), pts. 4 and 5.

7. Ibid. Also see Raymond E. Callahan, *Education and the Cult of Efficiency: A Study of the Social Forces That Have Shaped the Administration of the Public Schools* (Chicago: University of Chicago Press, 1964), chaps. 3–5; and Samuel P. Hays, "The Politics of Municipal Reform in the Progressive Era," *Pacific Northwest Quarterly* 55, no. 4 (October 1964): 157–69. For discussion of the development of the urban school superintendent see David B. Tyack and Elisabeth Hansot, *Managers of Virtue: Public School Leadership in America, 1820–1980* (New York: Basic Books, 1982), pt. 2.

8. Claudia Goldin and Lawrence Katz, *The Race between Education and Technology* (Cambridge, MA: Harvard University Press 2010), chap. 1; John L. Rury, *Education and Women's Work: Female Schooling and the Division of Labor in Urban America, 1870–1930* (Albany: SUNY Press, 1991), chaps. 2 and 3; Lisa M. Fine, *The Souls of the Skyscraper: Female Clerical Workers in Chicago, 1870–1930* (Philadelphia: Temple University Press, 1990).

9. Richard Hofstadter, *The Age of Reform* (New York: Vintage Books, 1955), 23. Also see David B. Danbom, *Born in the Country: A History of Rural America* (Baltimore: Johns Hopkins University Press, 1995), iv.

10. James N. Gregory, *The Southern Diaspora: How the Great Migrations of Black and White Southerners Transformed America* (Chapel Hill: University of North Carolina Press, 2005), chaps. 2–4.

11. Phillip G. Payne, *Crash! How the Economic Boom and Bust of the 1920s Worked* (Baltimore: Johns Hopkins University Press, 2015), chaps. 2 and 3. See slso Richard E. Fogelsong, *Planning the Capitalist City: The Colonial Era to the 1920s* (Princeton, NJ: Princeton University Press, 1986), chap. 7.

12. For an overview of urban development at this time see Eric H. Monkkonen, *America Becomes Urban: The Development of U.S. Cities and Towns, 1780–1980* (Berkeley: University of California Press, 1988), chaps. 7–9. On the character of city schools during these years see Mirel, *Rise and Fall*, chap. 2, along with Tyack and Hansot, *Managers of Virtue*, chaps. 11 and 12. On the treatment of African Americans in city schools see Tyack, *One Best System*, pt. 3, chap. 5; also see Judy Jolley Mohraz, *The Separate Problem: Case Studies of Black Education in the North, 1900–1930* (Westport, CT: Praeger, 1979), chap. 1; and James D. Anderson, *The Education of Blacks in the South, 1860–1935* (Chapel Hill: University of North Carolina Press, 1988), chaps. 5 and 6.

13. Mirel, *Rise and Fall*, chap. 3; David Tyack, Robert Lowe, and Elisabeth Hansot, *Public Schools in Hard Times: The Great Depression and Recent Years* (Cambridge, MA: Harvard University Press, 1987), chaps. 1–3.

14. Dolores Hayden, *Building Suburbia: Green Fields and Urban Growth, 1820–2000* (New York: Vintage Books, 2003), chap. 7; Jackson, *Crabgrass Frontier*, chap. 13; Chudacoff, Smith, and Baldwin, *Evolution of American Urban Society*, chaps. 7 and 8.

15. Goldin and Katz, *Race between Education and Technology*, chap. 6. Also see John L. Rury, "Social Capital and Secondary Schooling: Interurban Differences in American

Teenage Enrollment Rates in 1950," *American Journal of Education* 110, no. 4 (August 2004): 293–320.

16. James B. Conant, *The American High School Today: A First Report to Interested Citizens* (New York: McGraw Hill, 1959), chap. 3; David L. Angus and Jeffrey E. Mirel, *The Failed Promise of the American High School, 1890–1995* (New York: Teachers College Press, 1999), chap. 4. On black experiences see John L. Rury and Shirley A. Hill, *The African American Struggle for Secondary Schooling, 1940–1980: Closing the Graduation Gap* (New York: Teachers College Press, 2012), chap. 2.

17. On the 1950s as a time of stability and growth see Mirel, *Rise and Fall*, chap. 5, and John L. Rury, "Race, Space, and the Politics of Chicago's Public Schools: Benjamin Willis and the Tragedy of Urban Education," *History of Education Quarterly* 39, no. 2 (Summer 1999): 117–42. For a detailed account of changes in secondary education during this time see David L. Angus and Jeffrey Mirel, *The Failed Promise of the American High School, 1890–1995* (New York: Teachers College Press, 1999), chaps. 3 and 4. On minority group exclusion see Kathryn M. Neckerman, *Schools Betrayed: Roots of Failure in Inner City Education* (Chicago: University of Chicago Press, 2007), chaps. 3 and 4, and Jack Dougherty, *More Than One Struggle: The Evolution of Black School Reform in Milwaukee* (Chapel Hill: University of North Carolina Press, 2004), chap. 1.

18. Two classic accounts of this process are Thomas J. Sugrue, *The Origins of the Urban Crisis: Race and Inequality in Postwar Detroit* (Princeton, NJ: Princeton University Press, 1996), chaps. 3 and 4, and Arnold R. Hirsch, *Making the Second Ghetto: Race and Housing in Chicago, 1940–1960* (Chicago: University of Chicago Press, 1983), chap. 1. Also see Kevin Fox Gotham, *Race, Real Estate, and Uneven Development: The Kansas City Experience, 1900–2010*, 2nd ed. (Albany: SUNY Press, 2014), chaps. 4 and 5; and Fox, *Metropolitan America*, chap. 6.

19. Teaford, *Metropolitan Revolution*, chaps. 1–3. On early suburbanization and restrictive covenants see Robert M. Fogelson, *Bourgeois Nightmares: Suburbia, 1870–1930* (New Haven, CT: Yale University Press, 2005), pt. 2; and Jackson, *Crabgrass Frontier*, chaps. 10 and 11.

20. On urban and metropolitan development during these years see two books by Jon C. Teaford: *The Rough Road to Renaissance: Urban Revitalization in America, 1940–1985* (Baltimore: Johns Hopkins University Press, 1990), chaps. 1–3, and *Metropolitan Revolution*, chaps. 3–5. Also see Fox, *Metropolitan America*, chaps. 1–3.

21. Leah Platt Boustan, *Competition in the Promised Land: Black Migrants in Northern Cities and Labor Markets* (Princeton, NJ: Princeton University Press, 2017), chap. 4.

22. A classic account of this can be found in Hirsch, *Making the Second Ghetto*, chaps. 1–3. On debates about poverty in this era see Michael B. Katz, *The Undeserving Poor: America's Enduring Confrontation with Poverty*, 2nd ed. (New York: Oxford University Press, 2013), chap. 3.

23. Janet L. Abu-Lughod, *Race, Space, and Riots in Chicago, New York, and Los Angeles* (New York: Oxford University Press, 2007), chaps. 5 and 6; Gerald Horne, *Fire This Time: The Watts Uprising and the 1960s* (Charlottesville: University Press of Virginia, 1995), pt. 2; Malcolm McLaughlin, *The Long, Hot Summer of 1967: Urban Rebellion in America* (New York: Palgrave Macmillan, 2014), chaps. 1 and 2; National Advisory Commission on Civil Disorders, *The Kerner Report* (Princeton, NJ: Princeton University Press, 2016), pt. 2. On white attitudes being influenced by these events see Howard Schuman, Charlotte Steeh, Lawrence Bobo, and Maria Krysan, *Racial Attitudes in America*, rev. ed. (Cambridge, MA: Harvard University Press, 1997), 164; the authors suggest that these episodes of mass civil disobedience and destruction contributed to a substantial shift in white opinion about the sources of African American disadvantages.

24. Boustan, *Competition in the Promised Land*, chap. 4.

25. On these tendencies see Hirsch, *Making the Second Ghetto*, 216–17; Thomas J. Sugrue, *The Origins of the Urban Crisis: Race and Inequality in Postwar Detroit* (Princeton, NJ: Princeton University Press, 1996), chaps. 7 and 8; Kevin M. Kruse, *White Flight: Atlanta and the Making of Modern Conservatism* (Princeton, NJ: Princeton University Press, 2005), chaps. 4–6; and Eric Avila, *Popular Culture in the Age of White Flight: Fear and Fantasy in Suburban Los Angeles* (Berkeley: University of California Press, 2006), chaps. 1–3.

26. See James W. Loewen, *Sundown Towns: A Hidden Dimension of American Racism* (New York: New Press, 2005), 5, 10–12; Don Terry, "Chicago Neighborhood Reveals an Ugly Side," *New York Times*, March 27, 1997, http://www.nytimes.com/1997/03/27/us/chicago-neighborhood-reveals-an-ugly-side.html; Isabel Wilkerson, "Integration Proves Elusive in an Ohio Suburb," *New York Times*, October 30, 1988, http://www.nytimes.com/1988/10/30/us/integration-proves-elusive-in-an-ohio-suburb.html?pagewanted=all. On Wallace see Michael A. Cohen, *American Maelstrom: The 1968 Election and the Politics of Division* (New York: Oxford University Press, 2016), pt. 2. On racial beliefs see Schuman, Steeh, Bobo, and Krysan, *Racial Attitudes in America*, 153–66, which demonstrates how white ideas about African American disadvantages differed by levels of education at this time.

27. On the development of the black middle class see Rury and Hill, *African American Struggle*, 124. Data on changes in poverty rates, which affected both whites and blacks, can be found in Robert G. Mogull, "American Poverty in the 1960s," *Phylon* 33, no. 2 (1972): 161–68.

28. A compelling account of such concerns in this period can be found in Preston H. Smith II, *Racial Democracy and the Black Metropolis: Housing Policy in Postwar Chicago* (Minneapolis: University of Minnesota Press, 2012), chap. 5; Karl Taeuber, "Negro Residential Segregation: Trends and Measurement," *Social Problems* 12, no. 1 (Summer 1964): 42–50. Taeuber calculated that Kansas City had a segregation index of 90 in 1970, which was higher than its regional average and similar to cities in the South at the time. See Karl Taeuber, "Racial Residential Segregation, 28 Cities, 1970–1980," University of Wisconsin, Center for Demography and Ecology, March 1983, https://files.eric.ed.gov/fulltext/ED234107.pdf.

29. Rury and Hill, *African American Struggle*, chap. 4.

30. Black graduation rates generally remained below white rates, so the city schools usually registered an overall drop with white flight. But even crowded urban high schools in the North were an improvement over the haphazard educational opportunities available to blacks in the southern countryside at this time. See John L. Rury, "Attainment amidst Adversity: Black High School Students in the Metropolitan North, 1940–1980," in *Clio at the Table: Using History to Inform and Improve Education Policy*, ed. Kenneth K. Wong and Robert Rothman (New York: Peter Lang, 2009), 37–58.

31. For discussion of urban school desegregation and related problems in this era see Raymond C. Hummel and John M. Nagle, *Urban Education in America: Problems and Prospects* (New York: Oxford University Press, 1973), chap. 4; on overcrowding see Rury and Hill, *African American Struggle*, chap. 4.

32. Rury, "Race, Space," 131–32; Dionne Danns, *Something Better for Our Children: Black Organization in the Chicago Public Schools, 1963–1971* (New York: Routledge, 2002), chaps. 3–5; Dionne Danns, *Desegregating Chicago's Public Schools: Policy Implementation, Politics, and Protest, 1965–1985* (New York: Palgrave Macmillan, 2014), introduction and chap. 1; and Rury and Hill, *African American Struggle*, 158. On the Detroit walkout see Allie Gross, "Detroit '67: 1966 Student Walkout at Northern a Sign of Things to Come," *Detroit Free Press*, July 17, 2017, https://www.freep.com/story/news/local/

michigan/detroit/2017/07/17/detroit-67-1966-student-walkout-northern-sign-things-come/483019001/. Also see Barry M. Franklin, "Community, Race, and Curriculum in Detroit: The Northern High School Walkout," *History of Education* 33; no. 2 (2004): 137–56.

33. Boustan, *Competition in the Promised Land*, chap. 4. Also see Sugrue, *Origins of the Urban Crisis*, pt. 3.

34. Hummel and Nagle, *Urban Education in America*, 202–3. See chap. 7, "The Financial Condition of Urban Schools," for a comprehensive discussion of the fiscal problems facing large urban school districts.

35. Ibid., viii; Harvey Kantor and Barbara Brenzel, "Urban Education and the 'Truly Disadvantaged': The Historical Roots of the Contemporary Crisis, 1945–1990," *Teachers College Record* 94, no. 2 (1992): 278–314; also see Harvey Kantor and Robert Lowe, "Class, Race, and the Emergence of Federal Education Policy: From the New Deal to the Great Society," *Educational Researcher* 24, no. 3 (1995): 4–11. Although black graduation rates were on the rise, they still generally lagged the rates of whites who were leaving the cities. On this point see Rury and Hill, *African American Struggle*, chap. 4.

36. Robert J. Havighurst and Daniel U. Levine, *Education in Metropolitan Areas*, 2nd ed. (Boston: Allyn & Bacon, 1971), 84.

37. On the origins and evolution of ESEA see Gareth Davies, *See Government Grow: Education Politics from Johnson to Reagan* (Lawrence: University Press of Kansas, 2007), chaps. 2 and 3; see also Charles S. Benson and Kevin O'Halloran, "The Economic History of School Finance in the United States," *Journal of Education Finance* 12, no. 4 (Spring 1987): 495–515. On the question of state aid to districts see John Riew, "State Aids for Public Schools and Metropolitan Finance," *Land Economics* 46, no. 3 (August 1970): 297–304.

38. David K. Cohen and Susan L. Moffitt, *The Ordeal of Equality: Did Federal Regulation Fix the Schools?* (Cambridge, MA: Harvard University Press, 2009), 9.

39. Seymour Sacks, *City Schools / Suburban Schools: A History of Fiscal Conflict* (Syracuse, NY: Syracuse University Press, 1972), chaps. 4 and 7; Arthur Wise, *Rich Schools, Poor Schools: The Promise of Equal Educational Opportunity* (Chicago: University of Chicago Press, 1968). Also see Ryan, *Five Miles Away, a World Apart*, pt. 2.

40. On the Coleman Report see Adam Gamoran and David A. Long, "*Equality of Educational Opportunity*: A Forty Year Retrospective," in *International Studies in Educational Inequality: Theory and Policy*, ed. Richard Tees, Stephen Lamb, Marie Duru-Bellat, and Sue Helme (New York: Springer, 2007), 23–47. See also John L. Rury and Argun Saatcioglu, "Did the Coleman Report Underestimate the Effect of Economic Status on Educational Outcomes?," *Teachers College Record*, January 22, 2015, http://www.tcrecord.org, ID no. 17828.

41. The quote can be found in Gene I. Maeroff and Leonard Buder, *The New York Times Guide to Suburban Public Schools: Long Island, Westchester and Rockland, Connecticut, New Jersey* (New York: Quadrangle / New York Times Book Co., 1976), xvii–xviii.

42. For an overview of these historical issues and relevant research literature see John L. Rury and Jeffrey Mirel, "The Political Economy of Urban Education," *Review of Research in Education* 22 (1997): 49–110. Also see Robert P. O'Reilly, *Racial and Social Class Isolation in the Schools: Implications for Educational Policy and Programs* (New York: Praeger, 1970), chap. 7. The quote is from Sacks, *City Schools / Suburban Schools*, 172.

43. Mirel, *Rise and Fall*, chaps. 5 and 6; Rury, "Race, Space," 129–34. Also see Jack Dougherty, *More Than One Struggle: The Evolution of Black School Reform in Milwaukee* (Chapel Hill: University of North Carolina Press, 2004), chap. 4; Jean Anyon, *Ghetto Schooling: A Political Economy of Urban Educational Reform* (New York: Teachers College

Press, 1997), chap. 1; and Daniel H. Perlstein, *Justice, Justice: School Politics and the Eclipse of Liberalism* (New York: Peter Lang, 2004), introduction.

44. James T. Patterson, *Brown v. Board of Education: A Civil Rights Milestone and Its Troubled Legacy* (New York: Oxford University Press, 2002), chaps. 6 and 7; John Morton Blum, *Years of Discord: American Politics and Society, 1961–1974* (New York: W. W. Norton, 1991), chap. 7.

45. Ira Katznelson and Margaret Weir, *Schooling for All: Class, Race, and the Decline of the Democratic Ideal* (Berkeley: University of California Press, 1988), chap. 7; Kathryn M. Neckerman, *Schools Betrayed: Roots of Failure in Inner-City Education* (Chicago: University of Chicago Press, 2007), chaps. 3 and 4; Diane Ravitch, *The Great School Wars: A History of the New York City Public Schools* (New York: Basic Books, 1974), chaps. 23 and 24; and Ronald P. Formasano, *Boston against Busing: Race, Class, and Ethnicity in the 1960s and 1970s* (Chapel Hill: University of North Carolina Press, 1991), chaps. 5–9.

46. David Rogers, *110 Livingston Street: Politics and Bureaucracy in the New York City School System* (New York: Random House, 1968), chaps. 8, 9, and 11; Richard C. Kearney and Chandan Sinha, "Professionalism and Bureaucratic Responsiveness: Conflict or Compatibility?," *Public Administration Review* 48, no. 1 (January–February 1988): 571–79; Hummel and Nagle, *Urban Education in America*, 160–67.

47. Willis D. Hawley, "The New Mythology of School Desegregation," *Law and Contemporary Problems* 42, no. 4 (Autumn 1978): 214–33; Lewis M. Killian and Charles M. Grigg, "Community Resistance to and Acceptance of Desegregation," *Journal of Negro Education* 34, no. 3, Education and Civil Rights in 1965 (Summer 1965): 268–77; J. Harvie Wilkinson III, "The Supreme Court and Southern School Desegregation, 1955–1970: A History and Analysis," *Virginia Law Review* 64, no. 4 (May 1978): 485–559.

48. Hayden, *Building Suburbia*, chap. 7; Jon C. Teaford, *The American Suburb: The Basics* (New York: Routledge, 2008), chap. 1; John L. Rury and Argun Saatcioglu, "Suburban Advantage: Opportunity Hoarding and Secondary Attainment in the Postwar Metropolitan North," *American Journal of Education* 117, no. 3 (May 2011): 307–42.

49. Herbert Gans, *The Levittowners: Ways of Life and Politics in a New Suburban Community* (New York: Alfred A. Knopf, 1967), chaps. 1 and 2; Adam Rome, *The Bulldozer in the Countryside: Suburban Sprawl and the Rise of American Environmentalism* (New York: Cambridge University Press, 2001), chap. 1; Margaret Lundrigan Ferrer and Tova Navarra, *Our House: The Stories of Levittown* (New York: Scholastic, 1965), chaps. 2 and 3; Barbara M. Kelly, *Expanding the American Dream: Building and Rebuilding Levittown* (Albany: SUNY Press, 1993), chap. 7; Joseph Bensman and Arthur J. Vidich, "The New Middle Classes: Their Culture and Life Styles," *Journal of Aesthetic Education* 4, no. 1 (January 1970): 23–39; Shelley Nickles, "More Is Better: Mass Consumption, Gender, and Class Identity in Postwar America," *American Quarterly* 54, no. 4 (December 2002): 581–622.

50. Havighurst and Levine, *Education in Metropolitan Areas*, chap. 5; Gans, *Levittowners*, 97–101.

51. On these points see Reynolds Farley, "Components of Suburban Population Growth," and Larry H. Long and Paul C. Glick, "Family Patterns in Suburban Areas: Recent Trends," chaps. 1 and 2 in *The Changing Face of the Suburbs*, ed. Barry Schwartz (Chicago: University of Chicago Press, 1976), 3–68.

52. Steven Mintz, *Huck's Raft: A History of American Childhood* (Cambridge, MA: Harvard University Press, 2004), 277.

53. On the tendency of younger families to move to the suburbs at this time see Long and Glick, "Family Patterns in Suburban Areas," 40–68. For an informative study of a suburban school district see Daniel Linden Duke, *Education Empire: The Evolution of an Excellent Suburban School System* (Albany: SUNY Press, 2005), chaps. 1–3. Also see Paul Lyons, *Class of '66: Living in Suburban Middle America* (Philadelphia: Temple University

Press, 1994), chaps. 1 and 2; and Maeroff and Buder, *New York Times Guide to Suburban Public Schools*, introduction.

54. Frey and Speare, *Regional and Metropolitan Growth*, chap. 7; Jackson, *Crabgrass Frontier*, chaps. 13 and 14; David R. Goldfield, *Cotton Fields and Skyscrapers: Southern City and Region, 1607–1980* (Baton Rouge: LSU Press, 1982), chap. 6; Kruse, *White Flight*, chap. 9; Teaford, *American Suburb*, chaps. 1 and 2.

55. See Kathleen A. Brosnan and Amy L. Scott, introduction to *City Dreams, Country Schemes: Community and Identity in the American West*, ed. Kathleen A. Brosnan and Amy L. Scott (Reno: University of Nevada Press, 2013), 1–9. Also see David Rusk, *Cities without Suburbs* (Baltimore: Johns Hopkins University Press, 1993), 31–41.

56. Historically, significant educational differences had long existed between the North, South, and West of the country, as schooling conformed to the social and economic factors that distinguished them. The industrial and highly urbanized Northeast and upper Midwest, for instance, had traditionally invested more heavily in public education than the agricultural South, while the West exhibited the nation's highest levels of attainment. The development of national markets, however, along with improved transportation and communication networks, contributed to a gradual convergence in these regional characteristics. See John L. Rury, "American School Enrollment in the Progressive Era: An Interpretive Inquiry," *History of Education* 14, no. 1 (Summer 1985): 49–67; John L. Rury, Argun Saatcioglu, and William P. Skorupski, "Expanding Secondary Attainment in the United States, 1940–80: A Fixed-Effects Regression Model," *Historical Methods* 43, no. 3 (July–September 2010): 139–52.

57. James D. Tarver, "Migration Differentials in Southern Cities and Suburbs," *Social Science Quarterly* 50, no. 2 (September 1969): 298–324.

58. Argun Saatcioglu and John L. Rury, "Education and the Changing Metropolitan Organization of Inequality: A Multilevel Analysis of Secondary Attainment in the United States, 1940–1980," *Historical Methods* 45, no. 1 (January–March 2012): 21–40; Sukkoo Kim, "Economic Integration and Convergence: U.S. Regions, 1840–1987," *Journal of Economic History* 58 (1998): 659–83; F. Caselli and W. J. Coleman II, "The U.S. Structural Transformation and Regional Convergence: A Reinterpretation," *Journal of Political Economy* 109 (2001): 584–616.

59. Jackson, *Crabgrass Frontier*, chap. 8; Fox, *Metropolitan America*, chaps. 1 and 2; Kent P. Schwirian, F. Martin Hankins, and Carol A. Ventresca, "The Residential Decentralization of Social Status Groups in American Metropolitan Communities, 1950–1980," *Social Forces* 68, no. 4 (June 1990): 1143–63; John Fine, Norval D. Glenn, and J. Kenneth Monts, "The Residential Segregation of Occupational Groups in Central Cities and Suburbs," *Demography* 8, no. 1 (February 1971): 91–101; Carol A. O'Connor, "Sorting Out the Suburbs: Patterns of Land Use, Class, and Culture," *American Quarterly* 37, no. 3 (1985): 382–94.

60. Teaford, *American Suburb*, chaps. 1 and 2.

61. Frey and Speare, *Regional and Metropolitan Growth*, chap. 7; Goldfield, *Cotton Fields and Skyscrapers*, chap. 6. For more on this see Saatcioglu and Rury, "Education and the Changing Metropolitan Organization of Inequality," 21–24.

62. Douglas Massey and Nancy Denton, *American Apartheid: Segregation and the Making of the Underclass* (Cambridge, MA: Harvard University Press, 1993), chaps. 1–3; D. R. James, "City Limits on Racial Equality: The Effects of City-Suburb Boundaries on Public-School Desegregation, 1968–1976," *American Sociological Review* 54 (1989): 963–85; S. Welch, M. Combs, L. Sigelman, and T. Bledsoe, "Race or Place? Emerging Public Perspectives on Urban Education," *PS: Political Science and Politics* 30 (1997): 454–58. Mark Baldassare, "Suburban Communities," *Annual Review of Sociology* 18 (1992): 475–94; J. R. Logan, R. D. Alba, T. Mcnulty, and B. Fisher, "Making a Place in the Metropolis: Locational

Attainment in Cities and Suburbs," *Demography* 33 (1996): 443–59; V. J. Roscigno, D. Tomaskovic-Devey, and M. Crowley, "Education and Inequalities of Place," *Social Forces* 84 (2006): 2121–45.

63. Rury and Hill, *African American Struggle*, chap. 1. On the importance of parental education see W. Norton Grubb, *The Money Myth: School Resources, Outcomes, and Equity* (New York: Russell Sage Foundation, 2009), chap. 1.

64. On this point see Nan Marie Astone and Sara S. McLanahan, "Family Structure, Parental Practices and High School Completion," *American Sociological Review* 56, no. 3 (June 1991): 309–20; and Sheila Fitzgerald Krein and Andrea H. Beller, "Educational Attainment of Children from Single-Parent Families: Differences by Exposure, Gender, and Race," *Demography* 25, no. 1 (May 1988): 221–34.

65. Jackson, *Crabgrass Frontier*, chap. 7; Hayden, *Building Suburbia*, chaps. 6 and 7.

66. Caselli and Coleman, "U.S. Structural Transformation," 584–90; Saatcioglu and Rury, "Education and the Changing Metropolitan Organization of Inequality," 21–40.

67. Logan, Alba, Mcnulty, and Fisher, "Making a Place in the Metropolis," 443–53; H. L. Hughes, "Metropolitan Structure and the Suburban Hierarchy," *American Sociological Review* 58 (1993): 417–33; M. C. Brazer, "Economic and Social Disparities between Central Cities and Their Suburbs," *Land Economics* 43 (1967): 294–302.

68. Teaford, *American Suburb*, chap. 3.

69. Saatcioglu and Rury, "Education and the Changing Metropolitan Organization of Inequality," 36–37. Also see John L. Rury and Argun Saatcioglu, "Suburban Advantage: Opportunity Hoarding and Secondary Attainment in the Postwar Metropolitan North," *American Journal of Education* 117, no. 3 (Summer 2011): 307–42. In both these studies, enrollment in grade 11 or higher—or having graduated—was interpreted as a proxy for high school success and the likelihood of graduation. Both studies told the same story of a slight urban advantage in 1940 and a larger suburban advantage forty years later. Youth in the study were labeled suburban if they lived within an SMSA (Standard Metropolitan Statistical Area) but outside the central city. Some of these areas may have been rather rural in character in 1940, and much less so twenty years later.

70. On the challenges facing suburban children see Edward A. Wynn, *Growing Up Suburban* (Austin: University of Texas Press, 1977), chaps. 1 and 2.

71. On anti-city attitudes during this period see Steven Conn, *Americans against the City: Anti-urbanism in the Twentieth Century* (New York: Oxford University Press, 2014), chaps. 6 and 7; also see Campbell F. Scribner, *The Fight for Local Control: Schools, Suburbs, and American Democracy* (Ithaca, NY: Cornell University Press, 2016), introduction. See also Claude S. Fischer and Robert Max Jackson, "Suburbs, Networks, and Attitudes," in Schwartz, *Changing Face of the Suburbs*, 279–308.

72. Joseph F. Zimmerman, "The Metropolitan Area Problem," *Annals of the American Academy of Political and Social Science* 416 (November 1974): 133–47. For a concise discussion from a sociological standpoint see Amos H. Hawley and Basil G. Zimmer, *The Metropolitan Community: Its People and Government* (Beverly Hills, CA: Sage, 1970), chap. 1, "The Metropolitan Problem." On page 2 they noted, "Metropolitan growth has divided among many governmental units what are actually indivisible problems."

73. Vincent Ostram, Charles Tiebout, and Robert D. Warren, "The Organization of Government in Metropolitan Areas: A Theoretical Inquiry," *American Political Science Review* 55 (1961): 831–42; Luther Gulick, *The Metropolitan Problem and American Ideas* (New York: Alfred A. Knopf, 1962), chap. 1. On schooling see Warner Bloomberg Jr. and Morris Sunshine, *Suburban Power Structures and Public Education* (Syracuse, NY: Syracuse University Press, 1963), chaps. 5 and 6.

74. Hawley and Zimmer, *Metropolitan Community*, chaps. 5 and 6.

75. See the discussion of localism and its history, especially with respect to schools, in Scribner, *Fight for Local Control*, chaps. 1 and 2. Also see Hawley and Zimmer, *Metropolitan Community*, chap. 4; and Douglas S. Reed, *Building the Federal Schoolhouse: Localism and the American Educational State* (New York: Oxford University Press, 2014), pt. 2.

76. Basil G. Zimmer, "Suburbanization and Changing Political Structures," in Schwartz, *Changing Face of the Suburbs*, 165–202.

77. Robert Havighurst was a major contributor to this perspective. See, for instance, his following works: *Education in Metropolitan Areas* (Boston: Allyn & Bacon, 1966), "Metropolitan Development and the Education System," in *Education of the Disadvantaged*, ed. A. H. Passow (New York: Holt, Rinehart & Winston, 1967), and *Metropolitanism: Its Challenge to Education*, 67th Yearbook, National Society for the Study of Education, pt. 1 (Chicago: University of Chicago Press, 1968). See also the discussion of different examples of this in metropolitan Kansas City and Missouri in chapter 4.

78. Basil G. Zimmer and Amos Hawley, *Metropolitan Area Schools: Resistance to District Reorganization* (Beverly Hills, CA: Sage, 1968), chap. 1.

79. Ibid.; Basil G. Zimmer and Amos H. Hawley, "Factors Associated with Resistance to the Organization of Metropolitan Area Schools," *Sociology of Education* 40, no. 4 (Autumn 1967): 334–47. The survey was conducted by the University of Chicago's National Opinion Research Center to produce a probability sample of about five hundred respondents from urban and suburban zones in each of the six metro areas. The authors decided to focus on the North to avoid the confounding influence of regional variation, and selected metro areas in three size groups: large (total population around one million), medium (around half a million), and small (around 150,000). Some 630 public officials in both urban and suburban settings were interviewed as well, 45 in each city and 60 in each set of suburbs. This sampling strategy reflected Zimmer and Hawley's expectation that findings would differ across these varied metropolitan contexts.

80. On these points see Hawley and Zimmer, *Metropolitan Community*, chap. 1. The quote is from Richard E. Wagner and Warren E. Weber, "Competition, Monopoly, and the Organization of Government in Metropolitan Areas," *Journal of Law & Economics* 18, no. 3 (December 1975): 663.

81. Zimmer and Hawley, *Metropolitan Area Schools*, chaps. 7 and 8.

82. Ryan, *Five Miles Away, a World Apart*, 154.

83. Zimmer and Hawley, *Metropolitan Area Schools*, chaps. 7 and 8. For somewhat different perspective see Teaford, *City and Suburb*, chap. 5. Teaford suggested that resistance to unified government in metropolitan areas was greatest among blue-collar workers who feared racial change and higher taxes. Zimmer and Hawley did not explore the question of race, but they too found that less-affluent respondents were most worried about taxes. Unlike their study, however, Teaford's did not focus on the schools. For a study that mirrored many of the findings of Zimmer and Hawley, even though published six years earlier, see Roscoe C. Martin, *Government and the Suburban School* (Syracuse, NY: Syracuse University Press, 1962), chap. 4.

84. Zimmer and Hawley, *Metropolitan Area Schools*, 192. On the preferences of affluent suburbanites in this period see Sylvia F. Fava, "Beyond Suburbia," *Annals of the American Academy of Political and Social Science* 422 (1975): 10–24.

85. Patterson, *Brown v. Board of Education*, chaps. 2–5; Roger Goldman and David Gallen, *Thurgood Marshall: Justice for All* (New York: Carrol & Graf, 1992), 56–140.

86. Gamoran and Long, "Equality of Educational Opportunity," 29; Mildred A. Schwartz, *Trends in White Attitudes toward Negroes*, Report no. 119, National Opinion Research Center, University of Chicago, 1967, 9, http://www.norc.org/PDFs/publications/NOR

CRpt_119.pdf. American Presidency Project, Lyndon B. Johnson, Commencement Address at Howard University: "To Fulfill These Rights," June 4, 1965, https://www.presidency.ucsb.edu/documents/commencement-address-howard-university-fulfill-these-rights.

87. Patterson, *Brown v. Board of Education*, chaps. 6 and 7; Charles T. Clotfelter, *After "Brown": The Rise and Retreat of School Desegregation* (Princeton, NJ: Princeton University Press, 2004), chap. 1; Rury and Hill, *African American Struggle*, chaps. 4 and 5.

88. Kantor and Brenzel, "Urban Education and the 'Truly Disadvantaged,'" 278–314; Mirel, *Rise and Fall*, chap. 6; Rury and Mirel, "Political Economy of Urban Education," 73–81. On the misnomer that de facto desegregation represented see Richard Rothstein, *The Color of Law: A Forgotten History of How Our Government Segregated America* (New York: Liveright, 2017), xii.

89. Matthew L. Delamont, *Why Busing Failed: Race, Media, and the National Resistance to School Desegregation* (Berkeley: University of California Press, 2016), chaps. 1–3; Ansley T. Erickson, *Making the Unequal Metropolis: School Desegregation and Its Limits* (Chicago: University of Chicago Press, 2016), pt. 2; Gary Orfield, *Public School Desegregation in the United States, 1968–1980* (Washington, DC: Joint Center for Policy Studies, 1983), chap. 2; Clotfelter, *After "Brown,"* chaps. 3 and 4.

90. Joyce A. Baugh, *The Detroit School Busing Case:* Milliken v. Bradley *and the Controversy over Desegregation* (Lawrence: University Press of Kansas, 2011); Ryan, *Five Miles Away, a World Apart*, chap. 2.

91. Rury and Mirel, "Political Economy of Urban Education," 81–98; Jeffrey Henig, *Rethinking School Choice: The Limits of the Market Metaphor* (Princeton, NJ: Princeton University Press, 1995), chaps. 2 and 5.

92. Alejandro Portes and Rubén G. Rumbaut, *Immigrant America: A Portrait* (Berkeley: University of California Press, 1990), chaps. 1 and 2; Alejandro Portes and Rubén G. Rumbaut, *Legacies: The Story of the Immigrant Second Generation* (Berkeley: University of California Press, 2001), chap. 1.

93. Barry Bluestone and Bennett Harrison, *The Deindustrialization of America: Plant Closings, Community Abandonment, and the Dismantling of Basic Industry* (New York: Basic Books, 1982), chaps. 1–5; William Julius Wilson, *When Work Disappears: The World of the New Urban Poor* (New York: Alfred A. Knopf, 1996), pt. 1; also see Wilson's earlier work, *The Truly Disadvantaged: The Inner City, the Underclass, and Public Policy* (Chicago: University of Chicago Press, 1987). On debates about how to understand and label these developments see Michael B. Katz, *The Undeserving Poor: America's Enduring Confrontation with Poverty*, 2nd ed. (New York: Oxford University Press, 2013), chaps. 4 and 5.

94. On media representation of these issues as related to education see this 178-page compilation of articles from one newspaper: *Chicago's Schools: Worst in America* (Chicago: Chicago Tribune, 1988). A classic case of battles over desegregation leading to the decline of a city school system can be seen in Kansas City, described in Peter William Moran, *Race, Law, and the Desegregation of Public Schools* (New York: LFB Scholarly, 2005), chaps. 1–7.

95. The quotes can be found in Wilson, *When Work Disappears*, 8. See part 1 of the book for a discussion of the changing conditions that contributed to the heightened urban crisis of the 1990s. Also see Wilson's more recent book, *More Than Just Race: Being Black and Poor in the Inner City* (New York: W. W. Norton, 2009), chaps. 1 and 2.

96. Boustan, *Competition in the Promised Land*, 102; William W. Goldsmith and Edward J. Blakely, *Separate Societies: Poverty and Inequality in U.S. Cities* (Philadelphia: Temple University Press, 1992), chap. 4; Paul A. Jargowsky, *Poverty and Place: Ghettos, Barrios, and the American City* (New York: Russell Sage Foundation, 1997), chaps. 1 and 2; Kantor and Brenzel, "Urban Education and the 'Truly Disadvantaged,'" 310–12. On

inner-city ghetto communities see Tommie Shelby, *Dark Ghettos: Injustice, Dissent, and Reform* (Cambridge, MA: Harvard University Press, 2016), chap. 3. On overall trends in black standards of suburban living see Deirdre Pfeiffer, "Racial Equity in the Post–Civil Rights Suburbs? Evidence from US Regions 2000–2012," *Urban Studies* 53, no. 4 (2016): 799–817.

97. On African American suburbs and federal policy see Andrew Wiese, *Places of Their Own: African American Suburbanization in the Twentieth Century* (Chicago: University of Chicago Press, 2004), chaps. 8 and 9; Charles M. Lamb, *Housing Segregation in Suburban America since 1960: Presidential and Judicial Politics* (New York: Cambridge University Press, 2005), chaps. 2–5.

98. On these points see Nathan Glazer, "The Real World of Urban Education," *Public Interest*, no. 106 (1992): 57–75; Paula D. McClain, "Thirty Years of Urban Policies: Frankly, My Dears, We Don't Give a Damn!," *Urban Affairs Review* 30, no. 5 (1995): 641–44; and Lee Sigelman and Jeffrey R. Henig, "Crossing the Great Divide: Race and Preferences for Living in the City versus the Suburbs," *Urban Affairs Review* 37, no. 1 (September 2001): 3–18.

99. On these points see Alan Mallach, *The Divided City: Poverty and Prosperity in Urban America* (Washington, DC: Island Press, 2018), chap. 9.

100. Regarding the low state of public opinion regarding big-city school systems, and perceptions of bureaucratic control, see Dan A. Lewis and Kathryn Nakagawa, *Race and Educational Reform in the American Metropolis: A Study of School Decentralization* (Albany: SUNY Press, 1995), chap. 1.

101. On lessons to be learned from southern desegregation cases see Erickson, *Making the Unequal Metropolis*, conclusion; Ansley T. Erickson, "Fairness, Commitment, and Civic Capacity: The Varied Desegregation Trajectories of Metropolitan School Districts," in *The Shifting Landscape of the American School District: Race, Class, Geography, and the Perpetual Reform of Local Control, 1935–2015*, ed. David Gamson and Emily Hodge (New York: Peter Lang, 2018), 107–226; Genevieve Siegel-Hawley and Stefani Thachik, "Crossing the Line? School District Responses to Demographic Change in the South," in Gamson and Hodge, *Shifting Landscape*, 79–106; and Genevieve Siegel-Hawley, *When the Fences Come Down: Twenty-First-Century Lessons from Metropolitan School Desegregation* (Chapel Hill: University of North Carolina Press, 2016), pt. 3.

2. UNITING AND DIVIDING A HEARTLAND METROPOLIS

1. Aaron Tyler Rife, "Shifting Identities in South Kansas City: Hickman Mills's Transformation from a Suburban to Urban School District" (PhD diss., University of Kansas, 2014), 52.

2. For an overview of the area's development during this period see James R. Shortridge, *Kansas City and How It Grew, 1822–2011* (Lawrence: University Press of Kansas, 2012), chap. 5. For an account of a somewhat similar set of circumstances regarding school districts within city boundaries and its consequences see James C. Owen and Willbern York, *Governing Metropolitan Indianapolis: The Politics of Unigov* (Berkeley: University of California Press, 1985), chap. 6; and Shaina Cavazos, "Racial Bias and the Crumbling of a City," *Atlantic*, August 17, 2016, https://www.theatlantic.com/education/archive/2016/08/indianapolis-school-districts/496145/.

3. Shortridge, *Kansas City and How It Grew*, chap. 5; on the local history of racial conflict see Sherry Lamb Schirmer, *A City Divided: The Racial Landscape of Kansas City, 1900–1960* (Columbia: University of Missouri Press, 2002), chaps. 2–5; and Charles E. Coulter, *Take Up the Black Man's Burden: Kansas City's African American Communities, 1865–1939* (Columbia: University of Missouri Press, 2006), chaps. 7–9.

4. Growth rates are reported for the Kansas City metropolitan area in the *Statistical Abstract of the United States, 1951, 1961, 1971,* and *1981* (Washington, DC: Government Printing Office), section 1, population, which lists standard statistical metropolitan area population figures from each decennial census. These are available at https://www.census.gov/library/publications/time-series/statistical_abstracts.html.

5. On these points see Shortridge, *Kansas City and How It Grew*, chaps. 4 and 5.

6. Bill Gilbert, *This City, This Man: The Cookingham Era in Kansas City* (Washington, DC: International County Management Association, 1978), chap. 10.

7. Shortridge, *Kansas City and How It Grew*, 102–5.

8. "Area's Face Changes with Annexations," *Kansas City Star*, January 15, 1958, 1E.

9. Gilbert, *This City, This Man*, chaps. 10 and 11, which note that the referendum to annex the Northland passed by a margin of fewer than two thousand votes, out of nearly eighty thousand votes cast. Initially Cookingham felt the measure had failed, believing it required a two-thirds majority. But he soon discovered that only a simple majority was required. Opponents of annexation were dumbstruck to learn that it had passed despite the close vote. Also see Rick Montgomery and Shirl Kasper, *Kansas City: An American Story* (Kansas City, MO: Kansas City Star Books, 1999), 277.

10. "The Assembly Can Prevent a Local School Crisis," *Kansas City Star*, April 26, 1957, 50.

11. "School Bill Passed in Second Attempt," *Kansas City Times*, April 25, 1957, 3.

12. "A School Boundary Bill Passes House," *Kansas City Star*, May 9, 1957, 15.

13. Shortridge, *Kansas City and How It Grew*, 117. "Kansas City's Scattering of School Districts," *Kansas City Star*, September 7, 1958, 8; "No School Changes in Annexation Vote," *Kansas City Times*, March 3, 1960.

14. *One Hundred and Sixth Report of the Public Schools of the State of Missouri, School Year Ending June 30, 1955*, pt. 2, section 4, table A: Enumeration and Enrollment, 1954–55.

15. On the perceived advantages of larger school systems in this period see David L. Angus and Jeffrey E. Mirel, *The Failed Promise of the American High School, 1890–1995* (New York: Teachers College Press, 1999), chap. 4. On the advantage that urban high schools represented historically see William A. Fischel, *Making the Grade: The Economic Evolution of American School Districts* (Chicago: University of Chicago Press, 2009), 206–9.

16. Shortridge, *Kansas City and How It Grew*, 117.

17. On this point see ibid., 117 and 141.

18. Ibid., 86 and 87; also see Schirmer, *City Divided*, chaps. 3 and 4. The organization controlled by Thomas Pendergast dominated Kansas City politics between 1925 and 1939, when he was convicted of tax evasion. For an overview see Lawrence H. Larsen and Nancy J. Hulston, *Pendergast!* (Columbia: University of Missouri Press, 1997), chaps. 4–6.

19. Campbell Gibson and Kay Jung, *Historical Census Statistics on Population Totals by Race, 1790 to 1990, and by Hispanic Origin, 1970 to 1990, for Large Cities and Other Urban Places in the United States*, Population Division, Working Paper No. 76, February 2005, US Census Bureau, Washington, DC, http://www.census.gov/population/www/documentation/twps0076/twps0076.html.

20. Kevin Fox Gotham, *Race, Real Estate, and Uneven Development: The Kansas City Experience, 1900–2010*, 2nd ed. (Albany: SUNY Press, 2014), 98–99. US Census Bureau, *General Population Characteristics, 1980; United States Summary* (Washington, DC: Government Printing Office, 1983), table 69. At its height, the black population of KCK represented nearly a quarter of the city's population.

21. Shortridge, *Kansas City and How It Grew*, chap. 6. On ghetto formation during this period see Mitchell Duneier, *Ghetto: The Invention of a Place, the History of an Idea* (New York: Farrar, Straus and Giroux, 2016), chaps. 2 and 3.

22. Susan Hilliard, interview with John Rury, March 8, 2012. For other interviews see chap. 3.

23. Gotham, *Race, Real Estate*, chap. 5. Gotham suggests that school district attendance zones dictated black settlement patterns but also notes that a number of schools west of Troost eventually became integrated. He cites intact busing policies undertaken by the district as maintaining segregation, but these measures operated for a relatively brief time. As pointed out by Peter William Moran, integrated busing started in 1965. Gotham's analysis thus fails to explain why black residential settlement moved south—where predominantly white schools also existed—rather than west. On integrated busing see Peter William Moran, *Race, Law, and the Desegregation of Public Schools* (New York: LFB Scholarly, 2005), chap. 2. Also see "'Troost Wall' the Product of Kansas City's Long-Running Racial Plight: Racist Real Estate Practices Leave Urban Decay," *University News: UMKC's Independent Student Newspaper*, March 5, 2013, http://info.umkc.edu/unews/troost-wall-the-product-of-kansas-citys-long-running-racial-plight/. On the influence of real estate agents see Charles Hammer, "Nichols Fountain, 'Troost Wall,' Stories to Tell," *Kansas City Star*, July 3, 2017, 7A.

24. Moran, *Race, Law*, 27.

25. Gotham, *Race, Real Estate*, 97–111; Moran, *Race, Law*, chap. 4.

26. On racial change in the schools triggering neighborhood change see Moran, *Race, Law*, chap. 2. According to an examination of census tract data from the area on Social Explorer, in 1970 a somewhat higher proportion of the houses in predominantly white Tract 49, between Thirty-First and Thirty-Fourth Streets west of Troost, were valued below $12,500 than in predominantly black Tract 52 immediately to its east, 97 percent vs. 89 percent. A similar pattern was evident in Tracts 65 and 64 to the south between Thirty-Ninth and Forty-Third Streets. Overall, a majority of residences north of Forty-Seventh Street and west of Troost were valued below this benchmark, comparable to values on the east side of the dividing line.

27. A different set of factors appears to explain the persistence of the wall south of Forty-Seventh Street, where housing values were considerably higher west of Troost. This was Tract 74, which was proximate to the Country Club Plaza and included the local campus of the University of Missouri and affluent housing developments such as Brookside, with active homeowners' associations. With the assistance of the real estate industry, residents of these areas could more effectively bar African Americans from buying houses, especially those without the means to purchase more expensive homes. "Negroes: Do They Affect Property Values?," *Kansas City Star*, April 11, 1967. The *Star* article noted that the real estate industry itself was racially divided: "Several major firms which serve white home seekers have moved most of their operations out of southeast Kansas City. With a few exceptions, only firms which serve principally Negro buyers consistently show homes in the area." James Hazlett also recalled that the high price of homes in this area was a barrier to black families: James Hazlett deposition, March 9, 1983, box 109, file 154, 168–69, Arthur Benson Papers, Western Historical Collection, University of Missouri–Kansas City.

28. Stanley West, interview with John Rury, March 15, 2012.

29. Marvin Daniels, interview with John Rury, April 17, 2012.

30. Gotham, *Race, Real Estate*, chap. 6.

31. Deposition of Jack Casner, Arthur Benson Papers, box 106, file 143, Western Historical Collection, University of Missouri–Kansas City.

32. Hilliard interview, 2012; Shortridge, *Kansas City and How It Grew*, 143–45. On household income levels see Moran, *Race, Law*, 47.

33. David H. Klassen, *Survey of Black Residential Movement: Final Report, Kansas City Public Schools*, December 16, 1983, Part III; also see "Alleged FHA Custom Hurts Racial Shift," *Kansas City Star*, January 21, 1964.

34. "Still Barred in Home Buying," *Kansas City Star*, August 28, 1967; Daniels interview, 2012.

35. "Real Estate Ordinance Passed by City Council," *Kansas City Realtor*, January 30, 1964, 7.

36. Donna M. Davis, Jennifer Friend, and Loyce Caruthers, "The Fear of Color: 'Webb v. School District No. 90 in Johnson County, Kansas,' 1949," *American Educational History Journal* 37, no. 2 (2010): 331–45. Also see Rachel Devlin, *A Girl Stands at the Door: The Generation of Young Women Who Desegregated America's Schools* (New York: Basic Books, 2018), chap. 4; and Donald Bradley, "Before Landmark Desegregation Case, Another Brown Set the Stage," *Kansas City Star*, October 16, 2016, 6H. On schools in Independence, Missouri, see William J. Curtis, *A Rich Heritage: A Black History of Independence, Missouri* (Kansas City, MO: Better Impressions, 1985), 3–4.

37. Kevin Fox Gotham, "Missed Opportunities, Enduring Legacies: School Segregation and Desegregation in Kansas City, Missouri," *American Studies* 43, no. 2 (Summer 2002): 5–42.

38. See, for instance, "Negro Lynching (1rst report) Excelsior Springs, Missouri," *New York Times*, August 8, 1925, 2. Similar articles appeared in local newspapers, including the *Kansas City Star*.

39. Kansas City, Missouri, school superintendent James Hazlett observed from many conversations with African American parents that they wanted to send their children to schools where they would be accepted. In his words, "Blacks move into all white communities with feelings of insecurity, wondering how they are going to be accepted, wondering if their next door people are going to be neighborly, wondering if the teachers in their schools are going to really accept them." James Hazlett deposition, March 9, 1983, vol. 3, 344, Arthur Benson Papers, Western Historical Collection, University of Missouri–Kansas City.

40. Moran, *Race, Law*, chap. 6; Shortridge, *Kansas City and How It Grew*, 139–41.

41. A detailed account of this process can be found in Gotham, *Race, Real Estate*, chap. 5, although he focuses much attention on the influence of school attendance zones during the 1960s. For a more general discussion of neighborhood change see Michael J. White, "Racial and Ethnic Succession in Four Cities," *Urban Affairs Review* 20, no. 2 (1984): 165–83. Hoyt was from St. Joseph, Missouri, and graduated from the University of Kansas before going to Chicago for his doctorate. Regarding his sectoral thesis see Homer Hoyt, *The Structure and Growth of Residential Neighborhoods in American Cities* (Washington, DC: Federal Housing Administration, 1939). In his work for the FHA, Hoyt became one of the architects of housing policies that discriminated against African Americans; see Robert Beauregard, "More Than Sector Theory: Homer Hoyt's Contributions to Planning Knowledge," *Journal of Planning History* 6, no. 3 (2007): 248–71.

42. Poverty rates and income levels were calculated with Social Explorer, which was used to map the location of families living below the poverty line for African Americans and whites in 1970, along with average income at the tract level. The average poverty rate in the eighteen high-poverty African American tracts was 29.2 percent, and the average income was about $5,700 (about $32,000 in 2010 dollars). By comparison, average household income was considerably higher in Raytown (about $13,000, or $73,000 in 2010), North Kansas City (about $12,200, or $68,500 in 2010), and the Shawnee Mission area ($16,800, or $94,600 in 2010). The latter figure included a good deal of inequality too, as the wealthiest six tracts in Johnson County, mainly located in Mission Hills and Prairie Village, registered an average household income in 1970 of more than $27,500, or about $155,000 in 2010 dollars—more than four times greater than the poorest tracts just a few miles away. Figures provided in table 4.2 represent median

income levels and thus are a bit lower for the suburban districts. On the question of slums see Gotham, *Race, Real Estate*, chap. 4.

43. Ibid., chap. 2. The national poverty level for white families in 1960 was about 10 percent, less than a third of the black rate of 33.5 percent. See Robert G. Mogull, "American Poverty in the 1960s," *Phylon* 33, no. 2 (1972): 163. There was variation within census tracts, moreover, so that poverty often was more prevalent in some neighborhoods than others. On changes since the 1960s see Brad Plumer, "These Ten Charts Show the Black-White Economic Gap Hasn't Budged in 50 Years," *Washington Post*, August 28, 2013, https://www.washingtonpost.com/news/wonk/wp/2013/08/28/these-seven-charts-show-the-black-white-economic-gap-hasnt-budged-in-50-years/?utm_term=.bfc53bd91fe2.

44. Robert Neil Cooper, "Kansas City Missouri's Municipal Impact on Housing Segregation" (MA thesis, Pittsburgh State University, May 2016); see also "Racial Real Estate Steering," available on Sociology Research at http://sociology.iresearchnet.com/sociology-of-race/racial-real-estate-steering/.

45. Mark Gottdiener, *The Social Production of Urban Space* (Austin: University of Texas Press, 1987), chap. 3. This represented what Gottdiener described in the title of the book. Drawing on Henri Lefebvre's conception of social space as productive of class differentiation and conflict, Gottdiener argued that it is essential to studying social change.

46. Shortridge, *Kansas City and How It Grew*, 102–4; Gotham, *Race, Real Estate*, 14–22.

47. John L. Rury, "Trouble in Suburbia: Localism, Schools and Conflict in Postwar Johnson County, Kansas," *History of Education Quarterly* 55, no. 2 (May 2015): 135–40. Also see Shortridge, *Kansas City and How It Grew*, 80–85.

48. William S. Worley, *J. C. Nichols and the Shaping of Kansas City: Innovation in Planned Residential Communities* (Columbia: University of Missouri Press, 1990), chap. 10.

49. On Johnson County growth see *Johnson County Profiles*, University of Kansas Institute for Policy and Social Research, 2013, 2. For comparison of growth rates in different parts of the metropolitan area see Shortridge, *Kansas City and How It Grew*, 121 and 149.

50. On this point see Campbell F. Scribner, *The Fight for Local Control: Schools, Suburbs, and American Democracy* (Ithaca, NY: Cornell University Press, 2016), chap. 2.

51. Rury, "Trouble in Suburbia," 144–48.

52. Gotham, *Race, Real Estate*, 40–47; Shortridge, *Kansas City and How It Grew*, 122–29.

53. Joshua Dunn, *Complex Justice: The Case of Missouri v. Jenkins* (Chapel Hill: University of North Carolina Press, 2008), 2–7.

54. John L. Rury and Shirley A. Hill, *The African American Struggle for Secondary Education, 1940–1980: Closing the Graduation Gap* (New York: Teachers College Press, 2012), 151–52. On controversy regarding overcrowded schools see "Pupils Boycott Crowded School," *Kansas City Call*, November 7, 1952, 1.

55. Moran, *Race, Law*, chap. 2. See also "Adopt New Plan for Schools," *Kansas City Call*, November 6, 1964, 1.

56. Moran, *Race, Law*, chap. 3; Shortridge, *Kansas City and How It Grew*, 139–44. On the experience of other cities during this time see Jeffrey E. Mirel, *The Rise and Fall of an Urban School System: Detroit, 1907–1981*, 2nd ed. (Ann Arbor: University of Michigan Press, 1999), chap. 6; and Jean Anyon, *Ghetto Schooling: A Political Economy of Urban Educational Reform* (New York: Teachers College Press, 1997), chap. 6;

Daniel H. Perlstein, *Justice, Justice: School Politics and the Eclipse of Liberalism* (New York: Peter Lang, 2004), chap. 1.

57. Gotham, *Race, Real Estate*, 99–103; Shortridge, *Kansas City and How It Grew*, 190.

58. Edward T. Matheny Jr., *The Rise and Fall of Excellence: The Story of Southwest High School—R.I.P.* (Leawood, KS: Leathers, 2000), chap. 6.

59. See, for instance, Child Fund International, *The Effects of Poverty on Education in the United States*, November 11, 2013, https://www.childfund.org/Content/NewsDetail/2147489206/.

60. Data used in this portion of the study were drawn from the published Census of Population and Housing, which provides data in tract reports issued for 1960 and 1980: see US Census Bureau, *Census Tract-Level Data, 1960* (Washington, DC: US Department of Commerce, Bureau of the Census, 1971); US Census Bureau, *Census of Population and Housing, 1980. Census Tracts, Missouri (Selected Areas)* (Washington, DC: US Department of Commerce, Bureau of the Census, 1983).

61. Metropolitan Kansas City, including Johnson County, Kansas, is the principal point of interest. I have thus assembled a dataset to examine the distribution of educated adults across Jackson County in Missouri, which includes much of Kansas City and its southern suburbs, part of Clay County, Missouri, and Johnson County, Kansas. This enables assessment of the extent of geo-spatial inequality on a number of dimensions, with the census tract as the principal unit of analysis. Within the municipal boundaries of Kansas City, Tracts 1 through 96 were generally consistent in 1960 and 1980 census reports. Tracts outside the city that did not generally remain the same were adjusted to create comparable units across time. Tract data are weighted for population size. I have also assembled a 5 percent sample of seventeen-year-old residents of Jackson, Clay, and Johnson Counties in 1980, using US Census data from the Integrated Public Use Microdata Series (IPUMS) at the University of Minnesota. These data permit consideration of a range of factors affecting educational attainment, including residence in an affluent suburban area or the central city. Together with the tract-level data, this helps to provide a statistical portrait of how educational attainment was distributed unequally across the metropolitan area. The resulting sample included 958 individual cases, weighted to represent local population parameters.

62. This research is summarized in Norton Grubb, *The Money Myth: School Resources, Outcomes, and Equity* (New York: Russell Sage, 2009), chap. 1.

63. The movement of white families leaving Kansas City schools is discussed in chapter 4. On improving black graduation rates see Rury and Hill, *African American Struggle*, chaps. 3 and 4.

64. A statistical analysis of census tract data in each of these years reveals that the accumulation of educated adults in SMSD and Sunset Hills was independent of wealth in the area. In other words, more educated adults could be found in these parts of greater Kansas City than could be statistically explained by wealth or income alone. On this point see "Statistical Analysis of Uneven Educational Development," in the book's appendix, and the parallel discussion in John L. Rury and Sanae Akaba, "The Geospatial Distribution of Educational Attainment: Cultural Capital and Uneven Development in Metropolitan Kansas City, 1960–1980," *Histoire & Mesure* 29, no. 1 (2014): 219–46. One finding was the tendency of younger, highly educated families to move to affluent suburbs during this time. On this point nationally see "Trend Cited toward Purchase of Homes by Younger Couples Than Traditionally," *Kansas City Realtor*, May 13, 1965, 7.

65. On this point see Derrick Darby and John L. Rury, *The Color of Mind: Why the Origins of the Achievement Gap Matter for Justice* (Chicago: University of Chicago Press, 2018), chap. 2.

66. Moran, *Race, Law*, chap. 6.

67. On the persistence of poverty in segregated urban neighborhoods see Patrick Sharkey, *Stuck in Place: Urban Neighborhoods and the End of Progress toward Racial Equality* (Chicago: University of Chicago Press, 2013), chaps. 4–6.

68. See, for instance, John L. Rury and Argun Saatcioglu, "Suburban Advantage: Opportunity Hoarding and Secondary Attainment in the Postwar Metropolitan North," *American Journal of Education* 117, no. 3 (March 2011): 307–42.

69. The sample excluded those living in group quarters, such as orphan asylums, other residential institutions or jails, and those living in Wyandotte County, which included Kansas City, Kansas. Consequently, the analysis herein is limited to Jackson and Clay Counties in Missouri (including nearly all of Kansas City) and Johnson County in Kansas. It also excludes those attending private schools, which included many living in the Country Club district, home to the area's most elite nonpublic institutions. These data thus made it possible to focus on youth attending public schools. Because it is impossible to isolate KCMPS in IPUMS data, the entire city is assessed as a single geo-spatial entity, including annexed areas served by other schools. In the resulting analysis, Kansas City and Johnson County are included as fixed geo-spatial "dummy" variables, with suburban Jackson and Clay County residents serving as the comparison group. For additional points on this methodology and the data employed see Rury and Akaba, "Geo-spatial Distribution," 227–28.

70. Numbers are calculated from US Census data available through Social Explorer. In the city's most impoverished census tract, 45 percent of households were headed by single women. Altogether, an average of 27 percent were in this category across thirty-one predominantly black census tracts in 1980. On the other hand, in fourteen of those tracts more than 40 percent of families reported an annual income in excess of $15,000 ($40,000 in 2010 dollars), and in ten other tracts about 30 percent reported such income. On conditions in inner-city communities linked to family structure and poverty see William Julius Wilson, *The Truly Disadvantaged: The Inner City, the Underclass, and Public Policy* (Chicago: University of Chicago Press, 1987), pt. 1. For a somewhat different perspective see Adolph Reed Jr., "The Liberal Technocrat," *Nation*, February 6, 1988, 167–70. Regarding the challenges facing single-parent households, James Coleman observed that "we can think of the ratio of adults to children as a measure of the social capital in the family available for the education of any one of them." In other words, on average, single parents have fewer resources of all sorts to share with their children, and this showed clearly in data that he cited at the time. See James S. Coleman, "Social Capital in the Creation of Human Capital," *American Journal of Sociology* 94, Supplement: Organizations and Institutions: Sociological and Economic Approaches to the Analysis of Social Structure (1988): S112. A more comprehensive discussion of the topic can be found in Sara McLanahan and Gary D. Sandefur, *Growing Up with a Single Parent: What Hurts, What Helps* (Cambridge, MA: Harvard University Press, 1994), chaps. 1–4.

71. On these differences see Annette Lareau, *Home Advantage: Social Class and Parental Intervention in Elementary Education* (Lanham, MD: Rowman & Littlefield, 2000), chaps. 1, 6, and 9.

72. On this point see David Harding, Lisa Gennetian, Christopher Winship, Lisa Sanbonmatsu, and Jeffrey Kling, "Unpacking Neighborhood Influences on Educational Outcomes: Setting the Stage for Future Research," in *Whither Opportunity: Rising Inequality, Schools, and Children's Life Chances*, ed. Greg Duncan and Richard Murnane (New York: Russell Sage Foundation, 2011), 277–98.

73. On these points generally see William Julius Wilson, *More Than Just Race: Being Black and Poor in the Inner City* (New York: W. W. Norton, 2009), chaps. 1 and 2. On the history of policy and academic debates about this issue see Michael B. Katz, *The*

Undeserving Poor: America's Enduring Confrontation with Poverty, 2nd ed. (New York: Oxford University Press, 2013), chaps. 3–5.

74. Rury and Akaba, "Geo-spatial Distribution," 222–23.

3. FALL FROM GRACE

1. "Stresses Education's Role in the Area," *Kansas City Star*, August 31, 1962. As an example of this, in 1958 the Fred Liddy real estate office ran an ad in the *Kansas City Star* declaring "Johnson County has the tops in schools." Liddy's office was in Fairway, and the add appeared on page 29B of the *Star* on Sunday, May 4.

2. An example of this can be found in an article discussing the district's ability to attract and hold teachers compared to other districts: "City Is Losing Top Teachers," *Kansas City Star*, September 28, 1960.

3. "Stresses Education's Role in Area." Years later Hazlett recalled meeting with real estate professionals about these issues. James Hazlett deposition, March 9, 1983, 352–54, Arthur Benson Papers, box 108, file 157, Western Historical Collection, University of Missouri–Kansas City.

4. See, for instance, the following studies: Jeffrey E. Mirel, *The Rise and Fall of an Urban School System, Detroit, 1907–1980* (Ann Arbor: University of Michigan Press, 1993), chaps. 5 and 6; John L. Rury and Frank Cassell, eds., *Seeds of Crisis: Public Schooling in Milwaukee since 1920* (Madison: University of Wisconsin Press, 1993), esp. chaps. 1 and 3–6; and Jean Anyon, *Ghetto Schooling: A Political Economy of Urban Educational Reform* (New York: Teachers College Press, 1997), chaps. 5–7. Also see John L. Rury, "Race, Space, and the Politics of Chicago's Public Schools: Benjamin Willis and the Tragedy of Urban Education," *History of Education Quarterly* 39, no. 2 (Summer 1999): 117–42. For a more recent account see Alan Mallach, *The Divided City: Poverty and Prosperity in Urban America* (Washington, DC: Island Press, 2018), chap. 9.

5. James Shortridge, *Kansas City and How It Grew, 1822–2011* (Lawrence: University Press of Kansas, 2012), 138–41.

6. Peter William Moran, *Race, Law, and the Desegregation of Public Schools* (El Paso, TX: LFB Scholarly, 2005), chaps. 2–4. Also see Raymond C. Hummel and John M. Nagle, *Urban Education in America: Problems and Prospects* (New York: Oxford University Press, 1973), chap. 3. On the process of suburbanization see Jon C. Teaford, *The Metropolitan Revolution: The Rise of Post-urban America* (New York: Columbia University Press, 2006), introduction and chaps. 3–5.

7. John L. Rury and Shirley A. Hill, *The African American Struggle for Secondary Schooling: Closing the Graduation Gap* (New York: Teachers College Press, 2012), chap. 4.

8. For discussion of the *Jenkins* case see Joshua Dunn, *Complex Justice: The Case of Missouri v. Jenkins* (Chapel Hill: University of North Carolina Press, 2008), chaps. 2–5; and Moran, *Race, Law*, chap. 9.

9. For an overview of urban-suburban differences in education during this time see Argun Saatcioglu and John L. Rury, "Education and the Changing Metropolitan Organization of Inequality," *Historical Methods* 45, no. 1 (January–March 2012): 21–40. The results of this analysis demonstrate that urban youth prior to the Second World War had a higher likelihood of graduating from high school than their suburban counterparts. Forty years later the relative positions of the two groups had reversed.

10. District and population figures taken from *One Hundred Third Report of the Public Schools of the State of Missouri, School Year Ending June 30, 1952* (Jefferson City: Missouri Department of Secondary and Elementary Education, 1952), table A: Enumeration and Enrollment.

11. This point appeared in interviews with a number of local respondents.

12. For example, Russian was added to the Southwest curriculum in 1958: "Challenge of Study in Russian," *Kansas City Times*, March 18, 1958.

13. Rury and Hill, *African American Struggle*, 151–57. A sense of particular school strengths can be gleaned from yearbooks: *The Centralian*, 1950–1960; *Paseon*, 1950–1960; *Sachem*, 1950–1960.

14. "Kansas City Parents to Court in Booker T. Fight," *Kansas City Call*, December 12, 1952, 13. On inequality in resources in earlier times see Sherry Lamb Schirmer, *A City Divided: The Racial Landscape of Kansas City, 1900–1960* (Columbia: University of Missouri Press, 2002), 31.

15. As seen in table 3.1, white enrollments actually went down in KCMPS between 1955 and 1960, despite the baby boom, after increasing somewhat between 1950 and 1955. For a perspective nationally see "Study Shows Extent of School Crowding," *New York Times*, November 11, 1953, 29; Robert H. Anderson, "Crowding in the Schools: 1954 to 1961," Association for Supervision and Curriculum Development, 1961, http://www.ascd.org/ASCD/pdf/journals/ed_lead/el_196104_anderson.pdf.

16. "An Age Bar Down," *Kansas City Times*, January 20, 1956.

17. "Push on Schools," *Kansas City Times*, May 4, 1956.

18. Moran, *Race, Law*, chaps. 1 and 2; Rury and Hill, *African American Struggle*, 151–52. On the loss of jobs see "Reserve Teachers Have a Good Cause," *Kansas City Call*, October 14, 1955, 29.

19. Moran, *Race, Law*, 102–3.

20. "This Is Critical Year for Kansas City Schools," *Kansas City Star*, February 7, 1959.

21. "Asks a School Merger: Annexation by Kansas City Sought by Sugar Creek," *Kansas City Times*, January 10, 1955; "Sugar Creek In," *Kansas City Times*, May 12, 1955. KCMPS would annex the small Pleasant Valley district in 1973, marking an end to its physical expansion in this era. For an overview and list of annexations see Kansas City Public Schools, *Kansas City Public School History*, https://www.kcpublicschools.org/site/Default.aspx?PageID=4597.

22. "43 Integrated Schools," *Kansas City Call*, September 23, 1955, 29. The *Call* contrasted board policy in Kansas City, Missouri, with developments across the river in Kansas City, Kansas, where parents were blocked from enrolling their children in certain schools. See "NAACP Protests Discriminating School Policy," *Kansas City Call*, September 23, 1955, 2nd section, 1, and "Kansas NAACP Sues School Board," *Kansas City Call*, November 11, 1955, 13. With respect to the lack of teacher integration see "Reserve Teachers Have a Good Cause."

23. Rury and Hill, *African American Struggle*, chap. 5.

24. The *Centralian*, Central High School, 1956 edition, 10.

25. "Relieve the Load on Central Rolls," *Kansas City Times*, July 5, 1959.

26. "Color of the Class: Desegregating Kansas City Schools," *Kansas City Star*, May 8, 1990, 1. Kevin Fox Gotham, *Race, Real Estate, and Uneven Development: The Kansas City Experience, 1900–2010*, 2nd ed. (Albany: SUNY Press, 2014), chap. 5.

27. On this point see Robert J. Havighurst and Daniel U. Levine, *Education in Metropolitan Areas*, 2nd ed. (Boston: Allyn & Bacon, 1971), 221–39; and Hummel and Nagle, *Urban Education*, chap. 8.

28. Gotham, *Race, Real Estate*, chaps. 5 and 6. While map 3.3 appears to show a predominantly African American census tract extending into the Raytown School District in 1980, that portion of the tract is actually a large park that separated that portion of the district from black neighborhoods in KCMPS.

29. Joshua M. Dunn, *Complex Justice: The Case of Missouri v. Jenkins* (Chapel Hill: University of North Carolina Press, 2008), 36.

30. School District, Kansas City, Missouri, Office of the Superintendent, "Fifteenth Annual Report on the Progress of Desegregation in the Kansas City Public Schools," October 17, 1969, unpublished report.

31. Dunn, *Complex Justice*, chap. 2.

32. For a characterization of this area and the well-paying industrial jobs that sustained it see Shortridge, *Kansas City and How It Grew*, 117–22.

33. "Fifteenth Annual Report on the Progress of Desegregation in the Kansas City Public Schools."

34. "Negro Pupil Population Rises, Spreads," *Kansas City Times*, November 7, 1963.

35. Gotham, *Race, Real Estate*, 114–16. On conditions in the South see Rury and Hill, *African American Struggle*, chaps. 1 and 2.

36. Daniel U. Levine and Jeanie Keeny Meyer, "Level and Rate of Desegregation and White Enrollment Decline in a Big City School District," *Social Problems* 24, no. 4 (1977): 451–62.

37. Moran, *Race, Law*, 70.

38. On enrollment patterns east and west of Troost see Gotham, *Race, Real Estate*, 99–103. On enrollments at East and West, along with Westport High, see School District, Kansas City, Missouri, Office of the Superintendent, *Twenty Second Annual Report on the Progress of Desegregation in the Kansas City Public Schools*, School Year, 1976–77, table 1, Enrollment, 1954–1975. West High is not shown on the maps, as it was open for only about a decade, closing in 1980. See Moran, *Race, Law*, 96–102.

39. District leaders assured parents at Southwest that the school would not be affected by busing; see "Vow No Busing at Southwest," *Kansas City Times*, March 1, 1973.

40. There is a growing literature on the ways in which school authorities and other leaders in large cities could help to assuage white concerns about desegregation while also supporting African American desires for greater integration. On these points see Genevieve Siegel-Hawley, *When the Fences Come Down: Twenty-First-Century Lessons from Metropolitan School Desegregation* (Chapel Hill: University of North Carolina Press, 2016), chaps. 3–5; and Ansley T. Erickson, "Fairness, Commitment, and Civic Capacity: The Varied Desegregation Trajectories of Metropolitan School Districts," in *The Shifting Landscape of the American School District: Race, Class, Geography, and the Perpetual Reform of Local Control, 1935–2015*, ed. David Gamson and Emily Hodge (New York: Peter Lang, 2018), 107–26. Also, for evidence of white racism expressed in response to the racial changes in KCMPS see the discussion of South Kansas City in chapter 4, especially with regard to the Spainhower Commission.

41. Moran, *Race, Law*, 82–83; Dunn, *Complex Justice*, 42–43.

42. Susan Hilliard, interview with John Rury, March 8, 2012; Marvin Daniels, interview with John Rury, April 17, 2012.

43. Hilliard interview, March 8, 2012.

44. Stanley West, interview with John Rury, March 15, 2012.

45. Daniels interview, April 17, 2012.

46. Patrick Elard, interview with John Rury, March 27, 2012.

47. On this point see Sylvia L. M. Martinez and John L. Rury, "From 'Culturally Deprived' to 'At Risk': The Politics of Popular Expression and Educational Inequality in the United States, 1960–1985," *Teachers College Record* 114, no. 6 (2012): 1–31. On the less tolerant racial attitudes of individuals with lower levels of education at this time, including ideas about racial differences in ability, see Howard Schuman, Charlotte Steeh, Lawrence Bobo, and Maria Krysan, *Racial Attitudes in America: Trends and Interpretations*, 2nd ed. (Cambridge, MA: Harvard University Press, 1997), 164–65.

48. Quoted in Moran, *Race, Law*, 56. Also see *Kansas City Times*, October 3, 1964; *Kansas City Times*, October 10, 1964.

49. "Plan to Help Poor Scholars," *Kansas City Star*, January 6, 1967.
50. Rury and Hill, *African American Struggle*, 154.
51. Elard interview, March 27, 2012.
52. "Facing Tough Recruiting Class," *Kansas City Times*, January 3, 1963; "Wages Spur Teacher Migration," *Kansas City Times*, December 30, 1965; "Hurt by Teacher-Go-Round," *Kansas City Star*, January 16, 1967; "Positive School Move on Teacher Integration," *Kansas City Star*, September 4, 196; "Pay Not Luring Top Teachers," *Kansas City Star*, January 8, 1967; "Will Need 60 More Teachers," *Kansas City Times*, July 18, 1969.
53. "Faculty Integration: Teachers, Parents Join the Protest Teacher Shift," *Kansas City Times*, July 18, 1973.
54. "Defers School Probe Question," *Kansas City Times*, November 30, 1966, 1A.
55. Manny Stevens, interview with John Rury, March 27, 2012; Elard interview, March 27, 2012.
56. "Blacks' Frustration Growing Steadily," *Kansas City Star*, June 30, 1974, 1A; Stevens interview, 2012; West interview, 2012.
57. Moran, *Race, Law*, 128–29. Changes in extracurricular activities can be seen in comparing editions of *The Centralian*, published by Central High School (Kansas City, MO) between 1958 and 1966. For instance, see the number of groups presented in the sections on organizations, presented as part 5 in 1958 and part 3 in 1966. On national trends and debates about vocational education for black youth see Rury and Hill, *African American Struggle*, 133–36.
58. "Vandal Forays Hurt Schools," *Kansas City Times*, March 29, 1965; "Great Stone Barrage Rocks Schools," *Kansas City Star*, January 29, 1966; "Vandalism Costs High," *Kansas City Star*, May 4, 1969.
59. "Thorough Planning for a Special School," *Kansas City Star*, June 4, 1968.
60. "Schools Hit Hard by Vandals," *Kansas City Star*, December 4, 1968; "Destruction at Schools Carries Huge Price Tag," *Kansas City Star*, January 27, 1969; "School Vandalism Down," *Kansas City Star*, July 24, 1973.
61. "Students, District Fight Vandalism, Decaying Pride," *Kansas City Star*, May 19, 1975.
62. "Statistical Profile for Selected Characteristics of the School District of Kansas City, Missouri, 1980 Census," KCMPS Memorandum, September 29, 1983, Arthur Benson Papers, box 354.
63. In 1964 city council members complained about housing values being downgraded when African Americans moved into the city's southeast side. See "Allege FHA Custom Hurts Racial Shift," *Kansas City Star*, January 21, 1964. Also see "Real Estate Ordinance Passed by City Council," *Kansas City Realtor*, January 30, 1964, 7. On the problem in national terms see "Central City a Problem," *Kansas City Realtor*, July 13, 1961, 7.
64. There was a steady drumbeat of discouraging news reported about the district's budget, beginning in the latter 1960s. See, for instance, "School Money Crisis Feared," *Kansas City Times*, March 22, 1968; "The State and Kansas City's Crisis in the Schools," *Kansas City Star*, April 15, 1969; "Senate Bickers While Schools Headed Down the Drain," *Kansas City Times*, December 22, 1970; "Public Education Job Tougher," *Kansas City Star*, June 28, 1974; "School Here Hurt as Aid Bill Dies," *Kansas City Star*, May 14, 1975. On the "decay" of downtown retail enterprise in the later 1960s and the 1970s see Shortridge, *Kansas City and How It Grew*, 133.
65. "Presents Survey of Area Schools," *Kansas City Times*, October 21, 1964.
66. "City of Kansas City, Missouri, ½ Cent Sales Tax Intended for School Purposes," Arthur Benson Papers, box 444, Finance folder.
67. Moran, *Race, Law*, 104. The fact that Missouri required a two-thirds majority in such elections did not help matters.

68. "Summer School Disaster," *Kansas City Star*, June 5, 1969; "No Summer School in 1973," *Kansas City Star*, April 23, 1973.

69. Moran, *Race, Law*, 108.

70. Human Relations Task Force on Civil Disorder, *Three Year Report: The Quality of Urban Life*, Kansas City, MO, 1971, II-3.

71. Moran, *Race, Law*, chap. 1; on the process of neighborhood transition in Kansas City at this time see Schirmer, *City Divided*, chap. 8.

72. "Meet with 377 New Teachers," *Kansas City Star*, August 31, 1967.

73. Moran, *Race, Law*, chap. 2

74. "Rise in Negro Pupils," *Kansas City Times*, October 27, 1965, 1.

75. "Pride in Order at Southwest High," *Kansas City Star*, March 23, 1963. The magazine *Ladies' Home Journal* named Southwest one of the "25 best" high schools in the country. See also "Centennial Celebration—History of Southwest High," *Wednesday Magazine*, December 27, 1967.

76. M. Simon and B. Rodgers, "A High School That Just Lost Its Value," *Pitch Weekly*, November 13–19, 1997, 12–16. Rick Montgomery, "Erasing a Tragic History," *Kansas City Star*, June 6, 2010, A1, A10.

77. John L. Rury and Jeffrey E. Mirel, "The Political Economy of Urban Education," *Review of Research in Education* 22 (1997): 49–110.

78. R. J. Havighurst, "Problems of Integration in the KC Public Schools: A Report to the Board of Education," November 18, 1965. Among elementary school children, African Americans had become the majority.

79. Moran, *Race, Law*, 116–17.

80. "City Deprived Pupils Ahead in Reading Capabilities," *Kansas City Star*, March 19, 1971; "New Pupil Tests Here Rank Near Other Urban Centers," *Kansas City Star*, September 4, 1974; "Students' Reading Ability Down, New Tests Indicate," *Kansas City Star*, May 25, 1975.

81. "Rioting in City Takes Five Lives," *Kansas City Times*, April 11, 1968, 1; Mayor's Commission on Civil Disturbances, *Final Report*, 1968, Kansas City, MO, 5–32; Douglas E. Kneeland, "5 Die in Kansas City Riots; Snipers Hunted in Slums," *New York Times*, April 11, 1968; "And Then It Happened," KC History, Missouri Valley Collections at the Kansas City Public Library, http://www.kchistory.org/week-kansas-city-history/and-then-it-happened.

82. Brian Burnes and Glenn E. Rice, "Riots of 1968 Were a Watershed Moment for KC," *Kansas City Star*, April 6, 2008, A10; Glenn Rice, "Barriers Still Exist between Blacks and Whites," *Kansas City Star*, January 8, 1996, G1.

83. Moran, *Race, Law*, chap. 2; Gotham, *Race, Real Estate*, 117–18.

84. Human Relations Task Force, *Three Year Report: The Quality of Urban Life*, II-3.

85. US Commission on Civil Rights, *Racial Isolation in the Public Schools* (Washington, DC: Government Printing Office, 1967), 59.

86. On the impact of *Keyes* see James T. Patterson, *Brown v. Board of Education: A Civil Rights Milestone and Its Troubled Legacy* (New York: Oxford University Press), 161–63.

87. "Blacks' Frustration Growing Steadily," *Kansas City Star*, June 30, 1974, 1A. Gotham, *Race, Real Estate*, 101–3.

88. Dunn, *Complex Justice*, 40–41.

89. For example see "Southwest Students Take Integration in Stride," *Kansas City Times*, October 18, 1975.

90. Susan White, "Can the Kansas City Schools Be Saved? (or Is It Too Late?)," *Kansas City Town Squire*, June 1970, 12–20, 69–73.

91. Moran, *Race, Law*, 110–12.

92. "Desegregation Chronology," *Kansas City Times*, September 1, 1977, B4.

93. "Not Too Late to Build an Integrated School System," *Kansas City Call*, March 8, 1973, 8.

94. Dunn, *Complex Justice*, chap. 2.

95. School District, Kansas City, MO, *Twenty-Second Annual Report on the Progress of Desegregation*, table 1.

96. Moran, *Race, Law*, chap. 5.

97. Midwest Research Institute, *Decision Criteria and Policy for School Consolidation*, Final Report, March 15, 1974, 10.

98. "Filing Segregation Appeal a Waste of Taxpayers' Money," *Kansas City Call*, December 30, 1976, 10.

99. "A Moderate Busing Plan Is Adopted in Kansas City," *New York Times*, December 7, 1976, 32; Moran, *Race, Law*, chap. 5; Dunn, *Complex Justice*, chap. 6.

100. "Bad Day for Desegregation—Plan Takes Its Lumps," *Kansas City Times*, April 6, 1977, 34.

101. "Priest Splits with Group in Northwest," *Kansas City Star*, March 3, 1977.

102. "Northeast Sees Limited Choice," *Kansas City Times*, January 29, 1977, 7a.

103. "Adults Listen, Gripe on Desegregation," *Kansas City Star*, April 8, 1977; "Plan to Ease Busing Sought by Mayor King," *Kansas City Star*, April 7, 1977, 4.

104. "Grade Split Worries Southwest Patrons," *Kansas City Times*, April 13, 1977.

105. School District, Kansas City, Missouri, Office of the Superintendent, *Twenty-Sixth Annual Report on the Progress of Desegregation in the Kansas City Public Schools*, School Year, 1980–81, table 1; Moran, *Race, Law*, chap. 6. Only about 20 to 30 percent of the decline in white enrollments could be attributed to the end of the postwar-era baby boom.

106. "City School Survey Released," *Kansas City Times*, June 28, 1975.

107. "School Survey Shows Widespread Dissatisfaction," *Kansas City Star*, May 11, 1975.

108. Moran, *Race, Law*, 112–13.

109. "District Pay Hike OK'd," *Kansas City Star*, April 10, 1974.

110. "Teacher Strike Sends Parents Here District Hopping," *Kansas City Star*, March 1974.

111. "Waiting Lists at City's Private Schools," *Kansas City Star*, April 19, 1977. The *Star* found that while many parents called private schools to inquire about enrollment, most of these parents were not prepared to pay the relatively high cost of tuition, especially at the city's most elite institutions. Also see Moran, *Race, Law*, 109.

112. "Southwest Students Take Integration in Stride," *Kansas City Star*, October 18, 1975.

113. On this transition see Edward T. Matheny Jr., *The Rise and Fall of Excellence: The Story of Southwest High School* (Leawood, KS: Leathers, 2000), chaps. 6 and 7.

114. *Twenty-Sixth Annual Report on the Progress of Desegregation in the Kansas City Public Schools*, School Year, 1980–81, tables 1 and 10.

115. Rick Montgomery, "Erasing a Tragic History," *Kansas City Star*, June 6, 2010, A1, A10.

116. "Mixed Reactions to Area-Wide Desegregation," *Kansas City Call*, January 23, 1977, 2.

117. Dunn, *Complex Justice*, chaps. 3–5; for an alternative viewpoint see Preston C. Green and Bruce D. Baker, "Urban Legends, Desegregation and School Finance: Did Kansas City Really Prove That Money Doesn't Matter?," *Michigan Journal of Race and Law* 12, no. 1 (2006): 57–105.

118. Douglas N. Harris and Carolyn D. Herrington, "Accountability, Standards, and the Growing Achievement Gap: Lessons from the Past Half Century," *American Journal of Education* 112, no. 2 (February 2006): 209–38.

119. "Tests of Eighth Graders Shows Few Prepared," *Kansas City Star*, September 15, 1978, 1. Some outlying districts scored below 60 percent, such as Excelsior Springs, Grandview, and Missouri City, but these were relatively small and not major competitors with KCMPS.

120. "Inner City and Rural Students Score Lowest on Tests," *Kansas City Star*, April 30, 1978, 1a.

121. West interview, 2012.

122. Hilliard interview, March 8, 2012. Her youngest child, Erick, went to a Catholic high school because he wanted to avoid the problems then becoming associated with Southwest. She recalled him having "nothing but" white friends, unlike his sister.

123. On the history of controversy over curricular tracking at the secondary level see Samuel Roundfield Lucas, *Tracking Inequality: Stratification and Mobility in American High Schools* (New York: Teachers College Press, 1999), chaps. 1 and 2.

124. Daniels interview, April 17, 2012; Elard interview, March 27, 2012.

125. Stevens interview, March 27, 2012.

126. Arthur Benson Papers, SHSMO Research Center–Kansas City, UMKC Archives, box 320, file I.R.2.

127. On the general phenomenon or "white flight" during this period see William H. Frey, "Central City White Flight: Racial and Non-Racial Causes," *American Sociological Review* 44, no. 3 (June 1979): 425–48; Christine Rossell and Willis D. Hawley, *White Flight from School Desegregation: Magnitude, Sources, and Policy Options*, Final Report, US Department of Education, ERIC # ED245024, 1981; and Sarah J. Reber, "Court-Ordered Desegregation: Success and Failure Integrating American Schools since *Brown versus Board of Education*," *Journal of Human Resources* 40, no. 3 (Summer 2003): 559–90. For a cultural analysis of the general phenomenon of white movement see Eric Avila, *Popular Culture in the Age of White Flight: Fear and Fantasy in Suburban Los Angeles* (Berkeley: University of California Press, 2005). On tipping points see David Card, Alexandre Mas, and Jesse Rothstein, "Tipping and the Dynamics of Segregation," NBER Working Paper 13052, National Bureau of Economic Research, Cambridge, MA, April 2007.

128. "Waiting Lists at City's Private Schools," *Kansas City Star*, April 19, 1977. As noted earlier, the *Star* found that parents called private schools about enrollment but were not prepared to pay the high cost of tuition at elite institutions.

129. For a discussion of this see Jeffrey Mirel, "After the Fall: Continuity and Change in Detroit, 1981–1995," *History of Education Quarterly* 38, no. 3 (1998): 237–67.

130. Some fifty-six left for Kansas, but most probably went to schools in Wyandotte County, where the Kansas City, Kansas, public schools operated all-black Sumner Academy and also underwent desegregation.

131. Jennifer L. Hochschild, *The New American Dilemma: Liberal Democracy and School Desegregation* (New Haven, CT: Yale University Press; 1984), conclusion. For more recent accounts see note 40 above.

132. "Filing Segregation Appeal a Waste of Taxpayers' Money."

133. Dunn, *Complex Justice*, 41–42.

134. James Hazlett deposition, March 9, 1983, Arthur Benson Papers, box 108, vol. 3, 283. Hazlett hoped that African Americans could eventually be distributed across the metro area.

135. Levine and Meyer, "Level and Rate of Desegregation," 451.

4. RACIALIZED ADVANTAGE

1. "Raytown Shows Suburbs' Fear of School Redistricting," *Kansas City Star*, February 5, 1969, 4B. Longtime Raytown school superintendent Joe Herndon testified that a

study conducted by the district found that most of its clientele had moved from Kansas City. Joe Herndon deposition, April 18, 1983, p. 159, box 109, Arthur Benson Papers, Western Historical Collection, University of Missouri–Kansas City.

2. James Shortridge, *Kansas City and How It Grew, 1822–2011* (Lawrence: University Press of Kansas, 2012), 115–17.

3. On this pattern in the Postwar Era see Delores Hayden, *Building Suburbia: Green Fields and Urban Growth, 1820–2000* (New York: Pantheon Books, 2003), chap. 7. Kansas City developed one of the nation's most extensive systems of freeways to serve its expanded footprint. On this point see Shortridge, *Kansas City and How It Grew*, 106–9.

4. Kevin Fox Gotham, *Race, Real Estate, and Uneven Development: The Kansas City Experience, 1900–2000* (Albany: SUNY Press, 2002), chap. 5; Peter William Moran, *Race, Law, and the Desegregation of Public Schools* (New York: LFB Scholarly, 2005), chap. 6.

5. On events in 1968 see Donna Gardner and John L. Rury, "Suburban Resistance to District Reorganization: The 1968 Spainhower Commission and Metropolitan Kansas City and St. Louis," *Urban Review* 46, no. 1 (2014): 125–45; see also Moran, *Race, Law*, chap. 6.

6. Shortridge, *Kansas City and How It Grew*, 116–17.

7. Figures taken from Demographia: US Urbanized Areas, 1950–1990, http://www.demographia.com/dm-uad.htm (accessed March 29, 2016). Overall, greater Kansas City grew from roughly 800,000 to some 1.1 million.

8. On the somewhat complicated history of Kansas City's core during this period see Shortridge, *Kansas City and How It Grew*, chap. 6. The fact that KCMPS enrollment figures declined, however, is compelling evidence that families with school-age children were choosing other districts to live in, regardless of where they were moving from.

9. Ibid., 119.

10. While Shortridge lists the population of Raytown in 1970 at 33,306 (p. 121), some 26,280 school district residents lived in Kansas City, 44 percent of its population, according to figures provided by Daniel U. Levine, "Crisis and Opportunity: Education in Greater Kansas City," unpublished report, 1975, 29.

11. Aaron Tyler Rife, "Shifting Identities in South Kansas City: Hickman Mills' Transformation from a Suburban to Urban School District" (PhD diss., University of Kansas, 2014), 30–35. Also see Shortridge, *Kansas City and How It Grew*, 105.

12. Rife, "Shifting Identities," chaps. 2 and 3.

13. For an overview of the effect of family background and community characteristics on school performance in urban and suburban settings during this period see John L. Rury and Argun Saatcioglu, "Suburban Advantage: Opportunity Hoarding and Secondary Attainment in the Postwar Metropolitan Northeast," *American Journal of Education* 118, no. 3 (May 2011): 307–42. Federal free and reduced-price lunch subsidies went to students from households that qualified as below a low-income threshold, not just those in poverty. While poverty levels in the two Kansas City core areas were high, they did not constitute a majority of the student population in either of them.

14. On the development of Independence during this period see Shortridge, *Kansas City and How It Grew*, 119.

15. Adam Gamoran and David A. Long, "*Equality of Educational Opportunity*: A Forty Year Retrospective," WCER Working Paper No. 2006–9, Wisconsin Center for Educational Research, Madison, 2006.

16. Joshua Dunn, *Complex Justice: The Case of* Missouri v. Jenkins (Chapel Hill: University of North Carolina Press, 2008), 41–42.

17. "Suburban Schools Form Study Units," *Kansas City Star*, October 26, 1962, 4; Ted Warren, interview with John Rury, May 1, 2012; Leslie Wexler, interview with John Rury, May 1, 2012.

18. See, for instance, "Census Shows Increase of Blacks in Suburbs: But White Majority Large," *Kansas City Star*, February 18, 1971; and "Blacks Staking Claim to Good Life in Suburbs," *Kansas City Times*, May 26, 1976, 1a.

19. "Raytown as a City Is 7," *Kansas City Times*, July 17, 1957, 15.

20. "Raytown to Mark Booming Ten Years," *Kansas City Star*, September 7, 1960, 2B.

21. Shortridge, *Kansas City and How It Grew*, 121.

22. Roberta L. Bonnewitz and Lois T. Allen, *Raytown Remembers* (Clinton, MO: Printery, 1975), 72.

23. Shirley Wurth and Larry Nicholson, *Our First One Hundred Years: Raytown Consolidated School District No. 2* (Raytown Consolidated School District No. 2, 2004), 13–52.

24. "This Is Raytown," *Raytown News*, June 21, 1962, 1.

25. Ibid., 63; "Schools Opening Tuesday, September 7," *Raytown News*, August 26, 1954, 1.

26. Wurth and Nicholson, *Our First One Hundred Years*, 64–76.

27. "Big Retail Deal on U.S. 50 in Raytown," *Kansas City Star*, October 16, 1960, 2.

28. "This Is Raytown," *Raytown News*, 1. The rating was largely a measure of financial resources.

29. Barbara Caldwell, Sandy Crowley, and Jeanne Harrison, Raytown Historical Society, interviews with John Rury, March 1, 2012.

30. Caldwell and Crowley interviews, March 1, 2012.

31. Shortridge, *Kansas City and How It Grew*, 121.

32. Richard Alfred, interview with John Rury, March 1, 2012.

33. Wurth and Nicholson, *Our First One Hundred Years*, 73.

34. Ted Chitwood and Bud Lathrop were inducted into the Missouri Sports Hall of Fame in 2005 and 2002 respectively. Chitwood's inductee page can be found at http://mosportshalloffame.com/inductees/ted-chitwood/ and Lathrop's at http://mosportshalloffame.com/inductees/bud-lathrop/. Information about the stadium is provided on Chitwood's page.

35. Becky Montague, interview with John Rury, February 23, 2012. Wurth and Nicholson, *Our First One Hundred Years*, 53.

36. This was a theme in many of the Raytown interviews. On bonds formed between adults through their children and "social closure" see James S. Coleman, "Social Capital in the Creation of Human Capital," *American Journal of Sociology* 94, Supplement: Organizations and Institutions: Sociological and Economic Approaches to the Analysis of Social Structure (1988): S95–S120.

37. Caldwell and Harrison interviews, March 1, 2012.

38. Wurth and Nicholson, *Our First One Hundred Years*, 83.

39. "Student Decline Cited in Cuts," *Kansas City Star*, April 9, 1976, 4a; "Raytown School Enrollment Drops for Eighth Consecutive Year," *Kansas City Star*, October 4, 1977, 4.

40. Wurth and Nicholson, *Our First One Hundred Years*, 85–87; Alfred interview, March 1, 2012.

41. Rife, "Shifting Identities," chaps. 2 and 3; also see *Hickman Mills, Missouri: A Study of Conflict between Administrative and Policy-Making Agencies in a School System; Report of an Investigation*, National Commission for the Defense of Democracy through Education, Report to National Education Association of the United States and to Consolidated District #1, Hickman Mills (Washington DC: NEA, January 1960).

42. Rife, "Shifting Identities," 19.

43. "See Gain in Annexing," *Kansas City Times*, March 21, 1956.

44. "Grandview OK Anew on Annex," *Kansas City Times*, December 24, 1957.

45. Rife, "Shifting Identities, 31.

46. Shortridge, *Kansas City and How It Grew*, 153.

47. "Bias, Harassment Down, but Some Barriers Remain," *Kansas City Star*, January 23, 1977, 8e.

48. Manny Stevens, interview with John Rury, March 27, 2012.

49. Patrick Elard, interview with John Rury, March 27, 2012.

50. "Raytown Schools Announce Refusal to Play Central in State Tourney," *Kansas City Call*, January 18, 1973, 9; "Good Example of Poor Sportsmanship," *Kansas City Call*, January 18, 1973, 8. A decade later, Herndon acknowledged knowing the district's reputation for hostility to African Americans; Joe Herndon deposition, April 18, 1983, 154–55.

51. "High Race Barriers Linger," *Kansas City Star*, April 27, 1975, 25. This article quoted an assistant superintendent from Kansas City as declaring that suburban school officials worried that "if they allow that, there's going to be nothing to stop the black people from moving out here to live."

52. Superintendent Herndon acknowledged that the district had clear policies against outsiders using their schools; Joe Herndon deposition, April 18, 1983, 52. At least one former teacher described being sent to monitor bus stops near the district's border with Kansas City to observe possible violations of this position; Sandy Crowley, interview with John Rury interview, March 1, 2012.

53. Sally Westbrook, interview with John Rury, March 1, 2012; Caldwell, Alfred, and Harrison interviews, March 1, 2012.

54. Crowley interview, March 1, 2012. This form of surveillance apparently was practiced more frequently in the 1980s, as the African American population edged to the southeast parts of the city.

55. This map is a bit misleading, as it suggests that a large park that was included in the same census tract as an adjacent black neighborhood extended African American settlement into the district at this time. In fact, the park was a natural barrier that delayed the movement of black families into RSD.

56. For an elaboration of these points see John L. Rury and Aaron Tyler Rife, "Race, Schools and Opportunity Hoarding: Evidence from a Post-war American Metropolis," *History of Education* 47, no. 1 (January 2018): 87–107.

57. Rife, "Shifting Identities," 100. As noted in the previous chapter, the "31,000 culturally deprived children" figure came from KCMPS officials testifying at the state capitol, hoping to gain additional funding.

58. Rife, "Shifting Identities," chap. 4

59. Shortridge, *Kansas City and How It Grew*, 152–53; Rife, "Shifting Identities," 156–63.

60. Kansas and Missouri Advisory Committees on Civil Rights, "Crisis and Opportunity: Education in Greater Kansas City," unpublished report, 1977, appendix B, table B-2. Hickman Mills reported 211 African American students at that point, and Grandview 114, reflecting the movement of blacks into South Kansas City and the number of military families settling in the area. "Blacks Staking Claim to 'Good Life' in the Suburbs," *Kansas City Times*, May 26, 1976, 1a. Superintendent Herndon testified that Westridge Elementary School, located near African American neighborhoods in Kansas City, had the largest black enrollment for much of his time at the district's helm; Joe Herndon deposition, April 18, 1983, 205–6.

61. Shortridge, *Kansas City and How It Grew*, 75–76; Gary Littlefield, interview with John Rury, April 10, 2012.

62. *The History of the North Kansas City School District, 1917 to 1995* (Kansas City, MO: North Kansas City School District, 1995), chap. 2.

63. Warren interview, May 1, 2012.

64. *History of the North Kansas City School District*, chaps. 2, 3–5.
65. Bill Henry, interview with John Rury, May 1, 2012.
66. Littlefield interview, April 10, 2012.
67. *History of the North Kansas City School District*, chaps. 4 and 5.
68. "Looking Over Progress to the North, the Fast Growing Area of Kansas City," *Kansas City Star*, November 2, 1954; "A School Fund Rises: North Kansas City District Revenue Expected to Exceed Estimate," *Kansas City Times*, February 9, 1956.
69. "Schooling to New Job," *Kansas City Star*, May 11, 1955; "Dr. Schooling's Five Years," *Kansas City Star*, June 18, 1955.
70. Henry interview, May 1, 2012.
71. "The Neighborhoods of Clay County," *Northtowner*, June 21, 1962.
72. Shirley Albin, interview with John Rury, May 1, 2012; Warren interview, May 1, 2012.
73. *History of the North Kansas City School District*, chaps. 5 and 6; Henry interview, May 1, 2012.
74. Littlefield interview, April 10, 2012; Albin interview, May 1, 2012; Wexler interview, May 1, 2012; Henry interview, May 1, 2012.
75. *History of the North Kansas City School District*, chap. 8; Henry interview, May 1, 2012.
76. Shortridge, *Kansas City and How It Grew*, 149–50.
77. On the history of residential development and racial exclusion in Clay County see Gotham, *Race, Real Estate*, 61–62.
78. "State to Probe Lynching," *Kansas City Times*, August 10, 1925; "Mob of 1,000 Lynch Negro in Missouri, with Passengers on a Train as Witnesses," *New York Times*, August 8, 1925.
79. "Inquiry Ordered in Missouri Mob's Burning of Negro," *Albany Evening News*, November 29, 1933.
80. James Dempsy, interview with John Rury, March 22, 2012; Henry interview, May 1, 2012; clay.county.archives/photos/a.934620379912221.1073741828.11155937555 1663/934620393245553/?type=1&theater; http://www.civilwaronthewesternborder.org/map/liberty-missouri; http://www.kchistory.org/cdm4/item_viewer.php?CISOROOT=/Mrs&CISOPTR=712&CISOBOX=1&REC=4.
81. Darryl W. Levings, "Blacks Recall Long Trips to Segregated Schools," *Kansas City Star*, 1977. "To Transport Liberty High School Students," *Kansas City Call*, July 31, 1953. On the African American community in Independence see William J. Curtis, *Rich Heritage: A Black History of Independence, Missouri* (Kansas City, MO: Better Impressions, 1985), 48. On the southern character of Independence see "Just a Country Town," *Kansas City Times*, August 30, 1950.
82. Littlefield interview, April 10, 2012.
83. Warren interview, May 1, 2012; Wexler interview, 2012; Dempsy interview, March 22, 2012.
84. Stevens interview, March 27, 2012.
85. Marvin Daniels, interview with John Rury, April 17, 2012; Susan Hilliard, interview with John Rury, March 8, 2012.
86. Elard interview, March 27, 2012.
87. City Planning Department, Kansas City, Missouri, "Alternatives for Growth: Kansas City North," unpublished report, November 1966.
88. Shortridge, *Kansas City and How It Grew*, 104–6.
89. This was also noted in comments by longtime residents in interviews: Warren interview, May 1, 2012; Littlefield interview, April 10, 2012.
90. Henry interview, May 1, 2012.
91. Gardner and Rury, "Suburban Resistance to District Reorganization," 127.

92. The bulk of the opposition initially came from the mid-north-central part of the state, along the Missouri River, often characterized as "Little Dixie," together with the southeast, which had the largest African American population outside the major cities. In addition, the commission received hundreds of letters, roughly half of which were received before the report appeared. Principal reasons for opposition were that residents ultimately could not vote to end reorganization, and many did not want to pay for schooling other people's children. These were familiar points in resistance to school reorganization in other states. See Gardner and Rury, "Suburban Resistance to District Reorganization," 128; see also David Reynolds, *There Goes the Neighborhood: Rural School Consolidation at the Grass Roots in Early Twentieth-Century Iowa* (Iowa City: University of Iowa Press, 1998), chap. 6.

93. To establish a rationale for this interdistrict urban solution, Spainhower contracted with Clifford Hooker and Van Mueller from the University of Minnesota to prepare a separate report on the Kansas City and St. Louis area schools immediately after the full commission report was issued. This "urban" study was completed in late January 1969. It contextualized and provided data supporting the commission's recommendation to create nine local school units in the Kansas City area and sixteen in greater St. Louis crossing county lines and mixing urban and suburban schools. See Clifford Hooker and Van D. Mueller, *Equal Treatment to Equals: A New Structure for Public Schools in Kansas City and St. Louis Metropolitan Areas; A Report to the Missouri School District Reorganization Commission* (Jefferson City, MO, 1969).

94. Paul Van Osdol Jr., letter to the Honorable James I. Spainhower, January 29, 1969, in the Advisory Committee file, Missouri Department of State, Records Management and Archives Service, box 22070.

95. Hooker and Mueller, *Equal Treatment to Equals*, 8. Interestingly, the commission appointed to investigate the 1968 civil disturbance in Kansas City also recommended that all public schools in Jackson County be included in the Kansas City, Missouri, Public Schools, which would have meant effectively annexing districts such as Liberty, Raytown, Hickman Mills, Center, Grandview, Blue Springs, Lee's Summit, and parts of others. See Mayor's Commission on Civil Disturbances, *Final Report*, 1968, Kansas City, MO, 58.

96. See, for instance, Arthur E. Wise, *Rich Schools, Poor Schools: The Promise of Equal Educational Opportunity* (Chicago: University of Chicago Press, 1968), 199–205.

97. Mrs. Carl L. Tosspon, letter from Kansas City, MO 64138, to Reverend Spainhower, January 30, 1969, in "Correspondence K–Z," Missouri Department of State, Records Management and Archives Service, box 22070.

98. Clarence and Louise Swaidner, letter from Kansas City, MO 64129, to Mr. Spainhower, January 8, 1969, in "Correspondence K–Z," Missouri Department of State, Records Management and Archives Service, box 22070.

99. Mrs. P. G. Moore, letter from Oak Grove, MO, to Representative James I. Spainhower, October 24, 1968, in "Correspondence K–Z," Missouri Department of State, Records Management and Archives Service, box 22070.

100. Mrs. M. J. Aholt, letter from Raytown, MO, "To whom it may concern," undated, in "Correspondence A–I," Missouri Department of State, Records Management and Archives Service, box 22070.

101. Neighborhood Petition, of thirteen people living in the Center, Raytown, and Grandview school districts, 1969, in Petition file, Records Management and Archives Service, Department of Elementary and Secondary Education, Administrative Services, box 22070.

102. Petition from the Parents and Patrons of the Green Ridge R-8 School District, 1969. In "Correspondence A–I," Missouri Department of State, Records Management and Archives Service, box 22070.

103. Daniel J. Perin, director of Youth Education for the Association of Unity Churches, Lee's Summit, Missouri, to the Honorable James I. Spainhower, January 8, 1969, in "Correspondence K–Z," Missouri Department of State, Records Management and Archives Service, box 22070. On comparison of opposition in Kansas City and St. Louis see Gardner and Rury, "Suburban Resistance to District Reorganization," 140–45.

104. "Raytown Shows Suburbs' Fears of School Redistricting," 4B.

105. Jonathan Spears, interview by John Rury, March 8, 2012.

106. Deposition of James Spainhower, September 12, 1977, Arthur Benson Papers, Western Historical Manuscript Collection, University of Missouri at Kansas City, KC 250, box 354, 10.

107. Mrs. Margie McCoy to James Spainhower, March 3, 1969, Arthur Benson Papers, Western Historical Manuscript Collection, University of Missouri at Kansas City, KC 250, box 422.

108. "School Remap Weighed," *Kansas City Times*, November 16, 1968, 4C.

109. On Hazlett's response to the report see J. A. Hazlett deposition, Arthur Benson Papers, Western Historical Manuscript Collection, University of Missouri at Kansas City, KC 250, box 108, vol. 3, 361.

110. These reactions were consistent with an explanation offered by Peter Mieszkowski and Edwin S. Mills in "The Causes of Metropolitan Suburbanization," *Journal of Economic Perspectives* 7, no. 8 (Summer 1993): 137, who suggested that such perceptions "lead affluent central city residents to migrate to the suburbs, which leads to a further deterioration of the quality of life . . . which induces further out-migration." They also describe how this dynamic produced a certain type of suburban community: "Those who move to the suburbs often seek to form homogenous communities, for several reasons. There is the preference for residing among individuals of like income, education, race and ethnicity. By residing in income-stratified communities, the affluent avoid local redistributive taxes. . . . Homogenous groupings enhance the quality of education, as there is evidence that peer-group effects are important in the production of educational achievement" (137).

111. Mrs. Donald Hanes, [North] Kansas City, MO 64116, to the Honorable James Spainhower, February 5, 1969, in "Correspondence A–I," Missouri Department of State, Records Management and Archives Service, box 22070.

112. As Sacks, Ranney, and Andrews observed about the formation of suburbs, "These new communities . . . almost universally . . . 'felt' the necessity to provide an educational system consistent with their high personal income and aspirations. . . . The new suburban systems were conceived to provide a level of excellence which had no previous counterpart in terms of number of children involved." See S. Sacks, D. Ranney, and R. Andrews, *City Schools / Suburban Schools: A History of Fiscal Conflict* (Syracuse, NY: Syracuse University Press, 1972), 170.

113. Sacks, Ranney, and Andrews point out that "when suburban systems became sufficiently large, they competed . . . directly with large cities. [Eventually] suburban schools in general . . . emerged educationally equal to, or better than, their central city counterparts," ibid., 171.

114. H. Williams, superintendent, Smithville R-II Public Schools, to Mr. James I. Spainhower, November 25, 1968, in "Correspondence K–Z," Missouri Department of State, Records Management and Archives Service, box 22070.

115. Mrs. William Teal, Cass County, to Representative James Spainhower, January 9, 1969, in "Correspondence K–Z," Missouri Department of State, Records Management and Archives Service, box 22070.

116. Bi-State Committee on Education of the Kansas and Missouri Advisory Committees to the US Commission on Civil Rights, "Crisis and Opportunity: Education in Greater Kansas City," summary edition, 3.

117. Moran, *Race, Law*, 162–73.

118. "Area Districts Wary of School Merger," *Kansas City Times*, January 26, 1977, 1B.

119. "North District: No Part in Desegregation," *Kansas City Times*, February 9, 1977, 4A.

120. "Area Districts Wary of School Merger," *Kansas City Times*, 1B.

121. Many southern urban districts were organized on a county basis, offering lessons on how suburbanites could respond to well-crafted and carefully presented desegregation plans. On these points see Ansley T. Erickson, "Fairness, Commitment, and Civic Capacity: The Varied Desegregation Trajectories of Metropolitan School Districts," in *The Shifting Landscape of the American School District: Race, Class, Geography, and the Perpetual Reform of Local Control, 1935–2015*, ed. David Gamson and Emily Hodge (New York: Peter Lang, 2018), 107–226; Genevieve Siegel-Hawley and Stefani Thachik, "Crossing the Line? School District Responses to Demographic Change in the South," also in Gamson and Hodge, *Shifting Landscape*, 79–106; and Genevieve Siegel-Hawley, *When the Fences Come Down: Twenty-First-Century Lessons from Metropolitan School Desegregation* (Chapel Hill: University of North Carolina Press, 2016), pt. 2.

122. This point is acknowledged in Shortridge, *Kansas City and How It Grew*, 117. As suggested above, it eventually was less successful in Hickman Mills and Grandview.

123. For more on this see Rury and Rife, "Race, Schools and Opportunity Hoarding," 101–7.

124. A similar scenario unfolded after KCMPS lost its state accreditation in 2012, when in 2014 parents attempted to enroll their children in neighboring districts under the provisions of a state law permitting them to do so. The suburban districts were not cooperative, however, demanding full-year tuition payments up front before admitting such transfers. See Joe Robertson, "Transfer Law Confusion Keeps KC Families on Hold as School Year Approaches," *Kansas City Star*, August 5, 2014, http://www.kansascity.com/news/local/article1069939.html.

5. CONFLICT IN SUBURBIA

1. "Suburbia for Everyone?," *Album: Johnson County Museum* 21, nos. 2 and 3 (Spring/Summer 2008): 1, 5.

2. Ibid.; "Overland-Lenexa Council Hears Integration Causes," *Kansas City Times*, March 1, 1966, 32; "Donald Sewing: Housing Pioneer Improved KC Area," *Kansas City Star*, September 29, 2007.

3. Robert O. Self, "Prelude to the Tax Revolt: The Politics of the 'Tax Dollar' in Postwar California," in *The New Suburban History*, ed. Kevin M. Kruse and Thomas J. Sugrue (Princeton, NJ: Princeton University Press, 2006), 144–60; Lisa McGirr, *Suburban Warriors: The Origins of the New American Right* (Princeton, NJ: Princeton University Press, 2001), chap. 2.

4. Mindi C. Love, *Johnson County, Kansas: A Pictorial History, 1825–2005* (Shawnee, KS: Johnson County Museum, 2006), 162–64; "Shawnee Mission Schools Broke Much New Ground," *Johnson County Sun* special issue, *Bicentennial History of Johnson County*, July 2, 1976, 58.

5. "Outgoing Superintendent Explains Opposition to One Big District," *Johnson County Sun*, March 28, 1968 (Johnson County Library vertical file, "Shawnee Mission Schools, 1968"). Interestingly, there was no anticommunist rhetoric reported in connection with disputes in Shawnee Mission.

6. Robert Fishman, *Bourgeois Utopias: The Rise and Fall of Suburbia* (New York: Basic Books, 1989), chap. 5; on the role of Nichols as a suburban developer during this formative period see Kenneth Jackson, *Crabgrass Frontier: The Suburbanization of the United States* (New York: Oxford University Press, 1987), 177–78. Jackson described

Nichols as "qualitatively the most successful American developer" of suburban communities (177).

7. For an overview of desegregation struggles in the region see Joshua Dunn, *Complex Justice: The Case of Jenkins v. Missouri* (Chapel Hill: University of North Carolina Press, 2008), chap. 2. Major controversies over race and schooling occurred well after the events described in this chapter. Regarding the history of schooling for the local black community, which numbered around one thousand throughout the period, and the 1949 Kansas Supreme Court decision that ended segregated schooling there, see the Shawnee Sesquicentennial Committee, *A Pictorial History of Shawnee: Celebrating Shawnee's Sesquicentennial, 1856–2006* (Lawrence, KS: Sunflower, 2006), 37–38.

8. On the tendency of wealthy suburbanites to view local institutions in these terms, especially with respect to "hoarding of opportunity," see Kruse and Sugrue, *New Suburban History*, introduction. Regarding larger patterns of urban and suburban educational development see John L. Rury and Argun Saatcioglu, "Suburban Advantage: Opportunity Hoarding and Secondary Attainment in the Postwar Metropolitan Northeast, 1940–1980," *American Journal of Education* 118, no. 3 (May 2011): 307–42. The classic study of the development of urban school systems and the role of elite groups is David B. Tyack, *The One Best System: A History of Urban Education in the United States* (Cambridge, MA: Harvard University Press, 1974), pt. 4, where he described the "interlocking directorate" of like-minded civic leaders who promoted organizational reform in the schools. On page 149 Tyack quotes David Hammack's analysis of social groups supporting school centralization in New York, which identified "three over-lapping elites: aggressive modernizers from business and the professions, advocates of efficient, nonpartisan municipal government, and moral reformers determined to uphold Protestant values in polyglot New York City." These groups appealed to somewhat different constituencies but were united in support of bureaucratic reform. In short, centralization was supported by a coalition of affluent, well-educated, and elitist city residents determined to impose an ostensibly cosmopolitan vision on advocates of localism and the ward system.

9. Deanna Marquette, *The Historical Development of Johnson County* (Johnson County Center for Local History, Johnson County Community College, 1988), 12.

10. Love, *Johnson County, Kansas*, 96–97; "Taxes Turned Nichols toward Kansas Sites," *Johnson County Sun*, July 2, 1976, 39 (this article featured a lengthy interview with Nichols's son, Miller, about his father's approach to suburban development).

11. William S. Worley, *J. C. Nichols and the Shaping of Kansas City* (Columbia: University of Missouri Press, 1990), chap. 4. See also James R. Shortridge, *Cities on the Plains: The Evolution of Urban Kansas* (Lawrence: University Press of Kansas, 2004), 301–2. On the influence of Nichols, the Country Club District, and the Plaza see also Martin Mayer, *The Builders: Houses, People, Neighborhoods, Governments, Money* (New York: W. W. Norton, 1978), 57–59; and Robert Pearson and Brad Pearson, *The J. C. Nichols Chronicle: The Authorized Story of the Man, His Company, and His Legacy, 1880–1994* (Kansas City: Country Club Plaza, 1994), 91–106.

12. On the importance of exclusion see Jesse Clyde Nichols, "When You Buy a Home Site You Make an Investment: Try to Make It a Safe One," *Good Housekeeping*, February 1923, 38–39, 172–76. See the discussion of this in Becky Nicolaides and Andrew Wiese, eds., *The Suburb Reader* (New York: Routledge, 2006), chap. 8, "The Tools of Exclusion." On Nichols's openness to Jewish buyers see Worley, *J. C. Nichols and the Shaping of Kansas City*, 151. On the importance of Nichols's use of neighborhood associations see Richard Rothstein, *The Color of Law: A Forgotten History of How Our Government Segregated America* (New York: Liveright, 2017), 79. See also Pearson and Pearson, *J. C. Nichols Chronicle*, 57–63.

13. Shortridge, *Cities on the Plains*, 301–2; Love, *Johnson County, Kansas*, 115; Worley, *J. C. Nichols and the Shaping of Kansas City*, chaps. 7 and 8. Nichols's work was recognized by the National Association of Home Builders: "Prairie Village District Is Awarded First Place," *Kansas City Realtor*, February 9, 1950, 3.

14. Worley, *J. C. Nichols and the Shaping of Kansas City*, chap. 6.

15. Ibid., 83–84. Worley notes that in 1930 more than half the 1,325 individuals listed on the social register lived in Nichols settlements, and that by 1975 the proportion had increased to more than 80 percent of two thousand registrants, with a third living on the Kansas side of the border and 20 percent in Mission Hills alone. This was an unusually high concentration of wealth and social influence located at what would become the geographic heart of opposition to consolidation in SMSD.

16. James Shortridge, *Kansas City and How It Grew, 1822–2011* (Lawrence: University Press of Kansas, 2012), 122–29 and 154–58; Elizabeth E. Barnes, *Historic Johnson County: A Bird's Eye View of the Development of the Area* (Shawnee, KS: Neff, 1969), chaps. 6, 10, and 11; Love, *Johnson County, Kansas*, 125.

17. These factors were clearly correlated quite highly. In fact, all three are correlated at about .9, suggesting that they reflect underlying social status differences that clearly distinguished these settings. All these communities counted fewer than six thousand residents in 1960, with the exception of Prairie Village and newly established Overland Park, both with about twenty-five thousand. Some of the older Nichols communities, such as Westwood and Westwood Hills, were too small to be included in the published census tables.

18. Love, *Johnson County, Kansas*, 161; Worley, *J. C. Nichols and the Shaping of Kansas City*, 271–73; Franklin McFarland, interview with John Rury, April 2012.

19. Dave Farson, *Better Than Necessary: A Celebrational History of Shawnee Mission North High School* (Shawnee, KS: Shawnee Mission School District, 1981), 6. He reports the vote to establish the school at 1,027 to 952. Also see Love, *Johnson County, Kansas*, 161–62, and Barnes, *Historic Johnson County*, 28. Elizabeth Brooks, "Establishing the First Rural High School," *Johnson County Sun*, March 20, 1992, 4E. The school's establishment, of course, preceded development of most of the Nichols communities to the east and thus did not run afoul of localist sentiments that emerged later, during the postwar era.

20. "Dedicate Shawnee Unit," *Kansas City Times*, October 12, 1937, 1; "An Architectural Drawing of the New Proposed Shawnee Mission High School Building," *Suburban News*, May 2, 1941 (Johnson County Museum clippings file, "Schools").

21. "Shawnee Mission Schools Broke Much New Ground," 58; McFarland interview, April 2012.

22. Quoted in Love, *Johnson County, Kansas*, 163.

23. "Shawnee Mission Schools Broke Much New Ground," 58.

24. "The School Debt on Increase in Northeast Johnson County," *Kansas City Star*, January 3, 1954, 20E; Elizabeth E. Barnes, "Phenomenal School Growth," *Johnson County Herald*, September 8, 1960 (Johnson County Museum clippings file, "Schools"); McFarland interview, April 2012.

25. Donna Davis, Jennifer Friend, and Loyce Carruthers, "The Fear of Color: *Webb v. School District No. 90* in Johnson County, Kansas, 1949," *American Educational History Journal* 37, no. 2 (2010): 331–45; and Rachel Devlin, *A Girl Stands at the Door: The Generation of Young Women Who Desegregated America's Schools* (New York: Basic Books, 2018), chap. 4.

26. Myra F. Jenks and Irene B. French, *Historic Merriam: The History of Merriam, Kansas* (Lenexa, KS: Publishing Specialists, 2006), 123; Barbara Rein, "The Black Community of South Park–Merriam, Kansas, a Part of the Whole," in Student Papers in Local

History, Johnson County Center for Local History, Johnson County Community College, 1986, 145–55.

27. "Quiet Fund Drive Keeps an Area White," *Kansas City Star*, July 24, 1964. In another incident, longtime KCK resident Charles Oliver reported that he and several other African Americans were invited to a home in Johnson County, presumably to discuss local civil rights issues. Upon arriving they were ushered onto a side lawn, so that the neighbors could see them. The owner confessed that the purpose was to motivate the neighborhood association to buy the home, which was up for sale. Apparently such purchases were not so unusual in that part of greater Kansas City; Charles Oliver, interview with John Rury, Kansas City, Kansas, March 15, 2012.

28. "Move to Suburbs Not Easy: Negroes Consider Children First," *Kansas City Star*, March 6, 1968.

29. "Suburbia for Everyone?," 1; Oliver interview; JOCO History, "Civil Rights Pioneering in Johnson County," https://jocohistory.wordpress.com/2013/01/22/civil-rights-pioneering-in-johnson-county/.

30. *Kansas City Star*, May 4, 1958, 29B. A review of real estate advertisements published in Sunday editions of the *Star*, on the first two Sundays in May, was conducted for every year between 1948 and 1965. Shawnee Mission High School was mentioned in advertisements more than any other institution, typically four to six times each Sunday, although it should be noted that particular schools were named in a small proportion of hundreds of advertisements. Various SMSD elementary schools were regularly noted as well. City schools, particularly Southwest High, were mentioned also, although less frequently over time. For a similar analysis and discussion of suburban educational development see Jack Dougherty, "Shopping for Schools: How Public Education and Private Housing Shaped Suburban Connecticut," *Journal of Urban History* 38, no. 2 (March 2012): 2.

31. "Flood of Housing Spurs a Johnson County School Push," *Kansas City Star*, January 16, 1955 (Johnson County Public Library vertical file).

32. "Postwar Development in Johnson County, Kansas, Is Subject of Article in *Nation's Schools Magazine*: Building Problems Curriculum and Establishment of Junior High System Are Discussed," *Kansas City Star*, March 30, 1958 (Kansas City Public Library vertical file).

33. Ibid.; Love, *Johnson County, Kansas*, 149–51.

34. "Two Schools Here Win Praise for Excellence," *Kansas City Times*, October 11, 1957, 1; "What Makes Them Good?," *Time*, October 21, 1957, 54.

35. "Postwar Development in Johnson County, Kansas"; "Shawnee Mission Schools Broke Much New Ground," 58; McFarland interview, April 2012.

36. "S-M District Grows to 120,000 since '21," *Olathe News*, May 5, 1961 (Johnson County Museum clippings file, "Schools"); Patricia Jansen Doyle, "Shawnee Mission Northwest's New Passage to Learning," *Kansas City Star Magazine*, April 18, 1971; Roy Inman, "A New Plot in the Environment Story," *Kansas City Star Magazine*, May 30, 1971; Love, *Johnson County, Kansas*, 171–75. On the area's black population and their access to education see Shawnee Sesquicentennial Committee, *Pictorial History of Shawnee*, 37–38.

37. "Will Johnny Learn a Lot Next Year with More Kids in His Class?," *Squire*, February 5, 1970 (Johnson County Public Library vertical file), 10; Mayer, *Builders*, 59–60.

38. Kansas State Department of Education, "Unified School District Wealth, 1975–76," Kansas State Department of Education, Topeka, 1976, np. The taxable income per pupil in the district was $14,972, compared to $8,324 for Olathe and approximately $9,000 for Kansas City, Kansas, $11,000 for Wichita, and $13,000 for Topeka. Kansas State

Department of Education, "U.S.D. Report on Enrollments and General Fund per Pupil, 1974–5," Topeka: Kansas State Department of Education, 1975, 18.

39. "School Staffs in Good Shape," *Kansas City Times*, July 15, 1961, 1.

40. "Conservative Attitude Works as a Brake," *Kansas City Times*, September 16, 1967, 2B. The series was written by the *Star*'s education writer, Patricia Jansen Doyle, who also wrote about other districts in the metropolitan area. She raised a number of questions about whether the district's schools deserved their excellent reputation, noting that the district actually spent *less* per pupil than some other area school systems, and that some students complained that they had not been well prepared for college. Even if there was little question that Shawnee Mission was widely seen as the best district in the region, Doyle suggested that perhaps it was due to the high socioeconomic status of its clientele rather than the work of the schools. See "Both Facts, Fancy in Education Reputation," *Kansas City Star: This Week Magazine*, September 10, 1967, 1A, 10A.

41. "Kansans Face Vast School Change," *Kansas City Star*, May 25, 1964, 4.

42. Ghazal A. Husain, "Consolidation of School Districts in Kansas" (PhD diss., University of Kansas, 1966), 108; "School Consolidation History," Memorandum from Lauren S. Douglas to Senator Chris Steineger, Kansas Legislative Research Department, Topeka, November 2, 2009, http://www.scribd.com/doc/26316131/Kansas-School-Consolidation-History. See also "Finance Plan Keyed to Unification," *Kansas City Star*, May 28, 1964, 4; "Spur to Approval of a School Plan," *Kansas City Times*, May 29, 1964, 3; "Pros and Cons of School Unification," *Kansas City Star*, May 29, 1964, 4; "Hoping to End School 'Maze,'" *Kansas City Star*, May 31, 1964, 22.

43. On this point see "Solving the Rural School Problem: New State Aid, Standards, and Supervision of Local Schools, 1900–1933," *History of Education Quarterly* 48 (Spring 2008): 181–220, and David R. Reynolds, *There Goes the Neighborhood: Rural School Consolidation at the Grass Roots in Early Twentieth Century Iowa* (Iowa City: University of Iowa Press, 1999), chaps. 6 and 7. On early conditions in Kansas see E. T. Fairchild, *Bulletin of Information regarding Consolidation of Rural Schools* (Topeka, KS: State Print Office, 1908).

44. "A Study of the Public Schools of the Shawnee Mission District of Johnson County Kansas," March 1962, Shawnee Mission, KS, 30.

45. "Complex Issues in Unification Vote," *Kansas City Star*, May 27, 1964, 4A; "Push Approval of Unification," *Kansas City Star*, June 1, 1964, 4; "Johnson County Delays the Inevitable," *Kansas City Star*, August 19, 1964 (Johnson County Library clippings file).

46. "Another Blow to Unification," *Kansas City Times*, May 28, 1964, 4A; "The Best School Plan for Johnson County," *Kansas City Star*, June 1, 1964, 24; "Complex Issues in Unification Vote," 4A.

47. "Reject a School Plan," *Kansas City Times*, June 3, 1964, 4; "Complex Issues in Unification Vote," 4A. One local history suggests that the residents of affluent Westwood were solidly opposed to the unification plan; see Gene Culbertson, *The City of Westwood: Celebrating 50 Years of Progress, 1949–1999* (Shawnee, KS: Publishing Specialist), 25.

48. "Stride in School Vote," *Kansas City Star*, June 3, 1964, 4A.

49. "Kill a Merger: Mission–Roeland Park Consolidation Plan Loses Overwhelmingly in Election," *Kansas City Star*, September 27, 1953, 3A; "Vote on Merger Issue: Long and Sometimes Bitter Controversy over the Merger of Mission and Roeland Park," *Kansas City Star*, September 25, 1953, 14.

50. "Against a Merger," *Kansas City Star*, December 1, 1956 (Johnson County Public Library vertical file); "Plan Lengthy Bill Schedule: Move to Consolidate Johnson County Programs Will Await a Survey," *Kansas City Star*, January 3, 1957, 15. Interestingly, the straw vote was positive in this case, although it did not result immediately in consolidation. See "A Johnson County Tangle," *Kansas City Star*, September 13, 1958, 38. Mission

Woods was (is) a very small Nichols development immediately to the north of Mission Hills, on the Missouri border.

51. See Tyack, *One Best System*, pt. 4.

52. These points are taken from Husain, "Consolidation of School Districts in Kansas," summarized in chap. 5. A geographer, Husain conducted a statistical analysis of unification across all counties in the state, using multiple regression. Controlling for half a dozen other factors, including tax levels, farm products, and school costs, he found that the number of school districts was the strongest predictor of the rate of consolidation leading up to 1964 (p. 98). This logic did not appear to apply, of course, to Shawnee Mission in 1964, although Husain did not comment on it.

53. "Reject a School Plan," 4A.

54. "Mixed Views on Unification," *Kansas City Times*, December 4, 1968 (Johnson County Library vertical file). The quote about the danger in small boards is quite striking in light of Progressive Era measures backed by educated urban elites to drastically reduce membership on city school boards in the name of efficiency and nonpartisanship. On these points see Tyack, *One Best System*, pt. 4.

55. "School Plan Unit Studies Next Vote," *Kansas City Star*, June 5, 1964, 4; "Expect a Modified Unification Plan," *Kansas City Times*, June 5, 1964, 4.

56. "A School Unity Election Today," *Kansas City Times*, September 8, 1964, 10; "Johnson County Delays the Inevitable."

57. "Hails School Vote Results: Significant Step Seen Taken on Unification in Kansas," *Kansas City Star*, June 3, 1964, 4A.

58. Husain, "Consolidation of School Districts in Kansas," chap. 5, "Summary and Conclusions."

59. In 1968 just twenty-nine districts in the state had yet to consolidate, and thirteen of them were within the Shawnee Mission High School District attendance area. See "Outgoing Superintendent Explains Opposition to One Big District."

60. "Suggest Vote on Unification," *Kansas City Times*, February 13, 1968, 5; "Question Amrein on Vote Proposal," *Kansas City Times*, February 20, 1968, 4.

61. "Patrons Wary of Unity Plan," *Kansas City Star*, November 19, 1968, 4; "Official for Voluntary School District Union," *Kansas City Times*, February 3, 1968, 5A; "School Dispute Ends Smoothly," *Kansas City Times*, February 19, 1969, 12B.

62. "Editorial: Adding More Emotionalism," *Johnson County Sun*, January 8, 1969 (Johnson County Public Library vertical file, "Shawnee Mission Schools, 1969"); "For One School Unit," *Kansas City Star*, February 7, 1968, 4A; "Hits Material on Unification," *Kansas City Times*, February 16, 1968, 4A; "Bower Attacks Effort to Stop Shawnee Mission School Unity," *Kansas City Times*, March 12, 1968, 5; "Would Delay Unity for a Year," *Kansas City Times*, February 21, 1968, 4A.

63. Engelhardt, Engelhardt, and Leggett Inc., *Unification* (Johnson County, KS: Northeast Johnson County Public Schools, 1968); "Oppose Paying for Unification Study," *Kansas City Times*, December 12, 1968, 5C.

64. "For Unified District," *Kansas City Times*, January 21, 1969, 4; "School Unity Bill to Floor," *Kansas City Times*, January 28, 1969, 4.

65. "School Bill Is Passed," *Kansas City Times*, February 14, 1969, 4.

66. "Conservative Attitude Works as a Brake," 2B.

67. "Century of History Surrounds Closing of Linwood School," *Kansas City Star*, May 9, 1975 (Johnson County Public Library vertical file); "Closings Advised in Shawnee Mission," *Kansas City Times*, November 11, 1975, 4A; "School Closings to Be Topic Tonight," *Johnson County Sun*, November 19, 1975, 2A.

68. "Bill to Decentralize School District," *Kansas City Star*, February 12, 1973, 4.

69. Love, *Johnson County, Kansas*, 184–85; Florent Wagner, "1960–1980: Incorporation and Organization," in *Historic Overland Park: An Illustrated History*, ed. Norman Keech and Florent Wagner (San Antonio, TX: Historical Publishing Network, 2004), 72. On comparisons with Blue Valley and other districts see "State Competency Scores Improving but Not Great," *Johnson County Sun*, August 11, 1982, 8A; Rachel Bolton, "The Testing of the Shawnee Mission District," *Squire*, October 14, 1982 (Johnson County Library, Regional Reference vertical file, "Schools-Shawnee Mission, 1982"); "Some Teachers Find New Opportunities in District to South," *Kansas City Star*, June 9, 1985, 19A. The district also began to experience labor troubles in the later 1970s, as teachers complained about working conditions and salary levels. See "Shawnee Mission Teachers Sue," *Kansas City Star*, March 17, 1978, 4.

70. Under the terms of the state's school consolidation legislation, only city districts had the power to close schools without a vote of affected patrons. Since Shawnee Mission was originally a rural high school district, it had to abide by rules governing districts serving rural areas. See "Ball for Court Action to Clarify School Issue," *Kansas City Star*, March 5, 1976, 4.

71. "Impact of Keeping All Schools Open Studied," *Kansas City Star*, February 17, 1976, 4; "School Board to Turn to Courts," *Kansas City Times*, March 23, 1976, 4; "Parents Do Homework, Fight School Closings," *Kansas City Star*, December 4, 1975, 2W; "Board Can't Close Schools," *Kansas City Times*, February 6, 1976 (Johnson County Public Library vertical file); "Board to Renew Drive for School Closing Law," *Kansas City Star*, February 19, 1976, 4.

72. "Kansas House Defeats School Closing Plan," *Kansas City Star*, March 2, 1976, 4; "Shawnee Mission Again Faces Threat from School Closing Bill," *Kansas City Times*, January 26, 1978, 3B. For a legislative summary of the statute authorizing the district to close schools and the Kansas Supreme Court case upholding it see *1983 Cumulative Supplement to the Kansas Statutes Annotated, Volume 5A*, Article 81: Unified School District Provisions of Limited Application, "72–8136a. U.S.D. 512 authorized to close school buildings; conditions" (Topeka: Kansas State Printing Office, 1983), 72–7601.

73. "Shawnee Mission Hopes Feuding Is Over," *Kansas City Star*, November 11, 1987, 1; "The Education of Raj Chopra," *Kansas City Times*, November 5, 1988, AM Profile. The 1987 vote in favor of an increased levy was just 58 percent, a margin of victory that would have been insufficient in Missouri, where a two-thirds majority was required for approval of such measures.

74. "Shawnee Mission Board Gets Honor," *Kansas City Star*, October, 18, 1984, 5A; Shawnee Mission Schools, *Just the Facts . . . about Schools* (Fact Sheet distributed by the district in 1980).

75. Love, *Johnson County, Kansas*, 190.

76. On the propensity of earlier generations of civic leaders to promote bureaucratic, "nonpartisan" approaches to governance see Samuel P. Hays, "The Politics of Reform in Municipal Government in the Progressive Era," *Pacific Northwest Quarterly* 55, no. 4 (October 1964): 157–69, and William J. Reese, "The Control of Urban School Boards during the Progressive Era: A Reconsideration," *Pacific Northwest Quarterly* 68, no. 4 (October 1977): 164–74, in addition to Tyack, *One Best System*, pt. 4.

77. For a description of the study see Basil G. Zimmer and Amos H. Hawley, *Metropolitan Area Schools: Resistance to District Reorganization* (Beverly Hills, CA: Sage, 1968), chap. 1. Zimmer and Hawley found that college-educated, affluent suburbanites in larger metropolitan areas (Milwaukee and Buffalo in their study) expressed the greatest opposition to the idea of district reorganization or consolidation, favoring small, locally controlled and financed districts over other options (see chap. 7 for these

points). On "localism" see Amos Hawley and Basil Zimmer, *The Metropolitan Community: Its People and Government* (Beverly Hills, CA: Sage, 1970), chap. 4, "The Localization of Daily Life."

78. Matthew Lassiter, *The Silent Majority: Suburban Politics in the Sunbelt South* (Princeton, NJ: Princeton University Press, 2007), chap. 6; McGirr, *Suburban Warriors*, chap. 2; "Area Districts Wary of School Merger," *Kansas City Times*, January 26, 1977, 1B. Reverend Maurice Culver, president of the SMSD Board of Education, dismissed the idea of consolidating districts across state lines as "next to impossible," while the vice president of the Bonner Springs board declared that "nothing can be forced along this issue and make any real gains."

EPILOGUE

1. Mará Rose Williams, "Kansas City Public Schools Hits the Full Accreditation Mark for the First Time in Decades," *Kansas City Star*, November 7, 2016, http://www.kansascity.com/news/local/article113037663.html.

2. Joe Robertson, "As KC School District Ponders Big Moves, Southwest Students Are at the Forefront," *Kansas City Star*, April 19, 2015, http://www.kansascity.com/news/local/article18948126.html. In 2008 KCMPS lost a significant portion of its population when Van Horn High School and its feeder institutions were "re-annexed" to the Independence School District, a change that required—and received—approval from voters in both districts. On this point see James R. Shortridge, *Kansas City and How It Grew, 1822–2011* (Lawrence: University Press of Kansas, 2012), 181.

3. A listing of area districts and their size can be found at http://www.usa.com/kansas-city-mo-ks-area-school-district.htm. On perceptions of city schools, which may have improved a bit in recent years, see Joe Robertson, "KC Schools' Fight to Win Over Urban Millennials Touches Questions of Equity, Race," *Kansas City Star*, February 23, 2016, http://www.kansascity.com/news/local/article62077537.html.

4. A. G. Sulzberger, "Kansas City, Mo., School District Loses Its Accreditation," *New York Times*, September 20, 2011, http://www.nytimes.com/2011/09/21/us/kansas-city-mo-school-district-loses-its-accreditation.html. On an earlier crisis see "Kansas City Schools Lose Accreditation," *Los Angeles Times*, May 4, 2000, http://articles.latimes.com/2000/may/04/news/mn-26560.

5. Joe Robertson, "Lawsuit Likely If State Denies KC School District's Bid for Accreditation," *Kansas City Star*, October 20, 2013, http://www.kansascity.com/news/local/article329938/Lawsuit-likely-if-state-denies-KC-school-district%E2%80%99s-bid-for-accreditation.html. In 2013, Kansas City Star columnist Steve Rose wrote about a "private meeting" between area superintendents and Kansas City mayor Sly James, where it was reportedly proposed that KCMPS be divided up between the various "suburban" districts. Rose alleges that James opposed the idea, arguing that a "core district" was important to maintain. This, of course, was not accompanied by public statements from the participants, who did not have the power to make such decisions in any case. That sort of change would have required approval by school boards and voters in all the participating districts, a monumental undertaking, to say the least. Given the history of suburban animosity toward KCMPS, and the very public opposition of area school boards toward the transfer provision, the suggestion that this was a serious proposal strains credulity. See Steve Rose, "Rebirth of Van Horn High School Is a Sign of Hope," *Kansas City Star*, August 17, 2013, http://www.kansascity.com/opinion/opn-columns-blogs/steve-rose/article325444/Rebirth-of-Van-Horn-High-School-is-a-sign-of-hope.html.

6. Joe Robertson and Jason Hancock, "Few Families File for Transfers Out of Kansas City School District," *Kansas City Star*, March 29, 2014, http://www.kansascity.com/

news/politics-government/article341791/Few-families-file-for-transfers-out-of-Kansas-City-school-district.html; Lee's Summit R-7 School District, "Information about Kansas City Public Schools Loss of Accreditation and Its Impact on Lee's Summit R-7 Schools," January 28, 2014, https://lsr7.org/information-about-kansas-city-public-schools-loss-of-accreditation-and-its-impact-on-lees-summit-r-7-schools/.

7. National Public Radio, "562: The Problem We All Live With," https://www.thisamericanlife.org/radio-archives/episode/562/transcript.

8. A classic case of this occurred in Shelby County, Tennessee, which includes the city of Memphis: Erica Frankenberg, Genevieve Siegel-Hawley, and Sarah Diem, "Segregation by District Boundary Line: The Fragmentation of Memphis Area Schools," *Educational Researcher* 46, no. 8 (November 2017): 449–63. Also see Corey Mitchell, "Mostly White Alabama Town Can Split from Diverse District, Court Rules: Judge Says Move Is Racially Motivated," *Education Week*, May 9, 2017, https://www.edweek.org/ew/articles/2017/05/10/mostly-white-alabama-town-can-split-from.html; T. Keung Hui and Doss Helms, "A Split for CMS? Lawmakers Want to Study How to Divide NC School Districts," *Charlotte Observer*, April 12, 2017, http://www.charlotteobserver.com/news/local/education/article144231634.html; Gillian Edevane and Ian Cull, "Mt. Diablo Unified School District Split Doesn't Enhance Segregation, according to Independent Review," NBC Bay Area, August 11, 2017, https://www.nbcbayarea.com/news/local/Mt-Diablo-Unified-School-District-Split-Doesnt-Enhance-Segregation-According-to-Independent-Review-439920893.html. Also see Edward Buendia and Paul Humbert-Fisk, "Building Suburban Dreams: School District Secession and Mayoral Control in Suburban Utah," *Teachers College Record* 117, no. 9 (2015): 1–52.

9. Peter Mieszkowski and Edwin S. Mills, "The Causes of Metropolitan Suburbanization," *Journal of Economic Perspectives* 7, no. 8 (Summer 1993): 135; John Rennie Short, "Metropolitan USA: Evidence from the 2010 Census," *International Journal of Population Research* 2012 (2012), Article ID 207532, 6 pages, http://dx.doi.org/10.1155/2012/207532; Jed Kolko, "2015 U.S. Population Winners: The Suburbs and the Sunbelt," *CityLab*, March 24, 2016, https://www.citylab.com/equity/2016/03/2015-us-population-winners-the-suburbs-and-the-sunbelt/475251/.

10. Laura Lippman, Shelley Burns, and Edith McArthur, *Urban Schools: The Challenge of Location and Poverty* (Washington, DC: National Center for Educational Statistics, 1996), 4–11; quotes are from pages 5 and vi respectively.

11. On this point generally see John L. Rury and Jeffrey E. Mirel, "The Political Economy of Urban Education," *Review of Research in Education* 22 (1997): 49–110.

12. Lippman, Burns, and McArthur, *Urban Schools*, pt. 2.

13. William Julius Wilson, *The Truly Disadvantaged: The Inner City, the Underclass, and Public Policy* (Chicago: University of Chicago Press, 1987), pt. 1; William Julius Wilson, *When Work Disappears: The World of the New Urban Poor* (New York: Vintage Books, 1996), pt. 1; Paul A. Jargowsky, *Poverty and Place: Ghettos, Barrios, and the American City* (New York: Russell Sage, 1997), chaps. 3–6; Craig Reinarman and Harry G. Levine, "Crack in Context: America's Latest Demon Drug," chap. 1 in *Crack in America: Demon Drugs and Social Justice*, ed. Craig Reinarman and Harry G. Levine (Berkeley: University of California Press, 1997).

14. William H. Frey, "Melting Pot Suburbs: A Census 2000 Study of Suburban Diversity" (Washington, DC: Brookings Institution Press, 2001), 3–12. Also see his book *Diversity Explosion: How New Racial Demographics Are Remaking America* (Washington, DC: Brookings Institution Press, 2015), chap. 8.

15. Frey, "Melting Pot Suburbs," 4. A higher percentage of the Asian population moved to the suburbs, even if they numbered fewer than African Americans. Also see Richard Florida, *The New Urban Crisis: How Our Cities Are Increasing Inequality* (New York: Basic Books, 2017), chap. 8.

16. Mieszkowski and Mills, "Causes of Metropolitan Suburbanization," 137.

17. On this point see Jack Dougherty, "Shopping for Schools: How Public Education and Private Housing Shaped Suburban Connecticut," *Journal of Urban History* 38, no. 2 (March 2012): 205–24.

18. Andrew Wiese, *Places of Their Own: African American Suburbanization in the Twentieth Century* (Chicago: University of Chicago Press, 2004), chap. 9. See also Emily Strauss, *Death of a Suburban Dream: Race and Schools in Compton, California* (Philadelphia: University of Pennsylvania Press, 2014), chaps. 4–6. Recently, the term "slumburb" has been applied to some of these communities, although it has been critiqued as well. See Kriston Capps, "Minorities and the 'Slumburbs,'" *CityLab*, January 21, 2015, https://www.citylab.com/equity/2015/01/minorities-and-the-slumburbs/384680/.

19. Erica Frankenberg, "Understanding Suburban District Transformation: A Typology of Suburban Districts," in *The Resegregation of Suburban Schools: A Hidden Crisis in American Education*, ed. Erica Frankenberg and Gary Orfield (Cambridge, MA: Harvard Education Press, 2012), 27–44. On the status of blacks leaving the cities see Deirdre Pfeiffer, "Racial Equity in the Post–Civil Rights Suburbs? Evidence from US Regions 2000–2012," *Urban Studies* 53, no. 4 (2016): 799–817. On problems in suburban schools see Amanda Lewis and John Diamond, *Despite the Best Intentions: How Racial Inequality Thrives in Good Schools* (New York: Oxford University Press, 2015), chaps. 3–5; and Derrick Darby and John L. Rury, *The Color of Mind: Why the Origins of the Achievement Gap Matter for Justice* (Chicago: University of Chicago Press, 2018), chap. 7.

20. James E. Ryan, *Five Miles Away, a World Apart: One City, Two Schools, and the Story of Educational Opportunity in Modern America* (New York: Oxford University Press, 2011), chap. 8; Don Lee, "U.S. Population in Cities Growing Faster Than in Suburbs," *Los Angeles Times*, June 28, 2012, http://articles.latimes.com/2012/jun/28/nation/la-na-census-cities-20120628; Eric Jaffe, "Why You Should Be Skeptical of Statistics on City vs. Suburban Population Growth," *CityLab*, July 13, 2012, https://www.citylab.com/equity/2012/07/why-you-should-be-skeptical-latest-statistics-city-vs-suburban-population-growth/2571/; Joseph Berger, "Suburbs Try to Prevent an Exodus as Young Adults Move to Cities and Stay," *New York Times*, April 16, 2014, https://www.nytimes.com/2014/04/17/nyregion/suburbs-try-to-hold-onto-young-adults-as-exodus-to-cities-appears-to-grow.html; Richard Florida, "The Urban Revival Is Over," *New York Times*, September 1, 2017, https://www.nytimes.com/2017/09/01/opinion/cities-suburbs-housing-crime.html.

21. Ann Owens, "Inequality in Children's Contexts: Income Segregation of Households with and without Children," *American Sociological Review* 81, no. 3 (2016): 549–74.

22. Kris Hudson, "Generation Y Prefers Suburban Home over City Condo," *Wall Street Journal*, January 21, 2015, https://www.wsj.com/articles/millennials-prefer-single-family-homes-in-the-suburbs-1421896797; David Z. Morris, "Why Millennials Are About to Leave Cities in Droves," *Fortune*, March 28, 2016, http://fortune.com/2016/03/28/millennials-leaving-cities/; Haya El Nasser, "American Cities to Millennials: Don't Leave," *USA Today*, December 4, 2012, https://www.usatoday.com/story/news/nation/2012/12/03/american-cities-to-millennials-dont-leave-us/1744357/; Mike Lanza, "Suburb Hating Is Anti-Child," *NewGeography*, September 6, 2013, http://www.newgeography.com/content/003916-suburb-hating-anti-child; Alison Bowen, "Relax. Take a Deep Breath. Moving to the Suburbs Is Going to Be OK," *Chicago Tribune*, January 12, 2016, http://www.chicagotribune.com/classified/realestate/ct-mre-0117-relocate-suburbs-20160112-story.html. See also Alan M. Berger, "The Suburb of the Future, Almost Here: Millennials Want a Different Kind of Suburban Development That Is Smart, Efficient and Sustainable," *New York Times*, September 15, 2017, https://www.nytimes.com/2017/09/15/sunday-review/future-suburb-millennials.html?_r=0.

23. On this problem see Michelle Alexander, *The New Jim Crow: Mass Incarceration in the Age of Colorblindness* (New York: New Press, 2012), chaps. 2–4; and Becky Pettit, *Invisible Men: Mass Incarceration and the Myth of Black Progress* (New York: Russell Sage, 2012), chaps. 5 and 6.

24. Florida, *New Urban Crisis*, chaps. 2–5.

25. Ibid., chap. 8; Rolf Pendall and Carl Hedman, "Worlds Apart: Inequality between America's Most and Least Affluent Neighborhoods," Urban Institute, 2015, https://www.urban.org/research/publication/worlds-apart-inequality-between-americas-most-and-least-affluent-neighborhoods; Joel Kotkin, "Geographies of Inequality," *Third Way*, August 23, 2016, http://www.thirdway.org/report/geographies-of-inequality.

26. John R. Logan, Elisabeta Minca, and Sinem Adar, "The Geography of Inequality: Why Separate Means Unequal in American Public Schools," *Sociology of Education* 85, no. 3 (2012): 287–301.

27. Robert Balfantz and Nettie Legters, *Locating the Dropout Crisis: Which High Schools Produce the Nation's Dropouts? Where Are They Located? Who Attends Them?*, Center for Research on the Education of Students Placed at Risk, Johns Hopkins University, Report 70, 2004. More recently there has been a drop in the number of black and Hispanic students attending such institutions, although more than a million still attend them. See Chad Aldeman, "Great News: Fewer Students Attending Dropout Factories," *Education Next*, July 6, 2015, http://educationnext.org/great-news-fewer-students-attending-high-school-dropout-factories/.

28. Aaron Tyler Rife, "Shifting Identities in South Kansas City: Hickman Mill's Transformation from a Suburban to Urban School District" (PhD diss., University of Kansas, 2014), chaps. 4 and 5.

29. Eric Alder, Mará Rose Williams, and Savanna Smith, "KC Area Has Been One of the Most Racially Segregated in America. But Not Anymore," *Kansas City Star*, January 6, 2019, https://www.kansascity.com/news/local/article223888475.html. The local segregation index dropped from 71 to 60 in this time span, and the region fell from being the eleventh most segregated metropolis of greater than a million residents to the twenty-seventh.

30. Shortridge, *Kansas City and How It Grew*, chap. 7. On recent tensions see Mará Rose Williams, "Lee's Summit Schools Split over Training about Race," *Kansas City Star*, September 28, 2018, 4A, and "Lee's Summit School District Needs to Have a Tough Conversation about Race," *Kansas City Star*, September 29, 2018, https://www.kansascity.com/opinion/editorials/article219217130.html. Also see Mará Rose Williams, "Embattled Lee's Summit Superintendent Resigns," *Kansas City Star*, July 24, 2019, 1a, 6a, and the editorial published the next day, "Lee's Summit Students Are the Losers with Superintendent Dennis Carpenter Resignation," *Kansas City Star*, July 25, 2019, https://www.kansascity.com/opinion/editorials/article233068307.html. It states that "Lee's Summit, like much of the country, has a serious problem with race issues."

31. Mid-America Regional Council, *Fair Housing and Equity Assessment*, March 2014, chap. 2, "Segregation." On the continuing racialization of space in greater Kansas City see Kevin Fox Gotham, *Race, Real Estate, and Uneven Development: The Kansas City Experience, 1900–2010*, 2nd ed. (Albany: SUNY Press, 2014), conclusions. Also see Shortridge, *Kansas City and How It Grew*, chap. 7. The liberal views of residents in this area were discussed in oral history interviews: Franklin McFarland, interview with John Rury, April 2012, and David Cord, interview with John Rury, March 1, 2012.

32. Given the fact that white households were a minority in this part of the city, varying between 20 and 30 percent, it seems likely that many of them were also quite poor. Very few Hispanics lived in these census tracts. In largely black neighborhoods with lower levels of poverty, household incomes above $45,000 in 2010 dollars ranged between 30

and 45 percent of all families, suggesting a sizable black middle class. Data drawn from Social Explorer.

33. Shortridge, *Kansas City and How It Grew*, 182–84. On crime in the area see Robert A. Cronkleton and Ian Cummings, "Two Dead, 8 Injured Days after KC Police Pleaded for Help in Stopping Violence," *Kansas City Star*, August 5, 2018, https://www.kansascity.com/news/local/crime/article216130815.html, and Kelsey Ryan and Ian Cummings, "Crime Statistics Reveal Kansas City's Disturbing Homicide Trend," *Kansas City Star*, July 2, 2017, https://www.kansascity.com/news/local/crime/article159204444.html. Poverty levels in particular census tracts were taken from Social Explorer.

34. On the Hispanic community in Kansas City, Kansas, see Shortridge, *Kansas City and How It Grew*, 146–47.

35. See, for instance, Linda M. Burton, Marybeth Mattingly, Juan Pedroza, and Whitney Welsh, "State of the Union, 2017: Poverty," Stanford Center on Poverty and Inequality, https://inequality.stanford.edu/sites/default/files/Pathways_SOTU_2017_poverty.pdf.

36. The extent of single-parent households headed by women had increased, mainly in predominantly African American neighborhoods. In 2010, the American Community Survey showed some twenty census tracts in Kansas City, Missouri, where they numbered in excess of 30 percent of all households, and an equivalent number where they represented more than 20 percent. In tracts to the east of the historic ghetto area, their numbers were much lower. Data taken from Social Explorer.

37. For example see the editorial "Low Test Scores Show KC, Hickman Mills School Districts Falling Far Short of Goals," *Kansas City Star*, October 6, 2016, 8A.

38. Mará Rose Williams, "Students' ACT Scores in Missouri and Kansas Beat the National Average," *Kansas City Star*, August 26, 2015, http://www.kansascity.com/news/article32441295.html.

39. Joe Robertson, "Scores on ACT Point to Many Disparities," *Kansas City Star*, August 21, 2013, http://www.kansascity.com/news/local/article325697/Scores-on-ACT-point-to-many-disparities.html. Although veteran reporter Robertson was careful to discuss the various factors associated with variation in scores, especially the number of students taking the test, the list offered a ready means for ranking institutions across the region for anyone interested in doing so.

40. On local magnet schools see Andrew Vaupel, "These Are the Top High Schools in Missouri and Kansas," *Kansas City Business Journal*, April 19, 2016, https://www.bizjournals.com/kansascity/news/2016/04/19/top-public-high-schools-in-missouri-and-kansas.html.

41. Mará Rose Williams, "A Year after Hitting Mark, KC Schools Again Miss Critical State Measure," *Kansas City Star*, November 15, 2017, http://www.kansascity.com/news/local/article184867878.html. Although the district has improved its standing somewhat since then, it is unlikely to compete with high-performing suburban districts even if accreditation is eventually restored. See Steve Kraske, "Are KC Public Schools on the Verge of a Breakthrough? Full Accreditation within Reach," *Kansas City Star*, November 25, 2018, https://www.kansascity.com/opinion/opn-columns-blogs/steve-kraske/article222039045.html.

42. Regarding the effects of high mobility and its relationship to student poverty see Russell W. Rumberger and Katherine A. Larson, "Student Mobility and the Increased Risk of High School Dropout," *American Journal of Education* 107, no. 1 (November 1998): 1–35; Virginia L. Rhodes, "Kids on the Move: The Effects of Student Mobility on NCLB School Accountability Ratings," Penn GSE Perspectives on Urban Education, 2017, http://www.urbanedjournal.org/archive/volume-3-issue-3-spring-2005/kids-move-effects-student-mobility-nclb-school-accountability-r; and Janet D. Dalton, "Mobility and Student Achievement in High Poverty Schools" (PhD diss., East Tennessee State

University, 2013), Electronic Theses and Dissertations, Paper 1159, http://dc.etsu.edu/etd/1159.

43. For a clear summary of the racial dimensions of this see Thomas B. Edsall, "Integration vs. White Intransigence: Separate Has Never Been Equal," *New York Times*, July 17, 2019, https://www.nytimes.com/2019/07/17/opinion/integration-politics.html.

44. "On a Metropolitan Solution," James Hazlett deposition, March 9, 1983, 340–41, Arthur Benson Papers, box 108, Western Historical Collection, University of Missouri–Kansas City.

45. This process is summarized in Shortridge, *Kansas City and How It Grew*, chap. 7.

46. Basil Zimmer and Amos Hawley, *Resistance to Reorganization of School Districts and Government in Metropolitan Areas* (Thousand Oaks, CA: Sage, 1966), chaps. 1 and 2; Amos Hawley and Basil Zimmer, *The Metropolitan Community: Its People and Government* (Thousand Oaks, CA: Sage, 1970), chap. 1. Also see Stephen Macedo, *Diversity and Distrust: Civic Education in a Multicultural Democracy* (Cambridge, MA: Harvard University Press, 2000), pt. 1; and Roger B. Parks and Ronald J. Oakerson, "Regionalism, Localism, and Metropolitan Governance: Suggestions from the Research Program on Local Public Economies," *State and Local Government Review* 32, no. 3 (Fall 2000): 169–79.

47. Campbell Scribner, *The Fight for Local Control: Schools, Suburbs, and American Democracy* (Ithaca, NY: Cornell University Press, 2016), chaps. 1–4.

48. Hazlett deposition, March 7, 1983, vol. 1, 40–41, Arthur Benson Papers, box 108, Western Historical Collection, University of Missouri–Kansas City.

49. Interestingly, KCMPS superintendent Hazlett used the word "localism" to characterize suburban opposition to interdistrict cooperation. "Argue School District Plan," *Kansas City Times*, January 18, 1969.

50. For a discussion of these questions today see David D. Troutt, "Localism and Segregation," *Journal of Affordable Housing & Community Development Law* 16, no. 4 (Summer 2007): 323–47; Erika K. Wilson, "The New School Segregation," *Cornell International Law Journal* 49, no. 3 (2016): 139–210; and Richard C. Schragger, "The Limits of Localism," *Michigan Law Review* 100, no. 2 (November 2001): 371–472. Regarding opportunity hoarding in this context see John L. Rury and Argun Saatcioglu, "Opportunity Hoarding," in *The Wiley Blackwell Encyclopedia of Race, Ethnicity, and Nationalism*, ed. John Stone, Dennis M. Rutledge, Anthony D. Smith, Polly S. Rizova, and Xiaoshuo Hou (New York: Wiley Blackwell, 2015), 1–3, https://doi.org/10.1002/9781118663202.wberen435.

51. For elaboration of these comparisons see John L. Rury and Aaron Rife, "Race, Schools and Opportunity Hoarding: Evidence from a Post-war American Metropolis," *History of Education* 47, no. 1 (January 2018): 87–107.

52. Ibid., 96–105.

53. Joe Feagin, *Systemic Racism: A Theory of Oppression* (New York: Routledge, 2006), chap. 1.

54. On local liberalism, KCMPS superintendent Hazlett referred to Johnson County "bleeding hearts" who offered gratuitous advice on racial questions to city school leaders. See James Hazlett deposition, March 9, 1983, vol. 3, 320, Arthur Benson Papers, box 108, Western Historical Collection, University of Missouri–Kansas City. Regarding the role of shared norms as a form of social capital see James S. Coleman, "Social Capital in the Creation of Human Capital," *American Journal of Sociology* 94, Supplement: Organizations and Institutions: Sociological and Economic Approaches to the Analysis of Social Structure (1988): S104–5; on limitations to this conceptualization and a widely cited review of relevant literature see Alejandro Portes, "Social Capital: Its Origins and Applications in Modern Sociology," *Annual Review of Sociology* 24 (1998): 18–21.

55. Clifford Hooker and Van D. Mueller, *Equal Treatment to Equals: A New Structure for Public Schools in Kansas City and St. Louis Metropolitan Areas; A Report to the Missouri School District Reorganization Commission* (Jefferson City, MO, 1969); Bi-State Committee on Education of the Kansas and Missouri Advisory Committees to the US Commission on Civil Rights, *Crisis and Opportunity: Education in Greater Kansas City*, summary edition, 1977; Joshua Dunn, *Complex Justice: The Case of Missouri v. Jenkins* (Chapel Hill: University of North Carolina Press, 2008), chaps. 2 and 3.

56. Donna Gardner and John L. Rury, "Suburban Opposition to District Reorganization: The 1968 Spainhower Commission and Metropolitan Kansas City and St. Louis," *Urban Review* 46, no. 1 (March 2014): 125–45. My thanks to Professor Gardner for her meticulous research on these questions.

57. "Area Districts Wary of School Merger," *Kansas City Times*, January 26, 1977, 1B; "North District: No Part in Desegregation," *Kansas City Times*, February 9, 1977, 4A.

58. Robertson, "Lawsuit Likely."

59. Douglas S. Massey, *Categorically Unequal: The American Stratification System* (New York: Russell Sage Foundation, 2007), chaps. 3 and 4; Edsall, "Integration vs. White Intransigence."

60. On its expression in this era see Eric Foner, *The Story of American Freedom* (New York: W. W. Norton, 1998), chaps. 11 and 12.

61. Linda Darling Hammond, "Race, Inequality and Educational Accountability: The Irony of No Child Left Behind," *Race, Ethnicity and Education* 10, no. 3 (September 2007): 245–60. Also see Adam Gamoran, "Educational Inequality in the Wake of No Child Left Behind," Spencer Foundation Award Lecture, Association for Public Policy and Management, November 7, 2013, http://www.appam.org/assets/1/7/Inequality_After_NCLB.pdf.

62. On inequality between districts see Ann Owens, "Income Segregation between Districts and Inequality in Students' Achievement," *Sociology of Education* 91, no. 1 (2018): 1–27. On the importance of extending choice to the suburbs see James E. Ryan, *Five Miles Away, a World Apart: One City, Two Schools, and Educational Inequality in Modern America* (New York: Oxford University Press, 2010), chap. 8.

63. On the impact of *Milliken* see Jennifer Jellison Holme, Kara S. Finnigan, and Sarah Diem, "Challenging Boundaries, Changing Fate? Metropolitan Inequality and the Legacy of *Milliken*," *Teachers College Record* 118, no. 3 (2016): 1–40.

64. Genevieve Siegel-Hawley, *When the Fences Come Down: Twenty-First-Century Lessons from Metropolitan School Desegregation* (Chapel Hill: University of North Carolina Press, 2016), pt. 2.

65. http://www.tcrecord.org/library, ID no. 18247. An overview of the eight best-known such plans can be found at http://school-diversity.org/pdf/ASW-interdistrict.pdf, compiled by Jennifer Jellison Holme and Amy Stuart Wells. On the status of school desegregation nationally see Sean F. Reardon and Ann Owens, "60 Years after *Brown*: Trends and Consequences of School Segregation," *Annual Review of Sociology* 40 (2014): 199–218.

66. "Suburbs Reject Transfers," *Kansas City Times*, June 5, 1986, 1A. This began as a lawsuit to establish such a program and involved eleven districts on the Missouri side of the border. Two districts, Independence and North Kansas City, expressed openness to the idea once the lawsuit was resolved; the others rejected the notion wholly or refused to comment on it.

67. On these programs and others see http://www.onenationindivisible.org/wp-content/uploads/2012/09/ONI_Interdistrict_Overview.PPT.pdf. Also see Kara S. Finnigan, Jennifer Jellison Holme, Myron Orfield, Tom Luce, Sarah Diem, Allison Mattheis, and

Nadine D. Hylton, "Regional Educational Policy Analysis: Rochester, Omaha, and Minneapolis' Inter-District Arrangements," *Education Policy* 29, no. 5 (2015), at http://journals.sagepub.com/doi/abs/10.1177/0895904813518102.

68. On the history of the program in St. Louis, including suburban ambivalence about it, see Marquita L. Bowers-Brown, "The St. Louis Desegregation Transfer Program: Do African American Students Perform Better in an Integrated Suburban Setting?" (PhD diss., University of Missouri at St. Louis, 2015), chap. 3. Also see Elisa Crouch, "St. Louis Desegregation Program Headed for Phase Out," *St. Louis Post-Dispatch*, June 10, 2016, http://www.stltoday.com/news/local/education/st-louis-desegregation-program-headed-for-phase-out/article_9dadfa4c-3d49-5b80-b6ec-2b1c03d2e5c7.html. On a smaller but similar program in Boston see Susan Eaton, *The Other Boston Busing Story: What's Won and Lost across the Boundary Line* (New Haven, CT: Yale University Press, 2001), chap. 7.

69. Reardon and Owens, "60 Years after *Brown*," 207.

70. See, for example, Caitlin Howley and Kimberly Hambrick, "Interdistrict Cooperatives: They Improve Cost-Effectiveness and Make Common Cents," *District Administration*, July 1, 2011, https://www.districtadministration.com/article/interdistrict-cooperatives.

71. Chastity Pratt Dawsey and Mike Wilkinson, "School Choice, Metro Detroit's New White Flight," *Center for Michigan: Bridge Magazine*, September 13, 2016, http://www.mlive.com/news/detroit/index.ssf/2016/09/school_choice_metro_detroits_n.html; Urban Institute Student Transportation Working Group, "Student Transportation and Educational Access: How Students Get to School in Denver, Detroit, New Orleans, New York City, and Washington, DC," Urban Institute, February 2017, https://www.urban.org/sites/default/files/publication/88481/student_transportation_educational_access_0.pdf.

72. Raj Chetty, Nathaniel Hendren, and Lawrence F. Katz, "The Effects of Exposure to Better Neighborhoods on Children: New Evidence from the Moving to Opportunity Experiment," *American Economic Review* 106, no. 4: 855–902, https://doi.org. 10.1257/aer.20150572.

73. Mathew Desmond, *Evicted: Poverty and Profit in the American City* (New York: Crown, 2016), 308–12.

74. Siegel-Hawley, *When the Fences Come Down*, chap. 3.

75. On this point seen Derrick Darby and John L. Rury, *The Color of Mind: Why the Origins of the Achievement Gap Matters for Justice* (Chicago: University of Chicago Press, 2018), chap. 6.

76. Jennifer B. Ayscue and Gary Orfield, "School District Lines Stratify Educational Opportunity by Race and Poverty," *Race and Social Problems* 7, no. 1 (March 2015): 5–20. On the problem of fragmented school districts in a metropolitan area with less *community* fragmentation see Shaina Cavazos, "Racial Bias and the Crumbling of a City," *Atlantic*, August 17, 2016, https://www.theatlantic.com/education/archive/2016/08/indianapolis-school-districts/496145/.

77. For a recent review of themes in advancing equity in education see Erica Frankenberg, Lilliana M. Garces, and Megan Hopkins, "Which Way Forward? A Comprehensive Approach for Advancing Equity through Integration," in *School Integration Matters: Research-Based Strategies to Advance Equity*, ed. Erica Frankenberg, Lilliana M. Garces, and Megan Hopkins (New York: Teachers College Press, 2016), 215–22, although reorganizing districts or moving students across district lines are not major points of emphasis.

78. David F. Labaree, "Public Goods, Private Goods: The American Struggle over Educational Goals," *American Educational Research Journal* 34, no. 1 (January 1997): 39–81.

APPENDIX

1. John L. Rury, Argun Saatcioglu, and William P. Skorupski, "Expanding Secondary Attainment in the United States, 1940–80: A Fixed-Effects Panel Regression Model," *Historical Methods* 43, no. 3 (July–September 2010): 151, fn 2.

2. See, for instance, American Psychological Association, *Discussing Discrimination*, at http://www.apa.org/helpcenter/keita-qa.aspx.

Index

accreditation, 157–158, 171, 231n124, 242n41
ACT scores, 1, 168–171, 173, 179
adult education levels
    adult attainment, 32, 64–65, 67–75, 168, 186–192
    in black neighborhoods, 77
    in Johnson County, 137–138
    in Kansas City metropolitan districts, 109–111, 216n61, 216n64
    spatial organization of, 185–189
    and urban-suburban divide, 32–34, 64–69, 73–74
advantage, 2, 29–31, 168
    concentrated, 72–74, 168
    and gender, 191–192
    and Johnson County, 71–73
    and racial exclusion, 135
    suburban, 3, 14–16, 37, 43, 61, 128, 162–163, 171, 179
affluence
    and African Americans, 41, 54, 57, 163
    geographic distribution of, 178
    in KCMPS, 98, 106
    and localism, 12, 35, 173
    and suburbs, 6, 25, 27–28, 149, 145–155, 177–178
African Americans
    as "culturally deprived," 88–89, 93, 118
    and histories of education, 5
    and integration efforts, 38–42
    and Johnson County, 133, 140–142, 144
    and Kansas City development, 8–9, 50–57
    and KCMPS, 62–63, 77–89, 92–103
    and legacies of inequality, 158–167, 171–172, 174–177
    and localism, 13
    and metropolitan differentiation, 32–33
    middle class, 41, 72–73, 131, 164–165, 242n32
    and spatial inequality, 65–68, 71–73, 186–188, 190–191
    and suburban Missouri districts, 105–107, 110–111, 116–118, 122–124, 131–133
    teachers, 55, 62, 80, 171
    and US urban education, 21–26, 28

annexation, 14–15, 30–31, 124
    and Hickman Mills, 44, 50, 115
    and North Kansas City, 119–121, 123, 177, 212n9
    in postwar Kansas City, 46–48, 50
    and Raytown, 112, 118
    and suburb development, 58–59, 61, 108
    of Sugar Creek, 81
attendance zones, 29, 38–39, 51, 214n41

baby boom, 5, 22, 45, 84, 107, 189
Ball, Arzel, 151–152
Bedell, Mark, 157, 171
black people
    See African Americans
blue-collar communities, 8, 58, 99, 113, 117, 121, 174
Blue Springs, Missouri, 47, 164, 166–167, 170
Blue Valley School District, 60, 68, 152, 168–170
Bonner Springs, Kansas, 60, 129, 238n78
Boustan, Leah Platt, 24, 41
Brown v. Board of Education, 38, 55–56, 62, 81, 107, 141
busing, 38–39, 62–63, 86, 88, 95–96, 125, 213n23

Catholic schools, 100, 102, 224n122
Center District, 60–61, 82–83, 99, 108–110, 169–170
central city, 14–16, 23, 36, 158–159, 161, 179–181
    and KCMPS, 62, 69, 131
    and metropolitan differentiation, 32–34
    and the rise of the suburbs, 58
Central High, 79, 81, 88, 102, 117, 126, 176
Chicago, Illinois, 25–26, 29, 40–41, 62, 181
children, 1–4
    and educational inequality, 72–74
    and enduring inequality, 158–159, 165–168, 172, 181
    in Johnson County, 155
    and KCMPS, 63, 68–69, 86, 99–100, 102
    in Missouri suburbs, 118, 125
    and racial boundaries, 88–89

247

children *(continued)*
   and school integration, 39, 41, 96
   and school segregation, 55
city schools, 2–5, 11, 16, 19, 76–77
   crisis in, 77–78, 80
   and enduring inequality, 161, 182
   and Missouri suburbs, 127
   racial boundaries in, 88
   segregation in, 39
   and social change, 27–28, 34, 43
   and suburbs, 41, 43, 110
civil rights, 10, 25–26, 38–39, 62–63, 93–94
Clay County, Missouri, 60, 79, 216n61, 217n69
   race in, 122, 165
Coleman, James, 28, 38, 111
college education
   adults with, 37, 64–65, 67–69, 71–72, 185–189, 192
   college prep, 19–20
   and enduring inequality, 167–169, 173, 175
Commission on Civil Rights, US, 94, 98, 128, 155, 177
Conant, James, 18–19, 22, 24, 28
conflict
   and desegregation, 62–63, 74, 78, 95
   and enduring inequality, 163, 180
   and Johnson County, 134–135, 153, 155–156
   and KCMPS, 86, 93–95
   and metropolitan development, 11–12
   and Raytown, 115–118
   and suburban development, 64
   and urban education, 20, 29
consolidation, school district
   in Johnson County, 146–151, 155–156
   in Missouri suburbs, 15, 60–61, 112, 120–121, 124–125
   and suburban localism, 35–37, 43
Cookingham, L. P. (Perry), 14, 44–46, 48, 74, 115, 123
Country Club district, 64–65, 68, 74, 136, 186–189, 217n69
Country Club Plaza, 59, 136, 165
crime, 3, 11, 40–41
curriculum
   for African Americans, 89, 100
   of public schools, 22, 49, 78–79, 89
   and tracking, 20

Daniels, Marvin, 54–55, 87–88, 91, 100, 122
democracy, 125, 156, 178, 183
demography
   demographic changes, 14, 30, 58, 64
   demographic trends, 8, 69–70
   and suburbs, 41, 45, 58

Department of Health, Education, and Welfare (HEW), 94–95, 103
deprivation, 24, 72, 77, 159, 162, 169, 178
   concentrated, 165, 167, 172
desegregation
   after *Brown v. Board*, 38–40, 43
   and enduring inequality, 163, 171, 177, 179–180
   Jenkins v. Missouri, 10, 62, 78, 129, 157, 193, 232n7
   and Johnson County, 135, 157
   in Kansas City, 62–63, 78, 81, 84–86, 94–98, 102–105
   and Missouri suburbs, 128–131
   and urban education, 19, 26, 28–29
   Webb v. School District No. 90, 55, 141
   See also integration
Detroit, Michigan, 24, 26, 39, 102, 181
disadvantage
   and African Americans, 33, 68, 90, 92–93
   concentrated, 57, 72–74, 95, 168
   and urban-suburban divide, 42–43, 179
discrimination
   in cities, 5, 8–9, 13–24, 55, 57
   in education, 68, 107, 110
   and localism, 131
   ongoing, 160–161
districts
   assessments of, 91, 99, 196
   contemporary KC area, 1
   and desegregation nationally, 38–40
   and enduring inequality, 157–158, 160, 163, 165, 168–183
   and geo-spatial inequality in KC, 64–65, 68, 72
   interdistrict cooperation, 129–130, 180, 229n93, 243n49
   interdistrict transfer programs, 179–180, 183
   in Johnson County, 134–135, 138–141, 143–154, 156
   and Kansas City history, 10, 14–16, 47–50, 55–56, 60–63
   Kansas City Missouri Public Schools. *See* Kansas City Missouri Public Schools (KCMPS)
   and localism, 36
   mergers, 50, 119, 146, 148
   and metropolitan development, 30
   in Missouri suburbs, 105–115, 117–132
   in postwar US, 26–28
   unification, 146–156
   and urban-suburban divide, 42–43

East High School, 79, 82–83, 86–87, 89
East Side, Kansas City's, 53–54, 82, 92, 96, 102, 213n26
economy
  economic segregation, 8
  in Johnson County, 138, 152, 156
  in Kansas City, 46, 64–65, 75, 100, 109, 188–189
  in urban areas, 20–23, 32, 34
education
  adult. *See* adult education levels
  contemporary inequality, 158–159, 162, 168–169, 171–173, 178–181, 183
  and desegregation, 38–42
  golden age of urban, 19–22
  historical inequality, 4, 29–35, 42–43, 45, 58
  histories of, 6, 18–19
  impacts of, 1–2
  in Johnson County, 134, 140, 143, 155–156
  and Kansas City history, 9–11, 14–16, 45, 48, 61–75
  and KCMPS, 77, 79, 81, 88–89, 93–94, 98, 100
  in Missouri suburbs, 116, 120, 125, 127–129, 131
  and postwar social change, 22–29
  statistical analysis of, 185–189, 191–192
  and suburban localism, 36–38
Elard, Patrick, 87–89, 100, 116, 123–124
elementary schools, 22
  elementary districts, 48, 79–81, 119, 134–135, 145–151
  and Johnson County, 145–151, 234n30
  and KCMPS, 92–93, 95
Excelsior Springs, Missouri, 47, 56, 60, 79, 122, 224n119
exclusion
  and enduring inequality, 156, 161, 163, 175–176
  in Johnson County, 141
  localism and, 12–13
  and metropolitan development, 51, 54
  in Missouri suburbs, 105, 112, 117, 124, 130–131
  post-*Brown v. Board*, 39–40
expansion
  of African American population, 51, 56, 82–83, 178
  municipal, 10, 45–48, 51
  suburban, 19, 23, 59, 108, 139–140
extracurricular activities, 22, 49, 78, 221n57

Fairway, Kansas, 133–134, 137–138, 142, 148, 176
families
  African American, 28, 54–56, 57, 72–73, 142
  and enduring inequality, 169–176, 181–182
  family background, 28, 70
  family income, 65, 138
  family structure, 70, 72–73, 77, 160, 169, 191–192
  and the golden age of urban education, 22–23
  and inequality, 2–3, 70–73, 189–191
  and Johnson County, 137–138, 142, 161, 165
  and KCMPS, 76, 82, 86, 96, 99, 102–103
  and metropolitan development, 30, 56–57
  and metropolitan differentiation, 33
  and Missouri suburbs, 106–110, 118
  statistical analysis of, 189–191
female-headed households, 41, 71, 162, 190–192
Florida, Richard, 8, 161–162, 199n35
fragmentation
  and localism, 35–37
  of metropolitan areas, 48, 69, 182
  of school districts, 182–183
  of suburbs, 61, 135
Free or Reduced Lunch Program (FRL), 108, 110–111, 122, 162, 225n13
Frey, William, 160, 183

gender, 70, 190
  female-headed households, 41, 71–72, 162, 168, 190–192
  women teachers, 80
geo-spatial frame of reference, 11
  inequality, 43, 45, 64–66, 69–70, 74–75, 162, 183
  and metropolitan development, 31–32, 193
  and suburbs, 19, 58
  variables, 187, 190, 192, 217n69
Gotham, Kevin Fox, 54, 213n23
government
  centralized, 21
  and desegregation, 40
  and districts, 4, 50
  and localism, 35–36
  and suburbs, 116, 134–135, 249, 153–154, 176
graduation rates, 1, 159–160, 189–190
  African American, 24, 26–27, 67, 77, 93
Grandview, Missouri, 50, 58, 108–109, 115, 122, 126, 170
  African Americans in, 99, 227n60
  maps of, 47, 49, 60, 83, 164, 166–167
Great Depression, 21, 25, 137

INDEX

Hawley, Amos, 11, 36–37, 154–155, 172, 200n46
Hazlett, James, 76, 79–80, 127, 173, 178
   desegregation proposal, 86, 95, 103–104
   Hazlett huts, 94
   and race in KCMPS, 91–92, 171, 213n27, 214n39
Herndon, Joe, 115, 117, 227n50, 227n52
Hickman Mills District (HMSD), 15
   African Americans in, 16, 82–83, 112, 118, 163
   comparison to KCMPS, 99
   comparison to North Kansas City, 122–123
   comparison to Raytown, 115–116
   contemporary, 16, 169–170, 175
   development of, 108–110
   KCMPS annexation of, 44, 50
   and KCMPS out-migration, 101–102
   map of, 47, 83, 113
   poverty in, 122, 163, 165, 169–170
high schools
   and educational inequality, 70, 190
   and enduring inequality, 159, 162
   growth of, 20, 22
   KCMPS, 79, 81–83, 86, 90, 95, 99, 103
   in Johnson County, 61, 138–140, 143–147, 149
   and metropolitan differentiation, 34
   in Missouri suburbs, 114, 119–120
   public as superior, 15, 18, 22, 78–79
   rural, 48
   senior, 79, 95, 98
highway construction, 5, 19, 30–31, 51, 106, 225n3
Hilliard, Susan, 53–54, 87, 100, 102, 122
Hispanic population, 9, 40, 56, 124, 241n27, 241n32
housing
   and African Americans, 53–57, 90, 93
   and civil rights, 24–27, 93
   discrimination in, 9, 24–27, 59, 93
   and enduring inequality, 159, 173–175, 181–182
   home ownership, 5, 30, 33, 67, 70–71, 73
   home values, 34, 65–67, 143, 188
   housing markets, 5, 24, 27, 39, 115
   in Johnson County, 68, 134, 137, 139, 142
   in Missouri suburbs, 106, 108, 114–116, 118
   mortgage policies, 5, 9, 19, 23, 106, 123
   statistical analysis of, 186, 191–192
human ecology theory, 11–12

income, 27, 25, 34, 37
   and enduring inequality, 162, 165
   and Johnson County, 137–138, 145, 154, 156
   low, 27, 65, 225n13
   and Missouri suburbs, 109–110, 118, 123, 188
   and race, 54, 56–57, 118
   and spatial inequality, 65, 67
Independence, Missouri
   ACT scores in, 170
   African Americans in, 55, 83, 122, 129, 163–164
   and annexation, 47–49, 81
   college education in, 167–168
   Independence School District, 48–49, 78–79, 108–110, 113
   and KCMPS, 96, 99
   poverty in, 166
inequality, 2
   correlates of, 69–74
   economic, 63, 74–75, 125, 156
   enduring, 159, 162, 177–179, 182–183
   geo-spatial, 43, 45, 64–66, 69–70, 74–75, 162, 183
   histories of, 6, 32
   institutions and, 3–4
   in Johnson County, 140, 154, 156
   metropolitan, 32, 34
   in Missouri suburbs, 128, 132
   and race, 42, 102
   statistical analysis of, 187
   and suburban development, 36, 38
integration
   after *Brown v. Board*, 38–40, 43
   in cities, 25–26, 50, 105
   and enduring inequality, 163–165, 173–174, 180, 182–183
   and Johnson County, 55, 133, 140–141, 155
   in KCMPS, 62–63, 80–82, 84, 86, 92–97, 100
   and Missouri suburbs, 107, 117–118, 124–125, 127–133
   in secondary schools, 53

Jackson County, Missouri
   adult attainment in, 168, 216n61
   districts in, 49–50, 78–79, 157
   geo-spatial analysis of, 64–65, 67, 69
   poverty in, 165
   statistical analysis of, 186–187
   suburbanization in, 59, 61, 74
Jenkins v. Missouri, 10, 62, 78, 129, 157, 193, 232n7

INDEX

Johnson County, Kansas, 14–16
  adult attainment in, 64–65, 66
  African Americans in, 52, 55, 133–134, 140–142
  educational attainment in, 70–73
  and enduring inequality, 157, 164–165, 168–171, 175–177
  Johnson County District No. 55, 90, 140
  and KCMPS, 101
  school decline in, 152–154
  and Shawnee Mission high school, 138–140, 142–146, 152, 154–156
  statistical analysis of, 188–192
  suburban development in, 59–60, 67, 74, 135–138
  and unification conflict, 146–152
Johnson, Lyndon Baines, 24, 38

Kansas City, Missouri (KCMO), 1, 7–11, 14–16, 44–46
  correlates of inequality in, 69–75
  district transitions in, 61–63
  enduring inequality in, 157–160, 163–179
  expansion of, 45–50
  geo-spatial inequality and, 63–69
  and Johnson County, 134, 136–137, 143
  Kansas City Missouri Public Schools. *See* Kansas City Missouri Public School (KCMPS)
  and Missouri suburbs, 107–108, 112–113, 116–118, 123–131
  poverty in, 72
  race in, 50–58, 82–83, 87–88, 91–93, 97–98
  South, 58, 112–113, 116–118, 174
  statistical analysis of, 185–186, 188–192
  suburbanization and, 58–61
  See also metropolitan Kansas City
Kansas City Missouri Public Schools (KCMPS), 48–49, 76–78
  conflict in, 91–95
  decline of, 98–100, 102–104, 225n8
  desegregation failures and, 95–98
  and enduring inequality, 157–158, 168–169, 171, 178, 179
  exit from, 75, 100–102
  geo-spatial inequality and, 64–69, 72
  historical prominence of, 78–81
  and Missouri suburbs, 106–111, 116–118, 122, 126–132
  overcrowding in, 62, 78–80, 89, 92, 94, 96
  provisional accreditation of, 157–158
  race and poverty in, 81–86
  racial boundaries and, 87–91

statistical analysis of, 186–187, 189, 217n69
  and Sugar Creek district, 80–81, 96
  transition of, 61–62
Kansas City, Kansas (KCK), 1, 8, 45, 51, 110, 135, 141
  Kansas City KS public schools (KCKPS), 48, 109–110, 138
  race in, 51, 141, 166–167, 195n1, 212n20
  and suburban development, 59
  Sumner High, 141, 169
Keyes v. School District No. 1, 39, 94

Latinx population, 160, 162
Leawood, 137–138, 152–153, 164, 166, 167–168
Liberty, Missouri, 47, 60, 79, 120, 170
  ACT scores in, 170
  African Americans in, 55, 122
  and KCMPS, 99, 109
  Liberty School District, 61, 108–110
  poverty in, 110
Lincoln High, 56, 79, 82, 91, 93, 169
local control, 4, 35, 43, 155
  and Johnson County, 105, 126, 134, 148–149, 155
Localism, 11–13, 16
  and enduring inequality, 172–177, 182–183
  in Johnson County, 134, 147, 156, 233n19
  in Missouri suburbs, 107, 118, 124, 130, 132
  and suburbanization, 35–38
Logan, John, 162, 171
logistical regression analysis, 69–72, 190
Los Angeles, California, 24, 31, 40

magnet schools, 40, 42, 160–161, 169, 180
Manual High, 79, 81–82, 87
manufacturing, 7–8, 29, 31–32, 40, 45, 108
Massey, Douglas, 9, 178
McEachen, Howard, 139–140, 142, 144–145, 151, 155
Merriam, Kansas., 136–138, 141, 148
metropolitan areas, 2, 4–6, 12, 18–19, 42–43
  and history of public education, 21
  and integration, 38–42
  national development of, 29–32
  and social impacts, 23–25, 27, 32–34
  and suburban localism, 35–37
metropolitan Kansas City, 1, 6–11, 14, 16, 45–46
  and enduring inequality, 158–160, 162–168, 171–173, 178–183
  expansion of, 46–50, 63, 74–75
  geo-spatial mapping of, 63–69

metropolitan Kansas City *(continued)*
and Johnson County, 134, 137, 143, 145, 151, 155
and KCMPS, 85, 91, 97–98, 101–102
and Missouri suburbs, 106–109, 112, 122, 124–126, 128–131
racial development of, 50–58
and statistical analysis, 69–74, 188, 189
and suburban development, 58–61
middle class
African American, 24, 41, 72–73, 102, 131, 164
and enduring inequality, 161, 164–165, 188
and Johnson County, 137, 141, 144, 154
and KCMPS, 75, 90, 93, 102, 104
and Missouri suburbs, 106–107, 118, 121, 131, 188
and suburban development, 9, 13, 30, 61, 68
Mieszkowski, Peter, 160, 173
Milliken v. Bradley, 39–40, 43, 179
Milwaukee, Wisconsin, 28, 36, 39, 102, 179
minority groups
and enduring inequality, 158, 161, 168–170, 180
in Johnson County, 141
in KCMPS, 81, 95, 97, 101
and Missouri suburbs, 106, 109–111, 116, 118, 124
and poverty, 42, 169, 174, 180, 182
racial and ethnic, 3, 5–6, 21–23
Mission, Kansas, 138–139, 142, 148
Mission Hills, Kansas, 136–138, 142, 144, 148, 152–153, 165
Missouri v. Jenkins, 10, 62, 78, 98, 129, 157, 193
Moving to Opportunity (MTO) program, 181, 183

National Association for the Advancement of Colored People (NAACP), 9, 26, 38, 130, 141
National Merit scholars, 79, 92, 98, 143–144
neighborhoods
and desegregation, 38–41
and enduring inequality, 161–162, 164–165, 171, 174, 181
and geo-spatial inequality, 64, 67–68, 72, 188–189
and Johnson County, 127, 134–138, 141, 151–153, 155
and KCMPS, 62–63, 77, 79–82, 87–90, 96, 100–101
and localism, 13
and Missouri suburbs, 115–116, 121–122

neighborhood associations, 134, 136–137, 141, 165, 234n27
neighborhood schools, 29, 62, 80, 86, 127, 152
predominantly black, 55–56, 82
predominantly white, 6, 9, 23, 55, 86, 92
and race in Kansas City, 5, 8–9, 50–51, 53–57
and suburban development, 58
and urban education, 22–29
Nichols, J. C., 12, 58–59, 75, 134–137, 144, 186
and KCMPS, 63–64, 69
North Kansas City, 15
African Americans in, 67
and enduring inequality, 164, 170
and Kansas City, 47, 49, 60, 129, 131
North Kansas City School District (NKCSD), 64, 79, 108–110, 118–124, 177
Northland, the, 61, 120, 123–124, 165, 212n9

Olathe, Kansas, 60, 136, 169–170, 234n38
opportunity hoarding, 13, 15, 104, 174–176, 183
and Missouri suburbs, 107, 118, 131–132
oral history, 16, 185, 192–193
out-migration, 84–85, 92, 102, 107, 230n110
Overland Park, Kansas, 68, 133–134, 138, 152–153, 233n17

parental education, 28, 32, 70, 73, 109, 162, 171, 192
Park Hill district, 60, 170
Paseo Academy, 79, 82–87, 92–93, 101, 126
Pendergast, Tom, 8, 50, 212n18
police
and African Americans, 24, 53, 87, 93, 160
in Missouri suburbs, 116, 118, 176
politics, 19
big-city, 8, 11–12
dog-whistle, 131
local, 11–12, 29
and suburbanization, 19, 134
postwar era, 2–6, 12–15, 171–172, 191
and Johnson County, 135, 142, 146
in Kansas City, 50–51, 58–60
and KCMPS, 77, 84, 87, 106
metropolitan development in, 23, 29–31, 34
and Missouri suburbs, 112, 119, 124
urban-suburban divide and, 42–43
poverty, 9, 24–25, 27, 34, 41–42
concentrated, 159, 164–165, 175, 178, 181–182

INDEX

and enduring inequality, 158–172, 178, 181–182, 191
  extreme, 68, 182
  in Kansas City, 56–57, 68, 71–73
  in KCMPS, 76–77, 81–90, 102–103
  and Missouri suburbs, 111, 116, 127
  and students, 27, 88, 92, 103
Prairie Village, Kansas, 134, 137–138, 142, 148, 164–167, 214n42
predominantly African American institutions, 27, 169–161, 163, 174–175
  in KCMPS, 77–78, 81, 87–89, 93, 96, 100–102
predominantly white institutions, 39, 158, 161
  in KCMPS, 76, 86, 88, 90–92, 106
  in Missouri suburbs, 131, 135, 137
private schools, 63, 96, 98, 101–102, 138
property values, 26, 67, 88, 115, 144
  and enduring inequality, 173, 186–189
Public education, 3–4, 36, 42–43, 97, 173
  in Johnson County, 135, 155–156
  and Missouri suburbs, 128
  overcrowding in, 20, 39

race, 5–9, 13, 32–33, 45
  African Americans. *See* African Americans
  after *Brown v. Board*, 38–42
  Asian Americans, 160
  and enduring inequality, 163–65, 167, 172–178
  ethnic minority, 3, 6, 23, 106, 195n1
  Hispanic people, 9, 40, 56, 124, 241n27, 241n32
  and Johnson County, 134, 140–142, 155–156
  and Kansas City development, 50–58, 74–75
  and KCMPS, 62–63, 67–68, 77–82, 84–95, 100, 102
  Latinx population, 160, 162
  and Missouri suburbs, 105–107, 112, 117, 124–128, 131–133
  racism, 5, 11, 25, 86, 131, 175
  and social change, 22–29
  statistical analysis of, 69–70, 185–190
  and urban education, 21–23
Raytown, Missouri, 15–16, 105–106, 131–132
  African Americans in, 82–83, 112–118, 214n42
  comparison to NKCSD, 123–124
  and enduring inequality, 163–167, 170, 174–177
  and geo-spatial inequality, 66–67
  and Kansas City expansion, 47, 49–50, 58, 108–109

and the Spainhower Commission, 126
  statistical analysis of, 186–188
  See also Raytown School District
Raytown School District, 15–16, 105–106, 115, 219n28
  African Americans in, 83, 112–113, 116–118, 132, 163
  comparison to NKCSD, 120, 123–124
  and exit from KCMPS, 101–102
  and geo-spatial inequality, 64–65, 67
  and Kansas City expansion, 50
  poverty in, 165–166, 169–170, 214n42
  and the Spainhower commission, 126
  and suburban school development, 108–111
real estate
  and desegregation, 39
  and enduring inequality, 173, 176
  and Johnson County, 133, 142–143, 145
  and KCMPS, 76
  and Missouri suburbs, 117, 123
  and race, 5, 9, 53–57, 92
  restrictive covenants in, 5, 23, 59, 136–137
  and suburban development, 9, 19
  See also housing
rural districts
  African Americans in, 4, 15, 21
  in Johnson County, 146–147, 149, 153–154
  and Missouri suburbs, 112, 120, 126–127
  Shawnee Mission Rural, 139, 141, 237n70
  and urban districts, 2–3, 78
Ryan, James E., 37, 161

schools
  attendance zones in, 29, 38–39, 51
  consolidation of, 146–147, 149–150, 156
  funding of, 109–111
  overcrowding in, 20, 62, 78–80, 82, 92, 94
  school accountability, 168, 179
  school closings, 115, 120, 152–154
  school success, 32–33, 67, 70–72, 74, 190–192, 208n69
  and social capital, 13, 132, 176
  See also high schools
secondary schooling
  growth of, 20–22
  in Johnson County, 138–139, 141, 148–149
  in Kansas City, 48, 53, 62–63, 85–86
  in Missouri suburbs, 112, 114
  and race, 22, 53, 82, 89, 92
  See also high schools
segregation
  after *Brown v. Board*, 38–40
  desegregation. *See* desegregation

254   INDEX

segregation *(continued)*
  and enduring inequality, 159, 161, 163–164, 171–172, 178–180, 182
  and Johnson County, 134–135, 140–141
  and Kansas City history, 8–10, 51, 55–57, 62–64, 75
  and KCMPS, 78–82, 86–88, 91–98
  in Missouri suburbs, 123, 125, 129–132
  and suburban history, 5, 28
  and urban history, 24–26, 28–29
Sewing, Donald, 133–134, 142, 165, 174
Shawnee, Kansas, 137–138
Shawnee Mission School District (SMSD), 1, 60–61, 134–135, 154–156
  acclaim for, 144–146
  decline in, 152–153
  and district unification, 146–152
  and enduring inequality, 160, 169–170, 173, 175
  and geo-spatial inequality, 64–68
  Shawnee Mission High, 141–144, 149
  Shawnee Mission North, 1, 144
  Shawnee Mission Rural High, 138–141
Siegel-Hawley, Genevieve, 179, 182
social class, 2, 9, 11, 22, 37, 69, 156
social status
  and enduring inequality, 163, 183
  and institutions, 3–4
  in Johnson County, 138, 154
  and KCMPS, 62, 68
  and Missouri suburbs, 106, 114, 121
  and suburbs, 31
  and urban education, 6, 28, 74
socioeconomic status
  and race, 33, 42, 54, 68, 75
  and suburbs, 31, 58, 160, 162, 178
Southwest High, 79, 86, 90, 100–101
  African Americans in, 63, 68, 82–83, 92, 97–98
  and Johnson County schools, 138, 143
Spainhower Commission, 124–128, 130, 132, 148, 177
St. Louis, Missouri, 46, 48, 124–126, 158, 180
standardized tests, 16, 20
  and enduring inequality, 157, 159, 179, 186
  in KCMPS, 77, 93, 98, 110–111
  and poverty, 168–171
state line, Missouri-Kansas, 7, 128–130, 165, 168, 173, 188
statistical analysis, 64, 67, 69, 185–192
  and youth, 69–75, 189–191
Stevens, Manny, 89, 91, 100, 102, 116, 122
suburbs, 2–6, 18–19
  and desegregation, 39–43
  and enduring inequality, 158–163, 170–174, 177–182
  inner-ring, 42, 162–163
  Johnson County. *See* Johnson County, Kansas
  and Kansas City, 6–11, 46, 55, 58–61, 64–75
  and KCMPS, 76–78, 90, 98–99, 102–104
  local authority in, 153–154
  and localism, 11–14, 35–38
  Missouri, 106–107, 110–111, 117–118, 124–132
  and national urban development, 29–31
  social impact of, 22–28, 32–35
  suburban advantage, 3, 16, 29, 161–163, 170–179, 208n69
  suburban sprawl, 16, 31, 45, 58
  suburbanization. *See* suburbanization
suburbanization, 9–10, 21–24, 28, 30–31, 41
  of African Americans, 23, 199n35
  in Kansas City, 14, 58–59, 74–75, 158–160
Sugar Creek district, 80–81, 96
Sunset Hills, 63–64, 66–67, 79, 134, 138, 216n64
Supreme Court, United States, 10, 23, 38–39, 55, 94, 179

taxes
  and enduring inequality, 176
  and Johnson County, 143, 145, 149, 151–153
  and KCMPS, 77, 81, 91
  and Missouri suburbs, 109, 119, 125, 127–128
  and suburbanization, 28, 35
  urban, 26–27, 30
teachers
  African American, 55, 62, 80, 171
  after *Brown v. Board*, 41–42
  in KCMPS, 79–81, 88–89, 91, 97
  in Missouri suburbs, 114, 119–120
  urban historically, 19, 26, 49
Topeka, Kansas, 62, 143, 151, 153, 156, 234n38
transportation, 7, 19–21, 56, 112, 122, 181
Troost Avenue, 51, 53–54, 67–68, 85–86, 213n26
  and enduring inequality, 165, 189
Turner district, 60, 169–170
Tyack, David, 13, 20

unification, district, 156–154
urban spaces, 18–19
  and education post-*Brown v. Board*, 38–42
  and enduring inequality, 158–163, 172, 179–182
  golden era of education in, 19–22
  and Johnson County, 135–136, 138, 149, 155

and Kansas City history, 9–10, 46, 56, 62–63, 68
and KCMPS, 77–78, 82, 94, 120
and localism, 11–13, 36–37
and Missouri suburbs, 106–107, 110, 124–128, 130–132
national development of, 29–32
postwar social change in, 22–29, 32–34
statistical analysis of, 187, 189–190
urban education, 5–7, 19–22, 27, 42, 77, 125, 172
urban institutions, 5, 12–13, 22, 159, 162
urban-suburban divide, 42–43, 131, 179, 182

Van Horn High School, 81–83, 86, 92, 96, 98, 108
vocational training, 19–20, 81, 89–90

Warren, Michigan, 25, 117, 174
Webb v. School District No. 90, 55, 141
West, Stanley, 54, 87, 99
Westport High School, 53, 83, 86, 95, 101, 103
Westwood, Kansas, 137, 141, 148, 233n17, 235n47
white flight, 5, 24, 38–39, 78
 and Kansas City, 56, 62–64, 68, 74, 187
 and KCMPS, 78, 85–86, 97, 101–104, 157
 and Missouri suburbs, 105

white people
 and desegregation, 39, 41
 and enduring inequality, 158, 160–161, 163, 171–178
 and Johnson County, 140, 142, 144
 and Kansas City, 9, 53–57, 62–64, 74–75
 and KCMPS, 76–82, 84, 86–88, 90–98, 100–104
 and localism, 13
 and Missouri suburbs, 106–107, 117–119, 122, 131
 and postwar social change, 23–26, 28–29
 predominantly white institutions. *See* predominantly white institutions
 racism of. *See* racism
 and suburban histories, 5–6
 and suburbanization. *See* suburbanization
 white flight. *See* white flight
white racial frame, 5, 131, 175
working-class, 26, 54, 77
Wilson, William Julius, 40–41, 159
women, 41, 71–72, 80, 162, 168, 190–192
working-class people, 22, 26, 54, 77, 120–121, 135
Wyandotte County, Kansas, 59, 68, 133, 138, 169, 217n69

Zimmer, Basil, 36–37, 154–155, 172, 177

www.ingramcontent.com/pod-product-compliance
Lightning Source LLC
Chambersburg PA
CBHW032006230426
43672CB00010B/2265